Daschle vs. Thune

DASCHLE VS. THUNE
Anatomy of a High-Plains Senate Race

JON K. LAUCK

UNIVERSITY OF OKLAHOMA PRESS : NORMAN

Also by Jon K. Lauck

American Agriculture and the Problem of Monopoly: The Political Economy of Grain Belt Farming, 1953–1980 (Lincoln, Nebr., 2000)

Library of Congress Cataloging-in-Publication Data

Lauck, Jon, 1971–
    Daschle vs. Thune : anatomy of a High Plains Senate race / Jon K. Lauck.
        p.   cm.
    Includes index.
    ISBN 978-0-8061-3850-3 (hardcover : alk. paper) 1. Daschle, Thomas. 2. Thune, John, 1961– 3. Political campaigns—South Dakota—History—21st century. 4. Elections—South Dakota—History—21st century. 5. United States. Congress. Senate—Elections, 2004. 6. South Dakota—Politics and government—21st century. 7. Political candidates—South Dakota—Biography. 8. Political candidates—United States—Biography. 9. Legislators—United States—Biography. 10. United States—Politics and government—2001–   I. Title. II. Title: Daschle versus Thune.

    E840.8.D375L38   2007
    324.9783'034—dc22

2007005814

The paper in this book meets the guidelines for permanence and durability of the Committee on Production Guidelines for Book Longevity of the Council on Library Resources, Inc. ∞

1 2 3 4 5 6 7 8 9 10

To Jennifer and Anna Gross
and to the memory of
Marcus Don Gross, 1970–2004

Historians who wrote in aristocratic ages are wont to refer all occurrences to the particular will and character of certain individuals; and they are apt to attribute the most important revolutions to slight accidents. . . . Historians who live in democratic ages exhibit precisely the opposite characteristics. Most of them attribute hardly any influence to the individual over the destiny of the race, or to citizens over the fate of a people; but, on the other hand, they assign great general causes to all petty incidents. . . . Our contemporaries are but too prone to doubt of human free-will, because each of them feels himself confined on every side by his own weakness; but they are still willing to acknowledge the strength and independence of men united in society. Let not this principle be lost sight of; for the great object in our time is to raise the faculties of men, not to complete their prostrations.

—Alexis de Tocqueville

CONTENTS

Illustrations

PREFACE

I think we shall all agree that no historian can say the ultimate word.
—Frederick Jackson Turner

"Democracy," Henry Adams once wrote, "is the only subject for history." Despite Adams's desire to focus history's lens, historians have lost sight of the American democratic heritage. Campaigns and elections, the bone and sinew of democracy, seldom catch the historian's gaze. It is time to nudge historians out of their apolitical snooze and reopen their eyes to the basic mechanics of democracy, lest they be unable to help guide us through this day of democratic doubt. While democratic prospects in the Middle East fluctuate wildly, they dwindle in Russia, in former Soviet satellites, and in parts of Latin America. Islamic authoritarianism continues to stifle democratic hopes in Asia, Africa, and the Middle East and to disrupt the long-standing democracies of Western Europe. Stalinism reigns in North Korea. In the United States, some on the left sincerely fear the trampling of the nation's democratic traditions by a Bush administration bent, in their view, on dictatorial rule, a belief that some on the right attribute to a corrosive paranoia that can immobilize deliberative democracy. Such dire views justify a close examination of one of the republic's most critical electoral contests and a consideration of what it tells us about the health and direction of American politics. Reviewing an election that attracted a widespread following, pulled thousands of individuals into the electoral process, featured high-profile candidate debates over major issues, placed a premium on retail politics, recorded 80 percent voter turnout, and stoked intense democratic passions might even provide hope to those who have resigned themselves to a dark future for American democracy.[1]

During the celebrated 2004 Senate race between Tom Daschle and John Thune, I was an assistant professor of history at South Dakota State University and viewed the contest as an opportune confluence of civics and history. Thucydides, the Greek historian, served as an Athenian general in the Peloponnesian War, and his experience shaped his history of the conflict, even though he was demoted and forced to watch the finale from the sidelines (the Greeks demanded victory from their generals). He began writing his history "at the very outbreak of the war, in the belief that it was going to be a great war and more worth writing about than any of those which had happened in the past." I started making notes for this book in late 2003, and in January 2004 I started an Internet weblog, or blog—Daschle v. Thune—where I made daily comments on the race. After living through and then writing his history of World War II, Winston Churchill said, "I do not describe it as history, for this belongs to another generation. But I claim with confidence that it is a contribution to history which will be of service to the future." This book, I hope, contributes to our history.[2]

About halfway through the campaign, I became a paid research and debate consultant to the Thune campaign, so my allegiances were never in doubt. I had also supported and worked for Thune's 2002 Senate campaign, and I enlisted as a Thune staffer after the 2004 election. I supported Thune because we had both matured politically under Reaganism and sympathized with Reagan's critique of and resistance to the political turn of the 1960s, but I also admired John Thune for the moxie he showed by challenging the most powerful Democrat in the country. Thune's Senate bid could justify de Tocqueville's faith in the actions of individuals in democratic societies. If Thune could defeat the leader of the Senate Democrats, the existing legislative logjam in the U.S. Senate might loosen.

Some, because of my active support for one of the candidates, will question my analysis, but after years of reading academic tomes, I can assure readers that participatory history has advantages. Historian Richard Hofstadter agreed when he commended Henry Adams for the "mixture of . . . detachment and involvement" that underpinned his writing. Charles Beard once lamented that the historical profession was impaired by "too much calm, not enough passion . . . too many books, not enough strife of experience." More recently, historian

Christopher Lasch similarly criticized the "academic taste for abstract debates that have no political consequences, in which the participants are untroubled by any sense of political accountability."[3]

It is a fine thing for historians and other academics to have some skin in the game. They should enter the fray, say their piece, and record what they have seen before memories fade. Incisive books about the American left, historian Michael Kazin notes, were written by "scholars who were also activists in the politics of their day." A contemporary leftist historian argues that a "good dose of tear gas makes us think more clearly as historians." Socialist Michael Walzer made the best case for participatory history in his book *The Company of Critics.* "Closeness is the crucial quality of the good social critic," Walzer says in promoting the model of the "connected critic" over what Jacques Bouversee deems the "official marginality" of many university professors. Walzer also notes that "it is one of the discoveries of modern democracy—an advance that we have made over the Greeks—that by not killing the critic, we acquire the right not to admire him." Some will not like this history, but they are free to take their turn.[4]

The historian Arthur Schlesinger, Jr., a speechwriter for and advisor to Adlai Stevenson and John Kennedy, weathered criticism for being an "outspoken liberal." But Schlesinger's books stand as revealing masterpieces, despite their indulgence of FDR and JFK. Schlesinger's friend Theodore White, whose famous book *The Making of the President* (about Kennedy's victory over Richard Nixon) launched the campaign history genre and provides an obvious model for this book, even wrote speeches for Kennedy during the campaign he chronicled. White considered himself "an almost perfect specimen of American liberal thinking" and thought of Kennedy as a glimmering hero and Nixon as a snarling villain. With Mrs. Kennedy's direction and oversight, he created the myth of Camelot after her husband John's tragic end. White's books, as most political historians would concede, are nonetheless invaluable.[5]

Such ventures are not without perils, however. Consider Douglas Brinkley, whose admiring book about John Kerry's service in Vietnam ignited one of the most searing firestorms of 2004 when some of Kerry's fellow sailors contested its rendering of historical memory. "That's what set me off," said one retired Coast Guard captain. "It just upset me and made me seethe all over again, like it was in the early '70s." Kerry supporters tried early in the campaign to cajole C-Span into keeping footage of Kerry's 1971 Senate testimony (in which he compared the U.S. troops in Vietnam to the armies of Genghis Khan) locked in the archives. The Kerry campaign feared the unleashing of these old memories, which were less flattering than Brinkley's rendering of Kerry's Vietnam-era history. Brinkley commendably engaged the debate and helped frame and contextualize the historical currents at work in the elections of 2004, but he came away singed.[6]

Whatever the inevitable criticism, I wanted to take advantage of my unique vantage point and write an account of the Daschle-Thune race because it can tell us much about the practice of American democracy and the polarized political culture of our young century. Too often, Thomas Carlyle once lamented, "Battles and war-tumults which for the time din every ear, and with joy or terror intoxicate every heart, pass away like tavern-brawls." I wanted to ensure that the details of the Daschle-Thune race did not fade into the recesses of our memory too quickly, losing "some significance that once was noted in them, some quality of enchantment that once was theirs," as noted historian Carl Becker famously worried.[7]

This book blends historical narrative, political analysis, and personal reflection and relies on press accounts, interviews (both on and off the record), and my own observations and discussions with participants. The book helps explain the recent political success of American conservatism, a movement that historian Alan Brinkley deems "an orphan in historical scholarship" (in an inadvertent explanation for why it was disowned and relegated to history's orphanage, Brinkley renounces "any personal engagement with or sympathy for conservative politics"). One recent historical study found it necessary to grudgingly concede, "It is not a sin to be a conservative, nor does it make one less perceptive, analytic, or beneficial to society." Leo Ribuffo believes that "conservatives exert virtually no influence on the main course of American historiography." Historians of the United States, according to the old joke, know more about the Socialist Party than the Republican Party. Lamenting the "dull orthodoxy" of American history, Ribuffo believes that historians are guilty of "lumping conservatives into derogatory categories to highlight their perfidy." The "tendency toward glib moralizing from a left liberal or radical perspective," Ribuffo says, "has affected American historical writing for the worse."[8]

If liberals took political conservatism more seriously, however, their newfound understanding might bolster their power. Sociologist and popular writer Todd Gitlin believes that "many on the left do not recognize quite how they lost or understand how to recover." Richard Hofstadter once complained that in "the absence of a formidable and reasoned body of conservative criticism, liberals have been driven, for that exercise of the mind which intellectuals seek, to self-criticism, which has been of less value to them than powerful and searching opposition." The liberal academy is similarly diminished by an insular discussion, a variation of Michael Walzer's apt description of "professors writing for other professors." The president of the Organization of American Historians, Richard White, recently found it necessary to scold historians for their "reluctance to debate" and called on them to "celebrate scholars who draw strong reactions."[9]

A more robust dialogue and a wider diversity of political perspectives could also help revive the moribund field of political history, which can only bolster our democratic prospects. Historical study, Frederick Jackson Turner once wrote, affords "training for good citizenship" and is "one of the ways to create good politics." Turner imagined an ongoing and lively debate within the historical profession over a variety of historical interpretations. But in history departments at present, according to Elisabeth Lasch-Quinn, "the likemindedness of members generally rules out the kind of exchange possible in a context of open, but supportive, disagreement." This likemindedness is especially ironic given historians' loss of confidence in ascertaining The Truth about historical events. Hayden White, one of the leading skeptics of divining historical truth, notes that history "is never innocent ideologically or otherwise, whether launched from the political perspective of the Left, the Right, or the Center." In the face of this shrinking faith in historical truth, however, the political likemindedness of historians only grows, a trend that does not bode well for American democratic institutions. Such circumstances, Lasch-Quinn argues, are "a loss not only to the particular historian or to historical scholarship but to the large project of democratic deliberation, which relies on education, particularly of the sort history can provide, in order to function at all."[10]

Although the practice has fallen into disfavor in recent decades, American historians once spent most of their energy focusing on politics and civic institutions. The result was a large corpus of works that the general public consumed and therefore afforded the historical profession a much broader audience than other disciplines. These political histories deepened the public understanding of politics and helped citizens contextualize the political moment through which they were passing. At present, however, historians such as Sean Wilentz who still abide such interests mourn the "denigration of politics and political ideas that has become common among contemporary writers of political history" and have issued a call for a "sound and complicated understanding of American politics." While recognizing the efforts of scholars who work around the edges of unadulterated politics, Wilentz says, "It's fine to study the social history of politics, or the cultural history of politics, but neither one replaces the political history of politics—or, more simply, political history—which is essential."[11]

Jon K. Lauck
Sioux Falls, South Dakota
April 2007

ACKNOWLEDGMENTS

The advice and support of many people made this book possible. I especially want to thank Amy for her great patience as the book came together in the months after the election. As always, I thank my parents, pillars of the republic, for all their generosity and support. I also want to thank Mel Berger, Dan Domenico, Jason Duncan, Kerry Larsen, John Miller, Mark Milosch, Dave McMahon, George Nash, and Leo Ribuffo for reading all or parts of the manuscript and for their critical suggestions. I especially want to thank Don Simmons, executive director of the McGovern Center at Dakota Wesleyan University. Don may not have agreed with certain aspects of the book, but he still set a standard for civil repartee and open-minded debate. Finally, I want to thank Matthew Bokovoy of the University of Oklahoma Press. Matthew's vision and leadership were essential to the successful completion of the project.

This book is dedicated to the memory of one of my closest friends and to the wife and little girl he left behind. In May 2004, Marc Gross had a heart attack and died while working out at the gym at Creighton University, where he was attending law school after several years of mulling his professional options. My adventures with Marc—in our hometown of Madison, South Dakota, and beyond—are too many to count. Memory, it must be said, serves a higher calling than politics and history. Marc, who evolved from a small-town South Dakota Republican into an antiestablishment "Rage against the Machine" Naderite, took politics seriously and would have loved following the various skirmishes of the Daschle-Thune race. I still cannot believe he is gone.

Daschle vs. Thune

INTRODUCTION

POLITICS AND MEMORY

Every true history is contemporary history.

—Benedetto Croce

In 2004, for the first time in more than half a century, a party leader
in the U.S. Senate lost a reelection bid. Because the South Dakota
Senate race coincided with the famously contentious Bush-Kerry
presidential race, the *New York Times* deemed it "the *other* big race of
2004." The *Economist* and the *Wall Street Journal* called it the "second-
most important race in America" and said that it was "second only to
the battle for the White House in national significance." *Roll Call*
placed the South Dakota contest in the top ten Senate races of the
past fifty years. The backdrop for the Senate race was a republic
splintered into partisan camps and polarized by fevered clashes over
war and peace, moral codes and civil liberties, and the contours of
the New Deal economic order, skirmishes that colored the race and
brought international focus to the Dakota prairie. Historian Sean
Wilentz compared the nation's political divisions to the sectional strife
of the 1860s and the Populist rebellion of the 1890s.[1]

The schisms that roiled the nation were accentuated in the South
Dakota race, which featured Democratic senator Tom Daschle, who
served as titular leader of the opposition to Republican president
George W. Bush, an overt advocate of the Republican candidate, John
Thune. Control of the narrowly divided Senate also teetered in the
balance.[2] Senate GOP leader Bill Frist even flouted the Senate's genteel
traditions and ventured into South Dakota to campaign against his
fellow leader, fueling the animosity that had reduced the famed
deliberative body to a hothouse of squabbling, partisanship, and
obstruction. Throughout 2004, the nation was also convulsed by the

Bush administration's grandiose plan to build a democracy in the Muslim world, where no such governments existed, out of the ashes of a Stalinist dictatorship.

South Dakota, which boasts a recent history of barn-burner elections, offers an open window on the practice of democracy and the recent trends in American politics. Tom Daschle was first elected to the U.S. House of Representatives in 1978, when he lost the initial balloting by 42 votes but won the recount by 139. George McGovern, Daschle's mentor, won his first Senate race in 1962 by 597 votes. John Thune lost the 2002 senatorial election to Senator Tim Johnson by 524 votes. Relatively inexpensive airtime in South Dakota also fosters widespread television advertising, a staple of modern campaigns. Population sparsity (the number of residents in the state of South Dakota would constitute the nation's fourteenth-largest city) makes genuine retail politics and tightly focused get-out-the-vote drives possible. South Dakota, where intense contests for federal office have recently become the norm, offers a glimpse at democratic practice and the salient issues that animate contemporary American politics. In 2004, South Dakota became a central front in the continuing struggle between the nation's rival political traditions.[3]

The politics that animated the Daschle-Thune race of 2004 follow a long chain of shifting political coalitions. After the entrenchment of the democratic tradition in the United States in the decades after the Revolution, the Civil War and its aftermath ushered in a new political age. Although late-nineteenth-century politics continued to involve ethnic and regional clashes, the political debate widened with industrialization, the growth of unions, the Populist revolt, and arguments over economic inequality. During the Progressive Era, ethnocultural conflict persisted, and ongoing calls for economic reform triggered antimonopoly campaigns and the establishment of a federal regulatory apparatus. The growth of American involvement in global affairs, especially U.S. participation in World War I, also made foreign policy a prominent public issue.

The Great Depression finally shattered a thirty-year period of Republican Party dominance of American politics, which stretched back to the 1890s, a golden age that GOP strategists dreamed of reviving in the twenty-first century. In the 1930s, FDR's New Deal cemented a political coalition that allowed the Democrats to control American politics until the 1960s. The New Deal coalition included a solidly Democratic South, which had supported the Democratic Party as far back as Thomas Jefferson. The New Deal welfare state also fixed the Democratic loyalties of many workers and farmers who had supported the GOP in previous decades. When FDR transitioned from Dr. New Deal to Dr. Win-the-War during World War II, he also positioned the Democrats as the party of military preparedness and global interventionism. After World War II, Harry Truman crafted a foreign policy consensus around the need to aggressively engage Soviet communism.

The events of the 1960s shattered the foreign policy consensus, splintered the long-standing New Deal coalition, and created the dynamics of political debate that still shape American politics to this day. LBJ's ambition to expand the welfare state beyond the structure established during the New Deal caused a growing number of Americans to question the regulatory and tax burdens on the economy. LBJ's pursuit of civil rights laws designed to upend segregation and subsequent efforts to promote minority hiring preferences contributed to some southerners' abandonment of the Democratic Party. The coming of the counterculture (which was linked to some elements of the Democratic Party) and the social disorders of the 1960s also caused southerners and some working-class Americans in the North to abandon the Democrats. The deep divisions caused by the Vietnam War, which some prominent Democratic liberals opposed, also caused an enduring split among Democrats over the projection of the United States' military power. South Dakota senator George McGovern and his allies took much of the blame for fortune's abandonment of liberalism. McGovern, who personally endured the transition from liberal to conservative dominance in American politics, once conceded that his campaign for president opened the doors to the Democratic Party "and 20 million people walked out."[4]

A once-moribund political conservatism, which was routed by LBJ in 1964, slowly gained popularity in the later decades of the twentieth century. Ronald Reagan, who defeated a confirmed believer in New Deal politics to become governor of California, became famous with his critiques of creeping statism, the counterculture, and the Democrats' management of the cold war. Reagan helped craft a GOP platform of small government, traditional values, and a strong foreign policy that largely persists to the present day. Just as some GOP strategists such as Karl Rove hoped to re-create an earlier age of Republican dominance, some liberals such as Sean Wilentz hope that the "Democrats rebuild a new version of the grand Roosevelt coalition." The strength and persistence of Reagan's "hegemonic coalition," as political scientist Theodore Lowi terms it, was the broader question of political history at issue on the prairies of South Dakota in 2004.[5]

Early-twenty-first-century American politics follows the outline of criticisms advanced in the 1960s by the American left and countered by conservatives in the 1980s during the Reaganite ascendancy. In the 1960s, in a political environment similar to the current one, some on the left protested against what they perceived to be a corporate-sponsored "imperial presidency" waging an antidemocratic foreign war without popular support. The left also criticized American democracy for its subservience to plutocratic corporations, for being consumed by materialism, for pillaging the natural world, for being too exclusionary toward racial minorities, and for its belligerent foreign policy posture. The right argued that the post-1960s federal government became too bureaucratic, expensive, wasteful, and unresponsive to popular demands, that liberal elites leveraged government and judicial power into social engineering schemes that lacked popular support, that government sanctioned the erosion of individual responsibility and the moral code, and that the nation's international standing shriveled as foreign threats festered. The right won a major victory in this contest of visions with the election of Ronald Reagan in 1980.

The Daschle-Thune race of 2004 was largely shaped by the contours carved by 1960s liberalism and 1980s conservatism, both of which transformed the landscape of political debate. In the 1960s and early 1970s, in keeping with the nation's lurch to the left, South Dakota elected two of the most liberal members of the Senate: George McGovern and James Abourezk. As conservatives began to organize against the movements of the 1960s, however, both in South Dakota and nationally, the political appeal of liberalism withered. Senator Abourezk declined to run for reelection in 1978, and Senator McGovern met defeat in his 1980 reelection attempt as Reaganism surged nationally. Tom Daschle worked for McGovern's senatorial race in 1968 and his presidential campaign in 1972, then signed on as a staffer to Senator Abourezk. When he ran his own race for Congress in 1978, Daschle detected the mobilized forces of conservatism on the horizon and thus ran as a conservative Democrat, distancing himself from the increasingly unpopular liberalism of the 1960s. John Thune, who was in college when Reagan was elected as president, enlisted in the Reagan administration and worked for Senator James Abdnor, who upended McGovern in 1980 in another symbolic defeat for 1960s liberalism. The 2004 South Dakota Senate race was fought over the scarred battlefields left by the 1960s and the Reagan revolution, with Daschle defending a remnant of the old order while Thune carried the banner of Reaganism. The battle between Daschle and Thune showcased the traditions, ideas, and organizational networks of two warring political coalitions and the continuing skirmishes between them, a modern version, writ small, of Generals Montcalm and Wolfe, exemplars of their culture and times.[6]

Because the contemporary political conflict in the United States is rooted in the 1960s, which historian C. Vann Woodward called the "most historically minded of all ages," American politics often becomes a historical debate. Recollections of the 1960s are necessarily freighted with political meaning and, as historian David Farber notes, constitute "powerful acts of memory." When the first child of the 1960s, Bill Clinton, became president, the 1990s became an exercise in historical memory. Some on the right ascribed the unpopular countercultural tendencies of the 1960s to Clinton and his allies. Other critics, dipping into the well of national memory, questioned President Clinton's ability to serve as commander in chief because of his draft avoidance, his self-proclaimed "loathing" of the military, and his protesting during the Vietnam War, the most bitter social conflict during an age of rage and violence. Many conservatives preferred Clinton's opponents, President George H. W. Bush and Senator Robert Dole, in part because of their heroism during World War II, the unquestioned Good War, fought by what South Dakota native Tom Brokaw deemed the "greatest generation." The national reflection on World War II during the 1990s and memories of its moral clarity, in contrast to the divisive ambiguities of the 1960s, reinforced this preference, as did the killing of three thousand Americans on September 11, 2001, which again moved foreign policy to the center of American political debate.[7]

During the 2004 presidential primaries, many Democrats embraced Senator John Kerry, who had met and killed the enemy in Vietnam. They hoped thereby to diminish the drag of the 1960s on the Democratic presidential candidate and to sharpen their argument that

President George W. Bush had skirted military service during Vietnam. Kerry's actions during and after the Vietnam War, which came under scrutiny in the final throes of the presidential campaign, and their political-historical meaning exposed the persistent cultural chasm in American life first opened in the 1960s. The historical memory of Vietnam, which Kerry believed would confer battlefield gravitas, instead unleashed the furies of the 1960s. The heroic memories that Kerry summoned in 2004 contradicted his earlier efforts to stifle the memorialization of heroism in Vietnam. In the epilogue to the 1971 book *The New Soldier,* which was thrust into the 2004 presidential campaign in the fall, Kerry proclaimed, "We will not quickly join those who march on Veterans' Day waving small flags calling to *memory* those thousands who died for the 'greater glory of the United States.' . . . We will not take solace from the creation of monuments or the naming of parks after a select few of the thousands of dead Americans and Vietnamese. We will not uphold the traditions which decorously *memorialize* that which was base and grim." Opponents criticized Kerry for twisting this history during the campaign, for trying to have "it both ways: war hero and courageous war protester," according to one Naval War College professor. The episode made historian John Lukacs's point about the "deepening consciousness of the functions of human memory," which is "especially important in the democratic age in which we live," and its persistence as a potent force in American politics.[8]

Memories of the divisiveness of the 1960s pervaded the 2004 presidential race. Bush and Kerry each "saw the other as a symbol of the wrong side of the great post-1960s divide," according to *Newsweek.* During the Iowa caucuses, Kerry traveled with counterculture icon Peter Yarnow of Peter, Paul, and Mary and took inspiration from Yarnow's renditions of "Puff the Magic Dragon." CBS videotaped Kerry pretending to take a toke. In the fall, the Kerry campaign ran an ad criticizing President Bush entitled "Fortunate Son" and featuring the Creedence Clearwater Revival song of the same title in the background. Reliving the 1960s necessarily conjured memories of Vietnam— which Kerry imagined, given his military service, would deliver the Democrats from charges of foreign policy weakness. But political commentator Martin Peretz called Kerry's invocation of Vietnam "the first of his great mistakes." Peretz said that "no one—save Mr.

Kerry himself and his immediate circle—wanted to revisit Vietnam. It was the country's great nightmare, divisive, tormenting, politically paralyzing." Kerry's embrace of Vietnam and the hostile exchanges with the swiftboat veterans who opposed him kept the images salient, and Kerry became, as *Newsweek* noted, "living proof that the Vietnam War will never end."[9]

The 2004 elections also occurred in the wake of the 9/11 terrorist attacks and the nation's most decisive military operations since Vietnam, the toppling of the Taliban in Afghanistan and Saddam Hussein in Iraq, wars laden with allusions to Vietnam and the 1960s. The nation's major newspapers and magazines commonly portrayed Iraq as a "quagmire" tantamount to Vietnam and compared Baathist and al-Qaeda insurgencies to the Vietnam-era Tet Offensive. In the tradition of the 1960s, Senator Tom Daschle and others criticized what they saw as the stifling of dissent and attempts to question their patriotism for criticizing the war. A majority of voters in the Democratic presidential primaries of 2004 opposed the Iraq War, and many rallied behind the antiwar candidacy of Governor Howard Dean of Vermont, a 2004 version of a 1968 Eugene McCarthy or a 1972 George McGovern. Democrats in 2004 suffered from their embrace of the images and memories of Vietnam, which, as historian Matthew Dallek has explained, had "acted as a kind of political wrecking ball" on the Democratic Party in previous decades.[10] Supporters of the Iraq war considered themselves firmly within the Reagan tradition of projecting American power and supporting new democracies, which was again a reaction to the post-Vietnam miasma of the 1970s. Ronald Reagan's final passing in June 2004 and the outpouring of national commentary, sentiment, and criticism rekindled the historical memories of and debates about an aggressive military posture.

Although historical memory and the ghosts of the 1960s and Vietnam brusquely intruded on the 2004 elections, some elections remain devoid of broader meaning and a sense of the past. Historian Richard Hofstadter once lamented Americans' "grossly foreshortened sense of time and their recurrent disposition to look rather disdainfully upon the remoter past." Short memories can also impoverish the democratic process. Politicians can sometimes run "in the moment," tout their present power, use the mass media to boost their popularity and burnish their images, and rely on journalists to report on their present initiatives without scrutiny of how these might square with a candidate's personal and political record. This general tendency intensifies if the popular press favors a particular candidate and refuses to examine a past that might burden a candidate's present. The current critique of liberal bias in the media serves as the most prominent contemporary example of this problem. In the Daschle-Thune race, the largest newspaper in the state tended to be protective of Senator Daschle and his history, a favoritism that limited voters' access to the information—and memories—necessary to make a fully informed choice. When discussing how the British once protected the reputations of their politicians, noted historian Arthur Schlesinger, Jr., found the practice "surely injurious not only to history but to *democracy itself.*" In the Daschle-Thune and Bush-Kerry races, conservative bloggers and media critics often made Schlesinger's argument and pulled the historical past into the political present.[11]

The media's power to shape memories or to remind voters of a candidate's history carries risks for the politically powerful. "The struggle of man against power is the struggle of memory against forgetting," says one of Milan Kundera's fictional characters in *The Book of Laughter and Forgetting.* In Aldous Huxley's novel *Brave New World,* the regime waged a "campaign against the Past," including a ban on the teaching of history, to stymie the opposition's attempt to critique the present. Huxley's ominous vision finds modern parallels in Russia, where President Vladimir Putin, the former KGB agent, rigorously controls the media and historical memory remains buried. Anne Applebaum explains that there have "been no public truth-telling sessions in Russia, no parliamentary hearings, no official investigations of any kind into the murders or the massacres or the camps of the USSR." When the former communists came to power in Poland in 2001, they accordingly cut the budget of the Polish Institute of National Memory. Some prevail in the fight against memory loss, however. The French village of Oradour-Sur-Glane, where the SS randomly machine-gunned and burned 642 civilians in 1944, was preserved as a monument to the memory of Nazi brutality. During the sixtieth anniversary of the massacre in 2004, the French prime minister said that Oradour "is the justification for the *politics of memory,* resolute and innovative, that we follow."[12]

The expansion of the Internet allows individuals to circumvent the dominant media filter and provides an accessible platform for critiquing press coverage and discussing matters otherwise destined for the memory hole. Thus, 2004 would later be declared the "Year of the Blog," for in that year, the number of blog readers surged by 60 percent and the long-standing influence of mass media organizations on American elections began to erode. Merriam-Webster even chose *blog* as its word of the year for 2004. However, even though the novelty of political blogs caused the pundits to buzz in 2004 about the creation of an edgy new subculture of politics, they often revived and fueled old feuds. Blogs could be most powerful when poring over the remains of the past and conjuring memories of the unremitting political wars between the politics of the 1960s and Reaganism.[13]

CHAPTER ONE

THE CANDIDATES AND THEIR TIMES

*The sixties have preoccupied late twentieth-century America as much as
the Civil War preoccupied late nineteenth-century America.*

—John B. Judis

The events of November 21, 2003, became the clincher. On that morning,
fifty-eight U.S. senators voted for cloture, or to proceed to a final vote,
on the Bush administration's sweeping energy bill. A Democratic
filibuster necessitated a cloture vote, which required sixty affirmative
votes from the Senate's one hundred members. The successful filibuster
symbolized the partisanship that divided the Senate during the 108th
Congress. For the South Dakota Senate race, the consequential section
of the long-stalled energy bill included a provision boosting the
usage of ethanol, the corn-based fuel additive popular in the Corn
Belt. Thune called the bill "the holy grail for the ethanol industry."
Daschle reluctantly voted for the bill, according to *Congressional
Quarterly,* but he did not work for its passage. The *New York Times*
similarly noted that Daschle twisted no Democratic arms. The day
before the vote, *Congress Daily* reported that Daschle would not use
his leadership "position to press wavering Democrats into supporting
the bill." A Democratic source said that Daschle did not owe Republican Senate Majority Leader Bill Frist anything. The personal enmity
between the Senate leaders would propel Frist to South Dakota in the
spring of 2004 to campaign against his fellow leader, prompting wails
of denunciation for such partisan impudence.[1]

Daschle's handling of the ethanol measure bewildered political
observers. Back in South Dakota, Daschle had run television and radio
ads during the summer of 2003 touting his leadership on ethanol
legislation. The day before the vote on the energy bill, the *Sioux Falls
Argus Leader* also called for passage. The *Argus,* however, ran a

misleading headline referencing Daschle's vaunted Washington power on the same day he refused to press his fellow senators to vote for the law: "Daschle Lends Clout to Energy Bill." Daschle's press spokesman blamed Republicans who "went and wrote this bill behind closed doors" and left Daschle out of the negotiations, betraying one of the reasons Daschle did not promote passage of the measure. Other Democrats said that they opposed the bill because it exempted manufacturers of the fuel additive MTBE (methyl tertiary butyl ether) from certain lawsuits, a measure the pro-Democratic trial lawyer lobby opposed. After the removal of the MTBE provision, however, Senate Democrats still filibustered the energy bill.[2]

The 2004 South Dakota Senate race crystallized on the day of the energy bill impasse. Daschle's obligation to his Senate caucus had helped undermine a major piece of legislation important to farmers in South Dakota. Daschle faced a difficult choice: he could serve as the partisan leader of the Senate Democrats, thrust and parry with Senator Frist, and serve as the loyal opposition to President Bush in an age of partisan bickering, or he could fully represent his state's interests. But he could not do both. John Thune would spend the next twelve months criticizing Daschle for serving incompatible masters. The filibuster of the ethanol bill became Exhibit A in Thune's case against Daschle's Senate, where GOP legislation often languished.

The day after the energy bill vote, the Minnehaha County Lincoln Day dinner featured Virginia senator George Allen, chairman of the National Republican Senatorial Committee. Minnehaha County is the most populous county in South Dakota and the home of Sioux Falls, the state's largest city, named for the picturesque cascade of Big Sioux River rapids gushing through exposed pink quartzite bedrock on the city's northern edge. "Minnehaha" is Sioux for "water that laughs." At the end of his speech, Senator Allen said that Daschle had been signing copies of his new book in Allen's home state of Virginia the night before the energy bill failed by two votes. The *Sioux Falls Argus Leader,* which tended to filter damaging news to Daschle from the public, ignored the news about Daschle's promotion of his book, the publication of which signaled his presidential ambitions. But to those who heard about the revelation, it provided hard evidence that Daschle's priorities could cost his constituents. In the final crucial months of the campaign, Thune persistently jabbed Daschle for being "out signing autographs" when the ethanol bill was "on the one-yard line."[3]

On the day of the energy bill vote, some advisors from the National Republican Senatorial Committee landed in Sioux Falls to reveal the latest polling information on a possible match-up between Daschle and Thune. Their poll showed Thune trailing by five percentage points, an optimistic assessment that aided the Senate committee's effort to persuade Thune to run. Thune and his wife, Kimberley, were upbeat but wary of another arduous year in the campaign trenches battling the nation's most powerful Democrat, who had access to the deepest Democratic pockets in the country. A more realistic poll conducted by the Republican National Committee showed Thune trailing Daschle by eight points. Thune also considered a possible run for South Dakota's lone House seat, held by the state's former four-term GOP governor, Bill Janklow. A few months before, Janklow had driven through a stop sign and killed a motorcyclist. His trial on manslaughter charges would begin in December. Many observers concluded that Janklow would not run again, could not run another effective campaign, or might even go to jail. Polling showed that Thune could easily win back his former House seat. If he entered the Senate race, however, his personal pollster believed that he had only a three-in-ten chance against Daschle. But Thune could not believe that Daschle, a master of farm-state politics, had refused to push for the ethanol bill. It clinched Thune's decision to defy the electoral odds.[4]

Daschle's failure to orchestrate Democratic support for the ethanol bill caused a stir for several days. In early December, the state GOP ran an ad on farm radio stations needling Daschle for the ethanol bill's failure. The ad focused on Daschle's unwillingness to use his oft-touted "clout" and featured the state GOP chairman, a farmer who served on the board of an ethanol plant. Some Republicans thought that focusing on the "clout" issue presented dangers, because Daschle's leadership position served as his biggest political weapon. They wanted to concentrate on Daschle's allegiances within his caucus, which had prevented him from pushing through the ethanol bill. Daschle worried more, those critics argued, about alienating Senators Ted Kennedy, Hillary Clinton, Dianne Feinstein, and the core of his caucus than about delivering for South Dakota farmers. The campaign would ultimately focus on who benefited from the exercise of Daschle's power.

On December 8, 2003, twelve jurors found Congressman Bill Janklow guilty of manslaughter for colliding with and killing a motorcyclist in rural Moody County four months earlier. The defense characterized manslaughter as an absurd charge and argued that had Janklow suffered a diabetic reaction at the time of the collision. Prosecutors tried to cast doubt on Janklow's defense by presenting evidence of his proclivity for speeding across the state's wide prairies. In a strange moment, Daschle even testified as a character witness for Janklow, shaking his hand on the way into the courtroom. Janklow had long been a fixture of South Dakota politics and renowned for his spellbinding speeches. A populist but pragmatic ex-marine, Janklow started his career as a legal aide lawyer defending Indians on the Rosebud Indian Reservation in the 1960s. He inherited his legal prowess from his father, who had prosecuted Nazis at the Nuremberg war crimes trials after World War II. Janklow first became well known for prosecuting the leaders of the American Indian Movement, who led violent protests in South Dakota in the 1970s. After serving as South Dakota's attorney general, Janklow became a domineering four-term governor with a magnetic personality, either attracting or repelling. His advisors said that 30 percent of the people he met on the street hated him, 40 percent loved him, and the rest decided the election.[5]

The end of the Age of Janklow scrambled South Dakota politics in an odd way. In 1986, Janklow had challenged sitting Republican senator James Abdnor for the Republican nomination and the right to challenge Daschle, who sought to make the leap from the House to the Senate. Janklow lost a close primary, Daschle won in the fall, and the rifts within the GOP between the Janklow and Abdnor factions persisted for years. The *Wall Street Journal* called the Janklow-Abdnor primary a "blood feud." In the mid-1990s, when Janklow returned to the governor's mansion for another two terms, a Janklow-Daschle entente developed. The alliance began when Janklow defended Daschle's involvement in a plane crash investigation in which Daschle had intervened in the plane safety inspection process to help a friend, an episode that produced a predictably dramatic *60 Minutes* segment featuring reporter-dodging and allegations of document shredding. The alliance made political sense because Janklow and Daschle had the largest and most powerful competing political networks in the state. A ceasefire would benefit both of them. Daschle planned to showcase his close relationship with Janklow during the 2004 campaign as a sign of his conservative and bipartisan bona fides. Rather counterintuitively, the end of Janklow's career also undermined the Daschle campaign.[6]

Rumors also circulated in 2003 that Janklow and Daschle had made a deal in which Daschle would retire and aid Janklow's efforts to acquire his Senate seat, ostensibly precluding a Thune bid. According to one scenario, Daschle would take a poll in August that would presumably show his political strength and then Daschle would announce his retirement and take a valedictory lap around the state. The poll would signal to voters that Daschle was not retiring because he thought he was in political peril. Janklow also pressured the Republican Senatorial Committee to remain neutral and refrain from supporting a Thune candidacy, indicating that Janklow planned to make a Senate bid. Reports also circulated about Janklow running as an independent if he could not secure the Republican nomination. Some insiders dismissed a Daschle-Janklow "deal" as a ridiculous conspiracy as vigorously as others accepted it as a fait accompli: they argued that Daschle could do little to pressure rank-and-file Democrats into supporting Janklow, that Janklow could not beat Thune in a GOP primary, and that the odds of an independent bid by Janklow were long. The degree of truth in such rumors remains unknown, but speculation in political and journalistic circles remained intense during the summer of 2003. Despite the announcement of his intent to seek reelection to the Senate in January 2003, Daschle later conceded that he did not fully commit to seeking reelection until the late summer. The August car accident ended the rumors of a Janklow Senate bid and sent Janklow to jail for 100 days.[7]

Thune's advisors held different views about the wisdom of a bid against Daschle, but none doubted the grandiosity of such a race. Too many political races in the country, given the power of incumbency, can be predetermined in the absence of an anti-incumbent wave. During the 2002 and 2004 federal election cycles, only nine incumbents were defeated, the fewest in all of U.S. history. Politics benefits from nip-and-tuck Senate races over grand issues that draw young people into the political process and offer voters a substantive choice. The intensity of the Daschle-Thune race paralleled the famous 1952 John Kennedy–Henry Cabot Lodge Senate race in Massachusetts.

Kennedy, an ambitious three-term congressman, challenged a legend of Massachusetts politics and a national icon but did not obsess over his defeat. Family patriarch Joe Kennedy pressed the challenge: "When you've beaten him, you've beaten the best. Why try for something less?" Kennedy prevailed over Lodge in 1952, the last year in which a leader in the Senate went down to defeat.[8]

Similar to the situation in which Senator Lodge found himself in 1952, Daschle's obligations to his national party became a burden in 2004, one that he had skillfully avoided earlier in his career. In the early 1980s, Stuart Rothenberg noted that Daschle had "taken pains not to be identified as a classic Kennedy-McGovern liberal." But Daschle's accommodation of the Reagan revolution of the 1980s obscured his political roots. Daschle grew up the grandson of poor German immigrants in Aberdeen, South Dakota, the state's third-largest city (just to the north, immigrant Germans were drawn by the flattering decision of a North Dakota city to adopt the name of the German "Iron Chancellor," Otto von Bismarck). Germans were the largest ethnic group to immigrate to South Dakota; many of them, including Daschle's grandparents, had left Russia after 1871, when the Russian czars revoked the German immigrants' exemption from military service, which had first lured them to the agricultural heartland surrounding Odessa. During the socialist vogue of the early twentieth century, Brown County became one of the state's strongest outposts of reform sentiment. Father Robert Haire became a legend in Brown County for his charitable works, for organizing Catholic churches, and for his embrace of the socialist cause. Haire became a charter member of the Socialist local, and in 1900 he even served as an elector for Socialist presidential candidate Eugene Debs, reflecting the growing convergence between Catholicism and economic reform movements. The Yale historian Howard Lamar remembered Haire as "the radical Catholic priest who advocated socialism." Brown County also became a center of Populist ferment, and Aberdeen hosted massive rallies for William Jennings Bryan in 1896.[9]

Daschle's father, Sebastian "Dash" Daschle, was a teacher who later became an owner of Nelson Auto Electric, but he was "an artist at heart," according to one account. Daschle's mother, Betty, was an Aberdeen homemaker and Avon lady. The Daschles were Catholic, a religious subculture that tended to clump together in South Dakota and unite ethnically diverse groups of Germans, Irish, and Bohemians (unlike Lutherans, who divided into German Lutheran churches and Norwegian Lutheran churches). Daschle attended Sacred Heart Catholic grade school and, as with most Catholics of the time, naturally became a Democrat and a JFK-ophile in a Democratic Age. In public high school, Daschle overcame his shyness and fear of heights and became socially active, singing in the choir, joining the Young Cosmopolitans and the Young Democrats, playing tennis, and running and winning a race for senior class president. In 1963, Daschle's geometry teacher announced to the class that Daschle's idol, President Kennedy, had been assassinated. Despite the tragedy, Daschle announced during his high school years that he intended to enter politics: "I have a dream. I'd love to be a United States Senator someday."[10]

The Age of JFK nurtured young Catholic Democrats with reformist spirits. Presidential scholar James McGregor Burns argued at the time, "This is as surely a liberal epoch as the late nineteenth century was a conservative one." In 1964, South Dakota even voted for a Democratic presidential candidate, the only exception to the state's preference for GOP presidential candidates in the past seven decades. The crushing defeat of Barry Goldwater in 1964, along with the social disorders of the late 1960s, laid the groundwork for the future ascendancy of political conservatism, which would torment Daschle when he began to pursue his high school dream. The term "conservative" first entered the popular discourse when embraced by President Dwight Eisenhower in 1960, the year in which Daschle's political hero had won the presidency.[11]

Daschle went off to South Dakota State University (SDSU) in Brookings in 1965 and earned a degree in political science, becoming the first member of his family to graduate from college. During the chaotic year of 1968, while president of the Political Science Club, Daschle embraced the liberal wing of the Democratic Party. At a mock Democratic presidential convention, Daschle said that he was "appalled at the conservatism" of the delegates, who did not have the "true Democratic party spirit." To Daschle's chagrin, the convention repealed platform planks calling for federal gun control, a guaranteed annual income, termination of the bombing of North Vietnam, and abolition of the draft. Daschle led the effort, after the conservative elements of the convention had departed, to rescind the platform because he thought it "too conservative" and not in accordance "with the views of either McCarthy or McGovern," who were running for president that tumultuous year (McGovern, hoping to capture the Kennedy delegates, had entered the race after the assassination of Robert Kennedy). In the spring of 1968, in another sign of the broadening spectrum of the American left, the SDSU Political Science Club agreed to sponsor a visit by Minneapolis representatives of the Socialist Workers Party.[12]

Daschle's college activism coincided with the most intense political moments of the 1960s. In 1968, Daschle spent his spring break in Washington, D.C., where he "wound up in the midst of the riots that besieged Washington in the wake of the assassination of Martin Luther King, Jr." At the 1968 Democratic convention in Chicago, antiwar student protestors unfurled the "Viet Cong flag, the red flag of revolution, and the black flag of anarchy" and were met with the clubs of the Chicago police, with whom they fought "a pitched battle of hand-to-hand combat," according to one recent history. After one night of clashes, twenty reporters needed medical treatment. When nominating South Dakota senator George McGovern as a peace candidate, Connecticut senator Abraham Ribicoff famously said, "With George McGovern as president of the United States, we wouldn't have these Gestapo tactics in the streets of Chicago." During the week of the Democratic Convention, 308 U.S. troops died in Vietnam. It was 1968, James Traub later noted, when Vietnam "began moving the Democratic Party sharply to the left on issues of war and peace."[13]

The events of 1968 symbolized an age of political turmoil, and few politically inclined Americans lived through it unaffected. "Like so many politicians who came of age in the 1960s," the *New York Times* later explained, Daschle "was inspired by the activism of the age." The movements of the left also energized conservative critics, thus creating the chronic divisions in American life over the meaning of the 1960s that still shape the practice of politics. Daschle remained committed to politics and worked for George McGovern's South Dakota Senate campaign in 1968 and his presidential campaign in 1972, during which, McGovern said, Daschle "volunteered for anything we wanted him to do, making speeches on my behalf, going everywhere." In 1972, McGovern lost forty-nine states, including South Dakota, a hammer blow to the "New Politics" of 1960s activism that

McGovern came to personify. During these years, one reporter noted, Daschle "absorbed the liberal politics" of McGovern. Upon graduating from college in 1969, Daschle married Laurie Klinkel, whom he had met during the 1968 mock Democratic convention at SDSU. She supported Robert Kennedy and he supported Eugene McCarthy, the two senators who energized the anti–Vietnam War movement. Daschle was a child of 1968.[14]

After fulfilling his ROTC duties to the Air Force at the Strategic Air Command in Omaha, where he analyzed satellite photos, Daschle went to Washington in 1973. Along with his wife, he worked for the brash and populist senator James Abourezk, the son of a Lebanese peddler who hailed from Wood, South Dakota (population 66), and was considered one of the most liberal members of the Senate when the liberals in the body reached the apex of their power. Daschle supported Abourezk over the pro-life candidate in the 1972 Democratic Senate primary, and Abourezk subsequently gave Daschle "primary responsibility for Middle East and all other foreign relations matters." Daschle traveled to the Middle East with Abourezk, the first Lebanese-American elected to the U.S. Senate, who became best known as a fierce critic of Israel. Abourezk broke the tradition of reticence by freshman senators and immediately went to the Senate floor to denounce the Vietnam War and President Nixon, saying that the president had "single-handedly made this nation the bully of the world." Abourezk led an effort to break up the large oil companies and, along with the liberal lion Senator Howard Metzenbaum of Ohio, led a two-week filibuster of a natural gas deregulation bill, offering 508 amendments to stymie the bill's progress. Along with Senators Abourezk and McGovern, Daschle also supported Mo Udall, the candidate of the liberals, in the 1976 presidential primaries. Udall would take Daschle under his wing when Daschle made it to Congress and would help refine his "already considerable schmoozing skills."[15]

In 1977, Daschle and his wife returned to South Dakota to take command of Senator Abourezk's state operations and begin his long-planned ascent into elective politics. Daschle stepped on the toes of others in the state office (one coworker said, "Tom is getting involved in things over his head" and resented his control), but he managed to orchestrate a major overhaul of the office's press operation, which had failed to generate much publicity for the senator. Through this process, Daschle came to know, as one account noted, the "media gatekeepers" in the state. Daschle, a master of detail, understood the political moment, when the embrace of sophisticated media strategies reached its zenith.[16]

In the 1960s, as historian John Lukacs has explained, "many of the principal agents and aides of presidential candidates were publicity men" who specialized in "public relations." Joe McGinniss made the point in his famous book *The Selling of the President*, which detailed Nixon's successful 1968 presidential bid and his manipulation of television imagery. In the 1976 presidential race, Lukacs recounts, Jimmy Carter "depended on pollsters and public relations experts even more than had his predecessors." The 1976 contest, said one Democratic senator, had "all the issue content of a student-council race." Carter's gestures aimed at bolstering his image as a common man caused Garry Trudeau's *Doonesbury* syndicated cartoons to mockingly feature Carter's appointment of a "Secretary of Symbolism." According to historian Leo Ribuffo, "Carter had an intuitive feel for the techniques of symbolic politics" and relied heavily on his pollster Pat Caddell and his media expert Gerald Rafshoon (begetting more Trudeau depictions of "Rafshoonery").[17]

Although Carter earned the moniker "Southern-fried McGovern" from vice presidential candidate Bob Dole during the 1976 election, after he took office, liberals also skewered him for not promoting their agenda, precipitating a primary challenge from Ted Kennedy in 1980. South Dakota senator George McGovern also considered running as a man of the left in 1980 but deferred to Kennedy. Critics called Carter a "man of a thousand faces" who had "more positions than the *Kama Sutra*." When the famed campaign guru Bob Shrum quit the Carter campaign, he left the candidate a stinging departure note: "I am not sure what you truly believe in, other than yourself." During the Carter presidency, Vice President Walter Mondale complained to the president about his incoherent policy making and told him that people "don't know where you are going." But Carter maintained, according to historian Peter Carroll, a "respect for the power of the media" and cultivated the press. Carter later admitted, "I would not be where I am now had the press not accommodated some of my errors." Carter's attentiveness to the media paralleled Daschle's reconstruction of Senator Abourezk's press operation. Daschle became known for his savvy media operations, and the *New Republic* later emphasized that "Daschle displayed a sophisticated ability to use the media." In 1986, GOP governor Bill Janklow, before the beginning of the Janklow-Daschle rapprochement, deemed Daschle "a smooth politician. One of the new breed of TV-packaged, public relations kind."[18]

The 1970s spawned other developments that would shape Daschle's political career. The forces of the New Left scattered and weakened in the late 1970s, the radicalism of 1968 faded, and liberalism was increasingly under siege, leaving Daschle in a churning political environment. Living through the Vietnam War and the final collapse of South Vietnam in 1975 left him skeptical of the exercise of U.S. military power and therefore dubious of the arms buildup by the subsequent Reagan administration. President Carter's evangelical grounding also highlighted a new center of power in politics. Throughout the early 1970s, polls indicated the growing importance of religion in the lives of many Americans. By 1980, nearly half of Americans believed that family life had eroded during the previous decade. These Moral Majority sentiments, along with Carter's overt religiosity, helped propel the political organization of religious conservatives, who would criticize the cultural changes of the 1960s, aid Reagan's rise to power, and ultimately become steady critics of Daschle's voting record in Congress.[19]

A new form of personality politics also became prominent in the 1970s. While the violent man-the-barricades ideological politics of 1968 subsided, Daschle's politics paralleled the softer, *Love Story* undercurrent of the 1970s (the author of that novel, Erich Segal, was counseled to take a leave from Yale, however, because unrepentant radicals viewed his novel as a call "for a return to Eisenhower morality"). The 1970s, some historians have explained, transfigured the public behavior of some American males, a "shift from John Wayne to Alan Alda" (whom *Redbook* called "America's Sweetheart") and "from the strong, silent type to the sensitive New Age male." Bill Clinton later tapped this new sentiment with his famous "I feel your pain" politics. *Washington Post* reporter John Harris noted that Clinton's "willingness to talk about interior life perhaps was generational, a signature of the baby boomers." Daschle exemplified the transition from the cold warrior machismo of JFK and the podium pounding of Hubert Humphrey to the public persona of later political figures, who criticized the "meanness" and foreign policy bravado of Reagan's America.

Crusader liberalism and "takin' it to the streets" activism gave way to a "therapeutic sensibility," one side of the social dichotomy that political commentator Michael Barone divides into "Hard America" and "Soft America." By the 1970s, according to Barone, "it seemed that Soft America might eradicate Hard America entirely." But with the election of Ronald Reagan in 1980, Hard America won a victory. In subsequent decades, as Daschle advisor George Lakoff has explained, this imagery persisted as conservatives emphasized "discipline and toughness" while liberals focused on "need and help."[20]

In 1978, when Daschle launched his long-planned run for Congress, the Age of the Liberal was passing. George McGovern's chief of staff began writing ominous memos to his boss about the "drift to the right in South Dakota." In Senator Abourezk's office, where Daschle worked, staffers noted the potency of "redneck" issues in South Dakota. During the 1978 midterm elections, according to one study, "Democratic liberalism ran into a brick wall." In keeping with the rising tide of antigovernment Reaganism, Daschle tacked to the right and began criticizing the "bloated federal bureaucracy" and made a balanced budget amendment to the Constitution a centerpiece of his 1978 congressional campaign. President Carter also called for a balanced budget at the end of his first term, a promise that Republican presidents Richard Nixon and Gerald Ford had never made, which further infuriated the advocates of spending in the liberal wing of the Democratic Party. The *Sioux Falls Argus Leader* reported that Daschle "voiced conservative ideas" during his first campaign, including the balanced budget amendment to the Constitution, and that Daschle "acknowledged that such calls traditionally have come from Republicans." Such stances were popular in South Dakota. Cambridge Survey Research, run by Carter's pollster Pat Caddell, polled for Senators Abourezk and McGovern and found that 50 percent of South Dakotans even supported convening a constitutional convention to balance the federal budget. In keeping with the ongoing energy crisis of the 1970s, Daschle also criticized the oil companies for high gas prices (Caddell found that 74 percent of South Dakotans blamed the oil companies), called for a tax credit to promote insulation use and reduce energy consumption, and promoted gasohol, the forerunner to ethanol (which proved a decisive issue in 2004). In keeping with the prominence of farm politics in his agricultural state, Daschle also called for "100 percent parity" farm prices, a goal first set forth in the New Deal farm programs and an issue that George McGovern rode to Congress in the 1950s.[21]

The culture wars that shaped American politics in subsequent decades also undercut Democratic candidates in the late 1970s, including liberal senator Dick Clark in neighboring Iowa, who was defeated in 1978. Caddell's polling found that abortion was the "most potent 'single-issue' factor" in South Dakota and presented political risks for Senators McGovern and Abourezk. Daschle drew upon his Catholicism to deflect potential criticism on the issue. During the final weeks of the 1978 campaign, Daschle sent a letter to voters saying "I am opposed to abortion. I do not support it. I have never supported it. It is an abhorrent practice. As a citizen and as a lifelong member of the Catholic faith I will do everything in my power to persuade others that abortion is wrong." Daschle enclosed a letter from eight of his grade school nuns saying, "We know and we tell those with whom we speak of your abhorrence for abortion— and of your commitment to life." According to one account of the 1978 campaign, Daschle was "in free fall, until a group of Aberdeen nuns stepped in to help." Daschle neutralized the abortion issue and went on to win, but just barely. According to the *Sioux Falls Argus Leader,* which endorsed Daschle (and would do so every time he ran for office), Daschle had "built a 'nice guy' image" by knocking on 40,000 doors during the campaign with the help of his wife, Laurie (who, by all accounts, was instrumental to his success). On election night, with all the votes counted except for one envelope of absentee ballots, Daschle trailed by 42 votes. The last envelope of ballots gave Daschle a lead of 14 votes. After a year of lawsuits and recount battles, Daschle officially won by a mere 139 votes. House Speaker Thomas "Tip" O'Neill gave Daschle the "Landslide Award."[22]

During his early years in Congress, Daschle eschewed the 1960s liberalism that would lead to Senator McGovern's defeat in 1980. In Daschle's first legislative act, he sought the balanced budget amendment to the Constitution for which he campaigned. He also supported the famous Reagan tax cuts. In 1982, Daschle took flak from his own party for not identifying himself as a Democrat and for not running with the party. The chair of the Minnehaha Democratic Party openly blamed Daschle for the party's 1982 losses. The *Argus Leader* reported, "Daschle didn't campaign as a Democrat and didn't use the word

Democrat in his ads." Daschle said in his congressional races that he was "nonpartisan," and McGovern lent a hand by deeming him a "moderate." Stuart Rothenberg reported on Daschle's focus on small, noncontroversial issues, which opponents derided as "PR gimmicks," and explained Daschle's attempt to "reinforce perceptions that he is a hardworking, independent congressman." Daschle understood the politics of symbolism and the value of calling for popular legislation: "It's a way to say we accomplished something without doing anything at all." In the early 1980s, Daschle's media advisor Karl Struble, who would continue to work for Daschle throughout his career, used "feel good" ads organized around the theme of "Why I love South Dakota." Struble explained, "It's almost impossible to see an issue or an accomplishment in the first few ads we put together." Struble produced a famous ad with "Daschle driving around Washington in his old, smoke-belching Pontiac. No BMW for Daschle; he was an ordinary guy." Daschle had mastered what Alexander Hamilton called "the little arts of popularity." Daschle's avoidance of costly ideological battles during the early Reagan years helped him win three House reelection bids.[23]

When Daschle ran for the Senate in 1986, he was touted as a "New Western Democrat" and thus a precursor to the shriveled New Democratic centrism that Bill Clinton would later embrace. Daschle's opponent, Senator Jim Abdnor, was hobbled by the unpopularity of Reagan's farm policies in the midst of a heartbreaking farm crisis. Daschle pollster Mark Mellman, who served as Kerry's pollster in 2004, reported in the fall of 1986 that the "farm issue is also working strongly in Daschle's favor" and that eight in ten voters found farm prosperity "extremely important to everyone in South Dakota." Daschle's haunting television ads depicting farmers losing their land helped make farm policy the critical issue in the campaign. Abdnor also suffered from the brutal primary challenge waged by Governor Janklow and emerged from the primary with one-third of Daschle's financial resources. During the first half of 1986, Daschle had already spent twice as much as Abdnor and Janklow combined. Social Security also became an issue, and the Daschle campaign linked Abdnor to the national criticism of Reagan for allegedly undermining the program.[24]

On the social front during the 1986 Senate campaign, Daschle sent another letter to voters saying that he was "unalterably opposed to abortion on demand," and he cast the issue as "a battle over human life." He again enclosed a letter that he had received from a minister, who wrote, "You used expletives like 'repulsive' and 'gross' in underscoring your abhorrence of abortion. You even said it is a form of murder, and I believe you are right. The bottom line is you are as opposed to abortion as I am." On gun control, Daschle said, "I am against it. No representative of our state has ever supported restrictive Federal gun control laws written in Washington and there is a very good reason why. What makes sense in New York is crazy in South Dakota." In 1986 Daschle ran, as Howard Dean would later say, as a member of the Republican wing of the Democratic Party. He won the Senate seat with 52 percent of the vote.[25]

While Daschle's 1968 liberal idealism yielded to the rising tide of Reaganism, John Thune came of age in West River, South Dakota. Thune grew up in Murdo (population 679), a frequent pit stop for travelers along Interstate 90. A railroad town founded in the early years of the twentieth century, Murdo is in the center of the sparsely populated ranching country of Jones County. Murdo took its name from the Scottish cattleman Murdo MacKenzie, who shipped Texas steers to South Dakota in 1904. The *Murdo Coyote* once praised young pioneers with "the nerve to leave the drudgery of the mill and factory" behind to discover their "individuality" in the expanses of western South Dakota. Thune's grandfather Nicolai immigrated to South Dakota from Norway in 1906 with a meager eighteen dollars to his name, passing through Ellis Island, where he lost his Norwegian name Gjelsvik (which immigration officials said was too hard to pronounce) in favor of Thune, the name of the family farm near Bergen, Norway. Norwegians were the second-largest immigrant group to move to South Dakota, outpaced only by German immigrants such as the Daschles. After working on the railroad—often an immigrant's first job—Nicolai and his brother started a hardware store in Mitchell (where a Thune Hardware still stands, but under different ownership). Nicolai then branched off and started a store in Murdo, where the business barely survived the Great Depression.[26]

Nicolai Thune's son, Harold, became a Murdo sports star, winning the MVP award for the 1937 state Class B basketball tournament. Harold went on to play at the University of Minnesota, where he was MVP his junior year, becoming South Dakota's first major Division I athlete. He was later named South Dakota Sportsman of the Decade for the 1930s. Harold enlisted in the U.S. Navy during World War II, piloting an F6-F Hellcat fighter in the Pacific and organizing basketball games on the deck of the aircraft carrier *Intrepid*. He shot down four Japanese Zeroes in one day—just missing becoming an ace, which requires five. One day, when the *Intrepid* was set ablaze by kamikazes, the squadron was forced to land on the island of Leyte. When taking off from Leyte the next morning, a blowout on Thune's plane wrenched it off the runway. The underbelly of the plane scraped a boulder, and the plane burst into flames. Some of the other pilots in the squadron said, "Hey, we've gotta go back for Thune!" but the skipper said, "He didn't have a chance; that thing was in flames the minute he went off the runway. There's no use going back." Harold survived and finally managed to get back to the island of Ulithi, where the squadron reassembled. The skipper's "mouth dropped open" when he saw Harold, whom he had left for dead.[27]

After the war, when Nicolai's health began to fail, he wanted Harold to return to Murdo and give up his $500 a month navy salary for $150 a month working at the hardware store. Harold did his duty and returned home, but his monthly salary soon dwindled to $125, to $100, and on down. By the 1960s, like many other mom-and-pop businesses in High Plains towns, the hardware store had come to generate insufficient income to feed a growing family. Harold sold the store in 1963, went back to school to get a teaching certificate, and started teaching and coaching in Murdo in 1964. (John's brother Rich was the valedictorian of his class, despite getting his only "B" in high school from his dad, who believed in tough Norwegian standards.) Thune's mother, Pat, was the school librarian. Harold's transition to teaching was a time that John Thune later recalled as "the lean years." Faith bolstered the family in hard times, however, as Harold and Pat raised their five children in a household of religious conviction. In keeping with the postwar surge in church attendance and the growth of evangelical churches, Harold and Pat left the Methodist church and helped build the interdenominational Community Bible Church in Murdo in the late 1950s. The Thunes remained active in church, school, sports, and the social functions of Murdo. In her social history of neighboring Presho (population 654), Dorothy Schwieder explains how the "deepest impressions" in the small towns of West

River, South Dakota, are made by "family, friendships, school, and work"—the currents at work in Murdo and in the Thune household.[28]

Like Harold, John Thune excelled at high school basketball, football, and track. Sports helped lead him into public life and made him a competitor. His first brush with politics came when meeting Congressman Jim Abdnor, who, as a former West River farmer and high school coach from nearby Kennebec (population 286), was obsessed with one of South Dakota's most fundamental social institutions: small-town basketball. In 1976, Abdnor first saw one of Thune's games during the Murdo Invitational Basketball Tournament, an annual event that Harold had organized in the 1960s. Abdnor saw the freshman Thune make five of six free throws. Abdnor later said to Thune, upon meeting him on Murdo's main street, "I noticed you missed one."

Upon graduating from high school in 1979, Thune turned down in-state basketball scholarship offers and went to Biola University in Southern California, where his four siblings attended, and became a basketball walk-on. Thune's brother Bob had previously turned down a basketball scholarship at the University of South Dakota when an old Murdo friend of Harold's—who, like many other South Dakotans, had moved to California (various California cities hosted "South Dakota picnics" for the Dakota diaspora)—urged him to go to Biola, and the younger siblings followed. South Dakota historian John Miller has noted, "One of the most attractive destinations for former South Dakotans during the early 1900s was the Los Angeles area, where a huge South Dakota picnic became a yearly event." Biola is in Los Angeles County, a home to the postwar revival of conservative politics, and only a few miles from Orange County, which became "a hotbed of the taxpayers' revolt" in the late 1970s that helped propel Ronald Reagan to the presidency. A knee injury hobbled Thune's college basketball career, but he still managed to earn a basketball scholarship. Along with student loans and odd jobs on campus, the scholarship put Thune through college. Congressman Abdnor kept offering jobs to Thune, but he decided that he could earn more money during the summer working at the local diner in Murdo and living at home. At Abdnor's urging, Thune visited Washington, D.C., for the first time during the spring break of 1980. That fall, Thune cast his first vote for president, filling in the oval for Ronald Reagan, who carried 79 percent of the vote in Jones County, South Dakota (home of Murdo), over Jimmy Carter's 21 percent. "Reagan spoke to me," Thune recalled, and with the help of Abdnor, who defeated Senator McGovern that fall, Thune became part of the Reagan revolution. For conservatives such as Thune, as political commentator Bill Schneider once remarked, "1980 is the year one."[29]

Thune's parents, who were Democrats—as was Grandfather Nicolai—also began the slow transition from being New Deal Democrats to Reagan Democrats to registered Republicans, part of what Jonathan Rieder called a "maelstrom of defection" from the Democratic Party in the later decades of the twentieth century. In 1972, Harold still defended his fellow soldier George McGovern for his courage during World War II (Harold and McGovern both received the Distinguished Flying Cross), but he had decided by the late 1970s that McGovernism had become too extreme. The Democrats were no longer the party of the little guys and Harry Truman's fierce anticommunism, and the Republicans were no longer the party of the elitist country-clubbers. For Harold, the party of Reagan became the party of small-town values that challenged the "evil empire," while the Democrats remained wedded to the anarchic 1960s and liberal interest groups. By the 1980s, Harold had begun to vote Republican and left the Democratic Party. Or, as he said, the "Democratic Party left us; we didn't leave it."[30]

After college, Thune earned an MBA at the University of South Dakota, then joined Senator Abdnor as a legislative assistant on business and tax issues in Reagan's tax-cutting Washington. In 1984, when Reagan won forty-nine states on his way to defeating the liberal standard-bearer Walter Mondale of Minnesota (who wanted to raise taxes), Thune married Kimberley Weems of Doland, South Dakota (population 297). Doland was also the home of Hubert Humphrey, who had lost the 1968 presidential race to Nixon after turning back a convention challenge from McGovern, who was originally from nearby Avon, South Dakota (population 561). Two weeks after John and Kimberley were married in Huron (the church in Doland was too small), the new couple moved to Washington. Thune worked for Abdnor until the senator was defeated by Daschle in 1986; Thune then went to work for the Small Business Administration, which Reagan tapped Abdnor to lead. In 1989 Thune moved back to Pierre, South Dakota, at the urging of GOP governor George Mickelson, whose governorship was sandwiched between Janklow's four terms as governor. Before he was killed in a plane crash on an Iowa farm in 1993, Mickelson urged Thune to set his sights on a House bid in 1996, when Democratic congressman Tim Johnson was sure to challenge sitting GOP senator Larry Pressler. Thune served as a railroad commissioner for Mickelson and as executive director of the state party but was not well known when he made his first run for office in 1996.[31]

When the first articles appeared about the 1996 House race, Thune was not even mentioned as a possible candidate. After a dizzying blitz of chicken dinners at local Lincoln Day gatherings and with some help from his friends from the Abdnor days, Thune defeated Janklow's lieutenant governor to win the 1996 GOP nomination for the House seat. A poll released by his opponent six weeks before the primary showed the race at 69 to 15 percent, with Thune losing. Thune then beat Daschle's state director and protégé, Rick Weiland, in the fall of 1996 and won his 1998 reelection bid by the largest margin in South Dakota history. After another decisive win in 2000, Thune was a lock to succeed the (again) term-limited Janklow as governor in 2002. After the divisive presidential election of 2000, however, George Bush became president and the Senate was deadlocked 50 to 50 until Senator Daschle helped convince Senator Jim Jeffords of Vermont to leave the Republican Party and become an independent, making Daschle Senate majority leader in a Senate divided 50 to 49 to 1. With control of the Senate hanging in the balance, Thune walked away from an easy election for governor and challenged Democratic senator Tim Johnson. In early October, a month after the 9/11 attacks, Thune entered the race. In the Murdo gym across the gravel street from Harold and Pat's house, where his old 800-meter track record hung on the wall and where Senator Abdnor saw him miss that one free throw, Thune declared his Senate candidacy.[32]

The 2002 Senate race became a cliff-hanger. Senator Johnson adhered to the early Daschle model of avoiding costly ideological attachments to the national Democratic Party and highlighted his votes for the Bush tax cuts and the war in Iraq. He touted his ability to deliver money to the state using his seat on the Appropriations Committee and constantly said that he needed to win to "keep Tom Daschle as majority leader" of a Democratic Senate. Thune's candidacy suffered from a toxic GOP primary for governor, which redounded to the detriment of Republicans generally (one ad famously alleged that a candidate had invested in a firm that collected the skin of cadavers and used it, unbeknownst to the donor family, to fatten lips and flatten wrinkled skin). Democrats also blamed Thune for failing to convince the president, who visited the state five times to campaign for Thune, to support drought relief for farmers during an August visit to Mount Rushmore.

Thune held his own, however; at 4:30 A.M. the day after the election, voters who were still awake saw Thune leading by 3,200 votes. In midmorning, after the state Indian reservations had reported, Johnson surged ahead by 524 votes. On Pine Ridge Indian Reservation, Johnson picked up 2,856 votes to Thune's 248, winning the county 92 to 8 percent. Thune lost the Oglala precinct 390 to 44 and the Kyle precinct 512 to 48. In the wake of the 2000 presidential election and its electoral litigation and courtroom drama, problems of voter fraud made many headlines. After a week of teeth-gnashing over a potential recount allowed by state law in close elections, Thune chose to concede. Despite the results in South Dakota, the Democrats still lost control of the Senate, and Daschle once again became minority leader.[33]

Despite losing control of the Senate in the fall of 2002, Daschle was bolstered by Senator Tim Johnson's narrow victory and began assembling an impressive group of advisors for a presidential campaign in 2004. Political observers began reporting on Daschle's presidential campaign team and concluded that "he would have as good a chance to be the nominee as anyone else in the field." Pundits thought that Daschle would appeal to voters in the caucuses of neighboring Iowa and would make a strong bid for the nomination. His advisors devised an announcement schedule for Iowa and New Hampshire. But in early 2003, at the eleventh hour (the *Argus Leader* had already run a blazing headline: "HE'S RUNNING"), Daschle scotched his presidential bid. Speculation immediately began about a Daschle-Thune Senate battle in 2004. By the fall of 2003, the Janklow manslaughter verdict and the congressman's subsequent resignation put tremendous pressure on Thune to make a decision about his political future.[34]

As leader of the national Democrats, Daschle would not be able to run as a moderate in 2004 as Senator Johnson did in 2002 and as Daschle did early in his career. After his elevation to the Senate in 1986, Daschle had not been tested at the ballot box. His 1992 and

1998 reelection bids had been runaways against political unknowns, whom he outspent nine to one and fourteen to one. At the same time, his popularity grew among Democratic senators, and he narrowly won the post of Senate leader in 1994 by a vote of 24 to 23. In 2004, Daschle led the Democratic opposition to a GOP president who was popular in South Dakota in a time of war. While Thune served in the House in the mid-1990s after the GOP took over Congress, Daschle defended the Clinton administration's agenda and helped organize the Senate votes to prevent Clinton's removal after his impeachment by the House. Clinton's chief of staff, John Podesta, said that the denizens of the White House "absolutely put our fate in the hands of Tom Daschle." One veteran Democratic senator later said, "At any moment at that time, a negative signal from Tom Daschle would have brought down the presidency." When the problems that triggered impeachment first arose, Daschle's colleague Senator Kent Conrad of North Dakota informed the White House, "You are about three days from having the senior Democrats come down and ask for the President's resignation."[35]

After Bush was elected in 2000, according to Michael Barone, Daschle maintained an "all for one, one for all spirit in his caucus," convincing Democrats that "they had to hang together." All agreed that Daschle patiently massaged the egos of his caucus members and effectively maintained party discipline while offering effective resistance to the GOP, which increasingly lashed out at Daschle's tactics. Journalist Robert Novak reported, "Republicans who must deal with Daschle regard him as one of the coldest men they have met in politics, who truly subscribes to the Kennedy clan's axiom of 'Don't get mad, get even.'" Daschle understood political hardball (his campaign motto was "Only the paranoid survive"). Even after the 9/11 attacks, the friction between Daschle and the White House became so intense that post-9/11 breakfast meetings between White House officials and the congressional leadership were cancelled. Daschle's critics conceded his ability to block much of the GOP agenda. One government professor said that Daschle had "the style of a guy who sounds very reasonable, and when you look down, you're bleeding." A previous Democratic leader, Senator Robert Byrd, said that Daschle had "steel in his spine despite his reasonable and modest demeanor."[36]

Daschle's political positions also evolved as he climbed the leadership ladder. The balanced budget amendment that he had made central to his first congressional campaign in 1978, for example, failed in the Senate in the mid-1990s by one vote, and Daschle led the charge against it. Part of his historical legacy, the *Washington Post* noted, was "thwarting the Republicans' marquee initiative—a constitutional amendment to balance the budget." In contrast to his early invocation of his Catholic credentials on the abortion issue, Daschle also began feuding with the bishop of Sioux Falls in the 1990s over such matters as partial-birth abortion. By 2004, Daschle had returned to his political roots. He represented 1960s-era liberalism, battled the Bush administration (which carried the mantle of Reaganism), and served as the president's chief nemesis in an age of partisan rancor. Liberals such as Howard Dean and Michael Moore were also ascendant within Democratic circles. Political commentator Stuart Rothenberg noted during the 2004 Democratic convention that "the 1960s, socially liberal, anti-Vietnam generation is now solidly in control of the Democratic Party." McGovernism, the demise of which Daschle had personally witnessed in South Dakota in 1980 and assiduously tried to avoid, had been revived. Political analyst Ryan Lizza and moderate Democrats lamented the turn, arguing that the Democratic Party "has had to spend 30 years reorienting itself in response to the McGovern catastrophe and the rise of modern conservatism." In 2004, Reaganite conservatism would be represented in the South Dakota Senate race by John Thune. The traditions and memories of McGovernism and Reaganism would collide.[37]

In contrast to the ease of his 1992 and 1998 reelection campaigns, which were distinctly post–cold war affairs, Daschle's 2004 reelection campaign took place in a time of war. The cold war ended and the Soviet Union imploded in part because of the bloody war in Afghanistan, where a wealthy Saudi named Osama Bin Laden helped prosecute a jihad against the Red Army. After the war, Bin Laden held together his cadre of Islamic radicals, known as al-Qaeda, and began to build an international network of terrorists. Claiming to be insulted by the U.S. military presence in Saudi Arabia during the 1991 Gulf War and by U.S. support of Israel, in 1996 Bin Laden began to issue fatwas against the United States, which he deemed "the head of the snake."

From 1996 to 2001, the Taliban (the Islamic theocrats who ruled Afghanistan) allowed Bin Laden to train as many as twenty thousand Islamic fighters in their country. After Bin Laden's radicals used three planes to kill more than three thousand Americans, the Bush administration launched a war to depose the Taliban.[38]

Fearing the spread of weapons of mass destruction and hoping to promote a democratic alternative to radical Islamic theocracy in the Middle East, in 2002 the Bush administration began preparations for a war against Iraq. When Congress passed the Iraq War resolution in the fall of 2002, Daschle served as majority leader of the Senate. Some on the left fiercely criticized Congress for supporting the war resolution; critics such as E. J. Dionne felt that Democrats were intimidated into supporting the war. Although Daschle sought to postpone the vote until after the 2002 elections, he did vote to authorize the war. Senator Edward (Ted) Kennedy later criticized the "stampede to vote" on the war and said that many Democrats "got caught up in it." The strains of the Iraq War and the rancor of dissent would hover over the 2004 election season.[39]

A week after the Janklow manslaughter verdict in late 2003, Thune said that he would make an announcement about his future during the third week of December. He chose to challenge Daschle. The republic would witness a grand battle for a seat in the world's oldest deliberative body, a battle that crisply contrasted the views of the major parties at a crucial moment in the nation's history. Daschle would tout his congressional power and ultimately spend $21 million, dwarfing the per capita spending record of any previous congressional campaign, and deploy 315 full-time and 200 part-time staffers. Thune would spend $15 million, hire 18 campaign staffers, and rely on 70 campaign workers employed by the state party. It would be the most expensive race per capita in the nation's history. Daschle would spend $28 per voter, shattering New Jersey senator Jon Corzine's previous spending record of over $7 per voter (by contrast, in the Georgia Senate race of 2004, less than $1 per voter was spent). By the standards of American political history, the Daschle-Thune race would be monumental.[40]

The third week of December 2003 was not otherwise kind to Daschle. On Sunday, members of the Fourth Infantry Division found the bearded, lice-ridden Iraqi dictator Saddam Hussein in a rat-infested "spider hole" with a pistol and two AK-47s. Although he had been organizing and leading the Baathist insurgency, Saddam surrendered without firing a shot. The Fourth ID soldiers shouted down the hole, "President Bush sends his regards." While most observers celebrated, on Monday Howard Dean, the front-runner for the Democratic presidential nomination, declared that "the capture of Saddam Hussein has not made America safer." Instead, "The difficulties and tragedies which we have faced in Iraq," according to Dean, "show the administration launched the war in the wrong way, at the wrong time, with inadequate planning, insufficient help, and at the extraordinary cost, so far, of $166 billion." Dean's consistency and passion were admirable, especially when contrasted to the muddled message of his opponent for the nomination, Senator John Kerry. Nevertheless, many voters believed that the world was safer without Saddam Hussein on the loose, although still not safe. As Christmas approached, surface-to-air missile batteries were positioned around Washington, D.C., and New York City because of the rising level of electronic terrorist chatter. Despite the capture of Saddam and the continuing threat of terrorism, Dean continued his march to the Democratic nomination and even gathered the endorsement of former vice president Al Gore. Democrats were poised to nominate, as David Brooks said, the "Huey Long of the iPod set." A *Washington Post*–ABC News poll released in late December found that Bush would defeat Dean 55 to 37 percent, indicating the potentially disastrous drag of a Dean candidacy on Daschle's Senate campaign.[41]

In December, the Conference Board also announced its prediction of an economic growth rate of 5.7 percent for 2004. In addition to opposing the war in Iraq, the Democrats had been skewering the president's economic policies for three years. In his book *Like No Other Time*, released in late 2003, Daschle maintained that the economy was "floundering" and "plunging." As it turned out, the third-quarter growth rate for 2003 was 8.2 percent, the highest in twenty years, and just before Christmas, the Dow Jones Industrial Average hit 10,000.[42]

In mid-December, Democratic senator John Breaux of Louisiana announced his retirement from the Senate, contributing to Daschle's deteriorating political situation. Breaux had been elected to the Senate in 1986, the same year that Daschle made the leap from the House to the Senate. Breaux was a moderate, and the *New Republic* reported that Daschle was furious with Breaux for his deal making, which helped enable passage of the president's 2001 tax cuts and his 2003 prescription drug bill. Breaux's departure seriously undermined Democratic chances of retaking the Senate, which the GOP then controlled 51 to 48 to 1, during the fall 2004 elections. Breaux's seat might also go Republican, producing the first GOP senator from Louisiana since Reconstruction. The same scenario unfolded in North Carolina, where John Edwards was retiring; in Florida, where Bob Graham was retiring; in South Carolina, where Fritz Hollings was retiring; and in Georgia, where Zell Miller was retiring. The reddening of the South could make the Senate even redder after the fall elections.[43]

The departure of Democratic senator Zell Miller of Georgia, who went on to endorse President Bush during the fall campaign, surely did not bother Daschle. Miller's book, *A National Party No More: The Conscience of a Conservative Democrat*, was released at the same time as Daschle's book and overshadowed Daschle's in both sales and publicity. Miller claimed that Democrats such as Daschle were so unpopular that they could not even campaign in the ever-reddening South. Miller also took aim at Daschle's wife for lobbying the Congress in which Daschle served as a leader, and he compared the Democratic party's courting of special interests to "streetwalkers in skimpy halters and hot pants plying their age-old trade for the fat wallets of 'K Street.'" Miller blamed Daschle's assent to labor union demands for the defeat of his Senate colleague Max Cleland in the 2002 midterm elections. Miller "was appalled by the partisanship of Tom Daschle's Democratic Caucus," according to Michael Barone: "Just stick together, Daschle said, and don't worry about negative fallout; we'll be protected by the increasingly partisan pro-Democratic old media, and we can force the other side to give in." The same Sunday that Saddam Hussein was captured, the *New York Times Magazine* reported on the major ideas of 2003, which included a "write off the South strategy" for the national Democratic Party, which John Kerry also floated during the New Hampshire primary. As southerners such as Zell Miller wrote off the Democrats, political trends in the South increasingly favored the GOP.[44]

In addition to the capture of Saddam Hussein, the economic recovery, and the retirement of southern Democratic senators, Daschle's Senate leadership became the subject of increasing scrutiny. Many on the left called for an even more strident resistance to the Bush administration's agenda. The liberal website Buzzflash called for Daschle's resignation: "If you had to sum it all up, Tom is either totally ineffective AS minority leader because he is inherently inept at the position and unable to strategically battle the Republicans—or he is so conflicted by the red party politics of his state, his wife's role as a lobbyist, and his Democratic Leadership Council corporate ties that he is rendered a rollover patsy for the Bush Cartel." *National Journal* also quoted Democratic insiders and Democratic Senate staffers who seethed over the passage of the Bush administration's prescription drug bill during the fall of 2003 and concluded that Daschle's leadership "fueled much criticism." The *New Republic* similarly found Daschle's management of the fall 2003 energy bill vote "embarrassing."[45]

Daschle had also presided over the Democratic reversals during the midterm elections of 2002 and had allowed President Bush to advance much of his agenda, including large tax cuts, war with Iraq, large-scale education reforms, and the expansion of Medicare to include the new prescription drug plan. Daschle's advocacy of the Patriot Act also angered some civil liberties advocates on the left. Democratic senator Russ Feingold of Wisconsin, who voted against the Patriot Act, described Daschle's reaction to his dissent as "fairly brutal." Such actions fueled Democrats' fears that Daschle would "pay more attention to winning his race than unifying his caucus." Daschle's loss of his leadership post was at least possible in December 2003, but none of the unrest was reported by the *Argus Leader* in South Dakota, so criticism of Daschle back home was limited. Such dissension in the Democratic ranks was potentially career-ending for Daschle since his hold on a leadership position in Washington remained central to his reelection strategy. Daschle had been running ads for months trumpeting the importance of his post as Senate leader. A few South Dakotans also regretted the outcome of the 2002 election, in which Senator Tim Johnson's rationale for his reelection was to "keep Tom Daschle as majority leader." A postelection poll of South Dakotans showed that they would have voted out Johnson by a slim margin if they had known that the Democrats would lose the Senate and Daschle would not be majority leader anymore.[46]

Just before noon on Tuesday, December 16, 2003, a Thune advisor faxed a letter to the chairman of the South Dakota Republican Party stating that John Thune would not enter the House race and that any further political announcements would come after the first of the year. Most observers rightly concluded that Thune planned a Senate bid. Daschle's campaign manager began demanding that Thune immediately make his decision about entering the race. The Daschle camp had been conducting focus groups, polling, running ads, and identifying Daschle voters for six months in anticipation of a challenge. By late 2003, the Daschle campaign had already hired thirty staffers. Daschle attempted to dissuade Thune from running and repeatedly said that he had never been more prepared to run for reelection than he was in December 2003. He also crisscrossed the country collecting donations to fuel a $21 million campaign. In front of a "well-heeled crowd" at a Rhode Island fund-raiser, Daschle said, "My favorite people are those who live like Republicans and support Democrats." In December 2003, Thune had no campaign office, no campaign staffers, and no campaign money. One assessment called Thune's bid a "kamikaze mission."[47]

In South Dakota, people began digging in. After the holidays, people feared that the war would come. Throughout the battles of 2004, Daschle and Thune would represent warring political generations and reflect the broader national polarization between the nation's dominant political parties.

CHAPTER TWO

THE LAUNCH

Thune's decision to challenge Tom Daschle can only be seen as an act of political courage.

—Mitchell Daily Republic

On the evening of January 5, 2004, the windchill drove the temperature in Sioux Falls down to twenty-five degrees below zero. That evening, several hundred loyal Republicans in Lincoln County waited for Thune to announce his political intentions at the county's Lincoln Day Dinner, the annual fund-raiser held by county Republican organizations across the state. Before Thune announced his decision to the members of the Party of Lincoln, he welcomed Nebraska senator Chuck Hagel, whose state had named its capital for Lincoln. In his speech, Thune recalled how many of South Dakota's first immigrants were Union Civil War veterans and that 80 percent of South Dakota settlers in the 1860s registered as Republicans. Lincoln even appointed his own doctor as South Dakota's first territorial governor in 1861. South Dakota counties such as Grant, Meade, and McPherson took the name of Lincoln's generals, and Union County represented Lincoln's great mission as president. Thune's longtime political director, Ryan Nelson, even hailed from Gettysburg, South Dakota (population 1,169), named for the battle that turned the war against the Confederacy.

The Daschle-Thune race also rivaled the famous Lincoln-Douglas race. The *New York Times* reported in 1858 that Illinois was "the most interesting political battle-ground in the Union," a claim often made about the South Dakota Senate race of 2004. Like Lincoln and Douglas, Daschle and Thune would ultimately agree to seven debates in the fall (like Lincoln, Thune called for more). Lincoln also had to contend with a hostile *Argus*—in his case, the newspaper in the capitol of New York, the *Albany Argus*, which ridiculed him as "the ugliest man in the Union." At the Lincoln Day speech in Lincoln County, Thune invoked Lincoln's rallying cry after his wrenching loss to Douglas in the 1858 Illinois Senate race: "The fight must go on. The cause . . . must not be surrendered at the end of one or even one hundred defeats." Thune reconciled himself to his defeat in 2002, when he was nipped by 524 votes, and marched forward. Like Lincoln throughout much of that president's political life, Thune would be the underdog in the Senate race, a fact he openly conceded. Despite the long odds, a Thune victory could help break the logjam in Washington. During his announcement speech, Thune said, "I just flat don't know of a place where I could make a bigger difference or a place that is more in need of bold new leadership than the United States Senate."[1]

On the night of his announcement, Thune revealed a critical component of his early strategy. He started his speech by saying "I believe the last campaign season was way too long, that South Dakotans are still weary from it, and I don't sense that anyone is ready for the next campaign season to begin." Thune sought "a short, compressed campaign season," a strategic decision that would guide his campaign in the early months. The Daschle campaign, in contrast, had started running ads during the summer of 2003. Soon after the announcement, the Thune campaign rented an office, leased cell phones, and installed land lines and computers. Thune's campaign manager, Dick Wadhams, moved to South Dakota from Colorado, along with his deputy, John Wood, whom the press referred to as "Karl Rove's cousin," giving his presence a sinister cast (among Rove's detractors, at least). Wadhams had managed successful Senate campaigns for Colorado senator Wayne Allard in 1996 and 2002 and Montana senator Conrad Burns in 2000 and was known for his media skills and quotable quotes. The *Argus Leader* subsequently adopted a policy of not quoting spokesmen. Even before Wadhams arrived, Democrats circulated a memo outlining his history as an "attack dog." Long before Thune started campaigning, Daschle donned the mantle of persecuted victim, a tactic he had used in the past. During Daschle's prior competitive bid, in 1986, even the *Argus Leader* noted in its endorsement of Daschle that he would "whimper like a puppy when attacked."[2]

Some political analysts considered Daschle's campaign operation, which would enjoy a sizeable war chest, the most skillful in the nation. Daschle's campaign manager, Steve Hildebrand, had worked for

Daschle's 1986 Senate campaign and went on to become Midwest coordinator of the Democratic National Committee and political director of the Democratic Senatorial Campaign Committee. In 2000 he managed Al Gore's decisive win in the Iowa caucuses, and in 2002 he managed Senator Tim Johnson's narrow victory over Thune. Johnson's campaign spokesman in 2002, Dan Pfeiffer, would become the Daschle campaign's communications director in 2004. Daschle could also call on advisors whom he planned to tap for his presidential run and an assortment of veterans of past South Dakota campaigns. Mark Mellman, Kerry's pollster in 2004, had served as Daschle's pollster in his earlier Senate campaigns. Jim Jordan, the first campaign manager for Kerry's presidential bid (who later organized the efforts of Democratic-leaning 527 organizations), had served as Tim Johnson's spokesman in 1996. Joe Hansen, a direct mail and field organization specialist and a former executive director of the Democratic Senatorial Campaign Committee, had managed Johnson's 1996 and Daschle's 1998 Senate victories. Mitchell native Steve Jarding, an advisor to Senator John Edwards and a rural politics expert, had once served as executive director of the South Dakota Democratic Party. John Podesta, President Clinton's chief of staff during the Senate impeachment trial, planned to advise Daschle's presidential campaign and instead founded a new think tank called the Center for American Progress, which created and distributed information critical of the Bush administration throughout 2004.[3]

During the early weeks of January, the contest for South Dakota's only seat in the House of Representatives concentrated political minds in the state. The race became a focus of national attention as Democrats hoped that a victory would serve as a bellwether for the presidential contest. The Democratic candidate would be the young upstart Stephanie Herseth, who had mounted an impressive but unsuccessful bid against Janklow in 2002. After four rounds of dramatic convention votes, the GOP delegates chose state senator Larry Diedrich, a gregarious farmer from near Elkton (population 602) in eastern South Dakota. As the former president of the American Soybean Association and an ethanol investor, Diedrich drew attention to Daschle's handing of the ethanol bill. Diedrich also had a unifying personality—a boost to the South Dakota GOP, which had suffered from factional feuds in recent decades. At a breakfast speech during the January convention, his first public address since his announcement, Thune stressed party cohesion and again invoked Lincoln: "A house divided against itself cannot stand." Thune also emphasized outreach and noted his recent visits to the Pine Ridge, Crow Creek, and Lower Brule Indian reservations. Bruce Whalen, an Oglala Sioux from Pine Ridge, followed Thune at the podium: "I know there's a lot of Republicans out there on Pine Ridge. They just don't know it yet." The next week, Thune visited Eagle Butte on the Cheyenne River Indian Reservation and spent the day meeting with the tribal council, talking to schoolchildren, and helping with basketball practice. These were hopeful signs for the GOP in South Dakota: allusions to Lincoln, strong agricultural voices, party unity, and Indian outreach.[4]

Diedrich received the support of many GOP convention delegates concerned about "electability," which became the theme of January's other main event, the presidential caucuses in neighboring Iowa. Both the spillover effect of the South Dakota House race and the man whom Iowa Democrats would choose as their presidential favorite would help nationalize and define the South Dakota Senate race. The Iowa race had been viewed as a two-way brawl between Howard Dean and Congressman Dick Gephardt, with Dean given the edge after Gephardt, from neighboring Missouri, lost his early lead. However, when the votes were cast in the Iowa caucuses, John Kerry, aided by memories of glory revived by the late appearance of an old navy buddy he saved in Vietnam, and John Edwards, who emphasized his ability to win southern states, finished first and second and Dean a distant third. Gephardt had placed all his bets on Iowa; after receiving an anemic 11 percent of the vote, he quit the race. After a meteoric rise in the polls based on an antiwar and anti-Bush appeal to the Democratic Party's base, Dean complained of being the "pin cushion" of the media and the entire Democratic field in the run-up to the vote. After Dean's famous "I have a scream" speech on the night of the caucuses, many experts ignored his candidacy and pundits ridiculed his temperament. David Letterman ran a video of Dean's head exploding to make the point. A Dean candidacy would have yielded an even more fiercely ideological presidential race by presenting voters with direct clashes on core issues such as the war in Iraq and fiscal policy (most of the other candidates had tried to stake out a mushy middle ground), but Dean made many mistakes in his quest for the nomination. Prior to the vote, Dean's campaign manager admitted, "It's probably a f——g miracle we're even sitting where we're at."[5]

Within a few days of the Iowa vote, Dean's support plummeted in New Hampshire, where he had previously held a commanding lead in the polls over the increasingly erratic General Wesley Clark (the antiwar candidate of Michael Moore and George McGovern) and a third-place John Kerry. After his Iowa victory, Kerry opened up a wide lead over Dean in New Hampshire, and Clark faded. After losing New Hampshire to Kerry, Dean replaced his campaign manager and pulled many of his ads. Kerry, who had received little scrutiny in the previous months while mired in the polls, became the ABB ("Anybody But Bush") candidate, and many Democrats hoped that Kerry's service in Vietnam would bolster his foreign policy credentials in a national campaign focused on war and peace. Terry McAuliffe, chairman of the Democratic National Committee (DNC), wore an ABB pin in his lapel to make the point. Signaling their migration from passion to pragmatism, Democrats donned bumper stickers that read, "Dated Dean, but Married Kerry." Although Kerry prevailed, the Dean candidacy left a mark on the race. The *New York Times* reported that the "Democratic Party emerging from Iowa and New Hampshire is different from the careful centrism of the Clinton era." Dean had rallied the antiwar forces in the Democratic Party and ran ads criticizing Congressman Gephardt for supporting the war in Iraq. Senator Joe Lieberman, who supported the war, skipped the Iowa caucuses because of the hostile crowds he encountered while campaigning in the state. Michael O'Hanlon of the Brookings Institution worried that "the Democratic base is probably going to lose the Democrats the election in 2004."[6]

While the early Democratic primaries unfolded and Thune assembled his campaign team, the debate persisted over the Democrats' failure to block the president's prescription drug bill during the fall of 2003. During the month of January, Daschle traveled around South Dakota explaining his opposition. Daschle had already made the issue of prescription drugs a focus of his reelection campaign and worried that it might vanish as an issue after the passage of Bush's bill. Daschle also criticized the American Association of Retired Persons for supporting the administration's bill, which Daschle said aided the AARP's business interests. Newly arrived campaign manager Dick Wadhams noted to reporters, however, that Democratic senators Kent Conrad and Byron Dorgan of North Dakota and Ben Nelson of Nebraska had all supported the bill, in part because it aided rural hospitals. Democratic senator Max Baucus of Montana actually sponsored the bill, causing friction with Daschle over his willingness to break ranks. In a state that is increasingly gray, the cost of prescription drugs became a debating point in the campaign.[7]

Despite the support of Democratic senators from North Dakota, Nebraska, and Montana, Daschle still opposed the prescription drug bill, which many considered a major legislative victory for the Bush administration. Passage of the bill stoked the simmering rebellion in Daschle's caucus and generated calls for even more strident opposition tactics. Some Democratic senators sought to oust Senator Dorgan, a close Daschle ally, as chair of the Democratic Policy Committee because of his support for both the prescription drug bill and the energy bill (Dorgan was up for reelection in 2004). *The Hill* reported that Senator Harry Reid, the assistant leader, had the support of many caucus members and that, most ominously, Senator Christopher Dodd (another potential rival to Daschle) thought that the Senate leadership needed to be more aggressive. Some Democratic senators said that Daschle was distracted by the threat of Thune's candidacy at home. Senator Dianne Feinstein defended Daschle by saying that he would not allow his state's interests to interfere with his leadership duties. Back home, however, Daschle said that South Dakota took precedence. The state's leading newspaper, the *Sioux Falls Argus Leader*, ignored Daschle's difficulties, but more scrutiny of Daschle's political balancing act was inevitable as the national prominence of the campaign grew.[8]

Daschle faced the LBJ dilemma. In the 1950s, Lyndon Baines Johnson needed the support of northern liberals such as Hubert Humphrey to maintain his hold on his leadership post in the Senate, but back in Texas LBJ played the part of a southern conservative. LBJ, who did not have to worry about consistency-scrutinizing bloggers, managed the balancing act long enough to make an escape to the executive branch as vice president in 1960. Daschle had instead terminated his run for president in 2003 and in 2004 would try to run again in Republican-leaning South Dakota while serving as Senate leader.

Daschle also had a longer record of Senate leadership, serving for ten years, compared to LBJ's eight. Unlike Daschle, LBJ served as leader in the shadow of some frightening precedents. LBJ's immediate predecessor as Senate leader, Ernest McFarland of Arizona, was elected leader in 1951 and went down to defeat in 1952. McFarland's predecessor, Scott Lucas of Illinois, was elected leader in 1949 and went down to defeat in 1950. McFarland and Lucas both suffered from supporting an unpopular national Democratic agenda. McFarland lost to a forty-three-year-old conservative upstart from Phoenix named Barry Goldwater. In January 2004, a few days after Thune announced his candidacy, he turned forty-three. To avoid the fate of McFarland and Lucas, Daschle often reminded his South Dakota constituents how much he supported the president, which infuriated the national Democratic "Anybody But Bush" base. More articles questioning Daschle's ability to serve as Senate leader while running for reelection in a red state appeared in the *New Republic,* the *Nation, National Journal,* and the *American Prospect,* as well as on the liberal website Buzzflash, which openly called for Daschle to resign as leader. Such commentary failed to make the pages of the *Argus Leader,* however, so it failed to influence South Dakota voters unless they followed national magazines or local blogs.[9]

The "first major skirmish" of the Senate campaign, according to *Roll Call,* broke out in late January when the newspaper reported that Thune would continue to lobby for South Dakota ethanol and railroad interests while running for the Senate. Dick Wadhams responded by noting the hypocrisy of raising such an issue given the existence of "Daschle, Inc.," referring to the lobbying activities of the Daschle family, especially Daschle's wife, Linda. The *Wall Street Journal* ran a piece about the skirmish and noted that the potential criticism of his wife's lobbying explained why Daschle did not run for president. The Daschle campaign argued that Mrs. Daschle lobbied only the House and avoided the Senate, where Daschle served as leader. Reports also disclosed that Daschle's son and daughter-in-law were lobbyists.[10]

For Daschle, who had criticized "special interests" throughout his career, the lobbying controversy proved awkward. The Daschle campaign responded that "Thune plans not just to attack Tom, but Tom's family," but the issue became nonpartisan after stories in several liberal magazines proffered the most stinging criticism. In the final week of January, *Roll Call* reported that Daschle's deputy, Harry Reid of Nevada, favored a review of family lobbying by the Senate ethics committee. The Congressional Accountability Project concluded that if it "looks like a Senator's relatives are aggressively taking advantage of their ties to the Senator, then that makes the entire Senate look bad." The Daschle campaign hoped that the lobbying discussion would fade from voters' memories and that Thune's lobbying would neutralize the issue, but the January lobbying dust-up would be only a teaser.[11]

South Dakota's annual six-week legislative session also started in January. In his book, Daschle was dismissive of the Republican legislature, which had complicated his life in the past. In 2002, the legislature passed a law that prevented Daschle from running for both the Senate and president at the same time, a luxury that LBJ had enjoyed in Texas in 1960. The legislature also passed resolutions embarrassing to Daschle that called for federal judges to receive a vote on their nominations, for federal tax cuts, and for votes opposing federal gun control. Such were the perils faced by a national Democratic leader who represented a red state with a conservative legislature. In 2004, the legislature also attempted to outlaw abortion and force the U.S. Supreme Court to once again review *Roe v. Wade,* an indication of South Dakota's pro-life sentiments. After the 2005 legislative session, *Catholic World News* ran the headline "SD Adopts Strictest Abortion Restrictions in US." In 2006, the legislature succeeded in passing a law banning abortion. Following his election as Democratic leader, contrary to his early pronouncements on abortion, Daschle had become close to pro-choice groups such as the National Abortion Rights Action League (NARAL) and Emily's List. A major abortion discussion about banning abortion among his pro-life constituents during an election year would remind voters of Daschle's evolving position. Daschle's new stance on abortion had already created a rift with the Catholic bishop of Sioux Falls.[12]

By the middle of February, the Dean campaign had cratered, suffering one of the longest falls in American political history. On February 3, Kerry rolled over Dean in South Dakota's sister state to the north. North Dakota, for all its storied populist past and early experiments in state-based socialism, became a textbook case of the power of momentum and media trumping actual campaigning and signaled the degree to which the compressed presidential selection process constricts democracy. Kerry's campaign did not even open an office in North Dakota until a week before the caucus. On the Sunday before the vote, the Massachusetts senator made up for slighting North Dakota by watching the Super Bowl, featuring a dramatic win by the New England Patriots, in a bar in Fargo. Kerry's modest effort easily outdid Al Gore. In the 2000 general election, Gore stopped in North Dakota once, just long enough for some pizzas to be delivered to the Gore campaign jet in Grand Forks. Quick touchdowns for carry-out pizza do not foment democratic passion.[13]

The collapse of Dean, Kerry's early momentum, and the pressure to wrap up the race before Kerry received a serious grilling left the Democrats with an unvetted candidate as the front-runner. The Democrats could have benefited from a grueling nomination process similar to that of 1968 and 1972, when candidates were given a thorough going-over. Instead, party elders sought to frontload the selection process and quickly clear the field to save ammunition for the big battle in the fall. The Democratic logic was understandable but risky. Kerry was considered the *liberal* senator from Massachusetts, after all. The Swiss boarding schools, the sailing and parasailing, St. Paul's prep school, Yale, Skull and Bones, his antiwar activities during the Vietnam era, the East African–born ketchup heiress worth $500 million, and the multiple palatial homes all seemed a bit absurd in the Age of Dean and populist outrage. Kerry had told the *Harvard Crimson* after returning from Vietnam, "I'm an internationalist. I'd like to see our troops dispersed through the world only at the directive of the United Nations." Even by the standards of the Ivy League in the 1960s, such statements seemed extreme, but they were especially hard to explain in an age of UN ineptitude and corruption.[14]

Many Democrats, however, favored Kerry over Dean, who finally crashed during the Wisconsin primary. Dean fired his campaign manager Joe Trippi (who said that Dean was "just f——g not ready for prime time and he never will be"), lost his endorsement from the American Federation of State, County and Municipal Employees, or AFSCME (the union president called Dean "nuts"), and faded from media attention. After Dean finished third in Wisconsin, even losing liberal Dane County, home to the University of Wisconsin–Madison, he deactivated his campaign.[15]

The Dean boomlet, however, pulled the entire Democratic presidential field to the left. Dean revived what Minnesota senator Paul

Wellstone famously called the "Democratic wing of the Democratic Party" and shifted the party away from the centrism of Bill Clinton. Dean drew support from those who thought that Democratic leaders in Washington had been too timid in dealing with President Bush and had been steamrolled on the Iraq War vote, the Patriot Act, education reform, the prescription drug bill, and tax cuts. Despite losing, Dean changed the contours of the Democratic selection process. He was not merely a blip, as many presidential candidates have been, and he successfully tapped a strain of anger in the populace and brought new voters into the process. Later reports revealed the infighting in the Dean camp between the Vermonters, who viewed Dean as a moderate, and the Trippi faction, who wanted to press the antiwar cause and attack the "special interests." Dean's chief speechwriter quit when the Vermonters told him to put a lid on the populism, which they thought was not the real Dean. "I refused to believe it because I didn't want to," he said. "To believe that was to believe that Howard Dean was a fraud."[16]

The other major controversy in February involved President Bush's National Guard service during the Vietnam War, another early sign of the persistent power of the historical memories of the 1960s and Vietnam. Many stories implied that Kerry served in Vietnam and took enemy fire while Bush hid in the National Guard and shirked his duties. Filmmaker Michael Moore called Bush a deserter, and the DNC chairman said that Bush was AWOL, or absent without leave. It was a successful effort to create a media storm. The slow authorization by the White House of the release of old documents from the National Guard only increased suspicions of Bush. A *USA Today/CNN/Gallup* poll taken in mid-February showed Bush losing, with 43 percent of the vote, to Kerry's 55 percent. In addition to the National Guard story, Bush was hurt by the release of the report of former UN weapons inspector David Kay, who said that he did not find weapons of mass destruction during his investigation in Iraq. The intense coverage of the Democratic primaries, which focused on the dark side of the Bush administration, also eroded the president's standing.[17]

The national developments bolstered Daschle's campaign. The demise of Howard Dean certainly aided Daschle, who would have been hindered by a left-leaning Dean candidacy while running for reelection as Democratic leader in a red state. Bush's sinking poll numbers also helped Daschle. Republicans hoped for another big win for Bush in South Dakota in 2004, which would mobilize Republican voters and help Thune. But from August 2003 to February 2004, Bush's level of support in the state, according to *Argus Leader* polling, dropped from 58 to 47 percent. A November 2003 poll and an early February 2004 poll showed Daschle's level of support ticking up to 50 percent. Despite spending copiously on staff, fundraising efforts, and television ads, however, Daschle's poll numbers budged only slightly. Whereas Daschle had started running television and radio ads in the summer of 2003, Thune still had not run an ad in early 2004. Taking note of a state shell-shocked by ads in recent years, the Thune campaign stuck by its plan to delay ads into the distant future.[18]

In late January 2004, Daschle invited former president Bill Clinton to an all-day strategy caucus with Senate Democrats and said that Clinton was "somebody . . . whose judgment on these issues we respect." In early February, Clinton hosted a major fund-raiser for Daschle in Washington and raised more than $2 million for Daschle's campaign. Daschle and Clinton, who had shared the experience of working on the 1972 presidential campaign of George McGovern, had remained close. Clinton was first elected governor of Arkansas in 1978, the same year that Daschle was elected to the House, and they both sought to shirk the legacy of the 1960s and run as New Democrats. Daschle won his second term in the Senate in 1992, the same year that Clinton was elected president. In 1994, the Democrats lost both houses of Congress and Daschle became Senate leader, providing the Clinton administration's last line of defense against the GOP Congress. In early 1999, after the House passed articles of impeachment against Clinton, Daschle held together his forty-four Senate colleagues and foreclosed the possibility of removing the president, which required a two-thirds vote of the Senate. The *Washington Post* reported that "Daschle was determined to save Clinton's presidency."[19]

The Clinton fund-raiser again highlighted Daschle's role as a national leader of the Democratic Party. In addition to touting their long-running partnership in Washington, Clinton's February fund-raising letter for Daschle said that the GOP deemed Daschle "Public Enemy #1" for his staunch opposition to the Bush administration's agenda, which provided voters with another reminder of Daschle's defensive role in Washington. By the time of the fall election, Daschle counted on the fund-raiser and his connections to Clinton, who was unpopular in South Dakota, being forgotten. "It doesn't hurt Daschle now," Larry Sabato said. "People will never remember this in November . . . if you are going to have him raise money for you, this is the time to do it." But historical memory would remain a battleground in the campaign. The Daschle campaign hoped that voters would focus on Daschle's early congressional record of moderation, while the Thune campaign sought to turn the spotlight on Daschle's more recent activities opposing the GOP agenda and leading an increasingly strident Democratic caucus.[20]

In February, the U.S. Chamber of Commerce announced its endorsement of Thune, which created a contrast with Daschle's national allies such as Clinton. The national chamber said that if "we had the ability to replace one with the other, absolutely we would. John Thune is a friend of the chamber, very helpful. Tom Daschle is helpful about half the time, sometimes hurtful." The Daschle campaign responded by saying that they were not concerned about the chamber endorsement of Thune because Daschle had been standing up to the "special interests" for years. In the spring, however, *Roll Call* reported that Daschle had raised three times as much political action committee (PAC) money as Thune. A study analyzing the years 1998–2004 indicated that Daschle received more lobbyist and PAC contributions than any other senator. Daschle thought the situation with the Chamber of Commerce important enough to fly to Pierre for the annual meeting of the state organization, which Daschle had assiduously courted over the years. Instead of a productive effort to mend fences, however, Daschle triggered a blog eruption. In front of a relatively conservative chamber audience, the *Rapid City Journal* reported, Daschle "praised the Bush administration's war and nation-building work in Iraq and said he has no serious concerns about the lack of weapons of mass destruction." Daschle's stunning proclamation contradicted the strongly antiwar sentiments of many Democratic caucus-goers and primary voters in previous weeks. Opposition to the war and criticism of the Democratic enablers of the war in Washington had fueled the Dean candidacy and made Dean the front-runner despite his many flaws as a candidate. John Kerry and Daschle had also been criticizing the war. Indeed, Daschle, in his response to the president's

State of the Union address the month before, had said that the "President led us into the Iraq war on the basis of unproven assertions without evidence; he embraced a radical doctrine of preemptive war unprecedented in our history; and he failed to build a true international coalition." In Pierre, Daschle dismissed the difficulties in Iraq; in Washington, he viewed the situation in Iraq as scandalous.[21]

After Daschle's Iraq comments, the story rapidly migrated from the Dakota blogs to the Drudge Report, then throughout the blogosphere. Similar to the controversy over Trent Lott's comments at Strom Thurmond's hundredth birthday party, blogs intensified the scrutiny of Daschle's speech. The *Argus Leader* did not write a news story about the comments, but the story made its way across the country via the Associated Press. The episode reflected the influence of blogs in 2004 and provided a stark contrast to LBJ's years as leader, when he could differentiate his Texas statements from his pronouncements in Washington.

The war comments caused more observers to question whether Daschle could effectively serve as Democratic leader and chief opponent of President Bush while playing defense in his home state. A former Daschle staffer and *Washington Monthly* contributor, Amy Sullivan, noted on her blog how Daschle positioned himself to the right in South Dakota and explained how it would hurt Kerry and be used by White House strategist Karl Rove and company: "John Kerry says you should be outraged about the issue of weapons of mass destruction. But even Tom Daschle says that he's not concerned about it." She said that Daschle "may need to decide whether he can defend his seat and work to defeat Bush at the same time" (she also said that the Daschle camp tried to muzzle her criticism).[22]

More conflicts over his dual role awaited Daschle. When he returned to Washington, he blocked another version of tort reform in the Senate and was pressured by Senator Dianne Feinstein of California into adding gun control provisions to the National Rifle Association–supported legislation regarding gun manufacturers' liability. One of the provisions was a gun-lock requirement for new guns, which the NRA opposed. When the vote came, Daschle's Democratic colleague from South Dakota, Tim Johnson, defied Daschle and voted no. The vote delineated Daschle's dilemma—Johnson knew what position his constituents would take and voted no while Daschle, as Senate leader, toed the line with Senator Feinstein. Some gun groups in South Dakota noticed the difference between their votes, but the *Argus Leader* failed to report the split between Daschle and Johnson.

In the biggest story of the campaign to date, Russell Means endorsed Thune during a Pennington County Republican luncheon in Rapid City. Means, a famed activist and founder of the American Indian Movement, declared himself a "Lakota Libertarian Republican" and a Thune supporter. The Means endorsement, once again, was not reported by the *Sioux Falls Argus Leader* (but when a conflict developed between Means and the Thune campaign in the fall, the *Argus* found it newsworthy). Tim Giago—a longtime Oglala Sioux writer, editor, and owner of the *Lakota Journal*—also announced that he would challenge Daschle in a primary. Giago said that for too long the "Indian vote on the Indian reservations has been taken for granted" by the Democrats. Giago's comments reflected the sentiments of Russell Means, who criticized Indians for sticking to the Democratic "plantation." Given the importance of a large-scale Indian vote to Senator Johnson's 524-vote victory in 2002, Daschle's potential loss of some Indian support became a major concern to his campaign. Word spread that the Daschle campaign pressured Giago to leave the race, but Giago soon confirmed that he planned to run. Thune, meanwhile, continued his visits to the state's various Indian reservations to talk with the tribal councils. When on the Rosebud Indian Reservation, for example, Thune made a visit to the local Indian radio station, KINI, where he was given the microphone to talk about his candidacy, and attended the large powwow at South Dakota State University, where he was honored as a dignitary and again given the microphone. While the Daschle advertising campaign persisted and Daschle juggled his responsibilities to his national party, Thune wracked up miles on the ground visiting small towns and Indian reservations and shaking hands.[23]

The other major development on the South Dakota home front involved abortion. On February 10, the South Dakota House of Representatives passed a ban on abortion by a vote of 54 to 15. When the bill reached the floor of the Senate, it passed 18 to 15. Within a few weeks, the South Dakota legislature had voted to ban abortion and sent the legislation to the governor. Abortion made headlines again, highlighting a dangerous issue for Daschle, and it would return in dramatic fashion in the fall.[24]

On the national level, another prominent cultural issue unfolded. In early February, the highest court in the state of Massachusetts voted four to three to mandate marriages among gays and lesbians, rejecting state legislation that permitted same-sex couples only civil unions, which were first made permissible in Howard Dean's Vermont in the 1990s. The earlier Vermont action prompted the passage of laws in thirty-eight states defining marriage as between heterosexuals and also prompted a similar federal law, the 1996 Defense of Marriage Act, which Daschle supported. Because constitutions and the constitutional law crafted by judges trump statutes, the Massachusetts decision started another round of debate about constitutional amendments that would effectively ban gay marriage. President Bush also began to send signals that he would back such an amendment to the U.S. Constitution.[25]

In the wake of the Massachusetts ruling, cities such as San Francisco began allowing gay and lesbian marriages and sued the State of California seeking to overturn the state statute on the books that defined marriages as unions between heterosexuals. By the end of February, nearly four thousand gay and lesbian couples had been married in San Francisco. John Kerry said that he favored civil unions but opposed gay marriage, contradicting the holding of his state's highest court. Daschle also said that he opposed gay marriage but also opposed a federal constitutional amendment defining marriage, a policy combination some commentators criticized. Courts had ignored statutes defining marriage, critics argued, thus requiring a constitutional solution. Although Kerry, Daschle, and other Democrats said that they opposed gay marriage, gay rights groups such as the Human Rights Campaign remained silent, another sign of the left's effort to unify its opposition to the Bush administration in an election year. After the court decision in Massachusetts and the subsequent gay marriages in California, President Bush endorsed a gay marriage amendment to the U.S. Constitution in late February.

In the South Dakota House race, the Democratic candidate Stephanie Herseth quickly announced her support for the president's position on the marriage amendment, which angered some Democrats. Herseth said, "I agree with the president on this issue. Marriage should be between a man and a woman." One couple in Rapid City cancelled a fund-raiser for Herseth, and Daschle's campaign manager demanded that Herseth return his donation to her campaign over the issue. Herseth's strategy of running as a conservative Democrat, which was a throwback to Daschle's first campaigns for Congress, would cause additional friction with the Daschle camp in coming months. Later in the year, for example, Daschle helped filibuster the federal marriage amendment in the Senate while Herseth voted for it in the House.[26]

Back in Washington, Daschle shored up the Democrats' defenses in the Senate. Daschle tried to regroup after his failure to stop the president's prescription drug bill in December and called on his Senate colleagues to "put the past behind us. If we don't hang together, we hang separately." At the same time, Daschle put out the word that any senator who had voted for the prescription drug bill would be prevented from joining the coveted Senate Finance Committee, which would soon have some open seats. Daschle, according to *Time* magazine, planned "to craft a more combative legislative strategy" and oppose "bipartisan compromises." Daschle also hindered the convening of conference committees, which sort out the differences between House and Senate bills, and informed Senate Majority Leader Bill Frist that he would block legislation until his conference committee demands were met. "This place can't function without conference committees," GOP senator Chuck Grassley of Iowa complained. "Are they saying that we ought to have permanent gridlock?" Daschle then said that he planned to block any attempt to adjourn the body in March to prevent the president from making any recess appointments to the federal courts. This established the tone and setting for the world's oldest deliberative body during 2004.[27]

By the end of February, Dick Wadhams had taken command as Thune's campaign manager, overseeing a few other key staffers, some fund-raisers had been held, the computers were installed, and the rudimentary components of the campaign fell into place. The Daschle campaign, by contrast, had gambled that running enough television ads, touting Daschle's fund-raising prowess, and hiring dozens of staffers might bluff Thune out of an uphill battle. But Thune still entered the race, and Daschle's spending on television ads failed to have a demonstrable effect on the polling numbers. Daschle spokesmen were already denouncing "Republican negative attacks," even though Daschle was the only candidate running ads and Thune had just entered the race. Although the early months of

2004 presented some political pitfalls for Daschle, the candidacy of Howard Dean had imploded, which may have helped Daschle more than all the negatives hurt. In addition, President Bush's support had eroded, Daschle had one of the biggest fund-raising networks and best campaign organizations in the country, and the state's major newspaper was friendly.

In the early months, the Thune campaign declined to directly engage the opposition. While the Daschle campaign ran an advertising "air war," Thune ran a mobile ground war, hitting and running behind Daschle's front lines. Thune routinely visited Democratic strongholds in the state, including northeastern South Dakota and the Indian reservations, while Daschle battled the president's allies in Washington. As a master of retail politics, Thune knew that personal visits and voter contact in a small rural state such as South Dakota could counter large-scale media buys.

CHAPTER THREE

WHIPSAW

You can't have it both ways.

—Wayne LaPierre

The only time Tom Daschle ever initiated a call to John Thune was in 1997. A newspaper had asked newly elected, first-term Congressman Thune whether he would debate the issue of the federal balanced budget amendment to the U.S. Constitution with his South Dakota colleagues. As a supporter of the amendment and not wanting to say that he opposed such a debate, Thune offhandedly agreed. He soon received a call from Daschle, who scolded him for making such a challenge. Daschle opposed the amendment, which ultimately failed by one vote in the Senate, despite his early campaigns in which he promoted its adoption. Scrutiny of Daschle's similarly shifting positions on the Iraq War, tort reform, abortion, judicial nominations, and gun legislation would ultimately envelop his campaign.[1]

In recognition of the power of the gun rights vote in 1994, when the Republicans captured both houses of Congress, and in 2000, when it cost Al Gore rural counties in West Virginia and Tennessee, some pollsters had advised the Democrats to play down gun control issues. Others thought that Democrats such as Bill Clinton had successfully deployed the gun control issue in the 1990s by appealing to suburban "soccer moms" with such measures as the 1994 assault weapons ban. By 2004, those Democratic strategists who wanted to deemphasize gun control issues were winning the argument. In the fall of 2004, the Clinton-era assault weapons ban expired with barely a whimper.[2]

Democrats could appeal to gun owners by supporting a measure limiting lawsuits against gun manufacturers for injuries caused by guns, an increasingly popular area of litigation for trial lawyers. Daschle signed on to the bill in the fall of 2003 and promoted his support of the NRA-supported legislation back in South Dakota, where gun ownership and hunting are ubiquitous. One author, when noting the universality of gun ownership in South Dakota, sees it as part of an older American tradition "which says a boy becomes a man when he is given his first gun." After the introduction of the Chinese ringneck pheasant into South Dakota in the 1890s, the state became a pheasant-hunting mecca. In the early decades of the twentieth century, according to one biological analysis, South Dakota became the nation's "greatest center of pheasant populations." In 1957, the *Redfield Press*, a small-town newspaper in the heart of ringneck country, called pheasants "South Dakota's gift to the nation." The annual "governor's pheasant hunt" also became one of former governor Bill Janklow's major economic development initiatives. Several gun companies also moved to South Dakota to take advantage of a more friendly business environment. In recognition of Daschle's support for the gun-maker liability legislation, the NRA sent a postcard to South Dakota NRA members asking them to thank him, which the *Argus Leader* dutifully reported. *Argus* reporter Dave Kranz wrote that the postcard mailing "diminishes one possible Republican issue in the race." What seemed like a political coup, however, then turned into a disaster for Daschle.[3]

When the gun liability legislation came to the Senate floor in March 2004, liberal senators such as Dianne Feinstein of California (former home of some of the gun companies that had fled to South Dakota) and Chuck Schumer of New York, neither of whom liked the idea of allowing gun companies to avoid lawsuits, sought to add gun control amendments. When an amendment mandating trigger locks on guns passed 70 to 27, one of the two Democrats voting no, unfortunately for Daschle, was his colleague Tim Johnson. The vote reflected the sentiments of many of Johnson's and Daschle's constituents, but Daschle's leadership responsibilities limited his ability to oppose the requirement. Later amendments, adopted by much closer votes, extended the assault weapons ban adopted in 1994 and closed the gun-show loophole, which had allowed sales of guns between individuals at gun shows. The NRA opposed the amendments, and speculation spread that they were designed as "poison pills" to kill the overall liability protection legislation. The bill finally failed when Daschle refused to allow the Senate legislation to be reconciled in a Senate-House conference committee with the House legislation, which did not include the gun control provisions. Daschle sought to circumvent the conference committee process and force the full House to vote up or down on the amended Senate version. Ever since the prescription drug bill had passed the Senate with the help of supportive Democrats, Daschle had refused to allow conference committees to meet. Fellow Democrats had pilloried Daschle for allowing the prescription drug bill to pass after a conference committee reported a version of the bill favored by the GOP.[4]

After promoting adoption of the gun control amendments, Daschle informed the Republican sponsor, Senator Larry Craig of Idaho, that he opposed a conference committee. Daschle was concerned that, as had happened with the prescription drug bill, the conference committee would report a bill he opposed, perhaps without the Senate gun control amendments. Senator Craig blamed Daschle for not agreeing to a conference and for not recognizing the need for a clean bill, without the gun control amendments. Senator Feinstein had a commitment from Daschle, however, that the legislation would not go to conference unless Daschle had been assured that the assault weapons ban would remain in the bill. After the gun control amendments passed and the conference committee prospects looked dim, the NRA revoked support for the overall legislation. Many Democrats also viewed the bill as a special-interest giveaway to gun makers and opposed limiting individuals' right to sue. According to one observer, the NRA "said 'no' on the right, and the trial lawyers said 'no' on the left." Support for the bill thus collapsed; it failed 8 to 90, with Daschle as one of the eight yeas.[5]

In the end, Daschle's attentiveness to Senator Feinstein and those interested in gun control opened the door to amendments that killed the bill the NRA wanted. Not only did Daschle fail to pass the gunmaker liability shield, but he also voted for three different gun control amendments in the process. The NRA said that such votes would be used "in our future evaluations and endorsement of candidates." Asked whether Daschle's votes would be used against him, NRA vice president Wayne LaPierre said, "You bet. He was actively working for the amendments that he knew would take down the bill, and worked behind the scenes to cause trouble, while he's telling the people back home he's a big supporter of the bill. *You can't have it both ways.*"

Not only did Daschle alienate the NRA by allowing gun control amendments to the liability bill, but also his support for an NRA bill angered gun control advocates. Liberal columnist Eleanor Clift reported that Daschle's support for the liability shield prompted "calls from Democratic interest groups for his resignation as Senate leader."[6]

The NRA's criticism of Daschle helped alter the landscape of the 2004 race. In the 2002 Senate race, Thune won only 51 percent of the gun rights vote, to his opponent's 48 percent. The differences between the candidates in 2004, however, proved more stark in a state that was thoroughly anti–gun control. South Dakota allows concealed hand-guns with a state permit and became the first state to adopt a law prohibiting lawsuits against gun manufacturers, a state version of the federal legislation advocated by the NRA in 2004. In 2002, Senator Tim Johnson also relied on the endorsement of Tony Dean, a moderate Republican and longtime host of hunting and fishing television shows in South Dakota. Dean's television ads in 2002 supporting Johnson helped Johnson neutralize the gun issue. The tactic also worked in Arkansas in 2002, where the Democrats promoted the hunting creden-tials of Senate candidate Mark Pryor at NRA rallies and gave his bumper stickers a camouflage background, all part of a national Democratic strategy to win back rural whites and "NASCAR dads." After criticism from gun owners for his ads in 2002, however, Tony Dean decided to avoid politics in 2004. The collapse of the gun-maker liability bill further exposed Daschle on the gun issue. When the NRA made its major endorsement of John Thune in 2002, Dave Kranz of the *Argus Leader* instead wrote extensively about Tony Dean, the Repub-lican outdoorsman, backing Senator Johnson. In 2004, divisions between the candidates over gun control would be readily discernible. The houses of the South Dakota legislature also gave the gun issue some attention, specifically voting against gun show regulations 64 to 0 and 33 to 1. The Herseth candidacy for the House also prompted unfavorable comparisons to Daschle's voting record on gun control. By the end of the campaign, the gun control issue would mature into a clear liability for Daschle.[7]

Another costly issue for Daschle briefly surfaced in early April when Daschle stopped in Renner for a meeting with small-business owners to discuss the cost of health insurance. The owner of a seed-corn business told Daschle that he thought health care costs were driven by the high cost of medical malpractice insurance. Daschle agreed and said that such costs were "way too much." The *Argus Leader* report did not explain the donations that Daschle had received from trial lawyers—his biggest donor group—and his many efforts to block Republican tort reform proposals in Congress. When Daschle returned to Washington after his Renner visit, he filibustered a medical malpractice tort reform bill in the Senate. Daschle, once again, seemed to be on both sides of an issue. Unfortunately for the Thune campaign, no press outlets ran a story about the contradiction. At the end of the month, Daschle attended a banquet at the Waldorf-Astoria in New York City and accepted donations and an award from the New York Trial Lawyers Association. Daschle was "honored for his work in opposing tort reform." The issue of tort reform, like gun control, would linger until the fall.[8]

On March 2, John Kerry wrapped up the Democratic nomination for president and even defeated the southern senator John Edwards in Georgia. Both senators also attended the gun control votes in the Senate the same day in case of a cliff-hanger. After the primaries, Kerry quickly shifted gears and went to work campaigning, raising money, and bracing himself for the impending advertising salvos from the Bush team. The Drudge Report highlighted one important theme for the presidential campaign by reporting the *National Journal's* tabulation designating Kerry the most liberal senator in the chamber in 2003 (Daschle was considered more liberal than 80 percent of the Senate). The Bush team soon criticized Kerry's record of inconsistency on issues. In March, Kerry also made his famous statement about reconstruction funds for Iraq: "I actually did vote for the $87 billion before I voted against it." Even liberal commentators wrote devastating critiques of Kerry's opportunism and flip-flops on a series of issues, which became a constant theme of the national campaign. When Bush took his opening shot of the campaign, he made sport of the issue: "The other party's nomination battle is still playing out. The candidates are an interesting group, with diverse opinions. For tax cuts, and against them. For NAFTA, and against NAFTA. For the Patriot Act, and against the Patriot Act. In favor of liberating Iraq, and opposed to it. And that's just one senator from Massachusetts."[9]

Daschle remained vulnerable to similar criticisms. Daschle's situation proved more perilous than Kerry's, however. Kerry rose in politics in liberal Massachusetts and moderated his positions for the national stage in 2004. Daschle had to take two additional and confusing steps—he began his entry into politics as a young liberal activist in the 1960s and early 1970s, then ran as a conservative Democrat for Congress in 1978, then took liberal positions as a national party leader, then shifted gears to run as a moderate Democrat in South Dakota in 2004. Connections and comparisons between Daschle and Kerry on the consistency issue would continue to benefit Thune when at last they received attention in the state.

In the spring of 2004, Ralph Nader, who consistently criticized politicians for taking positions on both sides of issues, also entered the presidential race. Nader's attacks on "Republicrats" during the 2000 presidential race earned him nearly 3 percent of the national vote. In 2004, however, the left pursued a Popular Front strategy of unifying their sundry constituent groups to defeat the Bush administration, and the opposition from the left to Nader's candidacy became ferocious. Some critics denounced Nader as an egomaniac; Jonathan Chait discussed Nader's "ideologically motivated fanaticism." One study noted the "extraordinary lengths Democrats went to in 2004 to keep him off the ballot in many states." Before the end of April, Daschle would face his own Nader problem in South Dakota.[10]

In early March, Vice President Dick Cheney visited Sioux Falls and attended a Thune rally and fund-raiser attended by five hundred South Dakotans. Born in Lincoln, Nebraska, raised in Wyoming, and a frequent hunter of South Dakota pheasants, Cheney tended to draw a crowd in the state. In addition to offering a glowing assessment of Thune, Cheney also detailed many of the failures to act against Osama Bin Laden during the Clinton years of the 1990s and argued that John Kerry viewed the terror threat as a police enforcement action, not as a war. Striking one of the key themes of the Thune campaign, Cheney also said, "You'll never hear John Thune say one thing in South Dakota and something else in Washington, D.C." Cheney raised $250,000 for Thune, a far cry from the $2 million that President Clinton had raised for Daschle in Washington a few weeks earlier, but Cheney did it in South Dakota.[11]

In contrast to Thune's support from Cheney, South Dakota Democrats shunned their national leaders. Stephanie Herseth openly scoffed at the idea of a Kerry visit to help her congressional candidacy.

Daschle's campaign manager, Steve Hildebrand, said that no leaders of the national Democratic Party would visit South Dakota. Whereas Theodore White once described Republicans avoiding Barry Goldwater "as if he were bearer of contagion," Democrats in red states since the 1960s had adopted a similar policy of keeping their distance from the liberal leaders of their national party. Some Democrats viewed their national leaders as a burden: another sign of the two worlds inhabited by red-state Democrats and why Daschle's roles in Washington and in South Dakota often proved contradictory.[12]

During his introduction of Cheney, Thune once again needled Daschle on the ethanol bill. Instead of lining up two additional Democratic votes that would have allowed the bill to overcome a Democratic filibuster and pass the Senate in the fall of 2003, Daschle did not even make an effort. Thune said that the "night before the vote, [Daschle] was at a book signing at a Washington, D.C. suburb. . . . When it comes time to get votes for ethanol, I won't be signing books." Daschle's campaign manager said in response that it "was John's party that killed that legislation," a distortion of the record that the *Argus Leader* did not explain. For the rest of the campaign, the Daschle team blamed Republicans for the failure of the ethanol bill. In March, Daschle announced that he had secured the necessary votes to pass a scaled-down version of the energy bill through the Senate, but the month ended without any action. On the campaign trail, Thune continued to hammer on the failure of the energy bill, which had triggered his entry into the race.[13]

Immediately after the Cheney event, Thune and *New York Times* reporter Cheryl Gay Stolberg headed to Rapid City for a meeting with ranchers, then traveled to Pine Ridge Indian Reservation. They went to the village of Kyle and met with tribal elders and received a rousing welcome from local Thune supporter Russell Means. They also visited the reservation radio station KILI, where Thune talked for fifteen minutes. Thune then went to play basketball with the Pine Ridge high school team, the Thorpes, named after Jim Thorpe, the famous Indian Olympian voted the most outstanding athlete of the first half of the twentieth century. They also traveled just across the border to White Clay, Nebraska, a wide spot in the road with several liquor stores that exist solely to exploit the Indians on Pine Ridge, where alcohol sales are forbidden. Daschle also criticized the "Third World conditions" of many South Dakota reservations, and Russell Means denounced government control of reservation life, which he deemed "pure communism," a "dictatorship by the Bureau of Indian Affairs." Thune continued to campaign on the reservations while Daschle was tied down in Washington.[14]

During the Pine Ridge trip, Governor Mike Rounds announced that he would support the legislation banning abortions in South Dakota with a few tweaks of the statutory language. Rounds sought to revise the legislation to avoid the potential suspension of existing abortion laws after commencement of the litigation over the constitutionality of the bill. After the governor's "style and form veto," the bill sailed through the House but failed in the Senate 18 to 17 after two senators who had not voted the first time were present and another changed his vote. The intricacies of the voting process meant less to the race for the U.S. Senate than the overall attention it brought to the issue of abortion. The state of South Dakota, which Daschle represented in Congress, came within one vote of banning abortions, providing a contrast to Daschle's fund-raising efforts for NARAL and Emily's List. A poll conducted for South Dakota media outlets in late March indicated that 52 percent of South Dakotans supported the abortion ban.[15]

The abortion issue also received attention back in Washington. In late March, the Senate considered the Laci Peterson bill, named after a young mother in California who was murdered the year before while pregnant. The bill sought to make such an action two murders instead of one. Having already passed the House with White House support, the bill came to the Senate and became a repeat performance of the gun-maker liability legislation earlier in the month. During the debate, Senator Feinstein of California, repeating her actions on the gun-maker immunity bill, offered a "poison pill" amendment. The underlying legislation, formally known as Unborn Victims of Violence Act, applied federal penalties to acts of violence against unborn children, in addition to their mothers. Feinstein's amendment increased the penalties for crimes against pregnant women but deleted any mention of unborn children because such language legitimized the long-standing criticism of *Roe v. Wade* by deeming a fetus to be alive. NARAL and Planned Parenthood obviously supported the Feinstein amendment, and the National Right to Life Committee opposed it. Although Daschle wanted the amendment to pass, it failed 49 to 50. But Daschle then voted for the main Right to Life–supported legislation, which completely contradicted the Feinstein amendment. Even his Senate colleague Tim Johnson did not vote for the final Laci Peterson bill, because he had committed to opposing a law that "declares a fertilized ovum as an independent human being." Daschle said that both bills were "designed to protect pregnant women. I felt they both had merit, and that's why I supported both." The president of Planned Parenthood detected a critical difference, however, describing the bill as "part of a deceptive anti-choice strategy to make women's bodies mere vessels by creating legal personhood for the fetus." The legislation again elevated the issue of abortion, and one report explained that Daschle had aligned himself "on both sides of the fight" and voted "for two completely opposite approaches." The episode provided additional evidence that Daschle's loyalties were divided between the liberal tendencies of his national party and the conservative inclinations of his state.[16]

The day before the vote on the Laci Peterson bill, Daschle tried to allay the concerns of the party's liberal base about his attention to the interests of his red state. In a speech on the Senate floor, Daschle criticized the Bush administration's Iraq policy, which "may have made Americans less secure not more against terrorist threats." In contrast, the month before, Daschle had triggered a media storm when he appeared in Pierre and gave a contradictory assessment. The *Rapid City Journal* had reported that during the Pierre speech Daschle "praised the Bush administration's war and nation-building work in Iraq and said he has no serious concerns about the lack of weapons of mass destruction." While the national Democratic base demanded stronger criticism of the war in Iraq, the level of contradiction in Daschle's campaign approached the extreme. Although the National Republican Senatorial Committee issued a critical press release, the *Argus Leader* failed to report the contradiction. Daschle did, however, receive praise from Buzzflash, the liberal website, which had earlier called for his resignation: "We hope that this indicates a new trend in Daschle's stance, and that we will see fewer comments that end up being used on the Bush/Cheney weblog to indicate that Daschle supports many of Bush's policies, including his conduct of the Iraq War."[17]

March also marked the one-year anniversary of Daschle's criticism of the president's Iraq policy while the nation was on the eve of war.

On March 17, 2003, Daschle made his famous remarks to AFSCME, the large public employee union that had endorsed Howard Dean during the primary season: "I'm saddened, saddened that this president failed so miserably at diplomacy that we're now forced to war. Saddened that we have to give up one life because this president couldn't create the kind of diplomatic effort that was so critical for our country." After this criticism, a firestorm ensued, and Daschle fell behind Thune in a hypothetical South Dakota poll. Even the editors of the *Argus Leader* said, "Tom Daschle is out of line," concluding that "Daschle's comments at the 11th hour cannot possibly be viewed as legitimate dissent." While the *Argus Leader* was initially critical of Daschle for his pre-war comments, within a few weeks it adopted a policy of refusing to take letters to the editor critical of Daschle's comments.[18]

While both John Kerry and Daschle could be criticized for contradictory positions on the war, the Bush administration increasingly took fire over the situation in Iraq. During a meeting at the White House, Daschle had already had what the *Washington Post* called a "testy exchange" with President Bush over intelligence failures in Iraq. In March, after the al-Qaeda–inspired bombings of 3/11 in Madrid, the pro-war incumbent Spanish government lost the ensuing election, and the new government pulled Spanish troops out of Iraq. In early April, the Dominican Republic and Honduras also decided to withdraw their troops; other countries threatened to follow suit. The Mujahideen Brigades then captured three Japanese civilians and threatened to kill them if the Japanese troops did not withdraw. In the Sunni Muslim city of Fallujah in early April, four American private security guards were killed and the bodies of two of them were hanged from a city bridge. The founder of the liberal blog Daily Kos said, "I feel nothing over the death of mercenaries. . . . They are there to wage war for profit. Screw them." Such statements exemplified the left's extreme disdain for the war, which had underpinned the early success of the Dean campaign. Leftist commentator Christopher Hitchens had long since moved past such sentiments, however, and described the "Dantesque scenes from Fallujah," which he viewed as "a reminder, not just of what Saddamism looks like, or what the future might look like if we fail, but of what the future held before the Coalition took a hand." Hitchens underscored the importance of preventing Iraq from becoming the "property of *Clockwork Orange* holy warriors." The spokesman for the U.S. command in Iraq, General Mark Kimmitt, said that the Fallujah assassins were "people who want to turn Iraq back, to an era of mass graves, of rape rooms and torture chambers and chemical attacks."[19]

Nevertheless, events in Iraq continued to be used by the Democrats to conjure memories of Vietnam. In late March, as John Kerry reminded voters that his personal experience in Vietnam helped him understand foreign wars, Daschle publicly praised the memory of Eugene McCarthy, the hero of the anti–Vietnam War movement, whom Daschle had supported in 1968. At McCarthy's eighty-eighth birthday party, Daschle said that "when you hear someone question the reasons and costs of the war, you hear his voice." With the potential spread of the Iraqi insurgency to include Shiites, who constituted 60 percent of the population, the debate resumed over the need to add to the 130,000 U.S. troops already in Iraq. On the Senate floor, Senator Robert Byrd said that he heard "echoes of Vietnam" (he also recited "The Charge of the Light Brigade"), and Senator Edward Kennedy (who had called the war a "fraud") said, "Iraq is George Bush's Vietnam." The cover story of *Newsweek* in late April focused on "The Vietnam Factor"; the feature article was entitled "A Quagmire in the Making?" The *New York Times* editorial board compared the situation in April to the 1968 Tet offensive, after which a majority of Americans had turned against the Vietnam War. Daschle's praise of McCarthy infuriated some veterans of 1968 such as John MacArthur, the publisher of *Harper's Magazine,* who thought that Daschle's "singular cynicism" had permitted the Iraq War in the first place. McCarthy's politeness at his birthday celebration, according to MacArthur, "prevented any pointed references to Daschle's weak-kneed submission to the war party." Some liberals wanted 2004 to become 1968, when prominent liberal Democrats embraced the antiwar movement, and contrasted "Daschle's lack of gumption" with "old McCarthy's enduring courage."[20]

While Daschle and Thune practiced democracy in South Dakota and scoured the state's small towns for votes, the coalition authority in Iraq tried to cobble together rudimentary democratic structures in a country that had known only totalitarian horrors for decades. By mid-April the United States had delved deep into the details of democracy building in Iraq. Paul Bremer, the civilian administrator of the Coalition Provisional Authority in Iraq, had secured nearly $20 billion from a hesitant Congress for reconstruction efforts. Bremer also insisted that the money not be a loan, as congressional critics such as Daschle demanded, so the new Iraqi government could avoid a burdensome debt and the United States would not profit from Iraq. For the same reason, Bremer prohibited American companies from running Iraq's oil industry. Bremer also banned members of the top three layers of Saddam's Baathist ruling party, which had killed more than a million Iraqis, from government service and disbanded the Iraqi army, which caused concerns about unmoored soldiers becoming insurgents. Bremer paid them a stipend hoping to deter such behavior. Bremer also participated in the writing of the interim Iraqi constitution. He tried to accomplish in fifteen months what had taken General Douglas MacArthur seven years to complete in post–World War II Japan. The United States tried to avoid the spectre of another Aleksandr Kerensky, the Russian democrat whose government succeeded the Tsar and lasted only four months before Lenin's radicals took charge.

South Dakota felt the human cost of the Iraq War. In mid-April, two South Dakota National Guard companies had their tours in Iraq extended, and the first member of the South Dakota National Guard was killed in Iraq—the first to be killed in combat since World War II. Specialist Dennis Morgan, a 2000 graduate of Winner High School, died when a roadside bomb detonated. Morgan served in Company A of the 153rd Engineer Battalion, which supported the 1st Marine Expedition Headquarters south of Baghdad near the Euphrates River. He was married for two days before leaving for Iraq and had met his wife at the Black Hills Stock Show nine months before they were married. The Saturday before Morgan's memorial service, another man from the 153rd, Staff Sergeant Cory Brooks, age thirty-two and a University of South Dakota law school graduate, died in Iraq. Before being called up in December, Brooks had worked at a hardware store in the West River town of Philip (population 1,000). April 2004 brought the highest number of monthly deaths in Iraq since the invasion had begun.[21]

The 3,000 people in the West River town of Winner (so named because it had prevailed in the contest for the county seat), which Thune visited in April, had sent 40 soldiers to Iraq. They joined 1,200 South Dakota National Guard troops already serving in Iraq, the highest percentage per capita of any state in the union. Soldiers from rural counties died in Iraq at twice the frequency of those from large metropolitan counties. According to the Pentagon, 44 percent of military recruits came from rural areas compared to 14 percent from large cities. One woman quoted in the *Argus Leader* explained that Winner would pull together after the death of Specialist Morgan: "It's amazing, but small towns do that." Rodney Lanz, another Winner man serving in Iraq, said, "We see it escalating, but we're supportive of what we're doing because we understand that their new government is coming together. The majority of the people (in Iraq) are with us, it's just a few of them that don't want it to work." Lanz spoke of making Iraqi democracy work. South Dakota, which was in the midst of the biggest Senate race in decades in the world's oldest republic, sent its National Guard troops halfway around the world to help a nation ascend from Stalinist darkness into a democratic age. In late April, Winner National Guard troops assisted the Marine Corps' preparations for an attack on the insurgent stronghold of Fallujah, which had been under siege for nearly a month. The war loomed ever larger in the Senate race.[22]

As the Iraqi democratization process proceeded haltingly, conflict persisted between the Bush administration and Senate Democrats. In March, Daschle announced that all of President Bush's judicial nominations would be blocked unless the president promised not to make recess appointments of judges. Daschle had already led several unprecedented filibusters against federal appeals court judges and had delayed the consideration of trial court judges. Because the Senate Democrats would not allow Charles W. Pickering of Mississippi to have a confirmation vote in the Senate, in January 2004 President Bush made a recess appointment and put him on the bench, which allowed him to serve until the end of the congressional term. In a floor statement, Daschle said that no president has "ever used a recess appointment to install a rejected nominee on to the federal bench." Pickering and others, however, had never received a confirmation vote, thus had never been rejected. On the following Sunday, *60 Minutes* ran a story about Judge Pickering, noting that he had testified against a Ku Klux Klan boss in Mississippi in the 1960s, when such testimony usually triggered a firebombing of the witness's house, and had sent his children to majority black schools in the 1970s, a choice made by few well-to-do families. Local leaders of the National Association for the Advancement of Colored People (NAACP) in Mississippi and five of the six African-Americans on the city council of Pickering's hometown supported his nomination. A clip of Medger Evers's brother berating an NAACP official for his ignorance about Pickering even appeared in the *60 Minutes* segment.[23]

Democratic senator Chuck Schumer of New York assumed the task of criticizing Pickering on *60 Minutes* and depicted him as a closet racist. Pickering had reduced the sentence of a man convicted of cross burning because his coconspirators, who were much more culpable, had received a much lighter sentence. Schumer and Daschle and other liberals in the Senate used this decision to undermine Pickering. In his book, Daschle called Pickering an "apologist for racist cross-burners." The *New York Post* then reported that Daschle had strongly defended recess appointments during the Clinton presidency. In contrast to his opposition to allowing confirmation votes on Bush judges, when President Clinton was in office in 1999 Daschle had said, "I find it simply baffling that a Senator would vote against even voting on a judicial nomination." Such inconsistencies were not reported in South Dakota. Readers of the *New York Post* knew more about Daschle's activities in Washington than did the readers of the *Sioux Falls Argus Leader*.[24]

Throughout April, consistent with the battle over federal judges, the Senate deadlock continued. Senator Kennedy said that he had never seen the institution "so dysfunctional." After the failure of a welfare reform bill in the Senate, Morton Kondracke of *Roll Call* lamented the "rancid partisanship rife in all American politics" and reported that "moderate Democratic Senators [were] privately furious with Kennedy, Minority Leader Tom Daschle and other hard-liners." Daschle continued to block legislation from proceeding to conference committees and also announced that he would block a charity bill that was part of the president's faith-based initiative, a move that prompted a blistering editorial from the *Rapid City Journal* in the fall. Daschle had earlier promised the editors that he would work to pass the bill. Daschle finally announced that all presidential nominees would be blocked because he opposed the president's two recess appointments, another major development that went unreported by the *Argus Leader*.[25]

Senate GOP leader Bill Frist denounced Daschle's tactics as "clear-cut obstruction which can't be tolerated." During the last week of April, political columnist Robert Novak reported that Frist was "being urged by colleagues to threaten to close down the Senate for the rest of the year unless Senate Democratic Leader Tom Daschle ends his disruptive tactics." The national press corps also buzzed about Senator Frist's decision to visit South Dakota, which they viewed as a sign of the fevered partisanship of the Senate. The *New York Times* reported that Daschle was annoyed about Frist's visit. Although the Senate historian said that he had never heard of one leader campaigning in the other leader's backyard, *Roll Call* noted that Daschle had "been the single biggest thorn in Frist's legislative side, leading Democratic filibusters throughout the 108th Congress on numerous bills and nominations." Daschle's vulnerability, moreover, left him in a different position than recent Senate leaders. When Senator Frist sent out a fund-raising letter calling for donations to Thune, the Daschle camp complained ever more loudly about such a partisan breach of Senate etiquette. But Daschle also broke the Senate's "club" rules by campaigning against his colleague Larry Pressler in earlier years and took a memorable swipe: "A Senate seat is a terrible thing to waste." Daschle understood partisanship.[26]

Outside the Senate, the presidential race boiled over. John Kerry called the Bush administration "the most crooked . . . lying group I've ever seen" and branded Bush's foreign policy as "the most arrogant, inept, reckless and ideological" in modern history. The Bush campaign, meanwhile, prepared to engage Kerry by name in campaign ads, the earliest such assault in presidential history. A national poll in late March showed Kerry and Bush tied at 48 percent, indicating that Bush had closed the gap that existed earlier in the month. In April—while the president endured the 9/11 Commission hearings, the release of new books criticizing the decision to go to war, and the increasingly widespread uprisings in Iraq—Kerry suffered his own share of gaffes. After taking a skiing vacation in Idaho (where he swore at the Secret Service for getting in his way on the slopes), Kerry had to deal with tax day, April 15, and the inevitable questions about his wife's unwillingness to release her tax returns, which would highlight her $500 million ketchup fortune. In a precursor to the fall and yet another case of historical memories of Vietnam intruding on the present, the press disclosed that Kerry, while still performing service for the navy, met with Vietcong emissaries in Paris and that he also attended a meeting in Kansas City during which assassinating politicians supportive of the war was discussed (in the aftermath of these revelations, the Kerry campaign tried to persuade witnesses that Kerry had not been there).[27]

An old videotape of Kerry also surfaced in which he said that he threw his Vietnam medals over the White House fence in 1971. On the campaign trail, Kerry had been saying the opposite. When questioned on *Good Morning America* about the matter, Kerry said that the program was "doing the bidding of the Republican National Committee." Jeff Jacoby of the *Boston Globe* said that the "medal incident matters hardly at all. But as a surrogate for all the issues on which Kerry has ducked and dissembled, it matters very much." By the end of the month, the *Village Voice* even wondered whether Kerry should be the Democratic standard-bearer. In what could have been a cruel April for President Bush, Kerry made enough mistakes to neutralize the bad news from Iraq.[28]

While the debate over Iraq intensified and the sparks began to fly in the presidential campaign, Daschle faced another dilemma at home. Tim Giago, the founder of the *Lakota Journal*, announced that instead of challenging Daschle in the June primary he would run as an independent in the fall. The story quickly spread, and analysts predicted that Giago's candidacy could sink Daschle. Thune had faced a similar problem in 2002 when a third party Libertarian who actually wanted Thune to win (he dropped out late in the race, but his name remained on the ballot) received 3,000 votes in a race Thune lost by 524 votes. Daschle placed a frantic call to Giago the day after Giago's announcement, pleading with him to leave the race and arguing that he would have a Ralph Nader effect on the race (the *Washington Post* story was headlined "Daschle Gets His Own Nader"). Giago refused to yield. On the same day that Daschle made his telephone plea to Giago, his spokesman told the press that Daschle welcomed Giago's entrance into the race as a "good thing." Despite this public posture, Daschle again called Giago to convince him not to run, even offering the manpower necessary to file his primary petitions if Giago would run in the Democratic primary instead of as an independent. The national press quickly latched on to the Giago candidacy as evidence of Daschle's precarious standing. Even the liberal blogger Joshua Micah Marshall wondered whether the Giago candidacy might cause Daschle's defeat. Blogs first reported on Daschle's calls to Giago; only later did Dave

Kranz of the *Argus Leader* report the first Daschle telephone call in his column. Internet reporting, once again, outran the mainstream press.[29]

By the end of March 2004, the Thune campaign had still not taken a poll (despite what Dave Kranz of the *Argus Leader* had erroneously reported). No Thune ads had been run or produced or even planned. The Thune campaign organization amounted to six staffers and some volunteers who opened and sorted the returning fund-raising letters. During the 2002 race, Thune had announced his candidacy in early October of the previous year, but in 2004 Thune entered the race in January, and his campaign remained lean and conscious of voters' ad weariness. The Daschle campaign, by contrast, fought the last war. They had been running ads since the summer of 2003 and had hired dozens of staffers with only a modest lead in the polls to show for it. On April 1, a media-commissioned poll gave Daschle a 48 to 43 percent edge over Thune.[30]

The day after Easter, the Thune camp held its first major strategy session in Sioux Falls and reviewed its fund-raising to date. While some advisors had hoped that Thune would raise $1.3 million in the first quarter of 2004, he actually raised $2.2 million and had $1.85 million in the bank. In 2002 at the same time, the Thune campaign had only $618,000 in the bank and had already spent $350,000 on ads. During the strategy session, participants also discussed the ineffectiveness of Daschle's ad blitz and the problem of "ad fatigue" in the state. Thune in particular believed that South Dakotans were weary of ads, especially since Daschle had been running them since July 2003 and the impending House special election in June would bring even more ads. Everyone in the strategy session agreed to delay ads. The Thune campaign also planned to delay all polling until the summer.

After the strategy meeting in Sioux Falls, most of Thune's campaign advisors traveled by bus to DeSmet (population 1,100) to hear Thune's speech to the Kingsbury County Lincoln Day Dinner, another stop in Thune's early boots-on-the-ground strategy. As the campaign bus rolled through Volga (population 1,300), Lake Preston (population 700), and Arlington (population 1,000), campaign workers discussed the need to improve on Thune's 2002 showing in the small towns and rural counties of the agricultural heartland of eastern South Dakota. The town of DeSmet took its name from the Jesuit priest Pierre Jean De Smet, who was known as the "spiritual Christopher Columbus of the West," and featured a statue of the priest in the city park. Despite the Catholic moniker for the town, more than half of the residents are Lutheran. Kingsbury County, named after early territorial newspaper editor George Kingsbury (who wrote the multivolume *History of South Dakota*), epitomizes many East River counties: extremely rural with a few small towns, many farms, some prairie lakes, and many descendants of Norwegian and German immigrants, similar to Thune's and Daschle's grandparents. It is also very peaceful. According to FBI statistics, in 2000 there were zero murders, zero rapes, zero burglaries, zero robberies, and zero larcenies in the county. DeSmet also features one of the homes of Laura Ingalls Wilder ("The house that Pa built"), where Laura did battle against the evil Nellie Olson. Thune, the former basketball standout, spoke in the high school gymnasium directly under a basketball hoop; he gave one of his best speeches to date about the need "to get the Senate working again." To win, Thune had to do better in places like Kingsbury County. The odds remained long in mid-April, but morale remained high.

While the Thune campaign maintained its candidate-centered meet-the-voters ground strategy, the Daschle campaign continued a multi-pronged advertising offensive. By April, the Daschle campaign had run eleven different television commercials focusing on Daschle's clout in Washington and what it yielded for his state. In late April, the Daschle campaign also started running local radio and newspaper ads touting the appropriations the senator had secured for local institutions such as Dakota State University (DSU) in Madison and Mitchell Technical Institute (MTI) in Mitchell. Mitchell blogger Steve Sibson of Sibby Online began questioning the ads that were running in Mitchell, which sounded like an MTI endorsement of the Daschle campaign. The Mitchell paper reported, "Though much of the ad's message is attributed to MTI, the ad was paid for by A Lot of People Supporting Tom Daschle." Bloggers then disclosed that Daschle had voted against the appropriations package that included the funding for DSU and MTI. With the exception of a few voices in the wilderness, however, the Daschle campaign's media blitz went largely uncontested. Throughout the state, Daschle ads ran in local newspapers and on local radio and touted appropriations that Daschle had secured for smaller communities. Statewide television advertising supplemented the local media.[31]

The Daschle campaign also mobilized its defensive capabilities. While the Thune campaign stayed off the airwaves, a few third-party groups ran ads targeting Daschle in late April, and these triggered a quick response from the Daschle campaign. The Club for Growth criticized Daschle for opposing the repeal of the estate tax, and the Coalition for the Future American Worker, which nobody in the Thune campaign had ever heard of, criticized an immigration bill that Daschle had introduced in Congress. The Daschle campaign sent letters from its lawyers to South Dakota television stations demanding that the immigration ad be pulled. After the television stations refused Daschle's request, the Daschle campaign released a new commercial featuring people saying, "I don't like these negative ads attacking Tom Daschle. We don't need outside groups coming in telling us lies about Tom." The Daschle campaign also began a phone-calling campaign from a phone bank in Florida in which a woman, purportedly a Republican, advised people to "call John Thune's office . . . and ask him to stop his friends from polluting our airwaves." Since Thune had not run an ad yet and had no control over third-party ads, the calls seemed odd to some voters. Then KELO-Land News also reported that "Daschle's ads violate a new federal election law" because they did not include a mandatory disclaimer.[32]

Instead of being merely a campaign tactic, negative campaigning developed into an issue. It became a shield with which to deflect criticism and a sword to wield against opponents. Daschle claimed that he could prevent third-party groups from advertising in South Dakota (even though for campaigns to coordinate with third parties was illegal) and criticized Thune for not doing the same, thereby abetting negative attacks. Senator Kerry used the same tactic in the presidential race. Attempts to highlight Kerry's inconsistencies became a "negative smear" from the "GOP attack machine," and criticism of his votes on defense spending became a "negative attack" on his patriotism. In the case of the illegal phone calls, some voters were left with the impression that the Daschle campaign "went negative" first, but others surely blamed Thune.[33]

Daschle's superb political negotiating skills also brought an April victory. After a meeting in Rapid City in late April between third-party candidate Tim Giago and Daschle, Giago agreed to exit the race. In addition to securing a Daschle meeting with tribal leaders the following August, the *Washington Post* reported, Giago "wanted Daschle to open dialogue on returning the sacred Black Hills to the tribes of the Sioux Nation, and to help remedy the lack of economic opportunities on the state's reservations, the poorest in the country. Giago had expressed distress that Daschle did not seem open to discussing the Black Hills." The *Wall Street Journal* also reported that Giago had previously "said Mr. Daschle had spent 26 years in Congress ignoring pleas by Indian tribes to return the famous Black Hills to the Sioux Nation." *Roll Call* reported that Giago entered the race to force Daschle to address the issue of compensating Indians for the "theft of the Black Hills." But the Black Hills land return issue, which might have caused Daschle some political problems in South Dakota, was completely ignored by the South Dakota press. Many commentators viewed Giago's withdrawal from the race as a major victory for Daschle.[34]

Hairline cracks in the Daschle edifice were becoming noticeable, however. The attempt to link the Thune campaign to third-party advertising suffered when the violation of federal election law by Daschle's phone calls became known. Daschle's ads had also not substantially increased the gap between him and Thune in the polls. In addition to raising the largest amount of money of any challenger in the country, Thune, instead of running early ads, spent the month traveling the state and talking with voters while Daschle remained in Washington battling the GOP in the Senate, which had seized up in partisan gridlock, while the clashes between the Kerry and Bush camps intensified. The contrast between Daschle's early and later political positions also generated some attention. The editors of the *Rapid City Journal* pressured Daschle to release his tax returns by noting his past position on the issue: "Daschle has declined to release his income tax returns for the past two decades, despite repeated media requests. He has his own self to blame for our broaching the subject because he released his income tax returns in 1982 when he was running against Clint Roberts for South Dakota's newly combined U.S. House seat" (Dave Kranz was then an editor at the Mitchell newspaper, which followed Daschle's release with a demand that Roberts release his returns). Local blogs also gained increasing attention nationally because of links from national bloggers such as Instapundit, the Web's most popular blog (such links were deemed "Insta-lanches" because of all the hits they generated). Links from national blogs such as Powerline also boosted the hit totals for Dakota blogs. While the number of individual readers and voters in South Dakota may have been modest, reporters from the *Washington Post,* the *New York Times,* and *Roll Call* tuned in to the blogs. Some South Dakota voters and national reporters thus gained an alternative to the *Argus Leader.* Whether Daschle's defenses would hold once criticism of his consistency and his partisanship in Washington hit the general airwaves and Thune became more aggressive on the campaign trail remained unknown.[35]

CHAPTER FOUR

MAY DAYS

The Senate Shuts Down

The Senate is my home.

—Tom Daschle

On May 1, Thune attended the graduation of the largest class in the history of the state land-grant college, South Dakota State University, from which Daschle had graduated in 1969. At the ceremony, Thune's mentor, Jim Abdnor (ousted from his Senate seat by Daschle in 1986), received an honorary doctorate. Unlike the farm policy debate in 1986, when the Senate race focused on low commodity prices and gut-wrenching farm foreclosures, the debate in 2004 focused on the failure of the ethanol bill in the Senate. After the ceremony, Thune took a bumpy flight down to the Big Sioux River valley town of Hudson (population 400), which hosted the grand opening of a new ethanol plant, Sioux River Ethanol. The plant brought forty jobs to rural Lincoln County and would increase corn prices to local farmers selling to the plant by five to ten cents per bushel. The plant, designed to produce forty-five million gallons of ethanol a year from sixteen million bushels of corn, became the seventy-sixth ethanol plant built in the country since 1980 and the tenth plant built in South Dakota. One of every three rows of South Dakota corn being planted during the spring would be transformed into ethanol, and more than eight thousand farm families in South Dakota had invested in ethanol plants. The forward integration of farmers into commodity processing has been one of the biggest structural changes in agriculture in recent decades. In addition to congratulating the farmers who invested in the new ethanol plant, Thune emphasized the importance of making national leaders accountable for their promises to promote ethanol. The week before, Democratic filibusters had again killed the ethanol bill in the Senate.

By May 2004, the Senate had been practically frozen by filibusters—
a term derived from American mercenaries who fought in foreign
armies, most prominently in the pre–Civil War period. Originally a
Dutch word, *filibustero* was a term used by the Spanish to refer to the
West Indian pirates who sailed on "filibots." Historically, filibusters
often stymied action on major issues such as slavery, war, and civil
rights, not ethanol bills. The Senate abandoned limitations on debate
soon after the organization of the body, which became known for its
windy deliberation. After isolationists used filibusters to kill some
military spending bills prior to the United States' entry into World
War I, however, the Senate adopted a cloture rule, which allowed
two-thirds of the body's members to end debate and overcome a
filibuster. The first successful cloture motion, made in 1919, terminated debate on the ratification of the sweeping Treaty of Versailles,
which set the terms ending World War I. For the next four decades,
the Senate conducted only sixteen cloture votes. The filibuster became
most notorious when Southern segregationists infuriated reformers
by filibustering laws against poll taxes, literacy tests, and lynching. In
1975, Senate liberals successfully sought to reduce the cloture threshold
to sixty votes.[1]

Increased filibustering in subsequent decades reached a crescendo
in the 108th Congress during battles over President Bush's legislation
and federal appeals court nominees such as Miguel Estrada. In May
2001, President Bush nominated Estrada, a Honduran immigrant, to
serve on the D.C. Court of Appeals, but because of seven Democratic
filibusters, Estrada never received a confirmation vote. Thomas Mann
of the Brookings Institution considered the filibusters of Estrada
"highly unusual and extreme by Senate conventions." At a retreat for
Democratic senators in the spring of 2001, judicial experts had advised
Daschle that "Democratic senators could oppose even nominees with
strong credentials on the grounds that the White House was trying to
push the courts in a conservative direction." Estrada would finally
give up after twenty-eight months of waiting for a vote. He returned
to private practice and donated to Thune's campaign against Senate
obstruction. During his confirmation battle, Estrada's wife miscar-
ried, and in November 2004 she died of an overdose of alcohol and
sleeping pills.[2]

The filibuster of the energy bill, which contained the ethanol provisions that were frequently debated during the Senate race, symbolized the Senate gridlock of the 108th Congress. After passing the House with White House approval, the energy bill came to the Senate in November 2003, where Daschle's deputy, Senator Harry Reid, organized a Democratic filibuster against the bill, thus necessitating sixty votes to end debate and hold a final vote. In the end, the supporters of the energy bill secured fifty-eight votes, two short of the total needed to break the filibuster. Daschle failed to object. Instead, as Thune repeatedly argued on the campaign trail, Daschle traveled to Virginia and signed copies of his new book the night before the vote. On the morning of the vote, according to *Congressional Quarterly*, Daschle informed his colleagues that he "understood their choice to mount the filibuster and respected them for it." Noting the impending presidential election year, GOP senator Chuck Grassley of Iowa said on the Senate floor that the November bill was the "last train to leave town." Grassley warned, "Don't tell me you are for ethanol, don't tell me you are for biodiesel . . . don't tell me those things if you are not going to help us fight hard to get the 60 votes necessary to break the filibuster." The old farmer-senator from Iowa, the nation's corn and ethanol epicenter, blamed Daschle: "If a Democrat leader can deliver 46 out of 49 votes to keep the president's good judges from being approved, he surely ought to be able to deliver 15 out of 49 votes for the energy bill when it's so important to South Dakota."[3]

Broader partisan jockeying also contributed to the failure of the energy bill. *Congressional Quarterly* explained that the defeat of the energy bill "strengthened Daschle's hand [by] dealing Republicans in the White House and in Congress a stinging rebuke," making the energy bill part and parcel of what political commentator Morton Kondracke called the "rancid partisanship" of the Senate during the 108th Congress. Environmentalists also pressured Daschle to oppose the energy bill. Daschle had earlier put the energy bill at further risk by refusing to compromise on the inclusion of the Alaska National Wildlife Refuge (ANWR) provision, which would allow oil drilling in an Alaska wilderness area. In response to *Wall Street Journal* criticism, Daschle rejected the notion that he would favor "drilling in the wildlife refuge in order to advance the energy bill's ethanol provision" and said, "I will never make that trade." Republicans ultimately dropped the ANWR provision from the energy bill to promote final passage.[4]

After the House passed the ethanol bill and it came to the Senate, Daschle's position remained unclear. By not taking an early position as Democratic leader, Daschle sent a signal about the bill's shaky prospects, which allowed his caucus to organize resistance to the bill. While the proponents of the bill sought help from the Democratic leadership, Daschle said (according to *Congressional Quarterly*) that he "was not pressuring other Democrats to support cloture" and end the filibuster. Some Democrats objected to the MTBE liability waiver provisions in the bill, which originally triggered discussion of a filibuster by Senator Chuck Schumer of New York. GOP senator Pete Domenici of New Mexico, who spearheaded the GOP's effort to pass the energy bill, argued that the liability shield protected only those companies that did not act negligently. "The big lawyers are not happy with who is left over to sue," Domenici said. "That's it in a nutshell." Daschle and the Democrats, observers noted, were heavily reliant on funding from trial lawyers, who opposed efforts to limit lawsuits. With an eye to Daschle's home-state constituency, Domenici said, "Democrats are leading a parade to kill the most important provision ever" for farmers. "If I were a farmer," he went on, "I'd ask who threw it away? They're going to know." While *Congressional Quarterly* reported that Daschle only reluctantly voted for the ethanol bill and did nothing as Democratic leader to convince other senators to vote for it, the *Argus Leader* ran a contradictory headline: "Daschle Lends Clout to Energy Bill." Despite the opportunity in late 2003, Daschle let the ethanol moment pass. Passing the energy bill during the presidential-election year of 2004 would prove next to impossible.[5]

In April 2004, Senator Grassley reminded his fellow senators about the earlier Democratic filibuster, which had undermined the November 2003 ethanol bill: "Out of those 58 votes, we only had 13 out of 49 Democrats vote to break that filibuster. So there are another 36 Democrats that if they want to help us reduce the cost of energy, I would beg them to tell our leader that they are prepared to break that filibuster." Grassley's comments followed Daschle's surprise attempt in late April—"without warning," according to the *Washington Post*— to attach the ethanol bill provisions of the energy bill to an Internet taxation bill, which observers saw as a political ploy designed to mitigate the damage at home from the November ethanol vote. Daschle's attempt received only forty votes. Even the National Corn Growers Association opposed the maneuver, as did senators from ethanol states such as Minnesota, Iowa, Kansas, and Illinois (including nine Senate Democrats).[6]

Some viewed Daschle's April effort to pass the ethanol bill as political theater. He understood his vulnerability on the ethanol issue, owing to his inactivity in November 2003. Daschle sought to bring up the measure again in April, have a vote, garner a headline, and then use the failure of the bill against the Republicans by blaming them for its failure. Republican senator John McCain of Arizona immediately criticized Daschle's motives:

> And here we go, now we are going to spend late this afternoon jockeying back and forth. I am sure there may be a *headline in South Dakota that says: Senator Daschle fights for ethanol*. I bet there will be a whole lot of press releases, too, and maybe even the distinguished Senator from North Dakota will be fighting for ethanol, too. Out of those 58 votes, we only had 13 out of 49 Democrats vote to break that filibuster. So there are another 36 Democrats that if they want to help us reduce the cost of energy, I would beg them to tell our leader that they are prepared to break that filibuster.

Ethanol insiders on Capital Hill said that Daschle's ethanol bill was "designed to fail" and to score political points. First, Daschle had not contacted key senators such as Grassley or discussed the matter with Senator Bill Frist, the Republican leader and an original cosponsor of the ethanol bill. Second, Daschle did not contact key supporters such as the National Corn Growers Association, the Renewable Fuels Association, or the National Farm Bureau, who could have helped him lobby for and build support for the bill. Third, Daschle could have brought up the November energy bill, which included provisions relating to improving the electricity grid, oil and gas production, wind energy, and other items designed to generate broad support and final passage. Even the National Corn Growers Association opposed Daschle's bill and favored a comprehensive energy package. Instead of amending operable legislation, moreover, Daschle tried to amend a dead bill.[7]

After Daschle's ethanol bill received a mere forty votes, Senator Domenici offered the broader energy package for a vote. It received fifty-five votes but needed sixty to break the filibuster. The stated reason for Democratic opposition to the November energy bill was the MTBE provision, extending civil immunities to the makers of MTBE. Daschle blamed the November bill's failure on the MTBE provisions and said that if they were removed, he could deliver the votes needed for passage. To accommodate such objections, Domenici's April offering of the comprehensive energy bill excluded the MTBE provisions, another good-faith effort to pass the bill (similar to dropping the ANWR provision), but it still failed. Daschle then sent out e-mails and ran ads in South Dakota blaming the Republicans for failing to pass the ethanol bill. The *Washington Post* reported that the Daschle gambit on the ethanol bill "enabled him to blame Republicans for its failure. And he was quick to do so." The *Post* also reported that Daschle's surprise move was a stab at Senator Frist: "Several Senate aides from both parties said Daschle might not have ambushed Frist on the issue if Frist had not committed to working for Daschle's defeat." *Congress Daily* reported that when "laying the blame at the feet of Senate Republicans . . . Daschle also put special emphasis on the role of Senate GOP leadership in the amendment's failure—a not-so-veiled dig at Majority Leader Frist, who has been aggressively fund-raising for former GOP Rep. John Thune, who is challenging Daschle for his Senate seat."[8]

Despite the potential for political fallout in corn-covered South Dakota, the state press ignored the details reported by national publications. As Senator McCain predicted, the *Argus Leader* ran the headline "Ethanol Measure Discarded; Daschle Tacked Legislation onto Internet Bill." The lead paragraph said that the Senate "block[ed] Senate Minority Leader Tom Daschle's move to boost the fuel's production." The article then noted that both sides "traded accusations" over the bill's failure. The *Argus* ignored the vote totals, McCain's and Grassley's criticisms, the National Corn Growers' opposition to Daschle's bill, the *Washington Post*'s comment that the Daschle bill was designed to allow him to blame Republicans, Daschle's failure to line up critical support from farm groups and pro-ethanol senators, the opposition from several ethanol-state senators, and the attempt to undermine Senator Frist. The article also failed to explain Senator Domenici's compromise bill, which excluded any MTBE provisions but instead indicated that Daschle had made a good-faith fight for ethanol. The *Argus* story then migrated to the Associated Press and ran across the state. The *Argus* thus failed to give the voters of South Dakota all that they needed to know about Daschle and the politics of ethanol for them to make a fully educated vote in the fall.[9]

The ethanol debacle also revealed a rougher side to Daschle's practice of politics back home in South Dakota, where Daschle's campaign manager had vowed to "attack" any of the senator's critics. *Congressional Quarterly* reported in November that those "affiliated with [South Dakota's] burgeoning ethanol industry may also take out their anger on Daschle if an energy bill is not enacted this year, said Lisa Richardson, executive director of the South Dakota Corn Growers Association." Richardson said that Daschle, as Senate leader, was expected to ensure Democratic support for the energy bill and argued, "It will be hard to come back to South Dakota without it." Richardson quickly received strongly worded calls from Daschle and his staffers unhappy with her comments. In-state criticism soon diminished. The public inactivity of disappointed ethanol supporters underscored how Daschle's position of power in Washington muted criticism of his Washington activities. Behind the scenes, however, some leaders in the ethanol industry seethed.[10]

In May 2003, a year before Thune's speech at the Hudson ethanol plant, Daschle had said, "I am going to work as hard as I can and use every resource at my disposal to get [the ethanol bill] into law as soon as possible." In a letter to constituents, Daschle said that he thought of "the expansion of ethanol as a barometer of my congressional career." He ran radio and television ads during the summer of 2003 touting his work on ethanol. Although Daschle had been a promoter of ethanol throughout his time in Congress, when at the "one-yard line" in November 2003, as Thune constantly said, he failed to act. Daschle allowed the partisan friction of the Senate to defeat the ethanol bill. Thune tried to subtly make the point at the opening of the ethanol plant on May 1, but the media did not cover his comments, and the message did not reach beyond the small audience in Hudson. The *Argus Leader* refused to explain the machinations of the ethanol bill to voters.[11]

In late May, Grassley—"Mr. Ethanol"—went to the Senate floor and gave a long speech attacking Daschle for undermining the ethanol bill and for playing the "Block and Blame Game." Grassley said that Senate Democrats had informed lobbyists that "they were implementing a strategy to block all major legislation, except for some appropriations measures." The strategy sought to bolster the argument that "the GOP is getting nothing done." Reacting to Daschle's April ethanol maneuver, Grassley said that it was "inconceivable that the renewable fuels amendment offered by the Democratic leader on April 27 could have been designed any better to assure its failure. It was guaranteed to fail. If you understand Senate procedures, and the importance of passing a regionally attractive, comprehensive Energy bill, it is obvious to you that this amendment was *designed to fail.*" Grassley noted that "no pro-ethanol Republican ally was contacted in advance to help develop a strategy to assure that we secure enough votes" and that "the Democratic leader failed to contact the ethanol and corn grower lobbyists in advance. That, I know has never happened." Grassley also explained the procedural hurdles that Daschle's maneuver created and said that "adding an amendment to a bill to be taken to conference by Chairman McCain was the iron-clad guarantee it would be rejected." The *Argus Leader* did not bother to cover Senator Grassley's lengthy speech, even though several reporters were told numerous times about it. When the chairman of the Senate Finance Committee launched a major assault on the Democratic leader of the Senate on the Senate floor over an issue of critical importance to the state of South Dakota, the *Argus Leader* did not deem even that occasion newsworthy.[12]

The failure of the ethanol bill signified the deterioration of conditions in the Senate. A *Washington Post* story headlined "Senate Partisanship Worst in Memory" reported that the body was beset with "one of the worst Senate stalemates in history." The *Arkansas Democrat-Gazette* reported that Daschle "tried about every way possible this year to block legislation wanted by the majority. He has forced cloture votes (which require a 60-vote super majority to halt debate on matters and bring them to a vote), peppered bills with amendments he knew Republicans wouldn't want to vote on, and objected again and again to the appointment of conferees." The newspaper quoted Democratic senator Blanche Lincoln of Arkansas, who regretted that the Senate had "missed so many opportunities." The *Houston Chronicle* reported on the "bitter partisanship" and the "raging political war" within the

Senate and noted that "this year's battles have become too personal, biting and strident." The paper quoted Senator McCain's outburst during Daschle's ethanol maneuver: "Why don't we just go home . . . rather than go through this charade of telling Americans that we are legislating?" The *New York Times* also ran a long piece on the "election-year paralysis" and focused on the Democratic refusal to convene conference committees, which work out the differences between House and Senate bills. The May issue of *Harper's Magazine* even included a long essay calling for the abolition of the U.S. Senate. Daschle's spokesman responded by arguing that the "Republican leadership is running a do-nothing Senate." He did not explain that Daschle was the reason the Senate could not do anything. Despite the wide attention that the Senate deadlock was receiving around the country from newspaper reporters, the *Argus Leader* did not run such stories. In his floor statement in late May, Senator Grassley said that Daschle hoped "no one outside of Washington can figure out the nuances of the legislative procedures of obstruction."[13]

In early May, Senate Democrats announced that none of the president's judicial nominees would receive a Senate vote for the remainder of 2004. Republican senator Arlen Specter of Pennsylvania described a conversation with the Senate minority leader: "When I talked to Senator Daschle, he said, 'We will not take up any more judges unless the president says he will not use his Constitutional power to make interim appointments of judges.' Well, the president can't do that. He's sworn to uphold the Constitution, and the Constitution gives President Bush that authority." Specter said, "I was a district attorney long enough to know blackmail when I see it. You can't arrest them for it, but it's blackmail." Other commentators argued that Daschle had supported President Clinton's recess appointments and concluded that Senate Democrats simply sought a rationale for blocking the president's judges, a suspicion confirmed by confidential memos outlining the strategizing between Senate Democrats and liberal interest groups such as NARAL and People for the American Way (a GOP staffer had downloaded the memos from a shared hard drive in the Senate). The *Argus Leader* did not report on the Senate judicial blockade.[14]

In mid-May, *The Hill* reported that Senator Frist, in response to the judicial blockade and Daschle's refusal to allow conference committees to meet, contemplated invoking what was colorfully described as the "nuclear option" to break the deadlock. One plan discussed would raise a point of order in response to the Democrats' refusal to allow conference committees to meet or to allow a vote on judges. The chair of the Senate, Vice President Dick Cheney, would sustain the point of order, and the Democrats would object to the ruling. The Republicans would then move to table the nondebatable motion, which, unlike the sixty votes necessary for cloture, would require only fifty-one votes to prevail. Such a procedural ruling from the chair would effectively change the rules of the Senate. Republicans told the press that they would consider using such a maneuver in the future if the blockade persisted. Daschle's spokesman said, "What's their next power grab . . . replacing the President with a king?" Before the end of the month, the crisis passed when the White House relented and promised not to make any recess appointments in exchange for confirmation votes on twenty-five "noncontroversial" judicial nominees. Many questioned the blockade of noncontroversial judges in the first place.[15]

Senator Frist, the Republican leader in the Senate, was "fed up" with the Senate paralysis, according to *U.S. News and World Report*, and made his much-publicized trip to South Dakota in mid-May to help Thune. Just prior to Frist's visit to South Dakota, a new KELO/ *Argus Leader* Mason-Dixon poll showed Daschle ahead by a scant two-point margin, even though Thune had yet to run a single ad. When criticized for his "unprecedented" trip, Frist responded by noting Daschle's weak political standing, as indicated by the recent poll: "It may be rare, but these are rare times. It's rare that you have a leader who would not be very strongly supported by the people in his home state. That is almost unprecedented. Other leaders have simply not been in that situation." The *Rapid City Journal* picked up on Frist's dig at Daschle, as did the *New York Times*, the *Washington Post*, the national Associated Press, and others. The *Argus Leader* did not. Despite the widespread national attention paid to the Frist visit, the *Argus* put the story halfway down the page on B1. While the press focused on the unprecedented nature of the trip, forty-five-year Senate Democratic veteran Robert Byrd decried the breach of Senate tradition: "What has become of civility? . . . It used to be unheard of for Senate leaders to seek an active role against each other in campaigns. That time has gone." The *New York Times* reported that Frist's trip irked Daschle and that Frist's fund-raising letter for Thune had "strained relations between the men for a few days." The *Washington Post* also reported that the visit had "bruised some feelings." After the election, Daschle denounced Frist's visit as "wrong."[16]

During his visit, Frist criticized Senate Democrats for blocking legislation and, during a tour of a rural health facility in Dell Rapids, noted how many South Dakota seniors would benefit from the new Medicare prescription drug program passed by Republicans in December 2003. Frist also visited Ellsworth Air Force Base in Rapid City, which had lost thousands of personnel in previous decades because of the end of the cold war and the demolition of the nuclear missile silos that had dotted western South Dakota (if the Dakotas had seceded from the union during the cold war, they would have been the world's third-largest nuclear power). Frist hoped that more missions could be found for Ellsworth, which at the time hosted thirty B-1 bombers. Daschle ran several ads during the campaign arguing that his leadership post could prevent Ellsworth from closing and said that he had convinced President Clinton to save Ellsworth from closure in the 1990s. As early as May 2004, the Pentagon began making plans to close Ellsworth.[17]

The poll lead (49 to 47 percent) cost Daschle points in the political expectations game, and Frist's willingness to visit South Dakota further highlighted Daschle's vulnerability. Daschle's weakness also diminished his ability to dissuade potential Thune donors, which he had done prior to the Johnson-Thune race in 2002. In 2001, *Roll Call* reported that Daschle informed a Democratic lobbyist, "We are going to be watching how you and your industry do in the race in our state." The lobbyist told *Roll Call*, "I have never had anyone tell me I could not give to a candidate before." One GOP lobbyist said, "Daschle is being subtle and heavy-handed at the same time. He walks up, puts his hand on your shoulder, gives that Daschle grin and says, 'You know I am keeping track of people who give to Tim Johnson.'" By May of 2004, Daschle had collected three times as much political action committee money as Thune had; despite the recent poll results, moreover, his allies could still dissuade some Thune donors. During the summer, the insurance industry canceled a fund-raiser for Thune when, according to *Roll Call*, Senate Democrats "said they planned to drop their support for an industry-backed terrorism insurance bill if the industry went ahead with" the Thune fund-raiser.

The *Washington Times* criticized the "quid-pro-quo political power play that linked legislative action to campaign contributions" and concluded that "Mr. Daschle's fellow Democrats placed at risk the timely reauthorization of terrorism-reinsurance legislation."[18]

Despite such pressure, Daschle's second-quarter fund-raising and poll numbers did not impress many observers. Thune raised $1.4 million while Daschle raised $560,000. Daschle had raised significant funds overall, but he had also spent $8.3 million, which lowered his cash on hand at the end of May to $4 million, while Thune had about $2.5 million on hand. The recent poll and the fund-raising reports diminished observers' expectations of Daschle, an important component of contemporary politics. John Kerry won the expectations game during the Democratic primaries, for example, and analysts pointed out that it significantly boosted his support. Political analysts continued to see the Daschle-Thune race as a toss-up, aiding Thune's efforts to attract supporters and raise money. As Thune looked like less of a long shot, more insiders paid attention.

The ongoing contest for the June 1 special election for the House seat for South Dakota, which had closed from a thirty-point Democratic advantage to a ten-point race by late May, became the backdrop for the Senate race in late spring. The candidacy of Democrat Stephanie Herseth underscored a political dilemma for Daschle. Herseth employed the Daschle election model from the late 1970s and early 1980s and ran as a conservative Democrat, pledged to join forces with the "Blue Dog" conservative Democratic caucus in Washington, and promised to work with Republicans in a nonpartisan manner. She emphasized her winning, moderate personality, as Daschle had always done, and said that she supported the president's Iraq policy and his proposed marriage amendment to the Constitution, a decision that caused friction with the Daschle camp and gays and lesbians in South Dakota. Such moves put Herseth in a "conservative light," said Dave Kranz of the *Argus Leader,* so "she wouldn't be called your traditional Democrat right now." Many observers, however, considered Daschle a traditional Democrat in May 2004. The nonpartisan image that Daschle had projected in his early campaigns faded because of the interparty warfare in the Senate, his criticism of the president on the war, and his opposition to the gay marriage amendment. Herseth astutely distanced herself from Daschle and, in a telling moment, did not list him as one of her political mentors, although she did list Senator Tim Johnson, who still tried to assert moderate Democrat credentials. If Herseth won the House seat, 25 percent of South Dakotans, according to an *Argus Leader*/KELO poll, would be more likely to vote against Daschle to prevent the entire South Dakota congressional delegation from becoming Democratic. While a Herseth victory would contribute to national stories about Democratic momentum in Bush country, many insiders considered it a net liability for Daschle's reelection prospects.[19]

Herseth's support for the gay marriage amendment increased the attention given to the issue, as did happenings in Massachusetts. On May 17, gay marriage became legal in Massachusetts, and more than a thousand gay and lesbian couples sought marriage licenses. The next day, the Republican governor of Massachusetts, Mitt Romney, began demanding information about the licenses granted so that his office could verify that they were offered only to Massachusetts couples; Romney did not want the state to become "the Las Vegas of same-sex marriage." The governor of South Dakota sent a letter to Governor Romney asking him to deny marriage licenses to any South Dakota gays or lesbians who attempted to marry in Massachusetts. An earlier poll in South Dakota indicated that 63 percent of state residents favored the president's proposed amendment to the U.S. Constitution defining marriage. A poll conducted in May for various South Dakota media outlets found that 75 percent of South Dakotans rejected legalized same-sex marriage. Meanwhile, the director of the National Gay and Lesbian Task Force angrily challenged Daschle's commitment to opposing the federal marriage amendment, a charge that Daschle supporters in Washington vigorously denied. John Kerry, after announcing his opposition to gay marriage, also had to meet privately "with gay-rights groups to fortify a tenuous peace."[20]

An episode during the final week of the June 1 special election created another awkward moment for Daschle. Herseth and Senators Daschle and Tim Johnson attended a rally at which Johnson exclaimed "how sweet it's going to be" when the "Taliban wing of the Republican Party" gets news of Herseth's victory. Johnson refused to apologize for the remark and condemned those "who have attacked my religious faith, attacked my patriotism." Johnson incorrectly claimed that he had been compared to Saddam Hussein during the 2002 Senate race. The ad, which asserted that Saddam Hussein sought nuclear weapons, said, "Tim Johnson's voted against a missile defense system 29 different times. One of the most liberal records in Congress. Is this a question of patriotism? No. *It's a question of judgment.*" After the ad ran, Johnson berated Thune for such an "intensely over-the-top negative" ad and called it "despicable." After Johnson's Taliban comment in 2004, KDLT Television reported that Johnson said "he's sorry he wasn't more clear about who he was talking about when he made that comment. But, he didn't apologize for 'what' he said." The editors of the *Rapid City Journal* called it "classic non-apology, apology," and the *Mitchell Daily Republic* said that Johnson did not offer a "real apology." Even the editors of the *Argus Leader* thought that "Johnson's apology isn't good enough."[21]

Critics said that if the 2002 ad mentioning Hussein was despicable, then Johnson's direct Taliban comparison belonged in the same category. The hypocrisy charge received additional momentum from Daschle, who had given a major speech at Kansas State University a few weeks earlier denouncing the "startling meanness" of American politics. In his widely reported speech, Daschle once again repeated the false claim that Johnson had been compared to Hussein, which had become a basic component of Daschle's victimization mantra. He also said, "Demonizing those with whom we disagree politically does not serve the interests of democracy." Daschle, however, stood by and clapped during Johnson's jab at the Republican "Taliban." Daschle said later that Johnson had "apologized, and I think that's all that needs to be said." Daschle similarly refused to criticize Howard Dean, Al Gore, and John Kerry when they made intemperate remarks about President Bush. The *Rapid City Journal* editors said, "Note to Kansas State University: never mind." The episode undermined Daschle's ability to play the victim of negative attacks, which remained a core component of his campaign.[22]

Events on the international front took another turn for the worse in May. In the early part of the month, the Abu Ghraib prison abuse scandal broke open and seriously undermined the mission in Iraq, generating speculation about the firing of Secretary of Defense Donald Rumsfeld (it was reported after the election that he offered to resign) and calls for earlier Iraqi elections. Senator Daschle said that the abuse indicated a systemic problem and that the "resignation of one official" would not address the problem, a criticism echoed by Senator Kerry. Senator Edward Kennedy said that "shamefully, we now learn that Saddam's torture chambers reopened under new management: U.S. management." Al-Qaeda subsequently beheaded Nick Berg, a Jewish contractor from Philadelphia, and posted the grisly display on the Internet. The president's handling of Iraq cost him politically in May, just as it had in April. From December, when Thune made his final decision to enter the Senate race, to May, the number of Americans supporting Bush's handling of the Iraq War had dropped from 59 to 41 percent, according to a *Time*/CNN poll. Some Thune supporters feared that Bush's declining support would redound negatively to Thune, who shared the ballot with the president in the fall. The April *Argus Leader*/KELO-Land poll showed Bush winning South Dakota with 51 percent of the vote (to his opponent's 35 percent), but Kerry's negative rating since February had grown from 21 to 39 percent, reinforcing Daschle's problem of having Kerry on the ticket. Sixty-seven percent of South Dakotans, however, still approved of the president's handling of homeland security and the war on terror.[23]

Bush's weakening political support aided Daschle, who still remained in a strong position. A Zogby poll sponsored in part by the *Rapid City Journal* found Daschle leading 52 to 39 percent. The Daschle campaign touted its own poll showing the senator leading 55 to 42 percent to blunt concerns about the May Mason-Dixon poll showing a mere two-point lead. Some in the Thune campaign also viewed the two-point gap as an outlier and believed that Thune had to make up considerable ground. What was most important for Daschle was the continued obliviousness of the state's biggest newspaper to national stories that would have undermined his position in the polls. The newspaper even ignored the details of stories with local importance, such as the ethanol bill. Daschle's campaign organization also continued to grow, his advertising barrage persisted, and he continued to receive free media attention for introducing federal legislation and blaming Senator Frist for the failure of the ethanol bill. Finally, the Senate stalemate received virtually no attention in South Dakota. Few voters understood the details of Daschle's activities in the Senate. Still, some Washington Democrats began to fret. *The Hill* reported that "Democratic leaders were already developing plans to succeed

Daschle" but avoided maneuvers that "might be interpreted as a lack of confidence in Daschle." In response to a reporter's speculation that Daschle would step down as Senate leader after winning in the fall, MSNBC's Chris Matthews retorted, "You're betting he'll get re-elected? Don't."[24]

CHAPTER FIVE

THE POLITICS OF ASSOCIATION AND MEMORY

History is past politics and politics are present history.
—Herbert Baxter Adams

On June 1, 2004, Stephanie Herseth prevailed by fewer than three thousand votes in the special election to replace former congressman Bill Janklow. She defeated Elkton farmer and state senator Larry Diedrich by embracing Daschle's early political model. Dave Kranz of the *Argus Leader* reported that voters "who listen to Herseth and Diedrich side by side often say there isn't much difference between them." When the *Argus* endorsed the Democratic Herseth, the editors likewise noted that "there's hardly a whiff of difference between them on the key issues they would face in Washington, D.C." When the *Aberdeen American News* endorsed Herseth, the editors similarly concluded that "there's not much difference between the candidates." Herseth, as Kranz reported, "sought to discard the liberal label" by touting her A-rating from the National Rifle Association and by supporting the renewal of the Patriot Act, the war in Iraq, tax cuts, and the federal marriage amendment. An exasperated Diedrich told the *New York Times*, "She has done a very good job of running as a Republican." When asked about John Kerry, Herseth practiced what Kranz called the "politics of avoidance" and is described as having laughed at the idea of a Kerry visit to South Dakota: "I just don't see there would be any interest from my campaign or the national party."[1]

With few issues dividing the candidates in the House race, many voters focused on personality, which served Herseth well given her sunny demeanor, her name recognition, and her thirty-point lead in the polls. Political analyst Stuart Rothenberg reported that Herseth tried "to make the special election a popularity contest." Longtime local television anchor Steve Hemmingsen noted the difficulty of such a contest for Diedrich, who began the race as a "nobody except to legislators and soybean farmers." He also chided Herseth for her "Mary Tyler Moore Show innocent spunkiness" and took to calling her "Princess Stephanie"; the *New York Times* similarly reported that Herseth had "a star quality about her." Some reporters also said that Herseth's image benefited from the resignation of her 2002 opponent, former governor Bill Janklow, and the disclosure of some past Janklow pardons in the final days of the House campaign, which some thought aided Herseth and overshadowed her opponent.[2]

In a campaign focused on personality, Herseth emphasized niceness. A Dave Kranz piece for the *Argus Leader* entitled "'Nice' Image Appeals to Many S.D. Voters" captured Herseth's strategy. In her television ads, Herseth said, "I'm not going to tear my opponent down." Political analyst Charlie Cook said that Herseth "tried to set a trap for Diedrich with ads that call[ed] for a positive campaign." After a minor spat over the permanent extension of the Bush tax cuts, for example, Herseth ran an ad saying that she was "committed to a truthful campaign. It's clear that Larry Diedrich is not." The Herseth ad responded to a Diedrich contrast ad that Stuart Rothenberg deemed "downright wimpy." In his ad, Diedrich commented that "on tax cuts, I think they should be made permanent. Stephanie does not." Rothenberg concluded that "Herseth responded as if Diedrich just accused her of strangling kittens. She badly overreacted, making herself the one guilty of directing a 'negative attack.'" He added, "Herseth is like the little boy who cries 'wolf' when no threatening animal is in sight. . . . Herseth's response is a classic effort at inoculation. She is trying to make it impossible for Diedrich to identify differences with her, even if they exist." When the ad was widely perceived as snippy and undermined her image as a nice campaigner, Herseth quickly stopped running it.[3]

Despite Herseth's astute co-optation of Republican issues, her winning personality, and President Bush's slump in the polls, Diedrich's relentless hand-shaking helped boost his name recognition and close the thirty-point gap in the polls. He lost, 49 to 51 percent. The final tally, as the Associated Press reported, was "much closer than expected." Herseth joked that "compared to 524 votes" (the margin of Senator Johnson's victory over Thune in 2002), "over 2,000 is a landslide here in South Dakota." With higher voter turnout, however, Herseth might have lost. In the West River county of Pennington, the state's second-largest county (which Diedrich won with 59 percent of the vote), only 53 percent of voters went to the polls. Other West River Republican counties also had a low turnout: Butte, 50 percent; Meade, 52 percent; Lawrence, 46 percent. In Minnehaha County, by comparison, the state's largest county (which Herseth won by four points), 59 percent of voters turned out. Herseth also received huge majorities on the state's Indian reservations, a vote that would grow in the fall because of the large-scale get-out-the-vote effort by the better-funded Daschle campaign. The GOP nominated Diedrich again for the November race against Herseth, hoping that higher GOP turnout in the fall might put him over the top. A few weeks after the election, however, Diedrich announced that he required open-heart surgery, which relegated him to his farm near Elkton for much of the summer. In the ensuing months, the House race would fade into the shadows as the Senate race lit up the airwaves.[4]

The Herseth victory demonstrated the influence of the blogosphere. The Daily Kos blog, for example, which had organized national support for Howard Dean's presidential campaign, consistently supported Herseth. Markos Moulitsas Zuniga ("Kos" for short), who had organized Daily Kos in Berkeley, served as a consultant for Dean's campaign and other candidates. His loyal followers, who comment in long threads on his blog, have become known as "Kosacks." Many Kosacks contributed to the Herseth campaign, just as they had contributed to the Dean campaign, and traveled to South Dakota for the election to join forces with the nearly nine hundred out-of-state volunteers organized by the Democratic Congressional Campaign Committee. The *San Francisco Chronicle* called this new form of Internet activism "grassroots netocracy." Daily Kos significantly boosted Herseth's fund-raising and visibility. During election night, two of Kos's three servers melted down from all the attention given to the race nationally.[5]

Kos and his followers, who embrace liberal and progressive causes, scorned the accommodationist and moderate Democratic Leadership Council candidates for timidity, especially with regard to their lack of opposition to the war in Iraq. The election-night comments on Daily Kos exposed the anger of some on the left. Various Kosacks denounced South Dakotans as "racist"; referred to them as "fascists," "softball playing hicks," and "thugs" who wore "jackboots"; and ridiculed the generally "soulless forces of evil in the Republican party." Kos raised the issue of Diedrich's legislative voting "record on child abuse." As dedicated liberals, the Kosacks also had a lively debate about supporting Herseth. The purists deemed her unworthy of election given her support for the Iraq War, the Patriot Act, and the federal marriage amendment, but the Popular Front pragmatists argued that it was the best they could do in South Dakota. The unity of various component parts of the American left, a rare event in recent decades, signified the determination to defeat President Bush. Many Kosacks exhibited less charity toward Daschle, whom they viewed as a "squishy" Democrat and a Clintonesque corporate fund-raiser who had voted for the Iraq War, which many Kosacks and Dean supporters vehemently opposed, considering Daschle an uninspiring maintainer of the status quo. Some Daily Kos commentators favored replacing Daschle as Senate leader. Others wanted Daschle to win his reelection effort only to be subsequently replaced as leader, while others simply wanted him to lose. Some liberals and progressives on the front lines of politics professed little love for Daschle. The Kosacks exposed the rifts between the hardened base of liberal activists in the country and some of the established powers within the Democratic Party.[6]

Many commentators believed that Herseth's victory hurt Daschle. Steve Hemmingsen, for example, noted the consequences for Daschle's fall campaign when "inherently GOP South Dakota will be fence row–to–fence row with Democrats in Washington." For the first time since a month in the late 1930s, the South Dakota congressional delegation became completely Democratic. An *Argus Leader* poll found that 25 percent of voters would be less likely to vote for Daschle if Herseth won. The *New York Times* ran a story under the headline "Could Herseth's victory in South Dakota hurt Daschle?" In response to a question about the all-eggs-in-one-basket argument hurting Daschle, even South Dakota Democratic National Committeewoman Sharon Stroschein said, "I'm sure it would work to some degree." Herseth's crying wolf about negative ads also reduced the strategy's effectiveness for the Daschle campaign. Moreover, Herseth's "Blue Dog" platform, which followed the Daschle model from 1978, contrasted with Daschle's partisan sparring as a Democratic leader in 2004. Herseth's positions on guns, gay marriage, taxes, and the war made

Daschle's liberal positions more conspicuous. Comparisons between Daschle's and Herseth's record undermined Daschle, as would the memories churned up in early summer.[7]

June became a month of intense historical reflection. The first occasion involved the sixtieth anniversary of the D-Day invasion and the dedication of the World War II memorial on the mall in Washington. Consciousness of World War II burgeoned in the 1990s during the fiftieth anniversary of the D-Day landing, along with the publication of South Dakota native Tom Brokaw's book *The Greatest Generation*, the release of Steven Spielberg's movie *Saving Private Ryan*, several books by Stephen Ambrose (who once told me that he would not have "wasted" so many years writing Nixon books if he had understood the hunger for World War II history), and the HBO series *Band of Brothers*, which stemmed from an Ambrose book. The moral clarity of World War II intensified after the calamity of 9/11. Memorializing World War II again stiffened the spine of history in the nation's culture and politics. The inscription at the entrance to the new World War II memorial connected the war against Nazi Germany and Imperial Japan to the nation's founding ideals: "Here in the presence of Washington and Lincoln, one the eighteenth century father and the other the nineteenth century preserver of our nation, we honor those twentieth century Americans who took up the struggle during the Second World War and made the sacrifices to perpetuate the gift our forefathers entrusted to us: a nation conceived in liberty and justice."

President Bush projected the cultural power of World War II forward, comparing the conflict to the ongoing war against terror: "In their worship of power, their deep hatreds, their blindness to innocence, the terrorists are successors to the murderous ideologies of the 20th century." Bush linked the reconstruction of Iraq to the reordering of Nazi Germany into a Western republic after World War II. As late as 1947, Bush noted, "there was still starvation in Germany. Reconstruction seemed to be faltering. The Marshall Plan had not yet begun. Some questioned whether a free and stable Germany could emerge from the rubble." The battle over public support for the Iraq War became a contest of historical imagination, the president's historical allusions to the moral clarity of World War II competing against the skeptics' allusions to the ambiguity and futility of Vietnam.[8]

Memories of the nation's triumphs during World War II fused with memories of cold war victories when, on the day before the D-Day anniversary, Ronald Reagan died. After a viewing of the casket at the Reagan Library in California, where 80,000 mourners visited in twenty-four hours, Reagan was flown to Washington and his flag-draped coffin was taken to the capitol in a horse-drawn caisson to lie in state; there, another 200,000 mourners paid their respects. Reagan was eulogized at the National Cathedral six days after his death. Former British prime minister Margaret Thatcher, the other pillar of the 1980s conservative revival, said in starkly Reaganesque terms that Reagan sought to "free the slaves of communism." Sandra Day O'Connor, whom Reagan had appointed as the first woman on the Supreme Court, read from John Winthrop's "city upon a hill" sermon delivered in 1630, and former senator John Danforth invoked Reinhold Neibuhr's dichotomy between children of light and darkness. Attendees sang the "Battle Hymn of the Republic," "Ode to Joy," and "Amazing Grace." On the flight back to California, Reagan's plane dipped a wing over his boyhood home in Illinois.[9]

Before burial, a final ceremony was held in Simi Valley as the sun set, as Reagan had requested. The captain of the aircraft carrier USS *Ronald Reagan* presented Nancy Reagan with the flag from Reagan's coffin, and more than thirty-five million Americans watched the funeral on television. Reagan's death inspired a national conversation about his legacy and how he had shaped history, had fostered new democratic governments, and had given hope to those living under the boot of Soviet communism. The longtime defender of Jews in the Soviet Union, Natan Sharansky (whose book on democratization President Bush openly promoted), explained his embrace of Reagan while confined to a Soviet prison in Siberia. As Reagan's denunciation of the Soviet Union as an "Evil Empire" spread through the prison, Sharansky recalled, "We dissidents were ecstatic. Finally, the leader of the free world had spoken the truth—a truth that burned inside the heart of each and every one of us."[10]

The World War II commemorations and the Reagan funeral slowed the withering barrage of bad news from Iraq, especially the fallout from the Abu Ghraib scandal. They also conjured memories of remaking totalitarian states into functional, prosperous republics and freeing nations once held in bondage during a month when the United States prepared to transfer sovereignty to a new Iraqi government. Even before the transfer, President Bush touted the organization of political parties and courts of law, the establishment of a new currency, the opening of new businesses, the opening of schools and hospitals, and the publication of 170 newspapers in Iraq. The memory of Reagan and his legacy bolstered support for the effort to build the new Iraq. A Pew Research Center poll found that the number of Americans who viewed the U.S. military effort as succeeding jumped from 46 percent in May to 57 percent in mid-June. President Bush's approval ratings also increased after Reagan's death. The focus on Reagan's legacy stopped the hemorrhaging of Bush's support, which had become severe in April and May. The *New York Times* reported on "Bush's effort to wrap himself in the Reagan legacy" and the criticism it generated.[11]

Reagan's death proved an awkward moment for Daschle. In a strange turn, Daschle called for honoring Reagan's memory by passing the energy bill. Daschle also observed that the "civility and personal decency that we associate with [Reagan] seems, at times, to have all but disappeared from much of our public discourse. The elbows in politics have become sharper, the words have become meaner, and the accomplishments have become scarcer." Daschle's memory failed him. Reagan's upending of establishment liberalism and his frontal assault on the 1960s, the Great Society, and McGovernism—traditions in which Daschle had matured politically—had earned the president many bitter enemies. Political commentator Anthony Lewis had called Reagan "primitive"; John Oakes, a senior *New York Times* editor, had denounced his "mindless militarism"; historian Richard Reeves had identified a "whiff of moral fascism" stemming from Reagan's presidential candidacy; and Coretta Scott King, the widow of civil rights leader Martin Luther King, Jr., had said, "I am scared that if Ronald Reagan gets into office, we are going to see more of the Ku Klux Klan and a resurgence of the Nazi Party." During the 1980s, the New Frontier/ Great Society defender and historian Arthur Schlesinger, Jr., in an early attempt at shaping Reagan's history and memory, speculated that "a few years from now . . . Reaganism will seem a weird and improbable memory, a strange interlude of national hallucination." Political columnist Daniel Henninger recalled that the "ethos of Ronald Reagan and LBJ represent[ed] the two great political ideologies of our lifetime" and stated that when they clashed, politics got ugly:

"To any who were there, the first Reagan term was bloody" and the "air burned with antipathy." Henninger recalled that Senator Joe Biden had brought Attorney General Ed Meese's wife to tears during his confirmation hearing by twice calling the nominee "beneath contempt." "The Reagan wars," Henninger explained, "persist in our time."[12]

Daschle, who had contended with the rising tide of Reaganism as he started his political career, resisted Reagan's legacy as late as 2002. During the celebration of Reagan's ninety-first birthday that year, reporters noted that Daschle "criticized the former President's tax cuts and downplayed his role in winning the cold war" and "struggled to find something nice to say about the nation's oldest former president." Daschle had also tried to prevent the naming of Reagan National Airport a few years before. To concede the power and purpose of Reagan's legacy, after all, delegitimized much of the Democratic Party's agenda. In June 2004, Daschle and other critics of Reagan lost the popular argument over the historical memory of Reagan and, as a result, suffered politically. Political columnist Charles Krauthammer concluded that "rarely has a president been so quickly and completely vindicated by history." After Reagan's death, Jim Jordan, a past advisor to South Dakota Democrats who had served as John Kerry's first campaign manager, said, "I've been dreading this every election year for three cycles."[13]

The debate over Reagan's historical legacy also echoed in the Black Hills of South Dakota. The *New York Times* reported that Reagan's death created "ticklish situations for certain Democrats on Capitol Hill" and that "one of those in a delicate spot is Senator Tom Daschle." In response to calls for Reagan to be memorialized on the ten-dollar bill, Daschle demurred. Some advocated adding Reagan to Mt. Rushmore in Daschle's home state (the *Times* coyly noted that Daschle was not pressed on that "monumental question"). Peter Kirsanow, a member of the U.S. Civil Rights Commission, said that of all the possible Reagan memorials, "only Rushmore suffices." "When Doane Robinson first conceived the idea of Mount Rushmore," Kirsanow said, "he wanted to commemorate larger-than-life Western heroes." Kirsanow also linked Reagan to democratization, arguing that the sculptor "envisioned the monument as a 'shrine to democracy,' a national monument 'commemorating America's founders and builders.' No single person has done more to spread democracy in the last 100 years than Ronald Reagan."[14]

Daschle's embrace of a nonpartisan and tranquil political history of Reagan's 1980s served his purposes, however. It contrasted with what Daschle portrayed as the viciousness of politics under President George W. Bush and the "startling meanness" of contemporary political culture. Similar to Herseth, Daschle tried to inoculate himself against rigorous criticism in the Senate campaign and to claim the high ground in a state weary of television advertising and negative attacks. In early June, Daschle formally announced a "clean campaign pledge" and sent a letter to 130 liberal interest groups commanding them not to run ads in South Dakota, a move he constantly touted during the campaign. However, KELO Television commentator Steve Hemmingsen said, Daschle's "nicey-nicey ploy isn't going to work. It's just a stunt." To date, Thune had yet to run any ads, a fact that diminished the potential prominence of Daschle's announcement. The Daschle campaign wrongly believed Thune would start television ads after the House special election. Instead, the Thune camp responded with a proposal to limit campaign spending to $10 million per campaign in keeping with Daschle's calls in previous elections for a cap on spending. Daschle rejected the proposal and said that he needed a large war chest to fight off negative attacks. Campaign spending and the involvement of outside groups would remain sparring points in the campaign.[15]

Another week of jousting over history, politics, and memory began on June 20, when former president Bill Clinton appeared on *60 Minutes* to promote his new book *My Life*. Daschle's role in saving Clinton from removal from office following his impeachment by the House did not find its way into the pages of the Clinton book, which Daschle surely appreciated during an election year. Clinton used the history in his book, as Arthur Schlesinger, Jr., once said in a different context, "as a weapon," a way to settle scores with leaders of what Clinton deemed a "right-wing coup" attempt. Walter Isaacson of *Time* magazine explained that Clinton portrayed his presidency "as one filled with Herculean struggles by progressive forces to beat back that regressive right." Clinton lamented his failure to confront a major war or crisis during the post–cold war 1990s, which Charles Krauthammer described as a "holiday from history." Isaacson found the "psycho-logical introspection" in the book "suited for the Age of Oprah." The public discussion of the book often focused on Clinton's victory in the impeachment battle, which Clinton deemed "a badge of honor." Some critics dismissed Clinton's book as a work of history. *New York Times* reviewer Michiko Kakutani said that the book was "sloppy, self-indulgent and often eye-crossingly dull—the sound of one man prattling away, not for the reader, but for himself and some distant angel of history." Even Monica Lewinsky (the White House intern who helped trigger Clinton's impeachment crisis) weighed in on the book's historical import: "He could have made it right with the book. But he hasn't. He is a revisionist of history. He has lied."[16]

The media frenzy over the Clinton book soon passed as Michael Moore's movie *Fahrenheit 9/11* opened, another episode that produced risky associations for Daschle. The movie won the top prize at the Cannes Film Festival in France (where it received a twenty-minute standing ovation), and various enclaves of the American left eagerly anticipated its release. Moore said that he wanted "to make a movie where, on the way out of the theatre, the people ask the ushers if they have any torches." The movie opened on 868 screens across the nation, triple the attention given Moore's previous movie, *Bowling for Columbine.* Promoters of the movie spent $10 million on advertising, and Moore vowed to sue anyone who might write something defama-tory about his work: "Any attempts to libel me will be met by force." He also created a political "war room" run by Democratic opposition researcher, former Clinton staffer, and Gore spokesman Chris Lehane to respond to criticisms. The movie belongs in the category of history, however contestable. The *Washington Post* noted the power of past historical efforts at docudrama such as Oliver Stone's *JFK* and Spike Lee's *Malcolm X* but argued that "this time is different because the subject is living, unfolding history, four months before an election." Liberal columnist Christopher Hitchens, however, derided the movie as a "sophomoric celluloid re-writing of *history.*"[17]

Moore's history of 9/11 and the subsequent invasions of Afghani-stan and Iraq drew fire from critics for its eerie portrayal of President Bush as an incompetent flunky. According to Moore's rendition, Bush stole the 2000 election (Moore called him the "thief in chief," even though postelection newspaper recounts showed Bush the winner) and acted as an agent of oil companies, Saudi sheiks, and militarists. The conservative editors of the *Wall Street Journal* saw the film as propaganda and deemed Moore the "Leni Riefenstahl of our time." Frank Rich, the liberal *New York Times* columnist, concluded that Moore could justifiably be compared to Joseph Goebbels and ridiculed his portrayal of "a malevolent conspiracy of grassy-knoll dimensions." *Newsweek* said, "Moore twists and bends available facts and makes glaring omissions in ways that end up clouding the serious political debate he wants to provoke."[18]

Moore's personal comments generated even more criticism. In London, Moore had said that Americans "are possibly the dumbest people on the planet" and suffered from an "enforced ignorance." He condemned U.S. culpability in "many acts of terror and bloodshed." He viewed the Iraq War as an act of economic exploitation: "The motivation for war is simple. The U.S. government started the war with Iraq in order to make it easy for U.S. corporations to do business in other countries. They intend to use cheap labor in those countries, which will make Americans rich." In another historical allusion, Moore said that the bomb makers in Iraq should not be called "insurgents," but "Minutemen," and predicted that "their numbers will grow—and they will win."[19]

The Democratic Party openly embraced Moore's movie. Senator Daschle stopped work in the Senate on a defense appropriations bill so that senators and staffers could attend the Washington premiere. Daschle, Democratic National Committee chairman Terry McAuliffe, and other Democratic senators personally attended the premiere, "applauding throughout and giving Moore a standing ovation when it was over," according to the *New Republic*. Richard Ben-Veniste, whom Daschle had chosen to serve on the 9/11 Commission, also attended the premiere. Jason Zengerle explained that Democrats in the past had "kept Moore at arm's length, deeming him too controversial and mercurial to be of much political use," a policy that changed after Moore's attack on the president as a "deserter" during the New Hampshire primary aided the anti-Bush cause. After the movie, McAuliffe said, "I think anyone who sees this movie will come out en masse to make sure John Kerry is elected president this November. Credit to Michael Moore for taking time to put this together." Political commentator David Brooks noted that in previous decades, "American liberals have had to settle for intellectual and moral leadership from the likes of John Dewey, Reinhold Niebuhr and Martin Luther King, Jr.," but now the "liberal grandees Arthur Schlesinger Jr., Ted Sorenson, Tom Harkin and Barbara Boxer flock to [Moore's] openings." Brooks said that the "standards of socially acceptable liberal opinion have shifted." The *Economist* reported that "no prominent Democrat has seen fit to denounce" the movie and that "Tom Daschle and Terry McAuliffe attended the film's premiere in Washington, DC, and other Democrats have helped to publicize it." In contrast, Michael Barone of *U.S. News* wrote that "seldom have leaders of a political party promoted a commercial film so shamelessly" and found it "amazing that any politician, however opposed to Bush, would want to be associated with this film or its maker."[20]

Christopher Hitchens attacked Moore's inconsistencies, which he labeled "'let's have it both ways' opportunism." In 2002, for example, Moore thought it wrong for the so-called imperialist Americans to topple the Taliban. But in 2004, Moore claimed that he thought it irresponsible that more troops were not sent. After attacking the Bush administration for creating a climate of domestic fear and trampling civil liberties, Moore then derided the administration for woefully underfunding homeland security and for not implementing more vigorous security programs. The movie did not address Saddam's thirty years of crimes in Iraq and, as Hitchens observed, in "Moore's flabbergasting choice of film shots, children are flying little kites, shoppers are smiling in the sunshine, and the gentle rhythms of life are undisturbed." Political columnist Andrew Sullivan took columnist William Raspberry to task for inconsistently applauding Moore's "sly" movie for reaching the right conclusion but also conceding its dishonesty: "Raspberry cannot have it both ways. And the fact that he tries to get away with it says a lot about how corrupted the left has become in our national discourse."[21]

Despite the mounting objections to the movie and its potential misuse by hostile powers (for example, it was the first American "documentary" that the Chinese allowed to be shown in communist China), Daschle said nothing critical about it. After the movie, Daschle simply commented that "Michael Moore obviously intends to spark debate" (the *Argus Leader* reported that Thune was "unavailable to comment" about the movie even though the campaign had sent the *Argus* a statement six hours before the paper's call for comment). Daschle could have distanced himself from Moore's movies, especially since the movie portrayed him as a feeble enabler of President Bush. The *Washington Post* noted that "Moore hardly spares mainstream Democrats. He calls the party 'weak-kneed and wimpy.'" Daschle missed a Sister Souljah or Joseph Welch opportunity to separate himself from the movie, despite paving the way the month before when denouncing the "startling meanness" in American politics. Daschle chose to remain silent, thus empowering the conspiracy theorists of the left while preserving his own hold on power by not alienating the Michael Moore/Howard Dean/Daily Kos/Hollywood forces within his party. Daschle opted for survival as Democratic leader in the face of pressure from the leftist base of his party, which depended on Hollywood support. Along with unions and trial lawyers, according to one analysis, Hollywood constituted "one of the three pillars of the Democrats' financial structure."[22]

While the memories of World War II and Ronald Reagan and the latest work of Michael Moore animated the national discourse, on June 16 the Thune campaign held its second major strategy meeting. The discussion focused on the results of the Thune campaign's first poll. The benchmark poll (so named because subsequent polls could measure gains and losses from a fixed point) was conducted after the House election. According to the poll, Thune trailed by nine points and Senator Daschle's "clout" argument continued to resonate. The poll also showed, however, that a high percentage of voters viewed Daschle as a "typical politician" who would say anything to win and indicated that if voters knew about Daschle's positions on taxes, tort reform, abortion, and other issues, they would vote against him. Many voters, according to the poll, had made initial judgments about Daschle based on personality and clout and not with a full understanding of his record. During an afternoon of discussion, the Thune campaign decided to start running ads that would reintroduce Thune to voters in July. Most Thune campaign advisors took Daschle's nine-point polling advantage in stride, especially given Daschle's persistent television, radio, and newspaper ads, some stretching back a year. Other advisers worried about the contrast between the campaign poll and the *Argus Leader* poll in May, which had showed the race at 49 for Daschle, to Thune's 47 percent. After a solemn strategy session, Thune's advisors began preparations for a frontal assault on Daschle's record.

Some Thune supporters confessed to feeling overwhelmed in June. Daschle's advertising remained ubiquitous, and a reporter informed Thune that Daschle had already assembled more than one hundred staffers. Daschle also scored points on the agricultural front by calling for drought relief in western South Dakota and for investigations into Canadian beef that had slipped into the country despite the ban on Canadian imports imposed after a "mad cow" disease scare. Letters to the editor also poured in to South Dakota newspapers. Democratic campaigns in South Dakota produce streams of letters to the editor, which some voters read religiously. (One old-time operative told me about a "boiler room"—where campaigns write faux letters to the editor—he helped run in the 1970s. To avoid detection from newspaper editors who watched for multiple letters from the same style of typewriter, a staffer would travel the garage sale circuit buying old typewriters. Upon the exhaustion of their usefulness, the old machines would wind up in the river behind the campaign office.) The editorial page of South Dakota newspapers displayed the intensity of the Daschle campaign's letter-writing effort on a daily basis. The *Argus Leader* also continued to neglect news unflattering to Daschle, a practice that became a major strategic problem for the Thune campaign. Without press scrutiny and analyses of some of Daschle's positions and activities, the Thune campaign would have to explain to voters why they should not vote for Senator Daschle, generating criticism of Thune for "going negative." Thune's grassroots campaigning, however, showed tangible results. The Thune campaign organized a rigorous schedule of small-town picnics, which drew increasingly large crowds throughout June. Thune spent three days at the Sioux Falls Rib Fest, which draws in thousands of voters from around the Sioux Falls area. Despite restlessness among Thune supporters, the Thune campaign remained ground based and continued to stay off the airwaves throughout June.

The war in Iraq also continued to overshadow the entire campaign season. In mid-June, al-Qaeda beheaded another American, this time in Saudi Arabia, and displayed the photos on the Internet. Secretary of State Colin Powell called it an act of barbarism. Terrorists increased their attacks on Americans in the Saudi Kingdom, demanding the release of terrorists from Saudi prisons, and stepped up attacks on U.S. and coalition forces in Iraq in anticipation of the June 30 transfer of sovereignty. Daschle said that the United States had to minimize its "visibility" and that U.S. involvement could "no longer look like an occupation." On the Monday after Reagan's death, Daschle started running Charles Lindbergh–esque "America First" television ads reminiscent of the 1930s. On June 30, the United States was scheduled to transfer authority to an interim Iraqi government that would hold power until elections could be held in January 2005 and, subsequently, a final constitution written and adopted.[23]

In late June, coordinated terrorist attacks in Iraq mushroomed as insurgents hoped to disrupt the transfer of sovereignty. In a surprise move, the U.S. proconsul in Iraq, Paul Bremer, transferred sovereignty to the new Iraqi government on June 28 to avoid terrorist attacks scheduled for the day of the transfer. Bremer said that those with "any doubt about whether Iraq is a better place today than it was 14 months ago should go down to see the mass graves in Hilla, or see the torture chambers or rape rooms around this country." Great danger still awaited, however. Abu Musab al-Zarqawi, an ally of Osama Bin Laden's who coordinated the terrorist efforts designed to undermine the new Iraqi government, told the new prime minister, "We have prepared for you a full cup of death." The *New York Times* reported that "historians will be arguing for years" about the decisions made on the ground during the Iraq War and noted that "Mr. Bush is staking his presidency, and history's judgment, on the American experiment in Iraq." After the transfer of power, Senator Kerry criticized President Bush for the "ill-advised way that he went to Iraq," called for the spending of more reconstruction funds, and said that it was "critical that the president get real support" from allies. A Bush spokesman said, "Kerry revealed his cynicism when he complained that not enough of the money he voted against is being spent and that the contributions of NATO and our allies aren't 'real.'" Political reporter Ryan Lizza noted that the "problem with Kerry's Iraq plan is that Bush seems to be pursuing it himself."[24]

The Kerry campaign remained in a strong position because of its massively successful fund-raising efforts, which outdid Bush's efforts in 2000 and the efforts of any previous challenger, and by pro-Kerry

527 organizations, which would ultimately spend $200 million to oust Bush. Despite Bush's troubles in Iraq, however, Kerry did not pull away. A late June *New York Times*/CBS poll found that Bush's approval rating had fallen to 42 percent, the lowest point in his presidency, but Kerry led Bush by an extremely narrow margin, with 45 percent to Bush's 44 percent. The poll also found that more voters disliked Kerry than liked him. The Democratic base, however, remained united in its disdain for President Bush. In contrast, observers in South Dakota expected Bush to win decisively. Comparisons to the newly elected congresswoman Stephanie Herseth, revived memories of Reagan and Daschle's position on the wrong side of Reaganism, and associations with a political left animated by Michael Moore remained burdens on Daschle's candidacy.[25]

CHAPTER SIX

Disintermediation
The Dakota Blog Alliance and the *Sioux Falls Argus Leader*

American democracy is built around election campaigns that voters see and hear mainly through the press. Thus is the quality of our democracy directly connected to the quality of the coverage of those campaigns.
—*Columbia Journalism Review*

Throughout the campaign, South Dakota's largest newspaper, the *Sioux Falls Argus Leader,* ignored many stories that reflected poorly on Senator Daschle. By July, Thune campaign manager Dick Wadhams had begun to routinely clash with the *Argus.* During the national debate over gay marriage in July, for example, the *Argus* demanded to see Thune's television ads about gay marriage to scrutinize them in advance of their airing, even though the newspaper had never scrutinized any of Daschle's ads, which had been running for a year. The Thune campaign had neither planned nor produced a gay marriage television ad and had no intention of running such an ad, but the *Argus* believed the Daschle campaign's claims to the contrary. In response to the *Argus Leader*'s demand to preview Thune's television ads, Wadhams was to the point: "There's no f——g way you are going to see those ads in advance of the general public—you can wait to see them like everyone else." The *Argus* editor called Thune personally to complain and ran an editorial ridiculing Wadhams's response. In another contentious phone call over the newspaper's political coverage, Wadhams repeatedly asked the *Argus Leader*'s political editor, "Are you afraid of Daschle, or do you just want him to win?"[1]

South Dakota bloggers, meanwhile, continued to criticize the *Argus Leader*'s reporting and question its fairness. By July, the criticism had become so intense that the editor of the *Argus* announced the creation of an *Argus* blog to respond to "the steady stream of questions we receive about this newspaper's coverage of politics." In keeping with the presidential race, controversies over media bias and the attempt of bloggers to expose it animated the South Dakota Senate contest. Technology expert Lawrence Lessig viewed 2004 as a historic media moment: "When they write the account of the 2004 campaign, it will include at least one word that has never appeared in any presidential history: blog." In South Dakota, the friction between blogs and an established newspaper symbolized how the Internet scrambled long-time political practices.[2]

The political influence formerly enjoyed by the major media has suffered in recent years, and popular distrust of the media has deepened. In 1985, by a margin of 54 to 13 percent, people viewed the media as moral, according to the Pew Research Center. In 2004, as many people viewed the media as moral as those who did not.[3]

The Jayson Blair plagiarism scandal at the *New York Times* crystallized public skepticism. After the *New York Times* revelation in May 2003, at least ten major newspapers (including the *Minneapolis Star Tribune*, the *Chicago Tribune*, and the *San Diego Union-Tribune*) endured journalistic scandals. Criticism of the BBC caused the resignation of its two top officials in early 2004. In April 2004, after a fabrication scandal at *USA Today*, the managing editor, the executive editor, and the editor resigned. An independent review deemed that newspaper's editorial oversight "appallingly lax" and found a "virus of fear" in the newsroom that prevented reporters from speaking out. The *Wall Street Journal* blamed *USA Today* for "coddling a charming and charismatic star performer and ignoring repeated warnings about the reliability of his work from outsiders and insiders," a favoritism the *Wall Street Journal* called the "Golden Boy" syndrome. At the 2004 American Society of Newspaper Editors conference, *New York Times* publisher Arthur O. Sulzberger told newspaper editors to assume that corrupt reporters were present in their newsrooms. After the Jayson Blair scandal, the *Times* hired Daniel Okrent to act as ombudsman to a public increasingly skeptical of the newspaper. Okrent noted that "one reporter ripped me up and down about how offensive it was that the staff had to endure public second-guessing, how it makes reporters vulnerable to further attack, how the hovering presence of an ombudsman can hinder aggressive reporting." Some reporters did not appreciate scrutiny.[4]

Apart from actual fabrications, many Americans believed that the media favored the liberal cause—which some members of the press conceded. Andy Rooney, who referred to himself as "consistently liberal," said on *Larry King Live* that CBS News anchor Dan Rather was "transparently liberal." Longtime ABC News reporter Bob Zelnick similarly said that "Peter Jennings routinely attempted to insert his left of center editorial slant into correspondents' news copy." Walter Cronkite, after serving for decades as the face of television journalism, said, "I believe that most of us reporters are liberal." ABC's political editor said that the "political press corps" had "biases and predilections," which "include, but are not limited to, a near-universal shared sense that liberal political positions on social issues like gun control, homosexuality, abortion, and religion are the default, while more conservative positions are 'conservative positions.'" In July 2004, *New York Times* ombudsman Daniel Okrent (contrary to former *Times* editor Howell Raines's denials) asked and answered a critical question upon his departure from the *Times*: "Is the *New York Times* a liberal newspaper? Of course it is." The hammer blow fell in the fall when bloggers discovered that CBS's *60 Minutes* and Dan Rather had used forged documents in a story that tarnished President Bush's Texas Air National Guard Service record. *60 Minutes* terminated four producers after a subsequent investigation.[5]

Conflicts within the media also broke out, many sparked by anxiety over the success of the Fox News cable network and conservative-dominated talk radio. John Carroll, the editor of the *LA Times*, compared Fox News to Joe McCarthy. Liberal media mogul Ted Turner viewed the Fox News cable network as a propaganda tool of the Bush administration and compared the network's popularity to the election of Hitler. Comedian Al Franken started Air America Radio in early 2004 to counter conservative talk radio commentators such as Rush Limbaugh. On one of Franken's first shows, after Michael Moore apologized to Al Gore for voting for Ralph Nader in 2000, comedian Janeane Garofalo denounced Brit Hume's media-critic panel on Fox News for being an "Algonquin table of apologists." A think tank called Media Matters, headed by David Brock, a former conservative polemicist for the *American Spectator*, also received funding from liberal donors to critique the influence of Fox News and conservatives on the media. Studies indicated that CNN watchers leaned left and Fox

News watchers leaned right, confirming the fears of some political commentators that media polarization reinforced political polarization.[6]

In South Dakota, media scrutiny focused on the state's dominant newspaper, the *Sioux Falls Argus Leader*. In 1977, the *Argus* was purchased by the Gannett Corporation, whose former CEO, Al Neuharth, grew up in South Dakota. Neuharth considered Daschle "a longtime respected friend" and even promoted a future Daschle presidential bid during the summer of 2004. Neuharth frequently boasted about the monopoly power of his newspapers, telling Wall Street investors, "No Gannett newspaper has any direct competitors." The monopoly power of the Gannett-owned *Argus Leader* yielded considerable profits. According to documents filed in an out-of-state lawsuit, the *Argus Leader* enjoyed a 46 percent profit in 1997, making it the fourth-most profitable newspaper in the Gannett chain of 102 daily newspapers. Once asked how to pronounce "Gannett," Neuharth responded, "MONEY."[7]

Political reporting in South Dakota is remarkably thin, and much of it is driven by the *Argus*, which has further reduced the diversity of news sources by acquiring several small-town newspapers in the region surrounding Sioux Falls. The influence of an *Argus* story balloons when the Associated Press spreads it to the state's small-town newspapers, which do not have political reporters. The *Argus* remains especially dominant in the southeast corner of the state, a political swing region with a relatively large number of voters who often determine the outcome of statewide elections. What the *Argus* chose to cover and what it chose to ignore also influenced politics in the state by shaping the issue agenda. *Argus* editor Randell Beck recognized the power of the *Argus*, which he called "South Dakota's largest and most influential newspaper," and proudly proclaimed that his newspaper provided "news and information that formed the basis for the choices [voters] made." Dismissing concerns about his newspaper's monopoly on information, Beck said, "Nobody is standing next to those boxes forcing people to buy our newspaper." In the May 2004 issue of *the Atlantic Monthly*, former *New York Times* editor Howell Raines offered a thirty-three-page disquisition on the troubles at the *New York Times* and conceded the influence of "the reassuring but dangerously outmoded *Times* maxim 'It's not news until we say it's news.'" The *Argus* maintained a similar attitude. The Dakota blogs sought to break the *Argus Leader*'s near-monopoly on political news.[8]

In 1999, when Blogger began offering its software for free, only twenty-three blogs existed. In 2002, the number of registered users of Blogger software approached one million. By 2004, three million blogs had emerged. One commentator concluded that the "blogosphere had its grand opening on September 11th, when several million Americans who couldn't log onto the websites of CNN, the *New York Times,* and the *Washington Post,* instead began checking out alternatives whose servers weren't blown out from too much traffic." The most widely read blogger of 2004, law professor Glenn Reynolds of Instapundit, called the war in Iraq "the first Internet war" and detailed the rapid rise of the "blogs of war," or "warblogs." Reynolds frequently linked to the comments of soldiers in Iraq, who began "reporting all sorts of news without Big Media filters," providing readers direct access to news on the ground and a much different perspective on the war. While the major media outlets focused on the "Iraq-as-quagmire" theme, some bloggers offered extensive reports on the positive news from Iraq. Bloggers termed the process of circumventing established media gate-keepers "disintermediation."[9]

Many blogs gravitate toward commentary on politics and journalism. After Andrew Sullivan, the former editor of the *New Republic,* became a prominent blogger, other political blogs soon emerged and became frequent stops for the politically inclined. Glenn Reynolds started Instapundit in August 2001, Daily Kos started in May 2002, the anonymous Atrios started blogging in April 2002 (he was outed in July 2004 as working for David Brock's liberal think tank Media Matters), and in the same year, Powerline started by commenting on Minnesota's Senate race. In the fall of 2002, Senator Trent Lott became the first major victim of the blogosphere after his comments at Senator Strom Thurmond's one-hundredth birthday party. Daily Kos and other liberal blogs also energized the presidential campaign of Howard Dean during 2003 and 2004. Dean's campaign manager, Joe Trippi, made the case for the power of the blogosphere in his 2004 book *The Revolution Will Not Be Televised.* Some saw blogging as a distinctly American phenomenon with important precedents. Sociologist Alan Wolfe concluded that "if the technologies used by bloggers and hardballers are new, the form is older than the Republic" and "have their origins in the pamphlets of the colonial era."[10]

The designated political reporter for the *Argus Leader*, Dave Kranz, had tremendous influence on the state's politics and had been giving Republicans heartburn for decades. Kranz became a political reporter during the traumas of Vietnam and Watergate, when journalism reached the peak of its prestige. Kranz said that the "power of the news media was never more visible than during the Watergate fiasco" and praised Dan Rather's aggressive pursuit of the Nixon administration. The Watergate experience "overwhelms modern journalism," according to one study, and the "Watergate effect" helped explain the surge of college students, including Kranz, who became journalists. The *Argus Leader* frequently ran ads in bold letters touting the "Expert Insight" of Kranz: "With almost 30 years experience covering South Dakota politics, David Kranz is unmatched for expertise. His insights and analysis are a must-read for anyone." Liberal blogger Joshua Micah Marshall dubbed Kranz the "Jack Germond or Dan Balz of South Dakota politics," an endorsement that did not boost Kranz's credibility among conservatives. *Argus* editor Randell Beck called Kranz "a must-read for anyone seeking the 'how' and 'why' of state politics" and said that when "national television networks need an independent voice to decipher the political lexicon here in South Dakota, they call Kranz." Dakota bloggers, however, objected to the lionization of Kranz.[11]

In South Dakota, the blogging phenomenon originated with a law student at the University of South Dakota (USD) named Jason Van Beek, who started South Dakota Politics after the 2002 midterm elections. In keeping with Andrew Sullivan's "Raines Watch" feature about the embattled editor of the *New York Times*, Van Beek started "Kranz Watch" to track the reporting of the dominant political journalist in South Dakota. In early 2003, Steve Sibson of Mitchell started Sibby Online. Sibson was perturbed with Kranz's reporting on the gun control issue during the 2002 Senate campaign and worked up a thick dossier critiquing Kranz's reporting. In January 2004, I started Daschle v. Thune to track the daily happenings in the Senate race. At some point during the spring of 2004, the blogs collectively became known as the "Dakota Blog Alliance," in keeping with other blog clusters, including the "Northern Alliance," primarily based in Minnesota, and the "Rocky Mountain Alliance," primarily based in Colorado. Ryne McClaren of Ryne McClaren: A Weblog, who grew up in the

Black Hills, joined in April 2004. In the summer of 2004, another law student at USD, Quentin Riggins, who hailed from the small West River ranching town of Philip, started Quentin Riggins' Blog, and Wes Roth, another West River native, started his blog, which became the Roth Report. The number of blogs fluctuated, but the Dakota Blog Alliance usually included about ten active bloggers. One study later concluded that these "blogs created major messaging problems for Democratic Senator Tom Daschle."[12]

The Dakota Blog Alliance frequently criticized Kranz and the *Argus Leader*, but the first major confrontation came in May 2003. Steve Sibson of Sibby Online in Mitchell decided to visit the *Mitchell Daily Republic* archives and reviewed some old issues of the newspaper where Kranz had worked prior to joining the *Argus*. Sibson discovered that when Kranz left the Mitchell paper for the *Argus* in 1983, he wrote in his final column that he had "heard the disatisfaction [*sic*] and the *allegations of bias*. Yet I do not apologize for any one position I have stood for." In addition to finding evidence of bias complaints in Kranz's past, Sibson also found a direct link between Kranz and Daschle that had never been reported. When Daschle returned to the state from Washington in 1976, Kranz fondly recalled that he and Daschle had attended college together at South Dakota State University and discussed their efforts to organize a mock Democratic convention in 1968: "I remember our tireless search to find a renowned public speaker to address the convention such as McGovern, McCarthy, Humphrey or some other prominent Democrat."[13]

The blogs revealed that at the time Daschle and Kranz organized the 1968 convention, Daschle served as the president of the Political Science Club, which sponsored the convention, and Kranz served as his publicity chairman. Kranz also wrote an article about the convention for the college newspaper entitled "Daschle Was Workhorse for Political Convention," which explained that Daschle had "worked continuously" and spent "countless hours organizing." Kranz did not disclose his service as Daschle's publicity chairman for the convention, which he both participated in and reported on, which some bloggers interpreted as an eerie precedent for his later reporting. The incident was reminiscent of Walter Lippmann and James Reston helping Senator Arthur Vandenberg craft a famous speech, then reporting on the importance of the speech in their respective newspapers.[14]

Both Daschle and Kranz were supporters of John F. Kennedy in the 1960s, and both supported Eugene McCarthy for president in 1968, a logical choice for two young Catholic Democrats. Kranz came from a Democratic family, and Hubert Humphrey and George McGovern gave "eloquent tributes" to Kranz's grandparents—long-time devotees of Franklin Delano Roosevelt and Harry S. Truman—on their anniversary. Along with four other SDSU students, Kranz also went to Wisconsin in 1968 to campaign for McCarthy in the Democratic presidential primary process. Kranz recalled, "It was the McCarthy campaign that pushed my 'politically active' button for the first time"; he noted that "McCarthy became the official language of most of my college friends." Before leaving for Wisconsin, Kranz went home to collect his suit so that he could be "Neat and Clean for Gene." Eight thousand college students joined Kranz, according to presidential campaign historian Theodore White, who noted that "Wisconsin was to be the peak, the high-water mark, the Pickett's Charge of the McCarthy movement." Just before the vote, knowing that he was doomed, President Lyndon Johnson quit the race. Kranz and his friends "cheered" and awarded themselves "A's for forcing the hand of this powerful man." In subsequent years, as McCarthy faded but the antiwar movement persisted, Kranz became a George McGovern enthusiast.[15]

As Daschle began his ascent in South Dakota politics, Kranz continued his role as Daschle's "publicity chairman," using the pages of South Dakota newspapers. A survey of past Kranz columns in the *Argus* revealed his fondness for Daschle. Kranz termed Daschle "a master politician," deemed him "unbeatable," and described how he "stands in the middle of drought-stripped fields and bleeds for the American farmer." Kranz also defended Daschle's vote in favor of a congressional pay raise with an article under the headline "Daschle Shows Courage in Voting for Pay Increase."[16] Over the course of his career, Daschle came to expect a steady supply of positive stories from the *Argus* and Kranz and to expect little scrutiny of his actions. In contrast to his treatment of Daschle, Kranz aggressively reported on the previous Republican senator from South Dakota, Larry Pressler, as revealed by his writing during Pressler's 1990 reelection bid:

- "No one else comes close to filling the role of a public servant who uses slick marketing to make minor accomplishments look like world-saving ventures" (July 8, 1990).
- "To the kingmakers, Democrats and Republicans alike, he is a lightweight—holding his title with superficial rhetoric, unsubstantiated legislative success and a circle of friends who glitter from their wealth" (August 6, 1989).
- "Sen. Larry Pressler forfeited his chance to be considered a great Senator long ago. His obsession with image building and photo sessions has left him preoccupied and ineffective" (December 30, 1990).
- "Pressler has now been in Washington 14 years and still has no clear cause. He is controlled by public opinion, with a finger in the wind and a safe vote and press release to follow" (November 5, 1989).

In 1990, Kranz also wrote about Pressler's memory when early-onset Alzheimer's was a persistent campaign rumor and said that "it would be logical to challenge candidates to release their health records." In 1996, during Pressler's unsuccessful reelection bid, Kranz reported on an event organized by former Democratic senator Jim Abourezk that featured allegations that Pressler was gay. Despite such one-sided coverage, ironically, Kranz criticized other newspapers for bias. Kranz labeled my hometown newspaper, the *Madison Daily Leader,* a "partisan Republican voice" and a "glory and praise pamphlet for Republican policy."[17]

When confronted with the information about the old Kranz-Daschle connection, *Argus* executive editor Randell Beck said that he would not allow Kranz to get into a "pissing match" over information that was "made up." Beck did not explain what was "made up." The *Argus* never disclosed the connection between Kranz and Daschle and, in the beginning, did not take blogger criticism seriously. In June 2003, on a local radio station that featured an *Argus on Air* segment paid for by the *Argus,* Beck said that the blog criticism was driven by a "small cabal" and that it was a "well known political ploy" to "attack the media," dismissing the criticism as "falsehoods" and "crap." Beck also referred to such criticism as "despicable," "underhanded," and an attempt to "demonize those who don't agree with" the critics.

Beck said Kranz was being "targeted" and "subject to a personal attack" and maintained that Kranz had a "right to have a personal life"; in addition, Beck maintained that the *Argus* did not need to respond to blogs because the newspaper was not "on the public dole" and was a "private enterprise."[18]

National blogs also took notice of the revelations about the *Argus Leader*, given their proximity to the scandal at the *New York Times*. Andrew Sullivan wrote, "First the *NYT*: Now the *Sioux Falls Argus Leader*." Instapundit noted both the Kranz-Daschle relationship and the importance of local blogging, since "local newspapers, almost always monopolists and often with too-comfortable relations with local politicos, are ripe targets." South Dakota native and blogger Andrew Clem, a political science professor at James Madison University, said during the *Times* scandals that a "similar scandal is unfolding at the *Sioux Falls Argus Leader*, or as we prairie folk used to call it, the 'Argus Liar.' From what I hear, it's basically a mouthpiece for Tom Daschle and the Democratic establishment these days." The blog Powerline, under the headline "South Dakota Bloggers Break Through," concluded that "bloggers like South Dakota Politics have done a great job of exposing the incredibly biased reporting of the state's dominant newspaper" and noted that the editor "hasn't gotten past the point of hysterical attacks on the paper's critics." Powerline also called Kranz "Tom Daschle's Enabler" and his "crony of 35 years." After the first blog criticism in 2003, the editor of the *Mitchell Daily Republic* discussed "Kranz's long and friendly relationship with George McGovern" and concluded that "newspapers should have no reservations about their reporters' backgrounds being made public." With the exception of that single in-state editorial, however, no South Dakota reporters wrote about the Kranz revelations. One South Dakota reporter privately confessed that "nobody in South Dakota would report" such findings about a fellow reporter.[19]

Blogger research also revealed earlier complaints about the *Argus*. In 1990, even the *New York Times* had reported that the Democratic Senate candidate in South Dakota "seemed to take his campaign script from *the Sioux Falls Argus Leader*" and concluded that, ultimately, Senator Pressler "narrowly defeated two opponents: a well-financed Democrat and a vituperative newspaper." Bloggers discovered that when Kranz served as city editor of the *Argus* from 1986 to 1989, his

assistant city editor was Steve Erpenbach, the Democratic press spokesman during the 1990 senatorial election. Erpenbach went on to become
Senator Daschle's state director. During the 1990 Senate race, when
Kranz served as the managing editor of the *Argus*, *Roll Call* reported
that Kranz orchestrated the "hysterical bashing" of Pressler. *Roll Call*,
which entitled its story "Pressler Is Running for Re-election against a
Newspaper," noted that it received "a steady stream of anti-Pressler
Argus Leader clips sent to us by his opponent" and that the "bad blood
between Pressler and David Kranz, the *AL* managing editor and political columnist, is well known in South Dakota, according to sources
in the state press." The *Argus Leader* would run stories about Pressler
based on information provided by South Dakota Democrats, then the
same Democrats would call for an investigation of Pressler based on
the *Argus* stories. Pressler's chief of staff said that "the guiding hand
behind the *AL*'s treatment of Pressler is Kranz, the managing editor,
and this claim was backed up by two South Dakota reporters very
familiar with the paper's operation." One of the reporters said that
"sometimes the paper does appear to be working hand in hand with
the Democratic Party." Bloggers also found a 1986 opinion column
from the Republican lieutenant governor of South Dakota excoriating
Kranz for his Democratic bias: "When Dave Kranz was the editor of
the *Mitchell Daily Republic*, he was an unapologetic promoter of Democratic candidates for political office. During the golden years of the
Democratic party in South Dakota, folks like [Democratic Governor
Dick] Kneip, Jimmy Carter, and George McGovern beat a path to
Kranz's door. In Mitchell, they used to have a saying: 'When George
McGovern sneezes, it's Dave Kranz who catches the cold.'"[20]

According to the pattern detected by Dakota bloggers, Kranz would
receive ammunition from Democrats, which would quickly appear in
the pages of the *Argus* as "news." Instead of the Democrats engaging
in negative campaigning, the *Argus* would do the work for them, as
Daschle's longtime media advisor Karl Struble openly acknowledged.
In a 1997 article in *Campaigns and Elections* magazine, Struble described
how his media operation used the *Argus* in the 1996 Senate campaign
against Pressler: "The press ate it up. Our campaign systematically
doled out the information piece by piece to reporters in D.C. and
South Dakota. The result was a series of damaging articles. . . . We
used the headlines generated as *validators for our ads*." For Republicans

to inform voters about a Democrat's shortcomings, however, they were forced to "go negative" using television advertising, a tactic that could be unpopular with voters. Republicans would be criticized by the *Argus* for various matters but were then criticized by voters if they tried to similarly scrutinize their opponents.[21]

The scrutiny of Kranz accelerated with additional discoveries in the spring of 2004. The criticism originated with a column Kranz wrote in April 2004 entitled "Politicos See No Danger of Daschle Losing Clout," which included a quote from political analyst Stuart Rothenberg. Bloggers noted, however, that Rothenberg, one of the experts that Kranz often quoted, had recently said the opposite: "Tom Daschle (D-South Dakota) who has a terrific opponent in John Thune . . . *has lost the 'clout' issue* that saved his SD Democratic colleague, Tim Johnson, in 2002." Kranz did not quote Rothenberg when he said something that hurt Daschle but did when it would help Daschle. An article in *The Hill* also noted the rebellion in Daschle's caucus and mentioned that Senator Christopher Dodd of Connecticut, a likely opponent of Daschle's for the leadership post, called for more aggressive leadership, but Kranz did not report on the story in *The Hill*. Even former Daschle staffers opined in their blogs that Daschle should step down as leader if he continued to embrace conservative positions during his reelection bid, a suggestion that Kranz did not report. In a typical post, the blog South Dakota Politics said, "There have been rumblings about Tom Daschle's leadership in various publications for some time now. Articles in *Roll Call*, the *National Journal*, the *New Republic*, the *American Prospect*, the *Nation*, and the liberal website Buzzflash all have addressed this. Typically, the only publication that has NOT addressed this is the *Sioux Falls Argus Leader*, South Dakota's newspaper of record." When Kranz finally mentioned potential challenges to Daschle's leadership, he said that the speculation came from John Thune's campaign, when the speculation actually stemmed from statements by liberals and in liberal publications. In another damning moment, Senator Dianne Feinstein of California said that Daschle would not allow his state's interests to interfere with his leadership duties, a claim that contradicted the premise of Daschle's campaign. Kranz did not report on Feinstein's statement.[22]

In February, political analyst Charlie Cook traveled to South Dakota and gave a speech in which he argued, according to the *Rapid City*

Journal, that the "Daschle-as-power-broker argument [was] diminished." South Dakota Politics noted that Kranz had often quoted Cook in the past but—even though Cook was in South Dakota—when he said something unhelpful about Daschle, Kranz did not report his comment. After the Kranz column headlined "Politicos See No Danger of Daschle Losing Clout" was published, in keeping with Struble's past practice of using the *Argus* as a validator of campaign claims, the Daschle campaign quickly disseminated a fund-raising solicitation announcing that "an article in Sunday's *Argus Leader* found there was absolutely no evidence to support *Thune's claim*" (which actually stemmed from liberal publications) that Daschle might lose his leadership post. The Kranz column thus aided the Daschle camp's effort to dismiss speculation about Daschle losing his leadership post. Because Daschle's leadership position was the centerpiece of his election campaign, information about the prospects of his losing his position could have been damaging. Kranz's coverage, bloggers argued, therefore distorted the race.[23]

Additional hard evidence of Kranz's bias was revealed in April 2004. When Daschle and his first wife, who both served as staffers for Senator Abourezk, moved back to South Dakota in 1976 in preparation for Daschle's run for Congress in 1978, Kranz was the managing editor of the *Mitchell Daily Republic* and wrote a column trumpeting their return. The Daschles then took over the senator's state operation, aggressively reorganized his offices, and spent a large amount of time cultivating the press. According to an internal staff memo from the Abourezk archives reported on by South Dakota Politics, an Abourezk staffer dispatched to Mitchell reported back that the senator had received "good coverage" the previous week and that the paper's "Managing Editor is Dave Kranz, 30, formally of Austin Minn, and Watertown S.D. Went to SDSU (Mu U. with Tom D. [Daschle] and Tom Klinkel [Daschle's then brother-in-law] *Very much a strong Demo. and have been attending county demo. functions together.*" The memo also said that "Dave Kranz of paper is checking out some of the local biggees in Mitchell to see how much support we have to do something." Kranz also informed Democrats of his impending scrutiny of Republican congressman Jim Abdnor, who would ultimately lose the 1986 Senate race to Daschle: "Mitchell paper is going to expose Abdnor on rating by National Alliance of S. Citizens next week." The memo confirmed critics' worst fears about Kranz using his role as a reporter to promote Democratic candidates and undermine Republicans.[24]

A second memo disclosed by South Dakota Politics in April indicated that Kranz also gave the Daschle-led Abourezk organization advice on how to improve press coverage and win votes. Kranz urged that Abourezk do more "hokey things": "In addition, Dave feels Jim is not doing the hocky [sic] things necessary to be elected again. Like sending out calendars, X-Mas cards, birthday, marriages, weddings, and other hocky letters to SD people. The question is not if its hocky or not—but rather for many people its [sic] the only chance they will ever receive a personal card, greetings, or thank-you from someone they will or have voted for." The staffer also designated Kranz a "friendly editor" and noted that Kranz wanted confidentiality. Another memo explained how Kranz had worked with his sister, a McGovern staffer, to expose some Catholic priests' opposition to McGovern over the abortion issue by listening in on their conversation. The memo from Kranz's sister to McGovern's chief of staff explained that "my brother pretended to make a phone call to overhear" the priests; she added, "[W]ith a chuckle, I commented to Dave that I should have 'worked the meeting.' He said he finished it for me." McGovern later wrote a letter to Kranz saying, "I trust that you will do your best to keep the McGovern name in the headlines."[25]

The April revelations generated more attention from national blogs. An Instapundit entry was entitled "JOURNALISTS IN BED WITH THEIR SUBJECTS," and another noted that "some reporters are awfully chummy with Tom Daschle." Andrew Sullivan gave his post a more specific heading: "DASCHLE'S BEST BUDDY: Yep, he's a journalist—a very influential one in a very important paper in South Dakota. And he's been blatantly spinning for the Democrats for years." The blog Powerline was even more blunt: "David Kranz, Democratic Shill." The conservative *American Spectator* called Kranz an "old friend" of Daschle and the "David Broder of the upper Midwest" and reported that Kranz was finding "himself in the center of a growing and embarrassing scandal." The *Spectator* said, "Kranz is known to have carried his share of water for the Democrats in his career." Former Sioux Falls television news anchor Steve Hemmingsen, who posted commentary on his television station's website, said that his readers urged him "to take on that Daschle-loving David Kranz," but he declined because Kranz "buys ink by the barrel."[26]

In his last *Argus on Air* appearance on local radio in April 2004, *Argus* editor Randell Beck said that Kranz was "the best political reporter in the region" and "one of the finest, most honest, credible reporters in the region." Beck again said that blogger criticism was "crap" and driven by a "violent" internet "cabal" of "yahoos" and "jokers," who were full of "hatred" and "vitriol" and lacked "guts" because they hid "behind their computer screens" and would not face him "man to man." Beck said that some of the bloggers involved, including those of Powerline, were "people from outside the walls of South Dakota who are perpetuating this hate campaign" (John Hinderaker of Powerline was born and raised in South Dakota). Beck then went on to highlight the importance of debating issues "without calling each other names." Andrew Sullivan entitled his post on Beck's reaction to blogger criticism "AN EDITOR LOSES IT." Sullivan argued that Beck "cannot take any criticism from the outside about the blatant bias displayed by one of his key political reporters. Using blogs to criticize newspapers? How sad. How awful. How terrifying. I think we've hit a nerve here, haven't we? When you stumble into the truth, it sometimes hurts." Beck said after the election that he cancelled his radio appearances because "in a politicized climate where the bloggers would so manipulate the conversation that it was not worth it."[27]

For the Thune camp, the blogs' revelations rekindled memories of Kranz's coverage during the 2002 Senate race. When asked by national reporters for a local expert on South Dakota politics to interview, Johnson's campaign staffers had told reporters to talk to Kranz. At a 2002 parade in Kranzburg, a little town named for Kranz's ancestors, the Johnson campaign had handed out "I Love Dave Kranz" stickers that had been professionally printed. South Dakota native and conservative writer Jody Bottum later recalled that the *Argus Leader* "ran a long profile of Tim Johnson in 2002 so puffy and sweet it should be handed out in journalism school as a model of disingenuous advocacy." After the 2002 experience, Thune advisors advocated finding someone like Dick Wadhams who had significant experience handling difficult newspapers.[28]

In addition to the problems that critics detected in Kranz's reporting, the fact that the *Argus Leader* refused to assign reporters to cover certain stories and refused to run stories from national news agencies generated additional criticism. In January, for example, in the biggest story in the race to date, longtime Indian activist Russell Means endorsed John Thune. Both the *Rapid City Journal* and the Associated Press ran long stories that were picked up by other newspapers. The *Argus* ignored the endorsement story but later reported on a dispute between Means and the Thune campaign, which the newspaper deemed newsworthy. The *Argus* also ignored the constant stream of stories about Daschle's opposition tactics in the Senate and the numerous stories describing his handling of the ethanol issue. To make the point about the *Argus Leader*'s selectivity, South Dakota Politics analyzed four stories from *Roll Call*, two of which could be considered unflattering to Thune and two of which could be considered unflattering to Daschle. The negative stories about Thune in Roll Call appeared the next day in the *Argus Leader*; in contrast, the negative stories about Daschle were never published. "Every newspaper when it reaches the reader," political analyst Walter Lippmann once noted, "is the result of a whole series of selections as to what items shall be printed, in what position they shall be printed, how much space each shall occupy, what emphasis each shall have." The selections that the *Argus Leader* made during 2004 consistently benefited Daschle.[29]

Some critics thought that the lack of reporting on the unflattering aspects of Daschle stemmed from the personal biases of the *Argus* editor in charge of political reporting, Patrick Lalley. Lalley had formerly run an alternative leftist newspaper in Sioux Falls known as the *Tempest*, which was dubbed the "*Village Voice* of Sioux Falls." While editor of the *Tempest*, Lalley called Republicans "evil," derided President Ronald Reagan, criticized Daschle's opponents, and praised Daschle as a "*wunderkind*," highlighting his "quiet, confident demeanor, boyish charm, and populist politics." When traveling in 1990 with Senator Pressler's opponent and his press secretary (Daschle's state political director in 2004), Lalley noted the "good Democratic rhetoric" and said, "I ate it up." Ironically, before joining the Argus, Lalley acknowledged the potential distortion of the democratic process when citizens relied on a single, dominant news outlet: "What if all media and all the information you received was based on what a few powerful people in the community thought was fit for your consumption."[30]

Lalley's past writings demonstrated that he understood the monopoly power of the *Argus* and the newspaper's weaknesses and also indicated his sympathy for the political left. Lalley once wrote in the *Tempest*, "Since time eternal, it seems, people in Sioux Falls have been complaining about the *Argus Leader*, our daily newspaper. . . . [M]entioning the *Argus* anymore is about the easiest way to receive a sneer or half-hearted 'hrumph' in conversation. The paper doesn't have the best of reputations." He also said that he did not "like to admit that [he] read the daily paper in our fine city." When identifying the newspaper's problems, however, Lalley complained that the *Argus Leader* was not liberal enough. When he left his alternative newspaper, Lalley noted, "I have been critical of the mainstream for many years and I have come to the conclusion that I have an obligation to work *from the inside*." Lalley also denounced "right-wing hatemongers" and said that he had "been called many things: liberal, communist, homosexual, punk, trouble-maker, know-it-all, etc." Lalley asked readers to refrain from calling him a "commie (that's a bad one), pinko, taxin', spendin', gun takin', regulatin', Mondale votin', Quayle bringin' upin', Liberal." By the time of the 2004 Senate race, Lalley had come to make the political coverage decisions "from the inside" of the *Argus Leader*, the monopolistic newspaper that dominated South Dakota political reporting and shaped the state's political agenda.[31]

As blog criticism mounted, the executive editor of the *Argus*, Randell Beck, continued to dismiss it as "crap." One *Argus* reporter privately commented that "Beck can't fit blogs into his world view." James Fallows, the *Atlantic Monthly* correspondent, had noted that at a forum on the Iraq War "a network television producer finally tired of the torrent of criticism. If you don't like what you see, stop watching, he said. That was the way consumers could exercise 'choice.'" Beck maintained a similar position, which offered readers facing a monopoly few options. Beck thought that blogs tended to "hurl venomous attacks on those who dare disagree" and said that the Internet "allowed every fanatic with too much time on his hands to distribute half-truths to everyone on his buddy list." Beck also mocked blog criticism in his column about the "2004 Guide to Conventional Thought in Sioux Falls" by ridiculing the presumption that the *Argus Leader* was "In bed with Tom Daschle."[32]

In late July, Beck announced the formation of the *Argus* blog to answer public concerns about the newspaper's political coverage. During the announcement, he explained his view of blogs as places where the views of the "pinheaded" on the "political fringes" with "nutty opinions" can "spew forth," worsening the "polarized climate" in politics. Beck then said, "If Hitler were alive today, he'd have his own blog." National blogs—including Andrew Sullivan, Instapundit, Powerline, and Oxblog—again responded. Such "pinheads" (who included a former *New Republic* editor, a law professor, three Ivy League–educated lawyers, and three Rhodes Scholars) made sport of Beck's invocation of Hitler. Oxblog joked that if Hitler had a blog, he would probably have called it "Instafuehrer." Instapundit responded: "Ve haff vays of making you blog." One columnist for the British newspaper the *Observer,* who later wondered whether Daschle was "blogged into retirement," commented that a blogging Hitler would have needed "fewer Panzer divisions." John Fund, writing in the *Wall Street Journal*'s Political Diary, noted, "According to Godwin's Law, an Internet discussion-group dictum that long predates blogging, when one side in an argument invokes Hitler, it proves he's lost." The Dakota blogs, highlighting the irony of Beck's allusion to Hitler, also reported that after the *New York Times* debacle, Beck had opined, "From the top down, editors must set a moral compass for a newspaper."[33]

While Beck discounted blog criticism, the *Argus Leader* remained adamant about "government openness" and, in the context of prying loose information from law enforcement agencies, editorialized that "South Dakotans have a right to know what's going on."[34] The *Argus* editorial board opined "that in a democracy government works best in the pure and harsh light of day" and stated, "We need openness. Always."[35] Beck criticized the Minnehaha County Commission for "private planning," for its "willingness to do business in secret," for its "cynical abuse of what is generously called executive session," and for "relentless whining." Beck vigorously criticized Janklow's pardons and called the county commission and Janklow "examples of arrogance."[36]

While Beck held the *Argus Leader* to a different standard than he applied to South Dakota pols and institutions, bloggers requested the same scrutiny of Senator Daschle that the *Argus Leader* had meted out to Republicans such as Larry Pressler, the most recent Republican U.S. senator from the state. In 1990, the *Argus Leader* ran a series of long stories criticizing Pressler's Senate leadership. The series relied on interviews of dozens of hill staffers, senators (including Daschle), and journalists and even used *Spy Magazine* as a source. The *Argus* criticized Pressler's frequent press releases and reported that critics maintained that he "overtrumpets his accomplishments" and "flips around on issues." Such maneuvers, the *Argus* reported critics as saying, "masks a philosophical void, a man who often votes only after he has moistened a forefinger to gauge the prevailing political wind." The *Argus* also ran an article about Pressler entitled "Early Pledges Fall by the Wayside," which argued that Pressler had abandoned the stances he took when first running for office in 1974. The *Argus* proffered no such scrutiny of Senator Daschle. In a race that focused in part on Daschle's political migration to the left and the abandonment of his past policy positions, the *Argus* ignored the obvious importance of writing an analysis of Daschle's early political views, leaving them buried in the memory hole.[37]

In addition to gaining attention from national bloggers, the Dakota Alliance received recognition from the *Wall Street Journal*, the *Minneapolis Star Tribune*, the *Washington Times*, the *Weekly Standard*, South Dakota Public Radio, and other news outlets during the campaign. The conservative *World Magazine* wrote an article about the criticism of Kranz entitled "Daschle's Journalistic Gatekeeper?" The national blogger, radio talk show host, and law professor Hugh Hewitt wrote that the "influence of blogging on politics is nowhere more obvious than in South Dakota." Hewitt noted that Daschle's hold on power was maintained "with the assistance of a very friendly local press" but argued that local blogs, similar to national blogs, transformed the dynamic: "Reporters everywhere are getting the message: Agenda journalism isn't safe anymore. If you spin the facts, there are bloggers waiting to expose your partisanship. And the candidate you have been covering for." Hewitt also concluded that "the *Argus Leader* is in the tank for Daschle" and that the "paper's lead political reporter is a long-time Daschle booster."[38]

A *Time* magazine article on blogs concluded that "they represent—no, they are—the voice of the little guy. . . . Bloggers are inverting the cozy media hierarchies of yore." The Dakota blogs became a new form of populism, a movement that had earlier criticized the accommodationist corporate press. The Populists had formed their own network of newspapers, pamphleteers, and public speakers to circumvent the antireform establishment press, which resembled the Dakota blogs' criticism of the *Argus Leader's* friendly reporting on Senator Daschle. The *Argus Leader's* dominance over political reporting made the allusion to populism, a movement driven by antimonopoly sentiment, that much more appropriate. Patrick Lalley, who managed the *Argus's* political reporting in 2004, made a similar Populist argument about Gannett's outside ownership of the *Argus* during his days as a *Tempest* editor: "You need to ask yourself who better represents your interests in this community: this tiny publication, that is basically a few well-intentioned people with a couple Macintosh computers, or the huge media conglomerate that sucks untold millions out of this community every year, with the profits earmarked for the corporate coffers in Washington D.C. or wherever it is the Gannett fortress calls home?" The Dakota Blog Alliance discussed the problem of a monopolistic media at a conference at Augustana College in August 2004 entitled "The New Populism: Blogs, the Media, and Politics in South Dakota." The keynote speaker was John Hinderaker, who was from South Dakota and who blogged for Powerline, which would be named *Time's* "Blog of the Year" for exposing *60 Minutes'* use of forged documents in an anti-Bush story. Although invited, the *Argus Leader* staff declined to attend. John Fund's piece in the *Wall Street Journal* about the conference was entitled "A Prairie Revolt against the Lame-stream Media."[39]

By late summer, the *Argus* had begun to address some of the blogs' criticism. Kranz was pulled from daily coverage of the Senate race and assigned to cover the House race but was also given two columns per week in the newspaper instead of one. Because the column appeared on the news page and was not designated as opinion, many readers did not make a news/opinion distinction. After the election, Daschle campaign staffers confessed that they had been "shocked to learn that Kranz—who had routinely covered the state's biggest political stories for decades—would not be on the beat." The *Argus Leader,* however, never disclosed Kranz's past association with Daschle and his assistance to other Democratic candidates. Also, when the *Argus* cosponsored a Senate debate with the state's most widely viewed television station, it sent Kranz to serve as moderator. Executive editor Beck ultimately rescinded the Hitler comment about bloggers, and the *Argus* started a "blog" to respond to reader criticism, but the leading political editors and reporters did not participate and few criticisms were addressed. After eight posts—including one in which Beck made false statements that generated another national blogostorm (one of the Instapundit postings read, "Sometimes, I almost feel sorry for the *Argus Leader*")—the Argus blog died. After nearly two years of blogger criticism and a dramatic increase in the importance of blogs in South Dakota politics (as well as nationwide), the newspaper ran a story about blogs but did not explain the bloggers' detailed criticisms of the *Argus*.[40]

For the Thune campaign, the core problem remained the unwillingness of *Argus* editors to run stories critical of Daschle or to assign reporters to write stories scrutinizing Daschle. In his criticism of the *New York Times'* reporting on the existence of weapons of mass destruction (WMD) prior to the Iraq war, ombudsman Daniel Okrent made an important distinction between the bias in a particular story and overall coverage: "I use 'journalism' rather than 'reporting' because reporters do not put stories into the newspaper. Editors make assignments, accept articles for publication, pass them through various editing hands, place them on a schedule, determine where they will appear. Editors are also obliged to assign follow-up pieces when the facts remain mired in partisan quicksand." Therefore, Okrent concluded, the *Times'* failure on the WMD story "was not individual, but institutional." To make the point about the institutional bias of the *Argus*, one blogger noted that when the editorial page editor of the *Argus* departed in the 1990s, she made the easy transition to chair of the Minnehaha County (Sioux Falls) Democratic Party.[41]

In addition to the bias that was evident in Kranz articles, there was an institutional unwillingness by the *Argus* to report all the news about Daschle. Thune's campaign manager, Dick Wadhams (who had dealt with dozens of liberal-minded newspapers throughout three decades of campaigns), said that he had never encountered anything like the *Argus Leader's* "institutional bias for a candidate that they showed Tom Daschle." The Dakota blogs responded to this one-sided coverage, and the readership of the Dakota blogs grew exponentially into the fall along with the national blogosphere. More reporters also conceded the existence of press bias nationally. *Newsweek's* Evan Thomas said during the presidential campaign that the media's favoritism toward Kerry would boost his standing by fifteen percentage points. After the campaign, Howard Fineman of *Newsweek* declared that "the notion of a neutral, non-partisan mainstream press was . . . pretty much dead." A year after the election, a *Washington Post* editor confessed that the "elephant in the newsroom is our narrowness. Too often, we wear liberalism on our sleeve and are intolerant of other lifestyles and opinions. . . . We're not very subtle about it at this paper: If you work here, you must be one of us. You must be liberal, progressive, a Democrat. I've been in communal gatherings in *The Post*, watching election returns, and have been flabbergasted to see my colleagues cheer unabashedly for the Democrats."[42]

Despite such admissions and the criticism by the Dakota blogs, the *Sioux Falls Argus Leader* "was named one of the best newspapers in Gannett Co. Inc." and given a "Gold Medal" award for "quality of news content" during 2004. Executive Editor Randell Beck was awarded his third "President's Ring," which "goes to the top editors in the company."[43]

Daschle matured politically within a South Dakota Democratic Party dominated by Senator George McGovern. Daschle would eventually occupy the Senate seat once held by McGovern. Courtesy of Seeley Mudd Library, Princeton University.

Thune and former senator Jim Abdnor, who sparked Thune's interest in politics. Abdnor took the Senate seat held by George McGovern in 1980 and was defeated by Tom Daschle in 1986. Photograph by the author.

Senator Bill Frist of Tennessee, the GOP Senate leader, speaking in Sioux Falls, where he campaigned against his fellow Senate leader. Photograph by the author.

In contrast to Daschle's attendance at the Washington, D.C., premiere of *Fahrenheit 9/11*, Thune welcomed Timothy Watkins to Sioux Falls during the summer of 2004 for the premiere of Watkins's documentary *In the Face of Evil: Reagan in Word and Deed*. Photograph by the author.

Thune campaign manager Dick Wadhams having one of many arguments with the *Sioux Falls Argus Leader*, which supported Daschle. Photograph by the author.

During the 2004 Republican convention, the Daschle campaign began running a television ad that featured Daschle hugging President Bush. The ad alienated some liberals. Reproduced by permission of Getty Images.

Tim Russert of NBC News asked Thune and Daschle to participate in two national debates on *Meet the Press.* One debate was finally held on the morning of Sunday, September 19, 2004. Reproduced by permission of Getty Images.

The scene outside the federal courthouse in downtown Sioux Falls on election eve, when Tom Daschle personally sued John Thune. Reproduced by permission of the Associated Press.

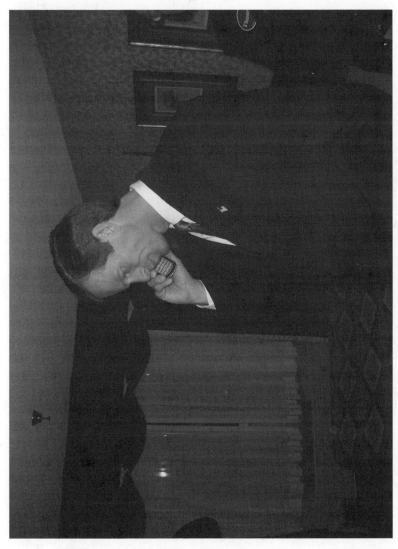

Thune takes the concession call from Daschle at 3:00 A.M. It lasted twenty-nine seconds. Photograph by the author.

Thune and Senator Pete Domenici of New Mexico outside the Senate chamber, where they celebrate final passage of the GOP energy bill in 2005. During the 2004 campaign, the energy bill became a major issue after Senate Democrats successfully blocked its passage. Domenici sponsored the bill, which included ethanol provisions popular in South Dakota. Photograph by the author.

Daschle and his mentor George McGovern in October 2006 during the dedication of the McGovern Library at Dakota Wesleyan University in Mitchell. Al Neuharth is seated behind. Photograph by the author.

George McGovern and John Thune at the dedication of the Vietnam veterans' memorial in Pierre, South Dakota, in September 2006. McGovern and Thune represented the liberal and conservative political movements, which have clashed during the past several decades in the United States. Photograph by the author.

CHAPTER SEVEN

THE END OF THE BEGINNING

Let's start the action!

—Frank Sinatra

While bloggers skirmished with the *Argus Leader* in cyberspace, the Thune campaign finally started to advertise on television in July. Many analysts expected Thune to launch an aggressive "air war," and *Argus Leader* reporters insisted that Thune's first ad would attack Daschle's position on the federal marriage amendment. Instead, Thune's first ad featured his teenage daughters jesting about their dad. The second ad featured Thune's parents, Harold and Pat, who proudly described their son's upbringing in the small town of Murdo. Thune's third ad discussed standing up for South Dakota and how "no party is right all the time." The Daschle camp responded by calling Daschle a "leader, not a follower," a phrase that accentuated Daschle's leadership post, and by deeming Thune too supportive of the national GOP. The next Thune ad focused on tax policy, a reflection of Thune's early embrace of Reaganism. After Thune began running television ads, the *Argus Leader* started an Ad Watch feature to scrutinize campaign ads. Daschle's television ads, which had started a year before, had received no scrutiny to date. Thune's entry into television advertising proved slow and subtle, leaving some observers wondering when the real battle would begin.

By the summer of 2004, the Daschle campaign had already run more ads than other candidates run during an entire election cycle. Throughout the summer, Daschle's ads persisted. One ad, designed to bolster Daschle's clout argument and appeal to farmers, featured a former president of the South Dakota Corn Growers Association crediting Daschle for his work on ethanol measures. Daschle also promoted health insurance buying pools—which, according to a testimonial, would be "a big deal for rural communities and would help families like ours afford coverage." Daschle had earlier opposed such measures in the Senate, while Thune had voted for them as a congressman. Daschle similarly emphasized the "health care squeeze" in his stump speech. Another television ad said Daschle supported the reimportation of prescription drugs from Canada, an issue popular with seniors and legislation that Thune had voted for while in the House. Daschle also called for all middle-income veterans to be given access to the VA health care system, which the *Argus Leader* dutifully reported.[1]

True to his campaign strategy, Daschle's television ads also continued to emphasize what he "delivered" for South Dakota, as did his previous radio and newspaper ads and direct mail to voters. In early August, one of Daschle's claims caused a public stir. A television ad saying that Daschle had secured funding for distance education triggered a letter from fifty state legislators who said that the legislature and the governor had been the moving forces behind distance education in the state. The letter also noted Daschle's vote against the bill that contained the distance education funding. Unlike earlier flaps, this one received significant attention in the state. The incident reprised the earlier controversy over Daschle's claim that he delivered for Mitchell Vo-Tech, in legislation he voted against. Daschle's claims about delivering for South Dakota could be thin at times and presented risks for a candidate depending on the "Daschle delivers" theme.[2]

In August, a debate about prairie dogs also highlighted the dangers of excessive credit-claiming and the "Daschle delivers" theme. Ranchers in western South Dakota despise prairie dogs, which dig up pastures, eat the grass needed by cattle, and spread disease. In 2002, Thune escorted Secretary of the Interior Gale Norton to South Dakota to meet with ranchers about the issue and to promote the removal of prairie dogs from a list of potentially endangered species, a designation that made ranchers' effort to kill them more difficult. In August of 2004, the prairie dog was finally delisted. Norton said, "I am thankful for the leadership of Gov. Rounds, Congressman Thune and the South Dakotans who have contributed to the resolution of this issue." Norton did not mention Daschle, whose campaign strategy was based on his being the person who delivered. Thune worked behind the scenes for months during the spring and summer of 2004 pressuring the administration to act on the issue. To some West River ranchers, the prairie dog issue symbolized the burdens of environmental regulation, for which they blamed activists in the national environmental movement along with their Democratic allies. In the fall, environmental groups filed a lawsuit to stop implementation of a prairie dog control plan, underscoring Daschle's connections to groups in the national Democratic coalition.[3]

Despite Thune's decision to delay television advertising until midsummer and his early positive ads, the Daschle camp repeatedly warned for more than a year of an impending "wave of negative attacks." In a manner similar to that of Stephanie Herseth prior to the June congressional election, they constantly demanded a clean campaign and portrayed Thune as a negative campaigner. The absence of any negative ads from the Thune campaign, however, made the Daschle campaign's criticisms seem frantic and overwrought. Like Herseth, Daschle was accused of crying wolf. During the summer, the only ads critical of Daschle were an ad by a California-based 527 imitating the Donald Trump show *The Apprentice*, saying that Daschle should be fired (an ad that many observers dismissed as absurd), and a national chamber of commerce ad. The chamber ad focused on the rising costs of medical insurance premiums and complained about Daschle's filibustering of tort reform in the Senate. The Daschle camp labeled the ad a "negative attack," but Daschle's record of blocking tort reform in the Senate was indisputable. Daschle's campaign manager dismissed the chamber of commerce, a fixture of civic boosterism in many South Dakota towns, as "right-wing extremists." The Daschle campaign again responded by running ads featuring people who called Daschle a "good man" who should not be subject to the "lies" of outside groups. While the Daschle camp hoped for blowback on Thune for the ads, the outcry was minimal. When Daschle portrayed himself as a victim of "outside attacks," he risked implying that he was above criticism, especially when the facts supported the chamber's claims.

Television ads are staples of modern politics, especially in South Dakota, where they are relatively cheap. Daschle planned an extensive seventeen-month-long barrage of seventy-five different television ads to burnish his image as someone who "delivered." Some voters hoped that the campaign could move beyond the sound bites of television advertising and that live debates between the candidates would begin. Daschle, however, preferred to rely on his television ads and avoid the risks of the live debate format, which could be unpredictable and would focus on differences over substantive issues. Daschle refused dozens of debate offers from television stations, fairs, and civic groups. In one instance, Daschle refused to debate Thune in front of a convention for vocational teachers and instead attended a "secret" fund-raiser hosted by trial lawyers in Oxford, Mississippi, that was kept "under the political radar."[4]

The trial lawyer fund-raiser was not reported in South Dakota, nor was Daschle's fund-raiser in the Hamptons a few days before, despite a long account of the event published in the *New York Times*. The *Times* headline revealed the reason for Daschle's trip by deeming the Hamptons "The Democrats' A.T.M.," and the article called the Hamptons a "Democratic Party candy store." The editor of the *Argus* insisted on the Argus blog that the newspaper had covered the Hamptons story "at least twice," which was untrue: the *Argus* had never covered the Hamptons story. The incident triggered another raft of commentary from national bloggers at the same time that the Associated Press was caught making up "facts" about one of President Bush's speeches in Wisconsin. After eight posts made over eight weeks, the Argus blog went dead, gone with a whimper. The *Argus* editor never admitted or addressed his misstatements about the Hamptons.[5]

During the August congressional recess, when Daschle planned to be on his county-by-county driving tour, Thune asked Daschle to debate in every county in the state. Daschle refused. The *Argus Leader* brushed off Thune's debate challenge with an article entitled "Debates May Not Change Election," in which an expert debunked the importance of debates. The Associated Press then spread the *Argus Leader* story around the state. The *Rapid City Journal* piece about the offer, in contrast to the *Argus Leader* report, was straightforwardly entitled "Daschle Turns Down Thune Challenge." In his first run for the Senate, Daschle had demanded "eight or more" debates with his opponent, Senator Jim Abdnor, and the *Argus Leader* noted that Daschle, "the smoother talker of the two, is scoring political points by keeping his eagerness for so many debates before the public." In 2004, however, the *Argus Leader* did not allow Thune to score any "political points" on the debate-ducking front but instead focused on an expert's opinion that debates did not matter. In the midst of the back-and-forth over debates, Dave Kranz of the *Argus Leader* reported that a fall *Meet the Press* debate had been arranged and that a "fuller debate schedule is coming together." Kranz did not mention Thune's offer of debates in every county or the fact that *Meet the Press* wanted two debates but that Daschle would only agree to one.[6]

Daschle's position on debates in 2004 provided direct contrast to his first run for Senate. In 1986, Daschle had said that he would stop all advertising in the race if his opponent would agree to six debates. He also said that he was "disappointed" that his opponent "refused to debate in any of the traditional debates in South Dakota." Daschle personally cornered his opponent at the 1986 state fair and challenged him to several debates, a confrontation that was captured on film and broadcast on the evening news. In the summer of 2004, by contrast, even while Daschle refused to debate, his campaign attacked ads from "third party groups" and said that "Senator Daschle believes that he and Thune should be talking about the issues important to the state and their commitment to South Dakota." The Daschle campaign nevertheless continued to reject proposals for a wide-ranging series of debates during August.[7]

Daschle agreed to only one live-audience debate, which was limited to farm policy and took place in mid-August in front of a crowd of 1,500 people at the Dakotafest farm show in Mitchell. Daschle remained on the defensive throughout most of the debate, which the *Argus Leader* dubbed "a raucous affair." Thune charged Daschle with impeding legislation in the Senate and said that when the crucial vote came on the ethanol bill in November 2003, "Tom walked off the field and was signing autographs," a reference to Daschle's book signing in Virginia the night before the ethanol vote, which failed to break the Democratic filibuster by two votes. Thune also said that when he left Congress, country-of-origin meat labeling (COOL) had been the law of the land but that it was delayed on Daschle's watch. When responding to the clout argument, Thune said that "any senator worth his salt" gets federal dollars and derided Daschle for saying "we won't survive without him." Daschle compared himself to Lyndon Johnson, who had said that when he acquired power in Washington he would use it. After noting what Senators Bob Dole and Robert Byrd had brought home for Kansas and West Virginia, Daschle said that South Dakota's "time had come." Daschle also denounced drug companies for "ripping off" seniors, called for the "break up of the big conglomerates" in agriculture, and criticized Thune for not delivering more drought relief in 2002. Daschle blamed Republicans for killing the ethanol bill by including an MTBE provision, even though during the April vote it had been removed and the Democratic Senate still filibustered the bill. Since the South Dakota press had not reported the details of the ethanol debate, however, few debate watchers understood the discrepancy. In his closing statement, Daschle said that the debate was "great" and that it represented "democracy in action."[8]

Despite praising the Mitchell debate, Daschle continued to reject the debate offers coming from South Dakota organizations. Thune's campaign manager called Daschle a "chickenshit" when he did not show up for a public forum and instead sent a staffer to videotape Thune. Daschle finally accepted four in-studio debates, including one of the two *Meet the Press* debates that Tim Russert had proposed, but he refused to consider more. Thune continued to apply pressure, however, and the *Rapid City Journal* also proposed weekly Lincoln-Douglas-style debates between the candidates that could transcend the television ads (designed to "manipulate reality") and serve as an alternative to scripted, in-studio television debates. The *Journal* also proposed a debate on an Indian reservation. The *Mitchell Daily Republic* and KSFY Television also called for a Lincoln-Douglas-style debate at the famous Corn Palace. The *Argus Leader,* by contrast, editorialized that most people had made up their minds about the race and that the debates already scheduled were enough. Despite the *Argus Leader's* defense of Daschle's position, the pressure grew; Daschle ultimately agreed to eight debates, but not in the public, Lincoln-Douglas format that some media outlets promoted. In one instance, the Daschle campaign agreed to the demand for a West River debate only a half hour before Thune planned to criticize Daschle's nonparticipation during a press conference. Other West River groups such as the Rapid City and Spearfish Chambers of Commerce also wanted debates, but Daschle refused. He also refused to participate in the proposed debate at the famous Corn Palace for "security reasons" and declined a public debate on the Freedom Stage at the State Fair, which had been a common ritual for candidates for decades, instead insisting on in-studio debates. The entire debate about debates made Daschle seem defensive, especially after his less-than-stellar showing at the farm show. The debates that were finally agreed to would take place during a compressed schedule in the final crucial weeks of the campaign.[9]

The fall debates would help determine what issues would affect the contest. Political consultants call the questions that tend to dominate a campaign its "issue matrix." Thune sought to address broad issues such as the procedural obstruction that undermined the ethanol bill in the Senate and the candidates' differences over economic policy, the federal judiciary, and social issues. Dave Kranz of the *Argus Leader*, however, said that the race was about clout—using his position as the state's dominant political reporter to define the terms of the race. Kranz generally focused on issues that would aid Senator Daschle, including clout and negative campaigning. Similarly, during Daschle's first run for the Senate in 1986 during the depths of the 1980s farm crisis, Kranz had deemed farm policy the defining issue in the race, which aided Daschle. Similar to the 2002 race, in 2004 the *Argus* tried to make drought concerns a major focus of the campaign. An *Argus Leader* headline shaped the parameters of the race by boldly asking, "Where's the Aid?" In July, a page 1A largefont, top-billing *Argus* headline blared "S.D. Denied Drought Relief" and continued, "Daschle says long-term assistance needed." In contrast, four days later, a three-sentence *Argus* blurb about flood relief headlined "Bush Makes Parts of S.D. Disaster Area" was relegated to a sidebar on 1B. What the *Argus Leader* chose to report, what it chose to ignore, and what it chose to emphasize helped define the contours of the race.[10]

Daschle hoped to steer the discussion away from issues that would hurt him politically. During the summer gay marriage debate, Daschle announced his plan to save rural America, which former television news anchor Steve Hemmingsen derided: "Daschle suddenly proclaims that he finds Rural America in decline and has a five-point plan to stop it. John Thune promptly asks where has our Tom been for the last thirty years. Heck, why not make it fifty." In August, Daschle similarly announced his plan for the creation of a "small farmer administration" similar to the Small Business Administration. Daschle provided no details and said that the legislation would not be introduced until the next Congress. Only twenty people turned out to hear Daschle's proposal at the Sioux Falls Stockyards. Thune said, "I can't believe it's the best he can do," then called it "an election-year stunt." The initiative served a purpose, however, by linking Daschle to the cause of small farmers and keeping the debate away from other issues that divided the candidates. After generating a few headlines, Daschle no longer mentioned the plan.[11]

Daschle had mastered the use of small, noncontroversial proposals with universal support to distract attention away from larger, more divisive issues that hurt him politically. In the 1980s, political analyst Stuart Rothenberg noted Daschle's agility with "PR gimmicks" that enhanced his moderate image and allowed him to avoid being "identified as a classic Kennedy-McGovern liberal." In July 2004, for example, Daschle began discussing a "dentist shortage" in rural America and announced the introduction of the Dental Health Provider Shortage Act. In South Dakota, there was one dentist per 250 square miles, Daschle said, while in Minnesota there was one every 28 square miles (although Minnesota has a lot more people). Daschle said that he did not know how much the measure would cost. The plan was announced on Daschle's weekly conference call with South Dakota reporters and was then widely reported around the state.[12]

Some national issues, however, were unavoidable in 2004. During the second week of July, the Senate considered the federal marriage amendment (FMA), the constitutional amendment defining marriage. Thune held a press conference to announce his support of the FMA, and the issue received newspaper and television coverage. Daschle continued to oppose the amendment and tried to raise counterissues to change the subject. The day after Thune's press conference, Daschle began talking about his plan for rural America, which did not include anything new beyond the meat labeling, ethanol, drought aid, and federal farm program legislation he had already proposed—all of which Thune agreed with. Daschle hoped that the plan would deflect attention away from the gay marriage issue, which the Daschle campaign downplayed as a serious concern. Daschle's spokesman said during the senator's July Fourth visits in the state that the marriage issue "didn't come up once," a claim contradicted by e-mails sent to the Dakota Blog Alliance by those attending Daschle's events. Daschle was vulnerable on the FMA issue because 63 percent of his constituents supported it, as did newly elected Democratic Congresswoman Stephanie Herseth. The governor of South Dakota also sent a letter to

Daschle urging him to vote for the measure. Contrary to his early statements, Daschle filibustered the FMA in the Senate.[13]

Daschle did say that he opposed gay marriage (generating a protest at the Democratic convention from a gay rights group) but also said that he opposed the FMA as unnecessary because of the existence of federal and state "defense of marriage" statutes. Daschle did not address the issue of judicial nullification of these laws, which had precipitated the gay marriage debate in early 2004. Daschle also said that he was a constitutional purist and opposed any tampering with the U.S. Constitution, arguing on the Senate floor that in "217 years we have only amended that sacred document 17 times" and that it was critical to "insulate" the Constitution from changes. In earlier years, however, Daschle had cosponsored thirty-seven constitutional amendments, which addressed such issues as limiting campaign contributions, adjusting the congressional pay raise, instituting congressional term limits, and eliminating the Electoral College. During his first campaign, Daschle also made a balanced budget amendment to the Constitution central to his campaign. Given the extreme pressure on Daschle from his caucus and gay rights groups, Daschle opposed the FMA, but his rationale for doing so, insulating the Constitution from change, contradicted his previous support for numerous constitutional amendments. Daschle's past support for the constitutional amendment process did not receive press coverage but was discussed by Dakota bloggers. Despite his stated opposition to gay marriage in South Dakota during the campaign, after the election the National Gay and Lesbian Task Force honored Daschle for defeating the federal marriage amendment.[14]

In addition to the debate on the FMA, presidential politics and the national conventions dominated the summer news. In early July, Kerry chose Senator John Edwards as his running mate. A strong media drumbeat preceded the selection of Edwards, and most commentators deemed him a wise choice. During the Democratic primaries, Edwards first ran as an electable southern moderate but then turned to a populist "two Americas" stump speech, which focused on the haves and have-nots in American life. In the primaries, Kerry had similarly adopted the Bob Shrum strategy of criticizing the "powerful interests," including the "influence peddlers, polluters, HMOs, the drug companies, big oil and the special interests who now call the White House home" but attempted to move to the middle during the summer. Kerry's choice of Edwards did not compare with John Kennedy's famous choice of Johnson, and the postannouncement "bounce" in the polls disappointed some Democrats. On the South Dakota front, the choice of Edwards (a small-town boy made good) helped Daschle more than some of Kerry's other potential choices would have. But it forced Daschle to run on a ticket with two fellow well-to-do liberal Democratic senators, which would put Daschle in awkward positions at times. Edwards's work as a trial lawyer also highlighted the copious donations Daschle had received from trial lawyers over the years—indeed, they were his biggest contributors for the 2004 cycle—and his work blocking tort reform votes in the Senate during 2003 and 2004.[15]

In mid-July, the danger of terrorism received heightened attention. Federal officials announced that intelligence reports indicated that al-Qaeda intended to disrupt the fall elections in the United States, just as the terrorist organization had done in Spain the previous March. In July, the Philippines withdrew its troops from Iraq to prevent the killing of a Filipino hostage captured by terrorists. Daschle found his July briefing on the renewed terror threat sobering. *Newsweek* also reported that counterterrorism officials were reviewing a plan to postpone the presidential election in case of a terrorist attack. Terrorists were attempting to undermine or at least influence the democratic process in the United States while at the same time resisting the effort to build a democracy in the Middle East. The idea of postponing the U.S. election was widely ridiculed, however, and soon had to be buried. The *New York Times* noted that even with the Civil War raging in 1864, the balloting had, according to Carl Sandburg, gone on "in quiet and good order."[16]

In July, the Democratic convention convened in Boston in Kerry's home state, a Democratic stronghold that reinforced Daschle's connection to East Coast liberalism. In a telling gesture, Daschle decided to leave the convention early and watch Kerry's acceptance speech in Sioux Falls: more photos of Daschle with Senators Kerry and Kennedy in Massachusetts would not help Daschle back home. The Democratic Senate candidates in the red states of North Carolina, Oklahoma, and Alaska skipped the national Democratic convention altogether. Kerry and the Democrats made no major mistakes at the convention (aside from a few flaps involving Hillary Clinton's speaking role and Mrs. Kerry telling a reporter to "shove it," which few Americans probably minded), and speakers received orders to limit their Bush-bashing. Kerry's speech received mixed reviews; he received only a small postconvention "bounce" in the polls. One postconvention poll by Gallup/*USA Today*/CNN actually found Bush leading, 50 to 46 percent. Commentators frequently noted that there was little love for Kerry but tremendous hatred of Bush in some quarters, which continued to motivate Democratic voters. *Newsweek* reporter Jonathan Alter warned Democrats about becoming "hyperventilating Moorecrats" and argued that "making Whoopi Goldberg mad doesn't win close elections."[17]

Kerry's agenda on major issues such as Iraq, about which he stated that he hoped for more international cooperation, also remained vague and largely consisted of process objections relating to the president's method of going to war and stabilizing Iraq. When Kerry announced that he still would have gone to war in Iraq despite the failure to find weapons of mass destruction, some on the left were furious. The Democratic rank-and-file remained thoroughly antiwar. Organizers of a national convention party for George McGovern planned for seventy-five people, but in another measure of Democratic sentiment, five hundred showed up to honor McGovern's antiwar legacy. The Democrats, in many ways, were still the party of McGovern.[18]

Kerry again invoked history during his convention speech, making his central selling point his military experience in Vietnam, for which he had been awarded five medals. He began his speech by declaring, "I'm John Kerry, and I'm reporting for duty!" and saluting. *Washington Post* columnist David Broder wrote that "Kerry and other speakers fixated on one brief shining moment in his prepolitical career: his valiant service as a Navy officer in Vietnam." When commenting on Kerry's invocation of his Vietnam service, Admiral William Crowe, a supporter of both Kerry and Daschle, said that "they pretty well drove it into the ground." In August, in keeping with Kerry's emphasis on his military service, a new book by Vietnam veterans entitled *Unfit for Command* began receiving attention in the blogosphere and developed into another contest over history and historical memory, which reopened old wounds first inflicted during the nation's most divisive twentieth-century moment. A group of 250 swiftboat veterans questioned how

Kerry had received some of his medals in Vietnam and said that Kerry's frequent claims that he had spent Christmas in Cambodia in 1968 were "complete lies"—on the Senate floor in 1986, Kerry had said that the Cambodia memory "is seared—seared—in me." The Kerry campaign then had to admit that this memory was wrong. When the swiftboat veterans began running an ad calling Kerry's Vietnam recollections untrue, the Kerry campaign threatened to sue stations that aired it, claiming that "your station is responsible for the false and libelous charges made by this sponsor."[19]

The controversy over the swiftboat veterans' television ads revealed how history and historical memory still animate contemporary politics, which remains a battle over the contested meaning of the 1960s, during which the Vietnam War was a central dividing point. Although President George H. W. Bush had said in 1991 that the country had "kicked the Vietnam syndrome," Vietnam War reporter Neil Sheehan argued that the "nation has yet to come to grips with what really happened in Vietnam." Daniel Henninger, a columnist for the *Wall Street Journal,* explained that Vietnam remained a "cauldron of memory" and that the swiftboat veterans' ads were "transforming history into today's news." David Broder asked, "Will we ever recover from the 1960s?" When the swiftboat veterans ran an ad about Kerry's testimony to the Senate in 1971, during which he claimed that U.S. soldiers in Vietnam were responsible for widespread Genghis Khan–like "crimes committed on a day-to-day basis with the full awareness of officers at all levels of command," the furious debate intensified. One man in the ad said that he had endured torture as a prisoner of war in Vietnam to avoid telling his captors the same untruths that Kerry had proclaimed to Congress. Former senator Bob Dole also entered the fray, saying that Kerry "should apologize to all the other 2.5 million veterans who served." The swiftboat blowup rekindled some toxic memories and, most commentators agreed, threw the Kerry campaign off-stride.[20]

Although Kerry did not carry the same amount of political baggage as Howard Dean, he proved an awkward ticket mate for Daschle. The Daschle campaign argued that South Dakota voters split their tickets and vote for individuals, and therefore the national ticket did not matter. Daschle also sought to focus on microissues rather than nationalizing the race, and he constantly criticized "outside groups" who might interfere in South Dakota politics. If Daschle could be consistently linked to Kerry, Kennedy, and coastal liberalism, it might cost him a few thousand crucial votes. In a retrospective on his 1996 defeat in a Senate race against John Kerry, former governor Bill Weld noted that the race was dead even until Kerry brought in Bob Shrum and Kerry began running "against Newt Gingrich, Jesse Helms and Bob Dole—in Massachusetts, a shrewd move." Clinton also boosted Kerry by winning Massachusetts by thirty-three points that fall. The Thune campaign similarly sought to link Daschle to unpopular national figures in his party.[21]

The Kerry burden for Daschle highlighted the politics of association that underpinned the Senate race. Daschle took pains to obscure his fund-raisers in the Hamptons and Hollywood (which the South Dakota press avoided reporting), because associating with wealthy liberal donors on the coasts presented risks in South Dakota. Daschle also avoided bringing Kerry and Kennedy and other national Democratic leaders to South Dakota. An analysis by *Congressional Quarterly* noted that "to continue leading his party nationally, Daschle must now distance himself from it locally." After the election, Kennedy said, "I told Tom I'd do anything to help him. He smiled and he hugged me and said, 'Thanks Ted—just stay a million miles away from South Dakota.'"[22]

The prominence of Michael Moore also intensified the politics of association, and his anti-Bush movie continued to makes waves in the Senate race. On July 5, a *Time* cover story entitled "The World According to Michael" included a Moore comment about Daschle: "At the Washington premiere, Moore sat a few rows behind Daschle. Afterward, says Moore, 'He gave me a hug and said he felt bad and that we were all gonna fight from now on. I thanked him for being a good sport.'" The story circulated widely on the Internet and spread to the *Washington Times* and the Internet arms of the *Weekly Standard* and the *Wall Street Journal.* Four days after the release of the *Time* story, Daschle denied that he ever hugged Moore. The Daschle denial, with the help of a Drudge Report link, then generated even more Internet commentary, as did Moore's insistence that he did indeed hug Daschle.[23]

"Huggate," as it became known, served as a reminder that Daschle had attended Moore's premiere, which lent legitimacy to the movie. Moreover, Daschle recessed the Senate, which was debating the National Defense Authorization Act for fiscal year 2005, to promote attendance of the movie. *Roll Call* finally reported that a K Street lobbyist who looked like Daschle was the one who had allegedly hugged Moore, but it was the national Democratic Party's general embrace of Moore and his criticism of the Bush administration that had the potential to hurt Daschle in South Dakota, where Daschle often said that he supported President Bush 80 percent of the time. To highlight the difference between the two candidates, Thune attended the documentary *In the Face of Evil,* which premiered in Sioux Falls and recounted Reagan's battle against communism. Thune mockingly hugged the director to underscore the contrast with Daschle's "embrace" of Moore.[24]

Daschle's problems with the national base of his party persisted as a subplot of the campaign. The base's dissatisfaction with Daschle's leadership, as indicated by Michael Moore's swipes at Daschle in his movie, triggered doubts about Daschle's ability to hold on to his leadership post in the Senate if challenged by more strident colleagues. Daschle's inability or unwillingness to speak out against his base or disassociate himself from it hurt him politically in South Dakota. Reinforcing the statements of Michael Moore, Al Gore gave a speech in late June denouncing President Bush's "deliberate campaign to mislead America" and, in a reference to the Nazis, said that the Bush administration worked with "digital brown shirts to pressure reporters and their editors" into not properly reporting the news. George Soros, a Daschle donor and financier of anti-Bush 527 groups, also said that the Iraq War had turned Americans "from victims into perpetrators" of terrorism. In July, at a $7 million celebrity fund-raiser in New York, Senators Kerry and Edwards were entertained by Whoopi Goldberg, Jessica Lange, Paul Newman, and other entertainers who offered up predictable denunciations of Bush. Daniel Henninger argued that the "world of celebrity and the world of the Democratic Party are now joined at the hip. They are one." Daschle was also the largest beneficiary of Hollywood donations during the 2004 election cycle. Despite his earlier denunciation of the "startling meanness" in politics, Daschle remained silent after the biting celebrity criticism of Bush.[25]

The war in Iraq remained an obvious presence during the summer campaigns. On July 1, Saddam Hussein faced hearings before a tribunal of the new Iraqi government, which had recently taken over control of the country from the provisional occupation authority. The new government faced another three-week rebellion in Najaf led by the Shiite cleric Moqtada al-Sadr, and the city of Fallujah threatened to become a "North Vietnam–like sanctuary" for terrorists, according to the *Wall Street Journal*, which opined that the cancellation of the impending U.S. Marine assault on Fallujah in April was a "terrible blunder." On the campaign trial, Kerry said that "we're going to get our troops home where they belong," triggering allusions to George McGovern's "Come Home America" sentiment of the early 1970s, a policy retreat by Kerry that the *New Republic* called "indefensible." Kerry then made his stunning statement that even if he had known there were no weapons of mass destruction (WMDs) in Iraq, he would have supported the 2002 war resolution, which prompted Bush to criticize Kerry for "sending mixed signals." The *New York Times* described Kerry's dilemma as attempting "to portray himself as tough and competent enough to be commander in chief, yet appeal to the faction of Democrats that hates the war and eggs him on to call Mr. Bush a liar." Kerry faced another awkward moment when former Clinton national security advisor and Kerry advisor Sandy Berger was found to be the subject of an investigation for improperly removing classified documents relating to the Clinton administration's antiterrorism efforts from the National Archives. After the election, Berger pled guilty to intentionally removing and destroying the documents.[26]

Daschle's position on the Iraq War remained less than clear, triggering more comparisons to Senator Kerry. Immediately prior to the war, Daschle caused a national stir by scolding the president for having failed at diplomacy and forcing the nation to war. In contrast to his earlier denunciation, while in South Dakota during the winter of 2004 he lauded the war effort and discounted the absence of WMDs. His position prior to the Senate vote on the war in 2002 was similarly confusing. Liberal political analyst Peter Beinart wrote in 2002 that "Daschle criticized the war endlessly, then voted for it on the flimsiest of pretexts, then went back to criticizing it," calling Daschle's confusing actions a "moral abdication" from the "meek and cynical center" that made "Democratic support for the war with Iraq synonymous with cynical calculation and ideological me-tooism." During the debate over authorizing the war, Daschle said that "Saddam's weapons of mass destruction are the principal threat to the United States and the *only threat* that would justify" war. But in July 2004 in South Dakota, Daschle said that he would still vote for the war despite the absence of WMDs, a precursor to Kerry's identical pronouncement the following month. Despite Daschle's vote in favor of the war, at White House meetings in September 2002, according to Senator Trent Lott, Daschle "made it very clear that he would not support the war resolution." But Daschle did vote for the war, which some liberals could not abide. John MacArthur, the publisher of *Harper's*, complained that he asked Daschle if he regretted his vote for the war and Daschle "responded with a political bromide not even worth quoting." Mac-Arthur turned to Eugene McCarthy, who told him to read William Butler Yeats for comfort in the age of "Daschle and the collapse of liberal courage."[27]

The summer ended with the Republican convention in New York, which again accentuated the politics of association. Thune spent the entire week at the GOP convention—unlike Daschle, who had quickly departed from the Democratic convention in Boston. Thune gave a speech focused on Daschle's obstructionism in the Senate, constantly invoking the *Wall Street Journal*'s description of the body as "Daschle's Dead Zone." The Daschle campaign also chose the week of the GOP convention to start running an ad in South Dakota featuring Daschle hugging President Bush after 9/11 to bolster his bipartisan image. When national commentators criticized Daschle after the ad appeared on the Drudge Report, Daschle said there was "nothing contrived" about the hug, which he called a "private moment in public view." Kerry's campaign manager said that the ad had "a lot to do with what's going on in South Dakota," where Kerry's negative ratings approached 50 percent. Political analyst Jennifer Duffy said, "I understand campaigns are cynical by their nature, but I'm sorry, this is a little too cynical for me." Duffy said that the Daschle campaign's decision to run the hug-ad indicated that they were nervous. The episode became known as "Huggate II" and drew comparisons to Daschle's alleged hug of Michael Moore, which then became known as "Huggate I." After the convention, both *Time* and *Newsweek* polls showed Bush opening up a double-digit lead over Kerry, another reason Daschle deemed it wise to show himself hugging the president in ads for South Dakota consumption.[28]

In late August, a *Washington Post* story questioned whether "Daschle fatigue" was growing in South Dakota. One Watertown man who tended to vote Democratic said, "I think it's time for somebody else to have a chance, see what they can do." Despite the steady din of Daschle's "clout" advertising, his support remained stuck around 48 to 49 percent in the polls. The debate over debates also made Daschle seem evasive. In addition, Kerry's candidacy continued to be a drag on Daschle's campaign. Thune continued his constant campaigning and appeared to make progress by assaulting Daschle's record, as he had done at the farm show debate. Thune still had many weapons that he had not fired, but Daschle continued to run ads denouncing negative campaigns in the hopes that Thune would hurt himself if he started a full-scale attack. In the fall, the war would come.[29]

CHAPTER EIGHT

THE FALL OFFENSIVE

The past is never dead. It is not even past.

—William Faulkner

The results of the Thune campaign's first internal poll, conducted in mid-June, showed Daschle ahead by nine percentage points. During the last week of July, another Thune poll showed Daschle ahead by four percentage points. Thune's light-hearted introductory advertising featuring his daughters, combined with his relentless schedule of small-town burger-and-brat picnics, had bolstered his standing. But he still trailed. Thune's polling also indicated, however, that Daschle's actual voting record was foreign to many South Dakotans and that they were willing to hear the other side of the story—and might change their minds if they did. As the fall campaign began, Thune had shaken hands with tens of thousands of voters, visited the state's Democratic strongholds, outlined his political agenda, and stockpiled resources for the final push. At the same time, Daschle remained at 50 percent or below in polls, even after *de minimus* scrutiny of his record and a deluge of pro-Daschle advertising. The eleventh hour came, and Thune began to press the case against Daschle.

Daschle campaign staffers had been bolstering their defenses for a year in preparation for a full-scale assault. They calculated that their constant criticism of Thune for "partisan attacks" and "negative advertising" would inoculate Daschle against the coming scrutiny and that voters would dismiss critical claims as the ravings of zealots. This defensive mechanism was invoked so often by the fall that it approached a Maginot Line level of obsolescence. A *Rapid City Journal* reporter noted that the Daschle campaign, in response to criticism, would send out calls for more funds with "the ink smeared by tears over the deplorable ads." Thune issued orders to focus on Daschle's history of votes, statements, and actions and to emphasize his own reform agenda and the importance of ending the deadlock in the Senate. The competing "Stop the negative attack!" and "Look at Daschle's record!" mantras became the central front during the fall campaign.[1]

The initial skirmish came in late August, when the national chamber of commerce launched a television ad criticizing Daschle for blocking tort reform votes in the Senate. The Association of Trial Lawyers of America had urged donors to give to Daschle, noting that in "recent years, probably no single Senator has played a more pivotal role in the fight against tort reform than Tom Daschle." Adhering to the battle plan, the Daschle campaign denounced the chamber's "conservative extremist agenda" and immediately fired off warnings about an impending "wave of attacks" from outside groups. The Dakota blogs disclosed that a man in a Daschle television ad denouncing the chamber's criticism was actually a lawyer whose business Daschle had promoted at the annual meeting of the Association of Trial Lawyers of America, where Daschle had denounced tort reform. The blogs also revealed an effort by Daschle's staff to coax South Dakota business owners into writing a collective letter criticizing the national chamber for scrutinizing Daschle. The effort fizzled after the blog disclosure.[2]

During the first week of September, the National Republican Senatorial Committee also ran its first ad, which explained that Daschle had voted with Senators Kerry and Kennedy to raise gas taxes several times. The ad was another attempt by the GOP to link Daschle to his liberal allies in his Senate caucus. Daschle initially said that he did not vote to raise gas taxes, but the record showed otherwise. He then countered by saying that lower gas taxes could limit the amount of federal highway dollars that came to South Dakota. The Daschle campaign again rolled out its biggest defensive weapon—a blistering ad attacking Thune for running negative ads, even though the GOP senatorial committee, not the Thune campaign, had run the ad. The Daschle camp hoped to create a confusing jumble of claims and counterclaims, a tactic that prompted Dick Wadhams to call Daschle a "pathological liar" and argue that Daschle ran the first untruthful negative ad. Daschle later admitted in a debate that the Thune campaign did not run the ad; Daschle's defensive weapons were misfiring.

Throughout the fall, the Daschle camp complained incessantly about Thune's "unwillingness" to stop "negative third party attacks," and the "negative ad" kabuki dance of charges and countercharges persisted. The first ad run by the Thune campaign that actually mentioned Daschle started during the third week of September and featured a Rapid City man criticizing Daschle for his gas tax votes and prodding Daschle for always claiming to be the victim of criticism, introducing a central theme of the Thune campaign: Daschle sent a confusing message about his power in Washington by embracing a strategy of victimhood. As the leaves fell and the harvest began, Daschle's ads denouncing Thune's "negative attacks" and "lies" continued. Even though Daschle had insisted for a year that Thune could force third parties to stop running ads against the senator and highlighted his own high-minded efforts to keep out third parties, in the final crucial weeks of the campaign the strategy was abandoned and the Democratic Senatorial Campaign Committee intervened to aid Daschle and ran ads attacking Thune. Daschle then admitted that he could not control outside groups. Daschle's basic defensive strategy—deflecting any criticism as a negative attack" and as unreliable and hyperpartisan agitprop—failed to blunt the arguments made in the first major campaign clashes, and the Thune campaign slowly gained ground.

During the Republican convention in late August and early September, the Thune campaign released a poll indicating that Thune had ticked ahead of Daschle, 50 to 48 percent. An independent Rasmussen poll (which the Daschle campaign condemned as unreliable), conducted during the second week in September, also showed Thune leading, 50 to 47 percent. Another Rasmussen poll in late September showed Thune leading, 50 to 46 percent. The only other Rasmussen poll of the race had been conducted in February and showed Daschle leading, 48 to 45 percent, indicating a seven-point swing to Thune in seven months. Thune's strategy of delaying his advertising until July and some Daschle miscues on debates had helped Thune's cause, while Daschle's attempts to deflect the first few contrast ads on tort reform and taxes had failed. Evidence of Daschle's record slowly snuck through the din. The tribulations of Kerry on the national front also weighed down the Daschle campaign. Several mid-September polls showed President Bush opening up a lead over Kerry and gaining ground in several battleground states such as Wisconsin and Pennsylvania. The slippage prompted the Kerry campaign to retool and bring several old Clinton hands on board in the early weeks of September after Kerry had a long call with President Clinton, who was about to undergo quadruple bypass surgery. In South Dakota, Daschle never mentioned Kerry's name.[3]

In early September, national bloggers discovered that Dan Rather and *60 Minutes* had relied on forged documents purportedly showing that President Bush had neglected his duties while in the Texas Air National Guard in the 1970s (even Michael Moore had rejected use of the documents). Rather and CBS dug in their heels and defended the documents while commentators savaged CBS's decision to run the story. Conservative bloggers relished the revelation about Rather, whom they viewed as a longtime GOP critic and Democratic Party enabler. The Dakota blogs also noted that *Argus Leader* reporter Dave Kranz had praised Dan Rather as a hero when CBS removed him from the White House beat, a decision Kranz called "an insult to standards we are to follow for good journalism." The *60 Minutes* episode confirmed the suspicions of those who thought the mainstream media favored Kerry. One study found that Kerry had "received better press than anyone since 1980, receiving a record breaking 77 percent positive evaluations" compared to 34 percent for Bush.[4]

The declining confidence in journalism nationally was reflected locally in South Dakota, where the *Sioux Falls Argus Leader* continued to draw fire. The editorial board of the *Wall Street Journal* noted that "in South Dakota, bloggers and the Web have challenged the dominance that Tom Daschle's pals at the *Argus Leader* have long had on that state's political dialogue." In October, the blog South Dakota Politics released a compilation of sixty-six stories critical of Daschle that had appeared in the national media in the previous year, all of which the *Argus* had ignored, underscoring the extent to which the state's largest newspaper obscured Daschle's history and voting record. In mid-October, the *Argus* endorsed Daschle, just as they had done every time he had run for office. The blog South Dakota Politics had started an "Argus Endorsement Countdown" in the early fall in anticipation of the inevitable moment. The *Argus Leader*'s preference for Senator Daschle did not surprise some voters. A Thune poll in late summer found that 55 percent of people in the Sioux Falls area thought that the *Argus Leader* was biased. The newspaper's ability to provide defensive cover for Daschle eroded as blog criticism persisted and gained a broader audience.[5]

September also brought a series of news stories relating to one-time third-party candidate Tim Giago's April departure from the race, which proved controversial for Daschle. When Giago originally entered the race, he said that "neither of the candidates running for the Senate will address the Black Hills settlement question" and that it would not be settled "until a politician with the guts to address it emerges and introduces a bill in the Senate to give back some of the land in the Black Hills and the money to the [Indian] people." After Daschle and Giago met privately in April and Giago left the race (with Daschle insisting that Giago would be the Ralph Nader of the race), the *Washington Post* reported Giago saying, "Every Lakota, Dakota, and Nakota will be shocked and surprised at some of the issues Senator Daschle will bring forth" as a result of the meeting. Giago also "said that he wanted Daschle to open a dialogue on returning the sacred Black Hills to the tribes of the Sioux Nation." The *Post* story was headlined "Daschle Rival Drops Bid after Promise on Land Return." After the April meeting, the *Lakota Journal* ran a blaring headline: "On Daschle's Word of Honor, Giago Drops Out."[6]

In late summer, the *Lakota Journal* started questioning whether Daschle had cut a deal with Giago to entice him to leave the race. Speculation focused on the possible return of some land, perhaps involving Wind Cave National Park, to the state's Indian tribes. KOTA Television in Rapid City ran a story entitled "Wind Cave Used as Bargaining Chip?" and reported that two sources "did confirm that a Wind Cave deal has been proposed." The blogs finally disclosed that a "Sioux Summit" would be held in the Black Hills in late September between Daschle and the state's tribes, and the Associated Press reported that Giago said "the return of the Black Hills" or "a small tract of land now controlled by the U.S. Forest Service" would be considered. Daschle campaign manager Steve Hildebrand maintained that "there was never a deal struck with Giago," but Giago said, "We shook hands on it. To me, that's a gentlemen's agreement." Giago added, "I don't know why Steve would say something like that." In the fall debates, Daschle denied that there was a "quid pro quo" and said that he was just "opening a dialogue," which seemed a far cry from the "shocking" announcement Giago had promised in April.[7]

The summit drew immediate criticism from state newspapers (except the *Argus Leader*). The *Aberdeen American News* asked, "Was it just a payback to get Giago out of the race?" The editors of the *Mitchell Daily Republic* opined that "with tax dollars in question, our belief is that those discussions should be public and open to review by the people who ultimately pick up the tab." The *Rapid City Journal* was also critical, as was the *Lakota Journal,* which wrote an editorial entitled "The 'Closed Door' Summit Leaves Much to Be Questioned." The *Lakota Journal* noted the return of the "Black Hills to South Dakota Sioux Indian Tribes—namely Wind Cave National Park—which was part of the original 'deal' made between Tim Giago and Senator Daschle. What has happened to that issue that was listed as the number one priority last spring?" At the same time, the *Argus Leader,* which completely ignored the summit story, criticized the Sioux Falls school board for "secret" meetings and questioned whether they might "violate the state's open meetings law."[8]

On the morning of September 19, Daschle and Thune met for a face-to-face debate on Tim Russert's *Meet the Press.* Unlike the earlier debate at Dakotafest in Mitchell, Daschle was unusually combative, animated, and abrupt, in contrast to his usual earnest and calm persona. Both candidates faced questions about past statements in the typical Russert fashion. Daschle admitted that his ad claiming Thune ran negative ads about gas taxes was wrong and that the ad was a GOP Senate committee ad. Daschle criticized the management of the Iraq War but would not say that the war was a mistake, and Thune called for staying the course. Daschle also said that John Kerry was wrong to vote against an $87 billion appropriation for Iraqi reconstruction. Daschle then defended his ad featuring his hug of President Bush. Kerry spokesman Jamie Rubin indicated the degree to which national Democrats would accommodate Daschle's difficult situation in South Dakota by dismissing Daschle's statement about Kerry's vote on the $87 billion appropriation for Iraq: "Well, Tom Daschle is in a close race in South Dakota. And there are certain things he has to say during that race." Noting an odd variety of boosterism, *The Hill* reported that Daschle used a seat pillow during the Russert debate: "Hill sources say an aide carries a blue pillow around for Daschle just in case the boss needs to avoid being looked down on." The blogs took to calling it "Pillowgate."[9]

Toward the end of the *Meet the Press* debate, Russert questioned Thune about a recent letter from the state GOP chairman claiming that Daschle's criticism of President Bush on the eve of war with Iraq gave "comfort to America's enemies." Thune criticized the timing of Daschle's statement, which he said "emboldened our enemies." In the spring, Thune also noted, Daschle had applauded when South Dakota senator Tim Johnson labeled the GOP the "Taliban." In a surprising turn, Daschle said that he regretted his comments on the eve of war, contrary to his earlier refusals to retract his statement: in late 2003, Daschle had said, "I feel vindicated. . . . I have no regrets whatsoever and would say it again." When Thune entered the race in January, Daschle again told the *New York Times* that he had "no regrets" about his pre-war statements. During the fall campaign, however, Daschle said he regretted his comments.[10]

After the row over Daschle's pre-war comments on *Meet the Press,* Daschle turned emotional and said that Thune's comments should earn him "a trip to the woodshed." Some voters sympathized with Daschle's response, while others viewed it as an overwrought and dramatic display of victimhood. A public radio story about college students' reaction to the debate reported that they "laughed and rolled their eyes" at Daschle's response. The reaction to the exchange probably depended on how one viewed the war. The *Meet the Press* altercation correlated with caustic clashes in the presidential race as the political salience of war and dissent persisted. Unfortunately for Daschle, support for the war remained steady in South Dakota, and support for President Bush remained strong, albeit fluctuating. A Zogby poll in late October found that 60 percent of South Dakotans supported the war, and John Zogby concluded that "there is more support for war in South Dakota than in most states." A Mason-Dixon poll in late October found that Iraq and homeland security were the top concerns of 40 percent of South Dakota voters.[11]

Rather than quarreling about Iraq, Daschle preferred to rely on his strongest offensive weapon, the power to deliver federal money to South Dakota, which he hoped would trump issues that counted against him. The *National Journal* reported that "Daschle's main campaign theme can be summed up in one word: CLOUT." As the Senate reconvened in early September, Daschle emphasized his leadership position and claimed credit for adding drought relief money to the Homeland

Security appropriations bill, which generated positive press for him in South Dakota. Senate action also presented perils for Daschle, however, as the Clinton-era ban on certain firearms expired in early September and John Kerry aggressively advocated an extension. Daschle also supported extending the gun ban but minimized his position in deference to both the hostility toward gun control in South Dakota and Thune's opposition to extension. The Senate spent much of the fall debating the recommendations of the 9/11 Commission and eventually approved the commission's recommended overhaul of the intelligence agencies by a 96–2 vote, which again pulled national security matters to the center of American politics. The Senate finally approved a drought relief measure and a large corporate tax bill that included some ethanol tax credits. Both provisions received wide attention from the press in South Dakota, and Daschle took credit for passing them. The Senate also extended some of Bush's tax cuts, which Daschle had originally opposed. Daschle, despite his earlier opposition, quickly began running radio ads touting his effort "to pass new tax cuts," but the South Dakota press did not highlight the contradiction. Thune called Daschle's stance on the tax cuts "an election-year conversion" and noted that Republican senators in Washington told him, "Daschle had never been so cooperative—you should have an election in South Dakota every six months." Daschle's suggestion during the campaign that he masterminded the tax cuts, according to one report, caused national Democrats who consistently opposed the Bush tax cuts to "wince at such tactics."[12]

On the presidential front, Bush stumbled in the first presidential debate in Florida on September 30. Several postdebate polls showed Kerry closing the gap with the president, and some showed Kerry pulling ahead. Thune's campaign polls indicated that he also suffered from Bush's poor performance. How much Bush would aid Thune in the Senate race, if at all, remained an unknown variable. During the second week in October, Bush and Vice President Dick Cheney delivered strong debate performances, however, which again boosted the GOP presidential ticket's standing. The Rasmussen presidential tracking poll after the debate showed Bush leading 50 to 46 percent, the first time Rasmussen had shown either candidate polling at 50 percent. After all of the presidential debates, polls collectively showed the Bush-Kerry race deadlocked, and analysts predicted a brutal stretch run. "These last couple of weeks," Kerry strategist Tad Devine promised, "are going to be reminiscent of the opening scenes of 'Scarface.'" Another Rasmussen poll in early October, after Bush's poor performance in the first debate, showed the Thune-Daschle race even at 49 to 49 percent. Some national experts such as Larry Sabato continued to preach the view that a large turnout for Bush would drive up the number of Thune voters and overcome the Republican ticket-splitters, who tended to help Daschle. "Coattails still matter," Sabato said in early October. "It will affect this race in South Dakota."[13]

During Bush's slip in the polls in late September, the Daschle camp fired its big artillery, running an ad that featured ranchers criticizing Thune for not "standing up to the president" in 2002 and delivering a drought aid package. Thune explained that he had arranged significant aid through the Department of Agriculture that year, but a discussion of the 2002 drought aid battle was a political negative. Daschle then began running ads saying that Thune wanted to undermine Social Security, a standard Democratic argument in a graying state such as South Dakota. In the October debates, Daschle similarly said that Thune supported the elimination of Social Security.[14]

Daschle also used paid media to promote actions taken in the Senate, including the extension of tax cuts he had earlier opposed. After the final adjournment of the Senate, Daschle returned to the campaign trail, claiming credit for drought aid and some ethanol provisions in a corporate tax bill that had long been stalled in Congress. Despite rumors at the time, the Senate Republicans did not schedule votes on issues that might have put Daschle and other Democrats running in conservative states in compromising positions. In addition to the positive press that Daschle received for events in Washington and his new ads, some Democrats buzzed about the persistent rumors of an "October surprise" in which former Republican governor Bill Janklow would endorse Daschle—while some Democrats favored the notion, others thought that support from Janklow (who had served a hundred days in jail earlier in the year after his manslaughter conviction) would hurt Daschle more than it helped.[15]

The Thune campaign suffered another setback during the second week of October. For several days in a row, Dave Kranz of the *Argus Leader* published stories about GOP campaign workers not properly notarizing absentee ballot requests. The articles focused on Thune's nephew Jeff Thune, which had the effect of directly implicating the Thune name. Jeff Thune was cleared of any wrongdoing, but the state party's "Victory" program, which registered new voters and arranged absentee ballots requests, was found to be notarizing ballot requests long after the requester had signed the form. Five individuals were eventually charged with one count of improper notarization and were fined $200. Former Governor Janklow ended a long public silence to criticize the Victory program (which he thought was not helpful to him during his 2002 congressional race), and a longtime state legislator and Janklow ally resigned from the party's executive board in protest. At a critical moment in the campaign, the notary fracas received enormous press scrutiny. Thune's former chief of staff and 2002 campaign manager, Herb Jones, was brought in to manage the Victory program. Despite the notarization problem, Jones was impressed with how much the Victory program had improved since 2002, as well as its highly organized get-out-the-vote effort.

Any momentary advantages that Daschle derived from the drought aid or the notary flap were soon overshadowed by issues detrimental to him. After the *Meet the Press* debate, the Daschle campaign continued to criticize Thune's "embolden the enemy" comment, inadvertently triggering a broader discussion about Daschle and the war. Daschle's allies in the Senate went to the floor to excoriate Thune for the comment, some pro-Kerry generals criticized Thune's lack of military service, and eight Daschle supporters went to Thune headquarters to protest. The pro-Daschle protesters were met by eighty Thune supporters defending Thune's comment and criticizing Daschle's remarks on the eve of the Iraq War in 2003. The GOP senatorial committee also began broadcasting an ad featuring Daschle's comments on the eve of war along with angry antiwar snippets from Senators Kennedy and Kerry, which again linked Daschle to the national Democratic Party's denunciations of the war. Daschle's Iraq comments were unpopular nationally (even Eleanor Clift had said Daschle overstepped) but were especially damaging in South Dakota. The discussion of the war again highlighted Daschle's association with the stridently antiwar left and his attendance at the Washington premiere of Michael Moore's *Fahrenheit 9/11*.[16]

Because the Senate was discussing a possible vote on a constitutional amendment to ban flag burning, the Iraq exchange became part of the wider national debate on war and dissent. The highest priority of the South Dakota American Legion was a constitutional ban on flag burning, a political issue that had lingered since the Supreme Court's 1989 5–4 decision declaring flag burning free speech. Daschle opposed the flag amendment and said that it was a distraction from more important matters, but he was put in an awkward situation by his South Dakota Democratic colleagues Senator Tim Johnson and Congresswoman Stephanie Herseth, who both supported the amendment, as did Daschle's deputy, Senator Harry Reid of Nevada. Retired army major general Patrick Brady, who was born in Philip, South Dakota, and represented 140 civic groups in the Citizens Flag Alliance, also traveled the state calling on Daschle to support the amendment; Brady received significant press attention.[17]

The debate about Daschle's eve-of-war comments and the flag amendment started just as John Kerry refocused his campaign on "the mess in Iraq." Although Kerry had planned to spend the fall talking about economic policy, *Newsweek* reported that Kerry changed his focus, "betting that the hard truths of Iraq will undercut Bush's soft-focus picture of a liberated nation, and ultimately the president's image as a war leader." By mid-September, the death toll of U.S. forces in Iraq passed one thousand as terrorist attacks surged, making war news a daily ritual. From early April to early September, terrorist attacks also killed more than three thousand Iraqi civilians, raising doubts about the overall experiment in Iraqi democracy. Andrew Sullivan questioned whether the "level of fear, anarchy and insecurity is conducive to a transition to democracy." Historian Victor Davis Hanson remained more hopeful, writing that "Islamic fascists are now fighting openly and losing battles, and are increasingly desperate as they realize the democratization process slowly grinds ahead leaving them and what they have to offer by the wayside." Hanson quoted the World War I–era French prime minister Georges Clemenceau, an odd invocation, to boost morale: "War is a series of catastrophes that results in victory." Others remained pessimistic about the ongoing struggle. A senior diplomat told *Newsweek* that the "idea of a functioning democracy here is crazy. We thought that there would be a reprieve after sovereignty, but all hell is breaking loose."[18]

When Iraqi prime minister Ayad Allawi visited Washington in late September and spoke to Congress, he said that fifteen of eighteen provinces were ready for elections "tomorrow" and that "doubters underestimate our country, and they risk fueling the hopes of terrorism." John Kerry dismissed Allawi's assessment, whereupon President Bush criticized Kerry for undermining an ally, saying that "you can embolden an enemy by sending a mixed message," a comment similar to Thune's on *Meet the Press*. In the end, the Kerry campaign's decision to focus on Iraq in the fall, Daschle's role as Democratic leader and his similar criticism of the Iraq effort, Thune's "embolden the enemy" comment during the *Meet the Press* debate, and the continuing friction over Daschle's eve-of-war comments gave the Iraq War a high profile in the Senate race. Kerry's inconsistent statements on the war, which became the primary focus of the presidential campaign, also undercut Daschle, whose views were similarly incoherent.[19]

In addition to the war, a number of issues emerged during the last month of the campaign, and these slowly eroded Daschle's standing and overran his defenses. Not only did Daschle's 2004 positions on the issues hurt him, but also the degree to which his positions on issues had changed since his entry into politics reinforced the notion that Daschle had "gone Washington" and would "say anything." The exposure of his dual positions on some issues also undermined his image of sincerity. Instead of conceding that Daschle's positions on some issues had changed, the Daschle campaign stood its ground, thereby generating another 60s-vintage "credibility gap" issue. On September 22, the Ave Maria List Political Action Committee, a conservative Catholic organization based in Ann Arbor, Michigan, began running a radio ad in South Dakota that some observers considered the most effective ad to date. The ad, entitled "Daschle Has Changed," focused on Daschle's abandonment of his support for a balanced-budget amendment and his differing positions on abortion and gun control. The ad also noted Daschle's vote against the federal marriage amendment in July. A woman with a whispery voice drove home the point: "Tom Daschle has changed. He just doesn't represent South Dakota values like he used to."[20]

The Ave Maria ad introduced several issues, including the balanced budget amendment, which would shape the political dialogue in subsequent weeks. Although the balanced budget amendment had not been a major issue nationally for several years, it provided a striking contrast between Daschle's first campaign in 1978 and his early career in Congress, when he consistently promoted the amendment, and his later years in the Senate. During his last competitive Senate bid in 1986, Daschle ran a television ad saying that "in 1979, Tom Daschle saw the damage these deficits could do to our country. His *first official act* was to sponsor a Constitutional amendment to balance the budget." In 1992, Daschle's campaign literature touted the "Daschle Plan," which included the balanced budget amendment: "In 1979, before it became popular, I was pushing a balanced budget amendment to the Constitution. It was my first official action, and I've authored or coauthored one every year." In 1995, the amendment had the support of sixty-six of the sixty-seven senators needed for passage, but Daschle voted against it because of opposition from the Clinton administration. In 1996, the *New York Times* noted that the Senate, in which Daschle served as Democratic leader, had become a "graveyard" of Republican proposals such as the balanced budget amendment "and Mr. Daschle has served as chief undertaker" (the metaphor persisted into the summer of 2004, when the *Wall Street Journal* dubbed the Senate "Daschle's Dead Zone"). When pressed on the amendment in the last television debate, Daschle said that he had opposed the bill in the 1990s because there were no provisions in the amendment allowing for emergencies such as war. But the record showed that there was an emergency clause. When Thune pointed this out, Daschle simply said, "That's not accurate." But unfortunately for Daschle, it was. Daschle's history was climbing out of the memory hole. His past was not dead.[21]

The Ave Maria ad also introduced the gun control issue into the Senate race and highlighted Daschle's "F" grade from the National Rifle Association (NRA). Daschle's grade created another detrimental comparison to Democratic congresswoman Herseth, who received the NRA endorsement and an "A" grade and had started to run frequent television ads touting her NRA support. The deeper point was Daschle's migration to the left on the issue of gun control. During his last competitive Senate race in 1986, Daschle said that "no representative from our state has ever supported restrictive federal gun control laws written in Washington and there is a very good reason why. What makes sense in New York is crazy in South Dakota." In 1990, Daschle said, "I am against gun control, period." In the forty-seven votes scored by the NRA since 1990, Daschle voted with the

NRA only seven times. In the final weeks of the campaign, the NRA ran television, radio, and newspaper ads criticizing Daschle and held a rally in Sioux Falls on the Saturday before the election. All were designed to resurrect Daschle's past.[22]

Daschle campaign staffers understood their candidate's vulnerabilities and attempted to repair the breaches in the line with television ads. In mid-September, the Daschle campaign began running an ad depicting Daschle in hunting regalia, shotgun in hand, weaving his way through tallgrass prairie (pheasant hunting season opens in October) to address the NRA's gun control criticism. "Where's Tom?" a man in the ad asked while spinning a Daschle hunting yarn. After hearing that his hunting group did not have its limit of pheasants, the man in the ad said, Daschle "went back out walking the fields." Respondents to an *Argus Leader* poll viewed the ad as phony. Hunters, the target audience, ridiculed the ad the most, but the Daschle campaign ran the ad for eight weeks. In another ad, designed to address criticism on the foreign policy front, Daschle criticized Thune's defense votes and Thune's support of a missile defense system.[23]

In mid-October, in one of the most audacious moves of the year, the Daschle campaign started running a television ad claiming that Daschle was antiabortion and anti–gay marriage and cited his votes against partial-birth abortion and for the 1996 Defense of Marriage Act as evidence. The ad did not mention Daschle's opposition to the partial-birth abortion ban prior to final passage, a posture that infuriated the Catholic bishop of Sioux Falls. Despite Daschle's filibuster of the federal marriage amendment the previous summer, the ad said that "Tom believes that marriage is a sacred union between one man and one woman." The ad had the effect of significantly raising the profile of the abortion and gay marriage issues, which had never been raised in Thune's television ads. Despite the ad's attempt to muddy the waters on two prominent social issues, the ad boldly proclaimed that "John Thune is being dishonest and he'll do anything to get elected." The Daschle campaign also began running an ad of Daschle standing in a barnyard in a red flannel shirt saying that he embodied South Dakota values, which he had learned by hunting with his dad and as an altar boy, an allusion Senator Kerry also made on the national level.[24]

Some observers found Daschle's altar boy reference especially odd, and it angered some individuals close to the Catholic Church.

The altar boy invocation revived memories of the late 1990s, when Daschle publicly bickered with the bishop of Sioux Falls over the issue of partial birth abortions. The bishop had called Daschle's position a "smokescreen" to "provide cover for pro-abortion senators and President Clinton"; Daschle, on the Senate floor, said that the bishop had become "more identified with the religious right than with thoughtful religious leadership." Daschle's staff assistant handling the issue of partial-birth abortions, Amy Sullivan, later recalled that Daschle "felt he had to change his position and cast a vote in favor of the ban," which she deemed "a sham of a bill." Daschle said that "it was time to move on." An article in the *Weekly Standard* in 2003 reported that the bishop of Sioux Falls had asked Daschle to stop listing himself as a Catholic in his political literature because of his positions on abortion. In August 2004, the bishop also published a lengthy article in the *Bishop's Bulletin* explaining why Catholics should not vote for pro-choice candidates: "You cannot vote for a politician who is pro-abortion, when you have a choice, and remain a Catholic in good standing." The *Argus Leader* did not report on the bishop's statement at the time. National newspapers, however, reported on the story as soon as the bishop made his statement. Three months after the bishop's statement, it was reported in the *Argus Leader* in the forty-first paragraph of a story about religion and politics. Some *Argus* stories during the year discussing Senator Kerry's relationship to the Catholic Church also mentioned Daschle's generally rocky relationship with the bishop, so some South Dakotans were aware of the situation. The bishop's opinion piece, entitled "Abortion Is Injustice of Modern Era," ran in the *Argus Leader* the day after the election.[25]

The abortion issue became prominent in the Senate race in October in part because of a fund-raising letter for the National Abortion Rights Action League (NARAL), written by Daschle during the closing days of the 2002 election cycle. In early October, reporter Kevin Woster of the *Rapid City Journal* published a lengthy article entitled "Abortion Letter Still an Issue" about the NARAL letter and the history of Daschle's position on abortion. In the 2002 NARAL letter, Daschle requested donations to NARAL six times and said, "As the Majority Leader in the U.S. Senate, I've stood up for a woman's right to choose, and the pro-choice leadership of the Senate has made a difference by safeguarding women's rights from the anti-choice agenda of the Bush administration." Despite such statements, Daschle refused to admit that the NARAL letter was a fund-raiser; further, according to the *Journal* story, "Daschle refuse[d] to say whether he [was] pro-choice on abortion." Instead, Daschle became irate with Woster, who later recalled that Daschle was "difficult and evasive" and that the "interview grew a hard edge and ended with an icy silence. In my years covering Daschle, I've never experienced that kind of interview." *Aberdeen American News* reporter Scott Waltman also thought that Daschle's "demeanor while discussing abortion didn't help. He was stern. And stern is fine, but it seemed as if he didn't think such questions were fair and they most certainly are." Despite his pro-choice statements in the NARAL letter, during the fall campaign Daschle declared, "I'm anti-abortion. I don't believe that abortion ought to be allowed." The *Rapid City Journal* article also noted that during his 1978 congressional race Daschle released a letter calling abortion an "abhorrent practice" and invoked his Catholic credentials on the issue by saying that he was "a lifelong member of the Catholic faith." In his 1986 run for the Senate, Daschle had also sent a letter saying that he was "unalterably opposed to abortion on demand" and enclosed a letter from a minister who said that Daschle had called abortion "a form of murder." The Drudge Report and many blogs linked to the *Rapid City Journal* piece, generating a raft of commentary about how far to the right Daschle was running in the Senate race. During the 2004 election, the *Argus Leader* did not report on Daschle's statements about abortion during his earlier campaigns.[26]

During the third week of October, the Ave Maria List (AML) held press conferences in four South Dakota cities. The AML distributed copies of Daschle's earlier campaign statements opposing abortion which the *Rapid City Journal* piece had discussed. The political action committee also circulated a letter that Daschle had received from eight of his grade school nuns, which Daschle had sent to voters in 1978 along with his letter calling abortion an "abhorrent practice." The nuns said in their letter to Daschle, "We know and we tell those with whom we speak of your abhorrence for abortion—and of your commitment to life." The AML press conference featured Sharon Gray, a South Dakota college professor who said, "I am ashamed to admit I worked to help Tom Daschle get elected when he first ran for Senate many years ago. I did so gullibly believing his assertion (along with the blessings of the Presentation Sisters) that he was pro-life." The AML also emphasized that contributions that Daschle had made to and received from the abortion-rights group Emily's List and showed a video of Daschle speaking to an Emily's List convention. The AML ran radio and newspaper ads on Daschle's past abortion letters and statements and set up a website for interested voters to visit to review the documents. Although the AML press conferences in Aberdeen and Rapid City were covered by the *Aberdeen American News* and *Rapid City Journal,* the *Argus Leader* did not report on the Sioux Falls press conference.[27]

The abortion issue burst onto the scene at an inauspicious time for Daschle and began to register as a liability for him in Thune's polling. In the final debate on KSFY Television, Thune highlighted Daschle's abortion record, saying that there were "83 votes in Tom's 18-year career in the Senate that National Right to Life rates. Seventy-five out of 83, Tom has voted against the position and yet comes out, you know, in an election year and says 'Oh, I'm opposed to abortion.' You can't square those two things. It's not possible." Some observers thought that Daschle lost more votes trying to finesse the issue than if he had simply said he was pro-choice, as Congresswoman Herseth had done prior to the June special election. Daschle responded by saying that Thune wanted to put women in jail, which was untrue and sounded absurd.[28]

As the gun control and abortion issues began to penetrate the public debate, the heavily viewed mid-October debates began. KDLT Television even aired its debate twice because of popular demand. The debates became an ordeal for Daschle. Thune noted the ascendant abortion issue in the KSFY Television debate: "Tom is in Washington, D.C., NARAL's poster boy, and in South Dakota runs TV ads talking about learning his values as an altar boy. I mean, it is awfully difficult to square those two things. And in an election year, he tries to become what he thinks people in South Dakota want him to be on some of these cultural issues." Thune transformed the issue into one of credibility: "Tom tries to be all things for all people, one thing in Washington and another thing in South Dakota. You can't have two sets of values." The failure of the energy bill—Thune's reason for entering the race—also remained a prominent issue, and Thune again charged Daschle with refusing to line up the two necessary votes for passage and for being "out signing books." On the KELO-Land debate, Daschle admitted, "There were books, but that wasn't the issue." He said, "I made that vote," referring to the energy bill. Thune had never claimed that Daschle did not vote for the bill. Instead he argued that Daschle did not use his highly touted power as Senate leader to get the bill passed. Thune also criticized Daschle for his change of position on the balanced budget amendment and on taxes, pulling out a copy of a pledge (subsequently broken) to never raise income taxes that Daschle had signed during the final weeks of his last competitive election in 1986.[29]

Daschle's past continued to be revived. In the public television debate, Thune said that "campaigns are about differences and records" and "not about what you say in an election year," pleading with voters to look to Daschle's history, not his statements on the campaign trail. In the KELO-Land television debate, Thune said, "Don't believe what Tom says, look at the record." In the KSFY debate, Thune criticized Daschle's cynicism, citing a Daschle quote culled from the *Washington Post*: "I dare say the first thing that comes to my mind in a vote is: Can it [the issue] pass the 30-second test, how successful will my opponent be in applying it to a 30-second ad? It's a screen that comes up whenever there is a vote." Daschle protested that the quote was "taken out of context." The exposure of Daschle's record during the debates proved that the Daschle campaign's early strategy of avoiding debates had been wise, but, unfortunately for Daschle, the pressure had been too intense to avoid participation completely. The Daschle campaign's delaying tactics had left the senator facing a compact series of painful debates at a crucial moment in the campaign. The debates also showcased Thune as a focused, articulate, and relentless debater who had memorized Daschle's record. Even the leftist British newspaper the *Guardian* reported that Thune was "a nimble and aggressive debater, arguably stronger than the softly-spoken Senator."[30]

In the final weeks of the campaign, attention literally turned to the home front. In the spring of 2003, *Forbes* magazine had reported that the Daschles had bought a "seven-bedroom house on Washington DC's ritzy Foxhall Road. . . . The property itself is described as a French country colonial home, with four stories." The *New York Times* reported that the house was located "in one of Washington's toniest neighborhoods." One news outlet sought the property-tax records for the house in the summer of 2003 and discovered that the Daschles had taken a homestead tax exemption on the Washington home. The *Washington Post, Roll Call,* and political columnist Bob Novak soon followed up with reports of their own, but the *Argus Leader* ignored the story in 2003. The Daschle campaign claimed in 2003 that Linda Daschle had signed the homestead documents because she also paid D.C. income taxes, which made the arrangement legitimate. During the fall of 2004, however, the results of a Freedom of Information Act (FOIA) request with the D.C. tax office indicated that *Tom* Daschle had applied for and signed the homestead exemption. The homestead exemption forms required him to declare that the District of Columbia was his principal place of residence. The FOIA documents exposed the "Linda signed the documents" story as false and fueled the "Daschle is out of touch" narrative.[31]

The blogs dryly called the switching of the tax documents "Mansiongate." South Dakota reporter Bob Mercer also wrote a story about whether Daschle could claim property tax exemptions on his D.C. house as well as his house in Aberdeen, which Daschle owned and where his mother lived. The Mercer story ran with two photos of Daschle's home, and a website featured views of all the parts of the house, including the so-called loggia. Some observers used Daschle's declaration of the District of Columbia as his principal place of residence to question whether he should vote in South Dakota. Other people questioned whether his wife should vote, since she was the final signatory of the tax documents that declared the District of Columbia as her principal place of residence, she paid D.C. taxes, and she had never lived in South Dakota. Still others focused on Daschle's right to take two homestead exemptions, especially one on an expensive home in the nation's capital while he criticized "tax breaks for the rich." When a news station asked Daschle about the situation and the tax treatment on his Aberdeen home, Daschle said, "Who knows, some day I may even retire there." While the Thune campaign never questioned the Daschles' ability to vote in South Dakota or the propriety of his property-tax deductions, it did argue that the house flap signaled Daschle's drift away from his South Dakota roots. After the election, Democrats similarly criticized Karl Rove for taking the D.C. homestead exemption, and he was investigated for illegally voting in Texas while taking the D.C. exemption, but no charges were filed.[32]

The Daschle house discussion was also elevated by reports about Mrs. Daschle's lobbying. On October 3, the *Argus Leader* ran a story about Daschle's wife that addressed a few of the controversies brought on by her lobbying work. However, the article did not address in any detail the questions raised by extensive articles in such liberal publications as the *Washington Monthly, Slate,* and *LA Weekly.* The *Washington Monthly* article claimed that the "landmines in Linda Daschle's professional portfolio will make Hillary Clinton's pork futures and law-firm billings look like mousetraps." The Daschles argued that Linda did not lobby the Senate so her lobbying was acceptable, but the *Washington Monthly* reporter thought otherwise: "[W]hen it comes to lobbying Congress, does it really matter whether a congressional spouse lobbies her husband? The House Democrats on whom Daschle focuses her attention aren't likely to ignore calls from the majority leader's wife."[33]

Although the *Argus* story was not critical, its front-page article in a Sunday edition put Mrs. Daschle's lobbying in the public spotlight, generating much Internet commentary and the circulation of the more extensive *Washington Monthly* piece. Despite this scrutiny, the Daschle campaign made the odd decision to run television ads criticizing Thune's lobbying after he left Congress, further elevating the lobbying issue. One Daschle ad featured an older man saying that Thune was a lobbyist for a firm that worked for "the big drug companies. We know what that means." The Thune campaign responded that Thune had never lobbied for drug companies and focused on the hypocrisy of Daschle for criticizing anyone for lobbying. The Daschle campaign also ran an ad saying that Thune lobbied for a "big meatpacker" that opposed country-of-origin meat labeling (COOL), which was untrue. Thune had lobbied for a South Dakota company that processed meat into hamburger but was not a big meatpacker, and the president of the company sent a letter to Daschle saying that his company had never even taken a position on COOL. The Thune campaign ran the letter in state newspapers, again casting doubt on the credibility of Daschle's claims.

The Thune campaign then sent out a mailing criticizing the Daschles' D.C. lifestyle stemming from the income from Mrs. Daschle's lobbying.

The campaign also ran the *LA Weekly* story as an advertisement in newspapers, which generated a heated response from the Daschle camp. A new Daschle television ad asked, "What does it say about a man's character when he attacks another man's wife?" The Daschle campaign also organized a press conference of women supporting Daschle who criticized Thune's mailer. One woman at the press conference dismissed the lobbyist issue by saying, "It is a discussion. You can discuss conflicts of interest and the ethics involved but not the last two weeks of a hotly contested Senate campaign." At a counter-rally organized by the "Women for Thune" organization, some members argued that elections were designed to raise such issues. Reports also appeared during October noting that Daschle had received more donations from lobbyists than any other senator seeking reelection in 2004 and had also received donations from firms his wife lobbied for.[34]

The activities of Mrs. Daschle also became linked to the fairness of the *Argus Leader* when the wife of former Republican senator Larry Pressler released an open letter to the *Argus* in late October. Harriet Pressler said that she had been "repeatedly under investigation by the *Argus Leader* and subjected to false accusations from Democratic Party sources" and that the *Argus* "had a reporter follow me around constantly sticking a microphone and camera in my face, called my business acquaintances and wrote negative articles about me." The *Argus* had responded to Pressler during its earlier scrutiny by saying, "It is our duty to explore and investigate the financial activities of a Senate wife." In 2003, however, when the articles about Mrs. Daschle appeared, the *Argus* said that it would not report on the spouses of politicians. Pressler's letter fueled local talk radio and kept the issue of Mrs. Daschle's lobbying in the spotlight. The *Argus* did not publish the letter, but the Dakota Blog Alliance did. In contrast to the absence of criticism of Mrs. Daschle, the *Argus Leader* criticized Newt Gingrich's wife in 1995, editorializing that the "spouses of U.S. leaders should be held to a high standard: Not only should they avoid impropriety, they should avoid all appearances of impropriety."[35]

As the Daschle campaign faced problems on several fronts, the Thune campaign rolled out its siege gun. During the final ten days of the race, the Thune campaign ran a television ad that represented a culmination of the previous weeks' criticisms of Daschle for doublespeak. Entitled

"In His Own Words," the ad featured several video clips of Daschle speeches, including comments lauding Hillary Clinton, which firmly connected him to the national Democratic Party establishment. It also featured Daschle speaking to a California Democratic Party function and loudly proclaiming, "We will not surrender sacred ground, and that includes a woman's constitutional right to choose," which under- cut Daschle's campaign statements on the abortion issue and his refusal to admit that he was pro-choice. The ad also included two snippets of Daschle saying, "I'm a D.C. resident," which underscored the criticism he had received for the tax break on his house. The ad supplemented a dizzying array of radio and full-page newspaper ads that the Thune campaign had run, arguing that Daschle's positions had changed since his early days in politics and that he had become increasingly out of step with South Dakota voters. In one radio ad, a Democratic attorney from Daschle's hometown said Daschle had changed and that the attorney was voting for Thune. Daschle was paying, as Robert Penn Warren once wrote, the "cost of having a history."[36] During the final weekend of the campaign, yard signs began appearing all over South Dakota echoing Thune's campaign theme about making a change: "It's Time."

In the final weeks, the Daschle campaign began sending obvious distress signals. In mid-September, Daschle still trumpeted his ability to stop outside groups from advertising on his behalf and said, "Not one group has come in on my behalf. In fact, three outside groups that ran ads in 2002 have specifically stated they'll respect my request— the Democratic Senatorial Campaign Committee, the Sierra Club, and the League of Conservation Voters." During the September *Meet the Press* debate, Daschle blamed Thune for Republican senatorial committee ads running in South Dakota and said "John has the ability to pull those ads. . . . John has a personal responsibility for those negative attacks and he is accountable for them." At the same time, the Democratic Senatorial Campaign Committee did reaffirm that it would "respect Senator Tom Daschle's request" to stay out of the race. Despite the centrality of Daschle's opposition to third-party advertising to his campaign, however, Daschle's situation became so dire in the final weeks of the campaign that the Democratic Senatorial Campaign Committee began running ads attacking Thune. After the senatorial committee's intervention, the headlines in the *Aberdeen*

American News and *Roll Call* read, "Daschle Reneges on Outside Help Pledge" and "Ad Violates Promise to Shun Third-Party Help."[37]

The intervention of the Democratic senatorial committee was not shocking, given Daschle's position in the polls. During the last week of October, four polls were released showing the race to be deadlocked or giving a slight edge to Thune. A McLaughlin and Associates poll found Thune leading, 49 to 45 percent, and Daschle receiving a 44 percent unfavorable rating compared to Thune's 35 percent. A Mason-Dixon poll for the *Argus Leader* and KELO-Land television had Daschle leading, 49 to 47 percent. A Rasmussen Reports poll released a week before the election showed Thune winning, 49 to 46 percent, as did a Zogby poll released the same day (the Zogby poll originally showed Thune winning by six points but was revised to a three-point lead). Most troubling for Daschle was a subpart of the *Argus* poll, which found Daschle's support among Republicans dropping to 13 percent. Analysts said behind the scenes that Daschle needed roughly 20 percent of GOP voters to prevail.[38]

In the days before the election, Democrats in the crucial electoral state of Florida filed nine lawsuits claiming that Republicans were "trying to scare people away from the polls," and the same siren was soon sounded in South Dakota. The Four Directions Committee—which was led by the former executive director of the South Dakota Democratic Party and donated to and advertised for Democratic candidates—sought and received a tribal court order on Pine Ridge Indian Reservation limiting the access of GOP poll watchers to polling places. Tribal Judge Marina Fast Horse signed the order without notifying GOP attorneys or officials. The U.S. Attorney soon said that "it would be my interpretation of that order that it does not comply with the law, and I have let it be known to law enforcement that they should not be enforcing any order on the reservation which purports to keep the Republican Party away from the polls." National newspaper reports indicated that "rule No. 2" of the Democratic election handbook urged poll watchers to launch a preemptive strike "if no signs of intimidation techniques have emerged yet." The handbook instructed subsequent Democratic press releases to quote "party/minority/civil rights leadership as denouncing tactics that discourage people from voting."[39]

At 8:00 P.M. on the day before the election, Tom Daschle personally sued John Thune in federal court in Sioux Falls. Daschle alleged that Indian voters had been intimidated and requested a court order restricting GOP poll-watching efforts. The complaint totaled thirty-three pages (indicating that it had taken several days to prepare) and claimed that poll watchers in Charles Mix County had written down the license plate numbers of Democratic vans transporting voters home from the polls. Thune campaign manager Dick Wadhams condemned the lawsuit and called it "nothing short of an attempt to steal an election Tom Daschle knows he is about to lose tomorrow." Wadhams's press release said that the "hearing will be before Federal Judge Larry Piersol who was appointed by Daschle to federal court and served as Daschle's personal legal counsel in 1978." Daschle had told the Association of Trial Lawyers of America in an earlier speech that during his 1978 recount, he was "fortunate to be represented by a great lawyer and dear friend, Larry Piersol." Judge Piersol's wife was a Daschle donor and ally and had recently convened the press conference that denounced criticism of Mrs. Daschle; she was also listed as a Daschle supporter in an ad that appeared in the *Argus Leader* on election day. Outside the courthouse in downtown Sioux Falls, two hundred Thune supporters started a protest rally, and former senator Jim Abdnor, whom Daschle defeated in 1986, arrived and said, "We need voters to decide this race not judges." Others held up signs featured on the eve-of-election television news saying "Shame on Tom" and "Don't Steal Tom"; another, featuring a giant clock, read, "It's Time For A Change." One man in a Santa hat held up a sign that read, "Santa Is Voting 4 Thune!"[40]

The Daschle legal team alleged that GOP poll watchers were intimidating voters because they "would make faces" and were "taking notes" near a polling place. Daschle's lawyers relied on the testimony of one man, who had been a Howard Dean campaign worker in the Iowa caucuses and had arrived in South Dakota from Virginia twenty-four hours before. The Daschle witness explained that a GOP poll watcher "wrote something down. I think that would be intimidating." No Indians or county election officials testified to the existence of intimidation, however, and a Republican poll watcher who testified during the hearing called the Daschle witness a liar and dismissed his charges as ridiculous. During the hearing, lawyers discussed the recent decisions of two federal courts that had limited poll watching in Ohio, and the judge had prepared copies of the decisions for the hearing. The Sixth Circuit Court of Appeals then suddenly overturned the decisions, which was communicated to the judge during his deliberation. A *Rapid City Journal* story filed just after midnight also became part of the legal battle and the judge's deliberation. The story discussed intimidation claims and allegations of vote-buying that had "been sweeping Indian Country." A GOP official said that people had been stopping at the campaign office in Pine Ridge: "We've had people burst through our door and demand money. We'll ask what candidate, and they'll say Democrat."[41]

At 2:00 A.M. on election day, the judge rejected the Daschle legal team's call for a sweeping reorganization of the GOP poll-watching operation and only ordered that poll watchers in Charles Mix County not write down license-plate numbers. The blogs "live-blogged" the entire hearing by reporting updates given by court watchers, and the national blogospheric reaction was immense. Mocking the '60s mantra, the blogger Will Collier wrote, "The Whole World Wide Web Is Watching"; MSNBC even linked to the Dakota blogs' reporting of the hearing.[42]

On election day, Joseph Bottum of the *Weekly Standard* wrote that "last night, Tom Daschle threw his campaign into the shredder." Bottum questioned whether "Daschle's lawyers had to make their candidate a laughing-stock by filing the case with Judge Lawrence Piersol—a strong personal friend who was Daschle's own lawyer in the court contests during the 1978 election and who only four days before had given a radio interview praising Daschle." Bottum concluded that "even your buddy Piersol was too embarrassed to give you more than an order banning the writing down of license-plate numbers." Even some in the *Argus Leader* newsroom thought that Daschle had sealed his fate with the last-minute lawsuit. Internet blogs, talk radio, and cable television obsessed over the Daschle lawsuit on election day, and Wadhams released a statement again lambasting the proceeding: "This sham ruling will not stand. Daschle's desperate move is nothing less than an attempt to steal this election in the dark of night by a political crony in a judge's robe." Some local lawyers cringed at the open criticism of the judge, while others objected to his hearing the case at all.[43]

Whatever the reaction, the lawsuit and Wadhams's criticism reverberated throughout the state and national media on election day. No commentator saw the Daschle lawsuit as a wise political move. Bottum concluded, "Everybody who can walk, hobble, or crawl in Rapid City's Republican environs is going to get themselves into the voting booth today to show what they think of Tom Daschle's attempt to steal the election by lawsuit." One commentator on the *Rapid City Journal* blog said, "It's one thing to rearrange the deck chairs on the Titanic, another to grab the helm and guide the boat into the berg yourself."[44]

The eve-of-election lawsuit exposed the fissures in the Daschle campaign. In the final weeks, the Daschle campaign put out a call for reinforcements to friendly lobbyists and Hill staffers. The *Washington Post* wondered whether Daschle was "getting panicky" when his campaign brought "a planeload of Democratic lawyers, lobbyists and loyalists" to Sioux Falls. Larry Sabato reported that Democrats "told me they're scared to death that Daschle will lose." The intervention of the Democratic Senatorial Campaign Committee, which was helping fight close-run battles on several other fronts for candidates with resources that paled in comparison to Daschle's, was the most dramatic warning flare. The move renewed charges of hypocrisy because Daschle had made the blockade of outsiders a central defensive strategy of his campaign. Indeed, during the last debate on October 18, Daschle was still arguing that the "thing that has troubled me the most is John's unwillingness to keep the third-party groups out." In September, Daschle had said that the Democratic senatorial committee would respect his request to stay out of South Dakota, but in late October, when the race was deadlocked, he declared that he was powerless to stop them.[45]

The Daschle campaign also conducted "push-polling" in the final weeks by calling voters and asking such questions as "Would you still vote for Thune if you knew he advertised on pornographic websites?" The calls referred to a snafu resulting from the Thune campaign's Web-advertising distributor, who had mistakenly put some Thune ads on some racy sites. The Daschle campaign also arranged for "pastors" to call voters to criticize Thune, a tactic that was quickly detected and reported by Thune supporters who received the calls and sent the information to national blogs.[46]

On November 2, the voting finally started. Daschle spoke on KILI Radio on Pine Ridge Indian Reservation and called for 60 percent turnout: "If we reach 60 in Pine Ridge, we win the election." He also promised additional housing on the reservation: "If we can send money to Iraq, we can send money to Pine Ridge to build houses." In dramatic contrast to his earlier avoidance of liberal Democratic figures, Daschle arranged for call-ins from Hillary Clinton, Ted Kennedy, and Jesse Jackson to spur reservation voting. Kennedy, invoking his brother Robert's famous visits to Pine Ridge in the 1960s, called Daschle "a very, very good friend of mine, and a friend of the Kennedys, and most importantly a friend of Native Americans." Tim Giago, the former third-party candidate, also broadcast a call for Daschle votes. Daschle's placards calling him "A Strong Voice For Indian Country" dotted the reservation. Thune also called in to the tribal radio stations, but he spent election day visiting towns east of the Missouri River, including Dell Rapids, Watertown, and Brookings. He ended his campaign in my hometown of Madison, home of Senator Karl Mundt— the only South Dakotan to be elected to four terms in the U.S. Senate, a record that was at stake on election day as Daschle sought his fourth term. The campaign war rooms were alive with reports of problems from the polling places. One Democratic lawyer on Standing Rock Indian Reservation interfered with election workers and when challenged said "F—— you, do something about it." A deputy sheriff soon removed the man from the polling place. There was also an attempt to keep the polls open late on the Pine Ridge reservation and other random reports of problems, which did not approach the level of problems reported in 2002. Daschle said on the nightly news that there was no intimidation during the election and stated that he thought his lawsuit had helped.[47]

The first returns signaled a close finish. After 363 of 827 precincts had reported, the race was tied, with each candidate at 50 percent. In comparison to the 2002 Senate race, however, Thune cut his losses in the rural East River counties. Daschle needed a solid lead when the West River precincts—which close later because they are in the mountain time zone—started to report. With 513 precincts reporting, Thune took a 51–49 percent lead, but the large Democratic precincts on the Pine Ridge and Rosebud Indian reservations had yet to report. The Thune campaign hoped that a sizeable lead in Republican-leaning Rapid City would counterbalance the heavily Democratic reservation returns. About 1:00 A.M., NBC called Ohio for President Bush, ensuring his victory and disproving the day's early exit polls. The final absentee votes were soon counted in Minnehaha, the state's largest county, where Sioux Falls is located. Thune lost Minnehaha County by a thousand fewer votes than in 2002, continuing the trend of better showings for Thune in East River counties. Confirming that Daschle's hopes were dwindling, Senator McGovern was interviewed on television in the early morning and said, "It's too soon to rule him out." In a ballroom at the Sheraton Hotel in Sioux Falls, the Daschle supporters (who had been treated to a boisterous performance by the local band Kory and the Fireflies earlier in the evening) slowly dissipated. With 16 precincts yet to report, including all of the large Democratic precincts on Pine Ridge, Thune held a nine-thousand-vote lead. The reporters began murmuring about the numbers not adding up for Daschle, and the blogs posted pictures of the Fat Lady. Daschle finally called his family together and reviewed the results: "This isn't going to happen." Daschle called Thune to concede at 3:00 A.M. The call lasted twenty-nine seconds.[48]

CHAPTER NINE

RECKONING

It's a staggering blow.

—George McGovern

After the terse concession call from Senator Daschle, Thune hugged his wife, his daughters, and his brother Rich. Harold, his eighty-five-year-old father, was sleeping in the next room and heard the commotion. Harold's Norwegian stoicism faded for a moment, and his eyes twinkled with pride after hearing of his son's victory. John Thune had won, 51 to 49 percent, defeating the most powerful and best-financed Democrat in the country by 4,508 votes. At 3:15 A.M., Thune greeted his weary troops. He claimed victory alongside former senator Jim Abdnor, who had introduced Thune to the world of politics. Election night was the eighteenth anniversary of Daschle's victory over Abdnor, whose defeat of the liberal icon Senator George McGovern had helped usher in the Age of Reagan and years of retrenchment for the American left. By embracing the legacy of Reaganism, Thune had defeated the man who had defeated his mentor. After Thune's early-morning remarks, the reportorial scrum charged the stage, pinning him down at the dais. At 3:25 A.M., the *Argus Leader* began printing its third and final edition of the morning newspaper. The headline: "THUNE WINS"[1]

The *New York Times* called Thune's victory a "historic political upset," and *USA Today* called it "a political seismic shock," noting that the last time a Senate party leader had lost a reelection bid was 1952. *Time* magazine headlined Thune as "The Giant Killer" and reported that Thune "will not just be another freshman Senator. He will be a conquering hero—the man who vanquished the G.O.P.'s 18-year obsession." The *Roll Call* headline was "John Thune: A Star Is Born." *Newsweek* ran a two-page photo of Thune's early-morning victory speech and, like *Time,* deemed him a "Giant-Killer." *The Hill* reported in subsequent weeks that Thune was the "highest-profile member" of the new class of GOP senators and had "already been a staple on television talk shows since the election." *Roll Call* reported that Thune had "already been accepted with open arms by the media as a new national spokesman for Republicans." The Sunday after the election, Thune appeared on ABC's famous *This Week,* the show that David Brinkley had made a pillar of establishment commentary and news, along with the Democrats' new star, Senator Barack Obama of Illinois.[2]

Thune's victory was a blow to the national Democratic Party. Daschle took a place in history alongside Tom Foley, the Democratic Speaker of the House, who had lost his reelection bid in 1994, thereby becoming the first Speaker to be defeated for reelection since 1862. Foley commented that Daschle's demise was a painful memory of a time he wanted to forget. The *New York Times* deemed Daschle's defeat "another glum marker for the party" and predicted a "huge psychological blow to Democrats." South Dakota Democrats agreed. Rick Hauffe, the former executive director of the state party, compared Daschle's loss to McGovern's in 1980: "This will hurt far, far longer than the last time South Dakotans thoughtlessly dismissed a great statesman in return for a phony campaign pitch that it's time for a change." Observed South Dakota Democratic activist Todd Epp, "We got our asses handed to us." Epp reported that a "long-time Democrat who is 'in the know' says this election may have set the Democrats back in this state 50 years." Nationally, the political editor of the *Progressive* endured "gut-gripping pain. The cold reality—Bush's margin in the popular vote, Kerry's wooden concession speech, Daschle's defeat in the Senate, every branch of government controlled by a band of emboldened rightwing Republicans—was almost too much to take in." The *Economist* reported that the fall election would be "remembered as the blackest of days for the Democratic Party."[3]

During Daschle's 1992 reelection bid, Democrats held a one-hundred-vote margin in the House of Representatives and fifty-seven Senate seats; moreover, they won the White House that fall. The Democrats' post-Reagan surge was short-lived, however. In 1994, the Democrats lost both houses of Congress. Thirty-two Democratic House incumbents were defeated, including Speaker Foley, and the Republicans gained fifty-two seats in the House. Two Democratic Senators even switched parties to become Republicans. Five Democratic governors were defeated, including three-term New York governor and presidential hopeful Mario Cuomo. During the next cycle, thirty-five-year-old John Thune defeated a Daschle protégé to become South Dakota's lone House member. In 1995, Daschle became the leader of the Senate Democrats; he helped save the embattled Clinton presidency in 1999 and became the face of the Democratic Party. After the GOP recaptured the White House in 2000, Daschle's Senate Democrats and their filibuster power became the main obstacle to Republican lawmaking in Washington.

Daschle's 2004 defeat thus became a symbolic as well as real victory for the critics of Democratic obstructionism in the Senate. With Daschle's defeat, the number of Democratic Senators dwindled to forty-four, the smallest Democratic caucus since the 1930s. The Republicans also gained ground in the House, and Bush became the first president since the New Deal to win congressional seats for his party during his reelection bid. Kimberly Strassel of the *Wall Street Journal* concluded that "the big daddy came with the overthrow of Mr. Daschle. That ouster, the first time in more than 50 years a Senate party leader was exiled, was as much a repudiation of obstructionism as it was Mr. Daschle's own record." Citing the "Ghost of Daschle's Past," she said not to "underestimate the psychological power Mr. Daschle's defeat will wield over middle-America Democrats." Michael Tomasky, editor of the liberal magazine the *American Prospect,* said that in 2006 some Democratic senators "won't want to risk what they inevitably interpret as what happened to Tom Daschle: He was obstructionist, and he lost."[4]

Beyond the symbolic and psychological consequences, Daschle's defeat would change the substantive workings of the Senate. Because Daschle served as "chief obstructionist," Senator George Allen of Virginia boasted that defeating Daschle was comparable to "picking up three Senate seats." When introducing the new Republican senators elected in 2004 (dubbed "The Magnificent Seven"), Allen said that "voters sent a clear message for less taxation, less regulation, and less litigation." The group included the first Cuban-American senator, the first Republican senator in history from Louisiana, a GOP replacement for Fritz Hollings (who had served as a Democratic senator from South Carolina since 1966), and Thune, the first challenger to defeat a

Senate leader in fifty-two years. Liberal columnist Al Hunt conceded that "Tom Daschle's loss does hurt three times as much" and would "change the landscape" of the Senate. Political analyst Charlie Cook said that Daschle's loss was "likely to reverberate around the chamber for some time to come." With the disappearance of southern Democrats, the Senate would also be more regionally polarized. The southern Democratic faction in the Senate, which had always kept Senate Democratic leaders Lyndon Johnson and Mike Mansfield busy unifying the Democratic ranks, was almost gone. The number of southern Democrats in the Senate declined from twelve in 1980 to four in 2005.[5]

Although the slow erosion of Democratic power in Washington since 1980 involved many losses, the defeat of the party's Senate leader was especially deflating. The Democrats' ability to advance a political agenda in Washington ebbed. The editors of the *New York Times* warily noted that the "Democrats' last redoubt in Washington—their minority outpost in the Senate—became considerably shakier last Tuesday with the fall of their leader, Senator Tom Daschle of South Dakota." The national Democratic Party, the *Times* reported, was "seen as lacking any obvious leaders in the wake of the November defeat of Tom Daschle."[6]

Thune's victory, as some hoped and others feared, promised to loosen the logjam in the Senate. Analysts predicted that some Democrats from GOP-leaning states might be more compromising in the aftermath of Daschle's demise. *The Hill* reported that "the verb 'to Daschle'" could "be loosely defined as 'to aggressively target for defeat a liberal Democrat who represents an otherwise solidly Republican state." The *New York Times* discussed being "Daschled," or the act of blocking Republican legislation and subsequently losing reelection in a Republican-leaning state. Senator Dick Durbin, the Democratic minority whip, conceded, "We have to pick our battles," signaling a departure from the previous policy of massive resistance all along the line separating the parties. The *Los Angeles Times* predicted that GOP gains in the Senate would finally enable passage of the long-stalled energy bill and the gun-maker liability legislation, both of which had animated the Daschle-Thune race. The new Senate dynamics would be a dramatic contrast to those of the 108th Congress, in which tort reform, welfare reform, the energy bill, judicial nominations, gun-maker liability legislation, the asbestos legislation, the faith-based initiative, and the highway bill had all been blocked. The *Great Falls Tribune* concluded that the chances of passing the energy bill, which had triggered Thune's entry into the race, "were enhanced by the electoral defeat of Tom Daschle, the minority leader from South Dakota who for the past three years orchestrated much of the Senate opposition."[7]

The list of bills blocked in the 108th Congress could have been even longer if Daschle had not been fighting to survive at home. A Democratic lobbyist, speaking of Daschle's role as opposition leader while representing a red state, said that "it hurt his effectiveness at home and in Washington." A Democratic aide said, "Daschle's organization became too focused on home-state concerns as Daschle's own Senate seat became increasingly in peril." With Thune as his opponent, Daschle's ability to give unqualified attention to opposing President Bush had eroded, and Senate Democrats did not have the option of replacing Daschle—his entire campaign depended on his having the clout of a Senate leader. The Thune challenge also dried up resources for other Democratic Senate candidates in 2002, when the Republicans regained the Senate and Daschle lost the majority leader post, and again in 2004, when Republicans consolidated their control of the Senate. Some critics in 2002 blamed Daschle for invoking a bland set of Democratic issues during the campaign; some thought these were designed to aid his South Dakota colleague, Tim Johnson (whose reelection Daschle had called his highest priority). At the end of 2004, despite earlier promises to the contrary, the Democratic Senatorial Campaign Committee also expended precious resources trying to save Daschle, resources that could have been used in other close-run battles in other states. Former Daschle staffer and *Washington Monthly* writer Amy Sullivan said after the election that it was foolish "to have a leader who hails from a hardcore red state" because it left national Democrats in an "untenable position." Because of the mounting pressure from Thune's challenge in the fall, Daschle embraced certain GOP policies such as extending Bush's tax cuts. Instead of attacking the president's foreign policy for failing "miserably," Daschle ran ads of himself hugging the president.[8]

Beyond the GOP's new legislative advantages, Republican Senate gains also came as the aged Rehnquist majority on the Supreme Court looked to retire their robes. Eight of the nine justices were over sixty-five years old, and there had not been a new appointment since

1994. Not since the 1820s had there been such long-term stability on the court, but vacancies were imminent. Chief Justice William Rehnquist announced eight days before the election that he needed chemotherapy, and the day before the vote, he announced that he would not be physically able to attend court arguments. Given the cumulative age of the Supreme Court justices, Bush would have the opportunity to reshape the court as Presidents Reagan and Franklin D. Roosevelt had done. On the future of the federal judiciary, Thune's defeat of Daschle was subordinate only to Bush's victory, according to Lyn Nofziger, Reagan's longtime political advisor. Nofziger called Daschle's defeat the "Republicans' most significant victory" and said that "Mr. Bush will probably no longer have to contend with Democratic filibusters preventing the Senate from voting on his judicial appointees." In the Daschle-led 108th Congress, the filibuster had been used for the first time to block confirmation votes on federal appeals court judges. Conservative political commentator George Will argued after the election that the president should renominate the ten appellate court nominees who had been blocked in the Daschle Senate and vow, in the words of General Ulysses S. Grant, to "fight it out on this line, if it takes all summer." The Bush administration agreed. The weakening of Democratic power in the Senate facilitated President Bush's attempt to leave what the *New York Times* called "an enduring conservative ideological imprint on the nation's judiciary."[9]

The Senate Democrats, who were the best positioned to halt GOP initiatives using the filibuster, regrouped after the election. Senator Harry Reid, at home in tiny Searchlight, Nevada (which Bush had won by twenty percentage points) received word of Daschle's defeat at 3:00 A.M. on the morning after the election and called Daschle to offer his condolences. "Well, I guess we're it," Reid said with what the *Washington Post* called "a dark laugh." He was on the phone to his colleagues by 6:00 A.M. and by 8:00 A.M. had secured the votes to become Daschle's successor. Reid, Daschle's deputy since 1998, showed early signs of defiance, saying after the election, "I would always rather dance than fight. But I know how to fight." Over the next several weeks, he set out to prove it. He soon said that he thought filibustering judges was appropriate. A few weeks later, Reid deemed Justice Clarence Thomas "an embarrassment to the Supreme Court"; he eventually called Alan Greenspan, chairman of the Federal Reserve, "one of the biggest political hacks we have here in Washington." Reid consolidated control over Democratic leadership committees and established a fifteen-person war room, headed by Senator Edward Kennedy's former press secretary, to combat the Republican message. Reid concluded that Daschle's defeat meant Reid had to bolster his ability to "fight the radical agenda coming from the White House."[10]

Although Reid prepared to fight, Senate Democrats lost leverage after the fall elections. Reid had four fewer Democratic colleagues than Daschle had the previous Congress. The *New York Times* urged Reid to filibuster when possible and "to seize the occasional chance for compromise" as he rallied "Democrats from their election day drubbing." Still, a *Times* reporter surmised, it remained "a time when Democrats can do little more on Capitol Hill than complain." The year 2005 brought final approval of several federal appeals court nominations and major pieces of legislation that had been filibustered and blocked in the Senate during Daschle's tenure. The sweeping energy bill that had been blocked throughout the Bush presidency finally passed during the summer after Daschle's defeat. The *Washington Post* reported that several bills passed in 2005 "after years of partisan impasses and legislative failures." Robert Novak reported that GOP Senate leader Bill Frist achieved more legislative victories in 2005 in part because he no longer faced "the implacable Tom Daschle as Democratic leader." After the death of William Rehnquist in 2005, Democrats in the Senate were not able to block Bush's appointment of John Roberts as the new chief justice.[11]

While Thune's victory scrambled the dynamics of power in the Senate, it also underscored the reasons for the nation's quarter-century drift to the right. Daschle's defeat, fundamentally, was caused by the continuing momentum of political conservatism. Although safely within the Democratic camp during the liberal ascendancy of the 1960s, Daschle faced the burgeoning strength of Reaganism when he made his long-planned run for Congress in 1978. After Reagan's victory in 1980, the Democrats began a long retreat. In Daschle's early House races and his bid for the Senate in 1986, he compensated for the shifting political environment by running focused and disciplined campaigns and projecting an image of moderation in keeping with the anti-1960s themes embraced by the New Democrats of the 1980s and 1990s. Without a serious challenger during the eighteen years after his first Senate victory, Daschle had climbed the leadership ladder. By 2004, Daschle found himself as the titular head of an increasingly strident Democratic Party, which had ended its 1990s flirtation with centrism, and the chief opponent of a president who was the heir of Reaganism.

The precariousness of Daschle's political standing became increasingly evident in 2004, as Daschle was whipsawed by an obligation to lead a national party tacking left and the demands of a red constituency at home. Memories of Daschle's earlier political positions, which underscored his migration to the left, also kept coming back to haunt him. The chickens came home to roost, in the earthy phrasing bandied about during the campaign. The editors of the *Rapid City Journal* said in late October, "Those footsteps Sen. Tom Daschle is hearing are from his own record catching up with him." Daschle's attempts to disguise his movement to the left made him appear cynical, an image reinforced by a Kerry campaign sustaining the same withering criticism on the national level.[12]

Daschle's leftward drift undermined his support in South Dakota. His first opponent in 1978, Leo Thorsness, said that Daschle was "an OK guy to start with" but decided that "he had become too partisan over the years, especially after becoming Senate leader." *Time* magazine concluded that "ultimately, the out-of-synch nature of Daschle's career may have been the most critical factor in Thune's victory." The *Washington Post* bluntly reported that "in the end, the conflict between Daschle's duties as the leader of a largely liberal Democratic caucus and his representation of a red state proved irreconcilable." One South Dakota voter put it simply: "I'm not a liberal Democrat. I'm afraid Tom is." Although National Public Radio reported that Daschle was a "self-described liberal," Daschle admitted in his book that "most South Dakotans are conservatives," betraying the central incongruity that bedeviled his campaign. The election day exit poll found that only 16 percent of South Dakota voters identified themselves as liberals, while 39 percent said that they were conservatives. Daschle, according to political scientist Larry Sabato, thus "had a conflict of interest with his red state."[13]

Daschle attempted to downplay his liberal stances during the campaign by claiming to be supportive of President Bush, saying that he did not believe abortions "ought to be allowed," praising the war effort in Iraq while dismissing the failure to find weapons of mass destruction, opposing gay marriage, and supporting extension of the Bush tax cuts. Such tactics prompted Thune's "say one thing here and do another thing in Washington" mantra and ignited a storm of commentary about Daschle's duplicity, which metastasized into a campaign issue. One blog reader in South Dakota said that he voted against Daschle "in protestation of his South Dakota/Washington D.C. alter egos." Another blog reader and South Dakota expatriate said, "Tom Daschle has brought new meaning to the term 'phony,' as a millionaire common man who is simultaneously a decrier and beneficiary of lobbyists, tax dodges, third-party political ads, crafty parliamentary tactics, and legislative gridlock. Claiming to be a pro-life Catholic, yet operating as a fundraiser for NARAL, he has been dealing identity politics from the bottom of the deck." A blog reader from Harrisburg said, "Daschle finally reached the height of hypo-crisy by bashing Thune for being a 'Washington lobbyist' while Daschle himself is married to one and reaping the benefits. And to keep insisting he is against abortion. . . . People are not THAT stupid." Scott Waltman, a reporter for the *Aberdeen American News,* believed that "abortion was the issue that started Daschle down a pretty steep slope" and thought that "Daschle should have simply said 'I am pro-choice and here's why.'" "But," Waltman noted, "his 'I'm anti-abortion' answer looked as if he was trying to work both sides of the fence." The communications director for Jim Abdnor in the 1980 campaign to defeat Senator George McGovern said that "both McGovern and Daschle have betrayed themselves with their quests for higher political power" and "became, out of the necessity to fulfill their ambitions, cynical and disingenuous."[14]

Such sentiments hardened into what University of South Dakota political science professor Bill Richardson called the "authenticity factor" in the race: "Thune and Bush weren't pretending to be any-thing they weren't (their strongly held religious beliefs being one obvious and visible example), but Daschle and, to a much greater extent, Kerry presented numerous 'visuals' that were almost hilariously pretentious." Dakota State University history professor Chris Maynard concluded that the "main thing Daschle has had going for him over the years is that people thought he was an average guy (his driving tours for example). When voters saw Daschle as just another politician, he lost his edge." Daschle supporter Sam Hurst conceded that Daschle "tried to put on an orange vest and talked about pheasant hunting, but it felt hollow." Hurst noted that Daschle did not tackle the question "Why have you changed?" According to Hurst, "Instead of having that conversation, we were forced to listen to his frail protestations that he had not changed at all." As a Daschle supporter, Hurst praised Daschle's new complexity but condemned his refusal to explain his transformation. Kevin Woster, a reporter at the *Rapid City Journal*, also noted "Daschle's failure in the authenticity area" and echoed the Hurst criticism: "Rather than facing those dangerous issues honestly—why not say, hell yes, I voted to increase the gas tax, and look what good came to South Dakota because of it—he tried doubletalk." Woster concluded that "more honesty and less spin would have served him well." Longtime Sioux Falls television anchor Steve Hemmingsen suggested that "the Democrats might try a little honesty with their candidates" and noted that "Senators Tom Daschle and Tim Johnson run under a 'don't ask, don't tell' banner" regarding their party and its positions.[15]

Daschle's tactics raised doubts about the sincerity of his beliefs, doubts that could not be papered over with advertising blitzes, a problem John Kerry also faced on the national level. The *New Republic* concluded that Kerry's "advantage in money did not offset a disadvantage in authenticity." Liberal commentator Tim Noah said that "Kerry didn't get anywhere with his hunting-trip photo op, or with frequent affirmations of his Catholic faith. Democrats, I fear, are doomed to be thought phonies whenever they play this game, even when they aren't." When Kerry the wealthy Brahmin tried to explain in Spring Green, Wisconsin, that he understood the financial difficulties of putting children through college, the farmers and laborers in the crowd "audibly laughed at him." At a meeting with farmers in Missouri, Teresa Heinz Kerry promoted organic food. A Missouri hog farmer, who was a Democrat and Kerry supporter, thought the meeting was disastrous. He said, "Mrs. Kerry, you've got to understand that hog farmers just freak out when they hear people telling them to go organic. . . . A lot of farmers think of those organics as some kind of elitist lunatic-fringe thing."[16]

The Republican strategist Lee Atwater once called Massachusetts governor Michael Dukakis an "honest liberal," a description also applicable to Daschle's mentor, George McGovern. Daschle sought to avoid the fate of Dukakis and McGovern by downplaying liberal positions and projecting an image of nonpartisan moderation early in his career, but such a strategy proved difficult to pursue in 2004, when he was Democratic leader and Howard Dean had resurrected the "Democratic wing of the Democratic Party." Dean's insurgency and his criticism of leading Democrats quickened the debate about the core principles of the Democratic Party, a debate that overshadowed the aftermath of Daschle's defeat and exposed the divisions between the organizations of Daschle and South Dakota congresswoman Stephanie Herseth. After the election, Democratic lawyer and activist Todd Epp said, "Herseth seemed embarrassed to be a Democrat," and he criticized his party for being "ashamed of our 'Democraticness.'"[17]

Herseth's conservative posture, most observers agreed, hurt Daschle. By voting for the federal marriage amendment (Daschle filibustered it), supporting the flag desecration amendment (Daschle opposed it), running ads touting her "A" rating from the National Rifle Association (Daschle received an "F"), and saying that she would vote for President Bush if the presidential race were thrown into the House of Representatives, Herseth consistently interfered with Daschle's effort to project the image of a moderate South Dakota Democrat. Daschle staffers were "furious" with Herseth and believed that "she undercut his position in trying to define her own" and "played into the anti-Daschle ads." Dave Kranz conceded that Herseth "alienated many Daschle loyalists who think her positions on gun issues and the marriage amendment undermined" Daschle. Herseth exposed Daschle's liberal positions more effectively than the GOP could; when Daschle tried to smooth over the differences, he widened his own credibility gap with voters. Daschle refused to adopt George McGovern's 1980 strategy of running for reelection as an unapologetic liberal, come what may. Instead, he tried to avoid the liberal image and substituted a focus on clout and Senate seniority, but Herseth's candidacy, along with GOP ads and bloggers, disrupted the delivery of his sanitized message.[18]

While this is an understandable political strategy, the Daschle camp's dependence on message control proved costly. Some who did not oppose Daschle's stances on particular issues nevertheless turned against him when his credibility declined. Rob Regier of the South Dakota Family Policy Council said that "for those who didn't care so much about the moral values, it was Daschle's duplicity on those issues that tripped him up—the two faces of Tom Daschle." Joe Cella of the Ave Maria List quoted Sir Walter Scott—"O what a tangled web we weave / when first we practice to deceive"—and pointed to Daschle's "opportunistic betrayal of his beliefs that he once shared with South Dakota voters, particularly on the pro-life and pro-family issues. When that happened, he began to weave a tangled web of deceptions of who he was, what he actually believed, and how he voted, which ultimately snuffed out his political career." According to the exit poll, 51 percent of voters listed being a strong leader, taking a clear stand on issues, or being honest and trustworthy as their most important quality in a candidate; they strongly preferred Thune. Daschle's perception as a double-talker was politically costly in the Age of McCain and the "Straight Talk Express," Howard Dean's blunt condemnations of Democratic vacillation, and Internet scrutiny, which diminished Daschle's ability to control the flow of information to voters via a friendly press.[19]

A central question for the Thune campaign was how to expose Daschle's contradictory record without validating the Daschle campaign's warnings of negative attacks. Thune started by aggressively making a case against Daschle at the August farm show debate, invoking hard evidence such as the ethanol filibuster. Although Daschle became more aggressive in the subsequent *Meet the Press* debate, the uncharacteristic deviation from his usually calm demeanor appeared awkward. In subsequent debates, which focused to a greater extent on issues that divided the candidates, Daschle's record became increasingly exposed. The *Argus Leader*'s Dave Kranz concluded that one of the Daschle campaign's flaws was that he agreed "to far too many debates, allowing voters to see too often the disdain the two men had for each other." The problem was not animosity during the debates, which were generally civil affairs, but Daschle's exposure on many issues, which made his conduct in the debates seem like a high-wire act. Patrick Lalley, the political editor of the *Argus*, also conceded that the debates proved to be "huge" in influencing voters' perceptions and that Daschle had performed poorly in them. Throughout the fall, the mutually reinforcing debates and television advertising slowly reconfigured Daschle's public image. The *Wall Street Journal* explained that "voters are being told about his Jekyll-and-Hyde routine."[20]

The debates corresponded with the onrush of television ads in the fall. One postelection letter to the editor from a man in Platte said that Thune's television ads "shined the bright light of truth on the dark nooks and crannies of [Daschle's] voting record on abortion, same-sex marriage and his blocking of conservative judicial nominees." Daschle supporter and *Rapid City Journal* columnist Sam Hurst thought that the "In His Own Words" ad—which featured Daschle talking about the "sacred" right to choose and saying, "I'm a D.C. resident"—was devastating: "The first time I saw the commercial, I knew the election was over. The Thune campaign ran it a hundred times, but once was enough. It was a dagger in the heart." Daschle's campaign manager, Steve Hildebrand, also said after the election that the "In His Own Words" ad was crippling, as did George McGovern's longtime chief of staff, George Cunningham. There was no way to respond. Statements in the ad from Daschle's own mouth contradicted the core claims of his campaign.[21]

Some observers believed that the Daschle campaign had mistakenly avoided the controversial aspects of Daschle's record early in the race. Denise Ross, a *Rapid City Journal* reporter, said that "Tom Daschle's campaign team failed him." She said that the 2002 NARAL letter "along with Daschle's criticism of President Bush's buildup to war in Iraq, the new $1.9 million house and the 'I'm [a] DC resident tape,' was lying around like an unguarded ammunitions pile in Iraq." Ross argued that while the Daschle campaign "couldn't stop Thune from firing away . . . they could have flushed him out earlier." Jennifer Duffy of the *Cook Political Report* rejected the "flush out early" theory and argued that Daschle's early advertising provided "ample evidence that Daschle's position was too weak to sustain the fallout from the revelation that perhaps he is not as pro-life as South Dakota voters had been led to believe."[22]

Denise Ross also pointed to the machinations surrounding Tim Giago's April abandonment of his third-party Senate bid and noted that the "Daschle campaign let Giago make all the public statements about what transpired during that meeting." In the fall, "people remembered that Giago had intimated big promises from Daschle, and they didn't like being shut out of the Sept. 25 gathering. By then, the buzz drowned out Daschle's assertions that he had not promised Giago anything." If the Daschle campaign had publicly defied Giago after the April meeting, however, Giago might well have stayed in the race, which they justifiably saw as a major threat. They had little option but to remain quiet and hope that the matter would pass, which, given the absence of reporting on the April meeting by the state's major newspapers, would likely have happened without the reporting of the *Lakota Journal* and the Dakota blogs. The house issue, first raised in 2003, also did not fade away. The national press and blogs often discussed the house when the issue reemerged in the fall. The *Argus Leader* conceded after the election that it was finally forced to cover the issue after the national newspaper and Internet scrutiny. After the election, national commentators routinely cited the house as a reason for Daschle's defeat.[23]

Other observers adhered to a psychological theory of the election and claimed that an inferiority complex explained the result. Daschle supporter Sam Hurst said that when politicians "lose touch with the soil," South Dakotans vote them out, which "fits our insecurities." The executive editor of the *Argus Leader* only half jokingly cited the "lutefisk factor," noting that "back here in South Dakota, the idea that our senior senator drove a Jaguar and lived in a $1.9 million house in Washington—the in-your-face message of [the] relentless ad campaign in the final weeks before the election—took root." Daschle had embraced "a lifestyle that appeared to be flamboyant and, in the end, un-Norwegian." The *Argus* editor cited the comments of the editor of the *Mobridge Tribune*: "We've got this inferiority complex in South Dakota. We think that when somebody gets too big for their britches, we have to knock them down." Chuck Raasch, a former South Dakota reporter who had joined Gannett News Service in Washington, found in the "Daschle and McGovern defeats the double-edged complex of inferiority and superiority" in South Dakota, which "produces a culture that rewards the conflicting traits of modesty, industry and success against the odds, while punishing inattention, self-importance and distance. Call it the 'Big Britches Syndrome.'" Dave Kranz of the *Argus* continued this theme, concluding that voters thought Daschle "was getting too big for his britches." Doug Grow, a former South Dakotan who went to work for the Minneapolis newspaper, also said that "Daschle got too big for his britches." From the Twin Cities, Grow sneered, "Modesty is the state's No. 1 value. Mediocrity is all South Dakotans feel they deserve. . . . Real South Dakotans don't join country clubs. They buy their suits at Penney's and sit down to dinners of roast beef and mashed potatoes."[24]

Such commentaries did not adequately address the inherent conflict between Daschle's increasingly liberal record, especially when compared to his early years in politics, and the conservative tendencies of his state. Moreover, what some observers saw as an inferiority complex, others saw as prairie populism, an aversion to Daschle's links to wealthy liberal donors. George McGovern's former chief of staff recognized the state's skepticism of "people who go to the country club" but linked the sentiment to the state's "old strain of populism," not a psychological malady. Beginning in the 1970s, conservatives increasingly donned the mantle of political populism when critiquing 1960s liberalism. In 2004, the political cost of Daschle's association with coastal liberalism and Hollywood elites indicated the continuing influence of conservative populism. A South Dakota Democrat who supported Thune said, Daschle's "been in DC too long. He's gotten away from his roots."[25]

National political trends also bolstered the Thune campaign. Political scientist Bill Richardson concluded that Thune benefited "because he and Bush ran symmetrical campaigns—many of their positions and issues were mutually reinforcing and appealed to the same constituencies. I can't recall where Daschle and Kerry ever hit harmonious campaign notes." Daschle's statements prior to the war in Iraq and the general debate over the war on terror also highlighted divisions between the national parties and hurt Daschle with some voters. A South Dakota truck driver said, "I'm tired of Daschle. The war on terror is the biggest reason. I'm pretty sure he's not helping the president fight this war. He fights the Republicans like hell in Washington, but comes back here with another story." While those who considered Iraq the most important issue in the campaign favored Daschle (probably because they opposed the war), 59 percent of South Dakota voters overall favored the decision to go to war in Iraq and 66 percent trusted Bush to handle the war on terrorism. Sixty-two percent of voters generally approved of Bush's job performance, and 69 percent of voters also said that the economy was "excellent" or "good." Bush carried the state by twenty points. The issues most important to voters in South Dakota and nationally favored the GOP. In South Dakota, 43 percent of voters listed moral values or terrorism as the issue most important to them in the election, while only 20 percent chose the categories of health care, the economy, or jobs.[26]

Bush's advantage over Kerry in South Dakota also underscored the politics of association and the danger of Daschle's embrace of Michael Moore's summer movie *Fahrenheit 9/11* and of indulging celebrities in general. After the election, political columnist Andrew Ferguson recalled that during the "gala premiere" in Washington, "Moore was greeted curbside by the chairman of the Democratic National Committee, Terry McAuliffe." Senator Bob Graham of Florida bragged that "half the Democratic Senate" attended the premiere, including Daschle, who had adjourned the Senate to attend. When John Kerry attended a celebrity fund-raiser at Radio City Music Hall, where John Mellencamp sang about Bush being a "cheap thug who sacrifices our young," Kerry said that the celebrities in attendance represented "the heart and soul of our country." Columnist Mark Steyn said after the election that the "American people don't want to be condescended to by ketchup heiresses, billionaire currency specu-lators, $20-million-a-picture Hollywood pretty boys, and multi-millionaire documentary-makers posing as bluecollar lardbutts." After the election, Daschle attended a gala awards ceremony at the Kennedy Center at which Alec Baldwin and Susan Sarandon received Defender of Democracy awards from People for the American Way. Chevy Chase, who spoke before Daschle, called President Bush a "dumb f——" and said, "I'm no f——g clown either. . . . This guy started a jihad." Daschle said nothing about the "startling meanness" of these comments. Another Joseph Welch moment passed. If Daschle had condemned the hyperbole of the left during the 2004 campaign, such comments might have helped him in South Dakota but also would have alienated the base of his party.[27]

The prominence of social issues in the race also hurt Daschle. Exit polls indicated that 25 percent of South Dakotans listed "moral values" as their greatest concern, and 81 percent of those voters preferred Thune. Family Policy Council executive director Rob Regier said "one need only look at how desperately Daschle tried to quiet the storm in the last couple weeks of the campaign to see what drove the vote. He conducted phone campaigns with 'pastors' plugging for the senator; sent mailings about how he used to be an altar boy and how he abhorred abortion; and ran ads claiming he was as pro-life and pro-family as the next guy." Daschle, said Regier, "knew where he was bleeding votes." The hemorrhaging prompted the Daschle campaign to run a stunning ad touting his pro-life credentials and his opposition to gay marriage. The Daschle ad did not mention his pro-choice votes, his work for NARAL and Emily's List, and his vote against the federal marriage amendment, and thereby fueled more charges of hypocrisy and contributed to the erosion of his credibility. A blog reader commented that "it was amazing to me that Daschle was the first candidate to mention abortion and marriage on TV. That opened the flood gates for Thune to bash Daschle on his record." Daschle's abortion and gay marriage ad significantly elevated the discussion of social issues in the race and spurred more voters concerned about social issues to go to the polls. Despite his past pro-life statements in South Dakota, after the election Daschle served as the keynote speaker at a California Planned Parenthood event entitled "Politics, Sex, and Cocktails," where he denounced limited access to abortions. Conservative Christian leader James Dobson also visited Sioux Falls and Rapid City during the first week of October, further highlighting social issues, and the South Dakota Family Policy Council also worked with churches to register voters and distribute voter guides.[28]

The interaction between religion and politics entered a new phase in South Dakota. One commentator and former South Dakotan noted that while a "vast majority of people in the state always have been people of deep Christian faith," it had largely been a "quiet faith" in previous decades. By 2004, it had become more public. Leo Thorsness, Daschle's first political opponent, recalled that he had "tried, mostly in vain, to get support from the fundamental church folks in 1978." Daschle's opponent in 1982, Clint Roberts, had been similarly disappointed with religious conservatives and said that the "churches were more concerned that they might offend some of their flock" and thus "were pretty much silent on issues or candidates." Liberal political commentator E. J. Dionne argues that a "polite disrespect for politics characterized much of the fundamentalist and evangelical movement" in the 1970s, but that changed. In some places, including South Dakota, the change was slow to develop. By 2004, those concerned about moral issues had become better organized and more vocal.[29]

Brad Carson, the Democratic Senate candidate in Oklahoma, recognized the importance of religious and moral issues in his 2004 campaign. Carson publicly distanced himself from Daschle during the fall by saying that he would not be a Daschle "enabler" if he was elected. Unlike some critics of religious conservatism on the left, however, he rejected the notion that religious voters were "deluded or uneducated. They simply reject the notion that material concerns are more real than spiritual or cultural ones. The political left has always had a hard time understanding this, preferring to believe that the masses are enthralled by a 'false consciousness' or Fox News or whatever today's excuse might be." In South Dakota in 2004, Daschle supporters organized a 527 entity named Focus South Dakota, which bought newspaper ads arguing in great detail that South Dakota voters were not as focused on moral issues as some analysts thought. They failed to stop the drift of churchgoers into the GOP camp, however, a trend that had been building for decades. George McGovern once considered the clergy part of his political coalition and actively sought out opportunities to speak to them early in his career. As the son of a Methodist minister and having also attended the seminary and embraced the Social Gospel, McGovern enjoyed a natural audience among the religiously inclined early in his career. The long-term impact of the politics of the 1960s (and, ironically, McGovernism) shriveled this audience for Democrats. When McGovern was first elected to Congress in the 1950s, Thune's parents, who were then Democrats, were leaving the Methodist church for a Bible-based church and beginning to reassess their politics.[30]

During the 2004 campaign, unlike his first race for Congress in 1978, Daschle could not successfully invoke his Catholicism, because of his conflicts with the Catholic bishop of Sioux Falls. Whereas George McGovern had won 90 percent of the Catholic vote in South Dakota when he was first elected to the Senate in 1962 (nationally, John Kennedy won 87 percent of Catholics in 1960), Daschle and Thune split the Catholic vote. The election confirmed the eclipse of the once-solid Democratic support among Catholics that began in the late 1960s and contributed to McGovern's loss in 1980—before which, his campaign manager had warned him about the need for "mending fences with South Dakota Catholics." Bush lost Catholics by a mere three percentage points in 2000, but won by five percentage points in 2004. The GOP presidential candidate increased his share of the white Catholic vote from 41 percent in 1996 to 56 percent in 2004. One commentator called the trend "Bob Casey's revenge." *Weekly Standard* editor Jody Bottum argued that "since the Clintons banned Pennsylvania's pro-life Democratic governor Robert Casey from the dais at the 1992 convention," the Democrats had become "entirely the party of support for abortion." Bottum cited a list of Democrats who had migrated to the pro-choice position: Tom Daschle, Al Gore, Richard Gephardt, Jesse Jackson, and Dennis Kucinich (the latter's "first act even as a protest presidential candidate with no real chance in the Democratic primaries last year was to renounce his previously staunch antiabortion position"). When Daschle was told by the bishop of Sioux Falls in 2003 to stop identifying himself as a Catholic because of his abortion views, the decision was based on a recent doctrinal note written by Cardinal Joseph Ratzinger, a critic of the radicalism of the 1960s, who went on to become pope in 2005.[31]

Postelection reports also noted that "Bush's share of the Catholic vote increased the most where bishops were outspoken about voters' moral obligation to protect unborn human beings," a phenomenon that included South Dakota. In the second presidential debate, John Kerry said that he had been an altar boy—as Daschle had done in television ads in South Dakota—but such invocations failed to rekindle the once-solid Democratic majorities among Catholics. Daschle's campaign manager complained after the election about "priests in this state who stood at the altar and said if you vote for pro-abortion candidates you shouldn't come back to this church." The Daschle campaign blamed the bishop of Sioux Falls for Daschle's defeat. The blitz of radio and newspaper ads from the Catholic Ave Maria List also emphasized issues important to Catholics. While Joseph Bottum downplayed the existence of a specific Catholic voting sensibility, he did note a growing coalition of the religiously inclined, finding "a horizontal unity that seems to cut across the vertical divisions of the old jarring sects." Devout Catholics and Protestants in South Dakota, who had once been bitterly split during campaigns in the early 1960s when George McGovern was running for the Senate, were increasingly united in their support of the GOP. When McGovern was defeated in

1980, one of the reasons was the increasing level of cooperation between conservative Catholics and Protestants, who had historically been divided.[32]

On the more practical level, the South Dakota Republican Party's get-out-the-vote effort noticeably improved over that of 2002, and many efforts were made to reach out to "undecideds" and "persuadables." The South Dakota GOP also relied almost exclusively on South Dakota campaign workers, unlike the Daschle campaign, which imported troops from the coasts (similar to the Kerry campaign's efforts). Howard Dean even lauded the GOP's national grassroots effort, noting that the Democrats "sent 14,000 people into Ohio from elsewhere" while the Republicans "had 14,000 people from Ohio talking to their neighbors, and that's how you win in rural states and in rural America." For the fall election, 10,400 new Republicans were registered in South Dakota, compared to 7,200 new Democrats.[33]

On election day, 79 percent of registered voters turned out, the highest level since the tumultuous year of 1968. Turnout in Minnehaha County, home to Sioux Falls, was 82 percent and in Pennington, home to Rapid City, it was 79 percent. The surge in Republican-leaning Pennington County turnout from 65 percent in 2002 to 79 percent in 2004 benefited Thune, but he only increased his Pennington margin by several hundred votes over 2002. In East River, however, Thune cut his 2002 losses significantly. In Minnehaha County, Thune cut his loss from 2,600 votes down to 1,600. In the twelve counties in the northeastern section of the state, Thune cut his losses from 6,800 votes down to 4,800. Thune also increased his winning margin by a thousand votes in rapidly growing Lincoln County (the nation's sixth fastest growing county), which might be considered an exurban county in some states because it borders on rapidly growing Sioux Falls. In my home county of Lake, Thune increased his percentage of the vote from 41 percent in 2002 to 44 percent in 2004, a harbinger of his improved performance in East River, which combined with strong victories in West River counties to give Thune the win. Thune's campaigning on Indian reservations also helped. In early October, Thune and Russell Means opened a GOP campaign office on Pine Ridge Indian Reservation, for perhaps the first time ever. Thune made six visits to Pine Ridge, and his percentage of the vote there grew from 8 percent in 2002 to 13 percent in 2004. In keeping with general GOP registration gains nationally since Reagan's ascendancy, Thune also benefited from a long-term erosion of the partisan balance in South Dakota. When Daschle was first elected to Congress in 1978 and South Dakota was represented by two of the most liberal members of the U.S. Senate, Democrats had a brief registration advantage in historically GOP-leaning South Dakota. A 1,500-person registration advantage for Democrats in 1978 disappeared, however, and in 2004, the GOP enjoyed a 47,000-person registration advantage.[34]

Although get-out-the-vote efforts are standard components of South Dakota campaigns, especially on the Democratic side, a unique twist in the 2004 campaign was blogging. In contrast to his performance in earlier elections, Daschle lost control of his ability to manage the flow of news in South Dakota through blog links to national stories and blogger criticism of the *Argus Leader*, the main source of political news in the state. The former anchor of the largest television station in South Dakota, Steve Hemmingsen, said that he thought blogs "had a lot of clout in this last election from Bush to Thune." Glenn Reynolds of the nationally famous Instapundit said that "one place where a weblog did make a difference, or at least a large part thereof, was in the defeat of Senate Minority Leader Tom Daschle of South Dakota." Reynolds pointed out that the blogs "played a big role in nationalizing that campaign, and in applying scrutiny to South Dakota's main political news outlet, the *Sioux Falls Argus Leader*, whose pro-Daschle slant had previously gone unchallenged. The *Argus Leader*'s sputtering responses are the best proof that this had an impact." The *National Journal* also published a long analysis after the election, noting that South Dakota bloggers "raised persistent questions about the objectivity" of the *Argus Leader* and "played a crucial role in shaping the news coverage of the race." One *Argus* reporter even said that a "siege mentality" took over at the newspaper. Dave Kranz, the *Argus* reporter criticized by bloggers for his past relationship with Daschle, refused to say that the blog claims about his connections to Daschle "didn't have some truth to them." The *National Journal*'s sources said that overall, "the campaign against the newspaper played a key role in the GOP's message-control effort to persuade voters to elect Thune over Daschle."[35]

Several national campaign reporters became loyal readers of the Dakota blogs (and were relieved to have an alternative to *Argus* reports), and some national news outlets also highlighted the work of the blogs during the campaign, further raising their profile. The *Wall Street Journal* wrote during the campaign that "the state's main news outlet, the *Argus Leader*—an unrelenting supporter of Mr. Daschle that had refused to report on the senator's inconsistencies—has been challenged by a wave of alternative media forums, especially bloggers." Michael Barone of *U.S. News and World Report*, who read the Dakota blogs, thought that they "played a critical role in the race" by highlighting "problems at the *Argus Leader.*" The British *Economist* reported that local bloggers "repeatedly highlighted Tom Daschle's partisan record in Washington, DC, something that the Democratic majority leader's friends in the local print media had never laboured to expose."[36]

The Dakota blogs energized civic life in the state by breaking the *Argus Leader*'s monopoly on what was "news." In addition to directly criticizing the *Argus Leader,* the blogs empowered thousands of readers, who became armed with information they never had before, to similarly criticize the *Argus* with calls, e-mails, and letters of protest, creating a blog-multiplier effect. Moreover, these readers had information about Daschle's statements in D.C. and from earlier campaigns that the *Argus* had not reported. Information spilled around the edges of the news filter that had benefited Daschle in previous years. Daschle could no longer keep his past buried in the memory hole. The *Grand Forks Herald* concluded that "conservative weblogs gave South Dakota voters access to news like never before" by "legitimizing criticism of the incumbent and using the media as a whipping boy," which "galvanized Daschle's opposition and gave them lots of material to rally around." The blogs also fueled local and national talk radio, and national bloggers and radio show hosts consistently publicized the Dakota blogs. In an early October visit, radio host Laura Ingraham was interviewed by bloggers, visited a Sioux Falls radio show, and then attended a GOP rally, making the point about blogger influence: "No longer can one newspaper fail to report the truth about one Senator and get away with it." Hoping to provoke a confrontation with the Old Media, she shouted to a thousand person rally in Sioux Falls: "Dave Kranz, are you here?" Dakota bloggers in turn appeared on national radio programs to give updates on the race.[37]

The blogs also drove stories such as Giago's third-party bid, Daschle's retreat on the balanced budget amendment, the old abortion letters,

Daschle's inconsistent statements on the war, the "huggates," the debate over debates, "mansiongate," "pillowgate," and Daschle's eleventh-hour lawsuit. Political scientist Bill Richardson said that the "blogs' success in getting all the news out about Daschle's [lawsuit was] an obvious illustration" of blog influence and proved "highly visible, effective and damaging to Daschle." When the blogs reported on national polls favoring Thune, including those by Rasmussen Reports, the Daschle campaign sought to boost morale by assuring staffers that such polls could not be trusted. In perhaps the boldest claim of the election postmortems, *World Magazine* concluded that the Internet scrutiny of Daschle's record "made him the second Senate leader [along with former GOP leader Trent Lott] to be brought down by bloggers." A *Rapid City Journal* report concluded that in 2004, "Thune supporters clearly won the battle of the blogosphere."[38]

The success of local blogs corresponded to the success of national blogs covering the presidential campaign, which became especially evident after the CBS forged memos fiasco and the blog-driven story about Kerry's alleged Christmas in Cambodia. Michael Barone was blunt about the impact: "Memo to future Democratic nominees: You can no longer rely on Old Media to hush up stories that hurt your cause. Your friends in Old Media don't have a monopoly any more." Randell Beck, executive editor of the *Argus Leader*, criticized blogs after the election for getting their facts wrong. Beck stated matter-of-factly, for example, that *Argus* reporter Dave Kranz had never worked for the Eugene McCarthy campaign in 1968: "It didn't happen." But Kranz's own lengthy recollections of campaigning for McCarthy disproved Beck's claim. Beck refused to correct his editorial or print a response, asserting that "further debate on the topic, in my judgment, serves no larger purpose." While the Old Media no longer maintained a monopoly, it could still control the facts that many readers saw in print.[39]

As the reporters and pundits discussed the various reasons for Thune's victory, some Daschle supporters rejected the assembled evidence. One Democratic aide conflated the various factors in Daschle's defeat into a simple rationale: "$20 million worth of lies was dumped in his lap." Such an explanation ignored the filibusters in the Senate, the fate of such measures as the energy bill and the gun-makers' liability legislation, the "flip-flopping" that similarly undermined the

Kerry campaign, social issues, the war, the diminished authority of a liberally inclined press, the legacies of the 1960s, the awkward associations with Michael Moore and other celebrities, the Herseth candidacy, and other factors. Critics may not recognize these factors as legitimate concerns for voters, but such a view does not make them lies. It makes them, for the critics, hard truths to be realized, lest the critics be bound to a delusion. But such critics surely prefer, in the words of historian Alan Spitzer, "a definition of truth as that which serves the cause." Popularizing the view that Daschle was simply smeared might have long-term utility, however. "Wars produce many stories of fiction," Ulysses S. Grant once warned, "some of which are told until they are believed to be true."[40]

After the election, Daschle did not want to discuss the reasons for his defeat, stating, "I don't want to go there. I just don't think it has any value or merit." But he hoped for final vindication: "I hope history will judge me well." In the history of the post-1960s political divide and the battles between the forces of the 1960s and Reaganism, history will probably remember Daschle's allegiance to the former and his hostility to the latter. After his defeat, he regretted that he had not been able to serve as an "offensive quarterback" in Congress in the manner of Democratic Senate leader Mike Mansfield, who had shepherded dozens of major laws through the Senate in the 1960s and 1970s when the Democrats controlled Congress. Instead, Daschle said that throughout most of his career, history had relegated him to "a defensive lineman," leaving him to tackle the advance of the Republican agenda. During the fall campaign, the Thune campaign also embraced the football metaphor through a corny television ad using old black-and-white football footage of "Tom the-blocking-machine Daschle," reminding voters of the legislation that Daschle had blocked. The ad featured Hillary Clinton and Ted Kennedy as Daschle's fellow defensive linemen.[41]

Even as Daschle attempted to persuade South Dakota voters that his legislative power should trump their tendency to support the GOP agenda, however, his record indicated that he did not become the bipartisan deal maker he had promised to be early in his career. The editors of the *Rapid City Journal* wrote that Daschle "has been one of the most partisan Democrats in Washington for 26 years, but it wasn't until media began reporting his every move as the top Democrat that Daschle's South Dakota constituents began scratching their heads and asking, who is that guy?" With his bipartisan image blurred by years of partisan warfare in the Senate, the support Daschle had enjoyed among South Dakota Republican voters in his early years slipped.[42]

The morning after the election, Daschle spoke to his supporters, many of whom wept: "I have a profound respect for the people of South Dakota. I respect their decision. I am grateful for the extraordinary opportunity that they have given me these many years." It was an emotional time and a stunning blow for many of Daschle's supporters. The Minneapolis newspaper reported that Daschle was "choking and tearing up" but told his supporters, "I don't want anyone in this room to be angry or sad." Back in Washington, Daschle's close allies in the Senate, with whom he had fought many pitched battles against the GOP, were solemn. After his farewell address to the Senate, Daschle said that "what mattered the most was to hear a colleague of yours say, 'I love you.' You know, it's not something you hear from a colleague all that often. But it melts you." The battles that Democratic colleagues thanked Daschle for fighting still lingered in the minds of Republican senators, and few came to the floor to hear Daschle's goodbye. The editors of the *New York Times* said that a "nastiness is in the air" after the election and noted that Daschle's farewell speech "was boycotted by a victorious, decidedly unsentimental majority." The Democrats, the *Times* noted, also vowed "never to forget Dr. Frist's foray into South Dakota to help unhorse his counterpart." Perhaps fittingly, Daschle exited the Senate in a cloud of bitterness and partisanship, a departure that symbolized his recent tenure.[43]

Back in South Dakota, the acrimony also persisted. Robert Penn Warren once noted that after the bitter election of 1860, "when the votes were counted, business was not resumed as usual." So too in South Dakota, where the *Argus Leader* described the persistence of the "eternal campaign" in an article entitled "Six Months Later, Campaignlike Mud Still Flying." During the summer of 2005, the *Rapid City Journal* reported on "the permanent campaign" and explained how "the Daschle team continues to wage political war against Thune." The political report the *Hotline* said that the Daschle campaign was "so indelible you'd have to sandblast it away." After the votes were counted in November, the editors of the *Argus Leader* had called for a "truce," "healing," and a "return to the idea that people who disagree with us aren't necessarily evil," but the call went unheeded by some Dakotans. One liberal website posted a cartoon of Thune tearing up the Constitution alongside a Grand Dragon of the Ku Klux Klan and Hitler, and others denounced "Bush Fascism" and claimed that Republicans relied on "a fuehrer to lead their party." *Roll Call* reported that after the election, Democrats had "spread a rumor like wildfire" that Thune was getting a divorce. One of several anti-Thune blogs started by former Daschle staffers promoted the purchase of "F—— John Thune" T-shirts and said that the blogger's goal was to "tear Thune's n—— off." One Daschle campaign aide called Thune an "old beast of the far right." Daschle's campaign manager Steve Hildebrand, who was still being paid from the Daschle campaign account and Daschle's political action committee, also pressured reporters to write stories critical of Thune and orchestrated protests outside Thune's Senate office. Some Daschle supporters and former staffers conceded that the anti-Thune efforts were driven by bitterness over Daschle's defeat and that such actions were motivated by their desire for revenge.[44]

By defeating the Democrats' leader and the chief opponent of the GOP agenda, Thune earned permanent foes. A Democratic strategist, according to *Roll Call*, said that the "party cannot afford to wait until 2009 to go after Thune." The Democratic Senatorial Campaign Committee also criticized Thune in early 2005, and Jim Jordan, John Kerry's first campaign manager, announced the formation of a new 527 organization to keep a "six-year drumbeat" on Republican senators. Conservative leader Paul Weyrich noted that Thune was "being attacked daily by the organized left," which was set on "avenging" the defeat of Senator Daschle. Daschle campaign manager Steve Hildebrand vowed that Thune would "have to watch his back." For some, the Daschle-Thune race would never end.[45]

Despite the intensity of his support in some quarters and his copious resources, Daschle was not in a good position to run for a fourth term. His vulnerability grew in Republican-leaning South Dakota after he became the leader of an intransigent and liberal caucus that dug in against the GOP majority. As one newspaper noted, Daschle had come "to epitomize obstructionism." If he had retired or run for president in 2004, Daschle could have mused in good conscience about the evolution of his political views since his first campaigns. He would have left the front with his party at low ebb but with the satisfaction of knowing that he had personally spent several years in the trenches fighting the good fight and blocking legislation he thought was wrong, a proud moment, recalling Milton's Samson:

Nothing is here for tears, nothing to wail
Or knock the breast, no weakness, no contempt,
Dispraise, or blame, nothing but well and fair,
And what may quiet us in death so noble.

Instead, Daschle chose to run for reelection to the Senate, believing that the disjunction between the Senate Democrats' stridency and the conservative tendencies of his state could be diminished by an advertising blitz and favorable press coverage.[46]

Prior to Senator George McGovern's 1980 defeat, his chief of staff had warned him about the dangers of a "dual track" strategy of keeping open the options of challenging President Jimmy Carter from the left and running for reelection in South Dakota: "Anything less than a full fledged, undiluted commitment to a Senate re-election campaign will result in your defeat." Daschle's service as Democratic leader in the Senate while seeking reelection to the Senate involved the same risks. Daschle showed signs of wanting to exit politics late in 2003, perhaps realizing that his recent record had complicated his ability to be reelected in South Dakota. Why Daschle ran in the end—perhaps because Bill Janklow was forced to leave politics because of the manslaughter charges and could not succeed him, or perhaps because his loyal supporters could not stand the thought of handing Thune the Senate seat held by George McGovern and Tom Daschle for thirty-six years—remains impossible to say.[47]

Daschle's expectation of victory spoke to his confidence in his ability to transcend his own protean politics. In a nationalized campaign during a year of political extremity, however, Daschle's mild public persona and appearance of goodwill could no longer obscure his fierce battles with the GOP in the Senate and his contradictory policy postures. Daschle could no longer rely, as Louis Menand once said of Bill Clinton, on "his tendency to let his intentions vouch for his actions." His actions and record were scrutinized in 2004, unlike the earlier campaigns, in which a supportive local media gilded his intentions and ignored his actions. In contrast, in 2004, Daschle seemed genuinely shocked and angered when a local reporter finally tried to pin down his position on abortion. Daschle's troubles began when the center of gravity in the campaign shifted away from Daschle's television advertising barrage trumpeting his clout and toward an examination of his long record in Congress. Denouncing any scrutiny of this record as a negative attack wore thin.[48]

Although Daschle lost the war against memory in 2004, he still contemplated another campaign. During an April 2005 trip to South Dakota, the first visit after his defeat, Daschle kept open the possibility of running for office once again. After an address by Daschle at the University of South Dakota, Dave Kranz reported that many observers "thought his remarks sounded like a campaign speech." Daschle said that he was "not going to be closing doors in my political life." Although his political future remained unknown, in the spring of 2005 Daschle joined the Washington lobbying firm Alston and Bird and became a fellow at the Center for American Progress, which was founded in 2003 by John Podesta, Bill Clinton's former chief of staff and Daschle's would-be presidential campaign advisor. Daschle also created a new political action committee to assist fellow Democrats and generally sought, *Roll Call* reported, "to re-establish himself as a political force." In 2005, Daschle donated a quarter of a million dollars to Democratic candidates around the country. In late 2005, Daschle ventured into Iowa to make the keynote address to the state Democratic Party's Jefferson-Jackson Day dinner and said that he was considering a presidential bid in 2008. By the end of 2005, Daschle had become a prominent critic of the war in Iraq, called for the withdrawal of U.S. troops, and pronounced the Bush presidency "essentially over."[49]

John Thune, meanwhile, assumed his duties in the Senate in early 2005. A child of the Reagan revolution from a small high-plains town in the heart of Reagan country, Thune made the difficult choices both to run and to scrutinize Daschle's drift to the left. "Sen. Daschle didn't like his record challenged," Thune noted after the election; "It's been a long time since anybody had the resources to challenge him." Daschle spent $21 million ($108 per vote he received), produced seventy-five different television ads, organized thirty field offices, and employed 515 staffers, one for every 375 votes he received. Daschle's laptop-wielding get-out-the-vote army "contacted every voter in the state, many several times, and [had] built up detailed profiles of all swing voters and their families." But Thune and his 18 campaign staffers delivered a strong message that exposed Daschle's history, and the 70 GOP staffers at the state party brought out the Thune voters. Despite Daschle's vulnerabilities, nobody in South Dakota could have defeated Daschle except Thune, given the immensity of Daschle's resources. As the leftist scholar C. Wright Mills once said, "Men are free to make history, but some men are much freer than others." Thune was the only person who could have made history by challenging Senator Daschle.[50] Thune's troops understood the historic victory and, after the votes were counted, circulated columnist Peggy Noonan's postelection invocation of Henry V, speaking on the day of battle, Saint Crispin's Day:

> He that shall live this day, and see old age,
> Will yearly on the vigil feast his neighbors.
> And say, "These wounds I had on Crispin's day."
> . . . .
> And gentlemen in England now a-bed
> Shall think themselves accursed they were not here,
> And hold their manhoods cheap while any speaks
> That fought with us upon Saint Crispin's day.

The 109th Congress began on January 4, 2005, when John Thune was sworn in as a U.S. senator by Vice President Cheney. Senator Tim Johnson (his 2002 opponent) and Thune's mentor Jim Abdnor (whom Daschle had defeated in 1986) escorted Thune to the Senate floor for the swearing in. At a reception for well-wishers that night, Thune pointed to Abdnor during his remarks and said, "It may have taken eighteen years, Jim, but we got your seat back."[51]

CHAPTER TEN

DASCHLE VERSUS THUNE
AS SYNECDOCHE

This is not the apocalypse.

—*New Republic*

Thune's defeat of the chief political nemesis of President Bush symbolized the durability of the post-1960s GOP resurgence. In an election with the biggest turnout since the riotous year of 1968, Bush overcame ferocious opposition and became the first president to win a majority of the popular vote since 1988. In addition to maintaining an emphasis on the frequent deflating reports from Iraq and the so-called jobless economic recovery, the American left was more united than it had been since LBJ's smashing victory in 1964. Liberal 527 organizations spent large sums trying to defeat Bush, augmenting the efforts of the Democratic Party and the Kerry campaign: Americans Coming Together raised $140 million; the Media Fund, $60 million; MoveOn.org, $12 million. In addition, two public employee unions gave their 527s $91.5 million. Overall, more than a billion dollars were spent on the 2004 presidential campaign (by contrast, in 1996, only $100 million had been spent). Many liberals also afforded Kerry latitude on thorny issues and avoided the temptation to defect to Ralph Nader. Democratic Party unity and fund-raising efforts in 2004 impressed many observers.[1]

Twelve days before the election, Democratic strategist James Carville said, "If we can't win this damn election with a Democratic Party more unified than ever before, with us having raised as much money as the Republicans, with 55% of the country believing we're heading in the wrong direction, with our candidate having won all three debates, and with our side being more passionate about the outcome than theirs—if we can't win this one, then we can't win shit! And we need to completely rethink the Democratic Party." Liberal columnist

E. J. Dionne said after the election that "what really irks Democrats is that they did a lot of things right this year and were still out-hustled by the GOP." After Kerry's defeat, the Democrats had lost seven of the previous ten presidential races. The three Democratic winners, however, ran as outsiders and promised southern centrism, not a return to 1960s-era liberalism. Political commentator and Washington wise man David Gergen said, "I think it's a mistake for Democrats to say, well, we just lost another one because we didn't have a very strong candidate. It strikes me that there is something much deeper going on here." The politics of 2004, including the Daschle-Thune contest, exposed the deeper dilemmas that continue to vex the Democratic Party.[2]

President Bush did not win reelection as a timid, triangulating moderate without an ideological agenda. During his first term, Bush enjoyed the most legislative success of any president since LBJ, winning passage of 80 percent of the laws he supported. Bush also said that he did not want a Nixonesque "lonely victory" in 2004 and instructed his advisors to increase GOP congressional majorities. "More than any in a generation," the *Economist* reported before the vote, "this is a big election, about big things." To advance his agenda after the election, Bush could point to a majoritarian mandate, a situation very different from that of his first term. Bush won by 4 million votes, carrying thirty-one states, including states that had supported Bill Clinton (such as Kentucky, West Virginia, Missouri, Arkansas, Tennessee, and Ohio), and he made small gains among Democratic constituencies. In the states that he lost, Bush improved his share of the vote by three percentage points. Compared to his showing in 2000, Bush's Jewish vote increased from 18 percent to 25 percent, his black vote increased from 8 percent to 12 percent, and more than 40 percent of Hispanics voted for him. He also won 10 percent of those who had voted for his opponent, Al Gore, in 2000; 59 percent of the nation's congressional districts; and John Edwards's home county. Bush also won white, working-class voters by twenty-three percentage points, which alarmed those on the left who considered the working class their core constituency. The "blue plutocracy"—those individuals worth more than $10 million—favored Kerry by 20 points, despite the perception of the GOP as a party of economic elites.[3]

A postelection Gallup survey found that 37 percent of the public identified themselves as Republicans and 32 percent as Democrats, a slight change from the Clinton years, when the Democrats had held a 6 percent advantage. By contrast, in 1976, when Daschle began planning his run for Congress, the Democrats' party identification advantage was three times greater, with 45 percent as compared to the Republicans' 28 percent. The GOP victories in the fall of 2004 continued a broader electoral trend that had first crystallized with Reagan's victory in 1980. Bush campaign manager Ken Mehlman said that the victory was "the ultimate continuation of the legacy of Reagan." Some Democrats recognized the troubling trends for their party. Simon Rosenberg, president of the centrist New Democratic Network, said that "we've woken up to the fact that Republicans have more power today than any other time since the 1920s. Things are not moving in the right direction for the Democratic Party."[4]

Despite the GOP gains, the nation remained politically divided. Forty-eight percent of the country had voted against President Bush, after all, and millions of Americans despised him. During the election, 90 percent of Republicans voted for Bush, 90 percent of Democrats voted for Kerry, and independents split evenly, a reflection of the nation's political polarization. Some academics believed that Bush's victory was the "last gasp" of a fading coalition of GOP-leaning voters that would soon melt away, but others noted that Bush had won ninety-seven of the nation's one hundred fastest-growing counties. E. J. Dionne instructed Democrats not to panic, arguing that Bush had won using "old strategies" and "familiar, Cold War–era stuff." Others dismissed the notion of a Bush mandate and urged the left to take heart from Rick Perlstein's book *Before the Storm*, which details the crushing defeat of the conservatives under Barry Goldwater in 1964 and their subsequent ascendancy. A leading historian of the 1960s, Todd Gitlin, believed that the massive organizational efforts of the left in 2004 were "not a figment of a utopian's imagination." The time of the liberals would eventually return.[5]

Others argued that the Republican gains could be quickly erased. A *New York Times* story warned that "history also suggests a perilous twist on an adage as old as Athens: Whom the Gods would destroy they first give control of both ends of Pennsylvania Avenue." Soon after the election, Republicans bickered over the elevation of pro-choice GOP senator Arlen Specter to chairman of the Judiciary Committee, and some GOP House members resisted a compromise plan to reorganize the intelligence services. *New York Times* columnist David Brooks saw the GOP coalition as unstable and predicted continued squabbling between the deficit hawks and tax cutters, neoconservatives and foreign policy realists, and cultural conservatives and libertarians. Some conservative activists also felt betrayed by Bush and his agenda, condemning what they viewed as his fiscal profligacy and global adventurism. Others argued that the GOP risked becoming too southern and culturally conservative and potentially losing moderate voters in the Midwest and Northeast. The authors of a history of modern American conservatism joked that "if you take away alcohol and adultery, there isn't a whole lot for stockbrokers in Connecticut to do." Others believed that the continuing conflict in Iraq could ultimately devour the GOP.[6]

Despite divisions within the GOP, many liberals were not optimistic after the 2004 elections. The editors of the *New Republic* said that the "convictions and the dreams of liberalism have genuinely failed to carry the day" and warned that "hard times, brutish times, lie ahead." They argued that "American liberalism did not die on November 2. It merely lost an election. . . . This is not the apocalypse. But it is the most formidable challenge to American liberalism in our time." They warned against the temptation to "wallow" in "Michael Moore leftishness." In the same issue of the magazine, liberal commentator Peter Beinart said that "American liberalism is going into a deep internal exile" and warned that liberals' "despair is so great it sometimes clouds out intelligent thought. And the fear of political oblivion can produce moral lapses." Beinart, fearing a "surge of cultural elitism" and a "spasm of liberal anti-Americanism that followed the failure to impeach Bill Clinton," cautioned Democrats to avoid the temptation to "revile conservative voters."[7]

Making Beinart's point by ignoring his advice, Andy Rooney of *60 Minutes* told an audience at Tufts University after the election that conservatives suffer from "a lack of education." The *Daily Mirror* headline in London after the election echoed the point: "How Can 59,054,087 People Be So DUMB?" The novelist Jane Smiley wrote that red-state voters "are virtually unteachable" and "prefer to be ignorant."[8]

Some Florida Democrats held group therapy sessions after the election to alleviate Post Election Selection Trauma, which caused people to tremble physically. A psychotherapist who attended a session noted,

"One person today said he thinks the country is now run by fascists." Democratic congressman Brad Carson, who lost his Senate bid in Oklahoma in 2004, said that the "well-heeled New York, Northern California world of Democrats considers nationalism a very discredited concept, that nationalism equals Brown Shirts." An online poll of readers of the Democratic Underground website asked whether 9/11 or Bush's victory was "more depressing"—73 percent chose Bush's victory. A *Time* writer reported on liberals' "paranoid fantasies about how evangelical leaders are at this very minute hunkered down in Bush uberadviser Karl Rove's office plotting to institute an Old Testament theocracy overseen by Attorney General Jerry Falwell." David Brooks compared liberals' reaction to the election to the "rage of the drowning man."[9]

Despair over their electoral losses caused some on the left to urge a fierce resistance to the GOP and a return to leftist fundamentals. The editors of the *Nation* concluded that the lesson for the Democratic Party was "that a posture of meekness, resignation and accommodation leads to failure." Other reports indicated that the leaders of the "party's left wing are planning a long-term campaign to move the Democrats to the left, just as right-wing activists took over the Republican Party and moved it to the right over the past 30 years." The *Economist* reported that leftist groups such as MoveOn.org were the "harbingers of a rebirth of left-wing politics that will return the Democratic Party to its radical populist roots." George McGovern, true to his history and his pronouncements since the 1970s, said that Democrats had to "stay with their convictions." The writers at Daily Kos and other liberals denounced moderates and the leaders of centrist organizations such as the Democratic Leadership Council (DLC) as "idiots" and "our party's version of the Flat Earth Society"; others ridiculed the DLC as a puppet of corporate America. Markos "Kos" Moulitsas of Daily Kos dismissed calls for unity and vowed to make the DLC "radioactive." Former Daschle staffer Amy Sullivan called for a purge of centrist pollsters and consultants who had presided over recent Democratic reversals, many of whom had been allied to and supported by Daschle.[10]

Others on the left mocked the liberal true believers and rejected a hard left turn: "What people really want is a Debs or LaFollette who will smite the corporations, turn swords into plowshares, share the wealth and banish John Ashcroft to a cabin in the Ozarks. But since the Democratic Party denies them their first choice, they will—naturally!—pick a hard-right warmaker of staggering incompetence and no regard for either the Constitution or the needs of the people." Dan Gerstein, a strategist for the centrist former Democratic senator Joe Lieberman, said that Democrats should confront "the painful reality that too many people are just not buying what we are selling." Other centrists dug in against liberals' support of Howard Dean's campaign to become Democratic Party chairman. Recalling Dean's performance on the night of Iowa caucuses, the editors of the *New Republic* opined that "if there's an image the Democratic Party is not looking to project to the country, 'unhinged screamer' would be at the top of the list." Prior to the vote for the chairmanship, Dean said, "I hate the Republicans and everything they stand for," a sentiment that mirrored the mood of some members of the Democratic base.[11]

Despite the objection of some moderate Democrats, Dean was elected party chairman. The president of the American Federation of State, County and Municipal Employees (who had called Dean "nuts" during the primary season when revoking the public employee union's endorsement) even supported Dean. After Dean became chairman, a former Republican National Committee chairman said, "I think it's a scream." The liberal base of the Democratic Party had won a major victory over the party's established powers. While the *Washington Post* reported that some Democratic strategists worried "that the influence of grassroots activists could push the party even further to the left," MoveOn.org announced that the Clintonian/DLC "era of triangulation is over." Political reporter Ronald Brownstein noted that MoveOn.org and liberal bloggers were "reshaping the Democratic Party" and were shifting the "balance of power" away from Clintonian centrism, which the head of MoveOn.org's political action committee pronounced "obsolete." Even though MoveOn.org had opposed the popularly supported war in Afghanistan after the 9/11 attacks, it still came to rival organized labor for control of the Democratic Party. As the centrist Democratic Leadership Council lost influence, however, it continued to warn that the Democrats "need to be the party of Harry Truman and John Kennedy, not Michael Moore." The DLC instructed the Democrats "to be choosier about the political company they keep" and urged them to avoid the "pacifist anti-American fringe."[12]

During the year after the election and the election of Dean as party chairman, the liberal wing of the Democratic Party and those who urged a more strident opposition to the Bush administration were ascendant. Dean catered to the base of his party, calling Republicans "evil," "corrupt," and "brain-dead," and he dismissed the GOP as a "White Christian Party." Democratic senator Ken Salazar called Christian conservative leader James Dobson "the anti-Christ," and Democratic senator Harry Reid called President Bush a "loser." The invocation of Hitler analogies also peppered liberal discourse. During the battle over judicial nominations, Democratic senator Robert Byrd compared GOP criticism of the judicial filibuster to tactics used in "Nazi Germany or Mussolini's Italy." When criticizing the Bush administration's handling of detainees at Guantanamo, the Senate's second-ranking Democrat, Richard Durbin, said on the Senate floor that "you would most certainly believe this must have been done by Nazis, Soviets in their gulags, or some mad regime—Pol Pot or others—that had no concern for human beings." Harsh criticism appealed to some hardened Democrats, who continued to be frustrated by the Bush administration's conservative agenda. Marc Cooper noted the growing fear of "fascism" among liberals, whose rhetoric was "increasingly laced with paranoia." Liberal columnist Kevin Drum commented that a "substantial faction of today's left thinks George Bush is only slightly preferable to Adolf Hitler." Such sentiments reflected the growing alienation of liberal critics from the mainstream of American public opinion.[13]

Democratic moderates and Dean critics who recoiled from a hard turn to the left started the Third Way organization in hopes of creating a "moderate majority" and promoting centrist policies. Southern Democratic senators also planned a centrist-led "New South" project to promote Democratic efforts in the South, a region that John Kerry, during the New Hampshire primary, had urged abandoning. These efforts approximated the Democratic Leadership Council's original strategy of moderation after the staggering defeat of Walter Mondale's liberalism in 1984. Similar to liberal criticism of centrism after the 2004 elections, in 1984 Jesse Jackson had denounced the DLC as "Democrats for the Leisure Class" who "didn't march in the sixties and won't stand up in the eighties." Conflicts between liberals and moderates continued to undermine Democratic Party unity. Divisions among Democrats were reminiscent of the age when Daschle first entered public office in the 1970s, when Speaker of the House Thomas "Tip" O'Neill famously quipped, "If this were France, the Democratic Party would be five parties." During the 2005 DLC convention, Senator Hillary Clinton called for unity and conceded that the Democrats were "split between left, right and center."[14]

Pragmatists within the Democratic Party simply wanted the party to formulate a coherent message. During the presidential race, former Clinton advisor Paul Begala met with the leaders of the Kerry campaign and presented various campaign themes, begging them to "choose one and stick with it." At a postelection gathering of Kerry's team in Washington, Kerry said "People are going to try and rewrite history and say we didn't have a message in this campaign. And let me tell you, the message never changed. The message we had in the final days of the campaign was the same as the one we had in the primaries." One strategist later said, "Everyone in that room was on edge because everyone wanted to know: What was that message?" Paging through a draft of a speech after winning the presidential nomination, Kerry himself had wondered, "What is our message?"[15]

Several commentators focused on the public's inability to discern a Democratic alternative to the GOP's agenda. Part of E. J. Dionne's advice to Democrats after the election was simple: "Stand for something." A postelection poll by former Clinton advisors James Carville and Stanley Greenberg found that Republicans had held a thirty-point advantage with voters in the category of "knowing what they stand for" and noted the power of the Kerry-as-"flip-flopper" image. One person polled, when ridiculing Kerry's indecisiveness, said, "He's the guy that holds up the line at McDonald's." Democratic strategist Ann Lewis conceded after the election that Kerry "ran what was basically an inconsistent campaign"; Greenberg continued to argue that Democrats suffered because they had "no core set of convictions or point of view." Throughout the South Dakota Senate race, Daschle similarly suffered from holding inconsistent policy positions. Throughout 2005, critics continued to argue that liberals were "bookless," or devoid of new ideas, and lacked a central organizing principle or "narrative" that could shape a broad-based Democratic agenda. *New*

Republic editor-in-chief Marty Peretz argued that the liberal agenda "looked and sounded like little more than a bookkeeping exercise. We want to spend more, they less." Political analyst Marc Cooper also condemned Democrats for "mere ankle-biting—quibbling on an ad hoc basis with this or that Republican initiative." When surveying the conservative policy agenda and condemning liberals' lack of imagination and obstruction of GOP plans, one liberal commentator concluded that "the left has become—there's no other word for it— reactionary."[16]

Many Democratic leaders understood that the party lacked a coherent policy program. Newly elected Democratic senator Barack Obama of Illinois conceded that Democrats had "lost their way" and were "trying to decide what [their] core values are." Even Democratic National Committee chairman Howard Dean proclaimed, "We need a message." John Kerry thought the problem was simpler: "We have to brand more effectively. It's marketing." An academic expert consulted by the Democratic leadership similarly thought that Democrats had to be better at "framing" issues. Political analyst Joshua Green concluded that Kerry and the Democrats were stuck in an "Olympian state of denial" that had "diverted them from a truth that ought to be perfectly clear: rather than being misunderstood, they were understood too well."[17]

The problems of the Democratic Party transcended miscommunication and could be traced to a fundamental and long-term burden. Too many Democrats were still wedded to the politics of 1968, a marriage that left them in a defensive crouch in the twenty-first century. The persistent antiwar sentiment of the Dean campaign and its supporters and the continued invocation of the Vietnam experience, which served as the lens through which many liberals viewed the Iraq War, confused Democratic foreign policy thinking. On the domestic front, the great liberal achievements such as the civil rights laws of the 1960s still deserved to be celebrated. By 2004, however, Martin Peretz thought that liberal thinking on race had become outmoded, trapped in an earlier age during which racial segregation and discrimination had been pervasive. Peretz criticized liberals for not recognizing the "tremendous strides" taken by African-Americans since the 1960s, and he pointed to the continuing "deference paid to Al Sharpton during the campaign," calling Sharpton "an inciter of racial conflict."

After the election, in another indication that liberal thinking remained imprisoned by the racial politics of the 1960s, New York congressman Charlie Rangel denounced President Bush as a contemporary "Bull Connor." During a Martin Luther King Day speech, Senator Hillary Clinton also condemned the Republican leadership in the House for running what she called a "plantation."[18]

By embracing the 1960s as their inspirational touchstone, Democrats suffered politically. Former Democratic senator Bill Bradley, in addition to criticizing liberals for not developing new policy approaches, blamed Democrats for relying on charismatic politicians instead of a consistent programmatic agenda, another carryover from the 1960s and the Kennedy mystique, which he said had hypnotized the party regulars. Liberal historian and author Rick Perlstein regretted that "most Democratic consultants [were] still telling stories about the 1960s." Daschle, who was inspired to enter politics because of President Kennedy, similarly saw those years as a benchmark, noting that "some of the most important things we've done in the last half century were done in the early years of the 1960s." The Democratic Party thus continued to be defined and animated by the divisive politics of the 1960s, which explained why some liberals sought to substitute the Progressive Era of the early twentieth century for the 1960s as the party's reference point.[19]

During the debate over the direction of the Democratic Party after the 2004 elections, Peter Beinart focused on foreign policy in a much-discussed manifesto in the *New Republic* that argued that liberals should be more aggressive on the war on terror and less sympathetic to the antiwar left. As precedent, he cited liberals' embrace of anti-communism and the purge of communists and fellow travelers from the Democratic Party and leftist organizations in the 1940s. Beinart specifically noted the purge of Henry Wallace and his followers in the left-wing Progressive Party, whose 1948 convention was attended by a young George McGovern. Beinart called for a similar distancing of the contemporary Democratic Party from the "Wallacite grass-roots that views America's new struggle as a distraction, if not a mirage." Beinart cited Michael Moore, who had argued that there was "no terrorist threat" and questioned why "has our government gone to such absurd lengths to convince us our lives are in danger." Beinart explained that "when Democratic National Committee Chairman

Terry McAuliffe and Tom Daschle flocked to the Washington premiere of 'Fahrenheit 9/11,' and when Moore sat in Jimmy Carter's box at the Democratic convention, many wondered whether the Democratic Party was anti-totalitarian."[20]

Beyond the antiwar signals sent by his tolerance of Michael Moore, Daschle's foreign policy views were otherwise difficult to discern, symbolizing the greater problem faced by the Democratic Party. In Daschle's farewell address to the Senate, David Frum noted, Daschle did not discuss the major wars in Afghanistan and Iraq. Frum called the omission Daschle's "party's problem: For all the Dems insist that they have overcome their dovish and isolationist history, it remains the case that the defense of the nation remains a subject about which they prefer not to speak." In his book, Daschle said that he found President Bush's post-9/11 rhetoric "worrisome" and declared that he had been uncomfortable with the president's "axis of evil" speech. The Democrats' foreign policy positions remained confused in part because of the deference afforded the antiwar forces within their party and the continuing power of the 1960s spirit.[21]

Beinart's critique of the antiwar movement and call for a Wallace-ite purge did not change the Democratic Party's direction, however. Arthur Schlesinger, Jr., after all, who codified the liberal anticommunist "fighting faith" of the 1940s with his book *The Vital Center*, later abandoned his faith. Beinart could not pierce the fog of the 1960s and Vietnam, when liberalism increasingly became linked with antiwar sentiments, a transitional experience that shaped the early lives of John Kerry's and Tom Daschle's generation. In the early 1970s, the Americans for Democratic Action (ADA), which had led the purge in the 1940s and which Beinart used as his model, enthusiastically supported George McGovern's "Come Home, America" foreign policy and questioned the anticommunist cause. In 1977, McGovern became the president of the ADA, symbolizing the organization's drift from the "vital center." Another symbolic action was taken by President Jimmy Carter—whose first major address on foreign policy condemned the nation's "inordinate fear of communism." John Kerry, in his famous 1971 Senate testimony, had said that he was the most angry about overblown fears generated by the "mystical war against communism." In 1973, Daschle's newly elected boss, Senator Jim Abourezk, immediately went to the Senate floor to denounce the Vietnam War and the nation's anticommunist foreign policy. Beinart's vision could not overcome the continuing power of the antiwar movement within liberal circles. The contemporary ADA rejected Beinart's call for a purge of the antiwar left. But he continued to counsel liberals to examine "how they grew estranged from large numbers of Americans in the post-Vietnam period."[22]

Vietnam and the 1960s reconfigured American liberalism and disrupted the post–World War II foreign policy consensus, a historical episode that Democrats could not escape. The editor of the liberal *Washington Monthly* said after the 2004 election that "today's Democratic political operatives, most of whom came up in the late 1960s to early 1970s and were essentially anti-war, have never been comfortable with national security." Liberals such as Kevin Drum wondered whether the danger of Islamic totalitarianism that worried Beinart was as "truly overwhelming" as many conservatives insisted. After the election, the head of MoveOn.org's political action committee, a bastion of antiwar enthusiasm and one of the targets of Beinart's criticism, criticized the Democratic Party's "professional election losers" and claimed control of the party: "We bought it, we own it, we're going to take it back." Despite Beinart's pleas, the antiwar left remained firmly entrenched in the national Democratic Party. In a review of conventional wisdom, the *Washington Post* reported that the Democratic Party "struggled to move beyond the antiwar legacy of the 1960s and 1970s." In one postelection survey of foreign policy attitudes, Americans in general ranked the destruction of al-Qaeda as their highest priority; among liberals, it tied for tenth. Martin Peretz said that such attitudes among liberals were another "leftover from the '60s."[23]

As critics of the Iraq War grew more strident after the 2004 elections, they continued to rely on the personalities and images of the past. During the summer of 2005, former senator Gary Hart, who had served as George McGovern's presidential campaign manager in 1972, began demanding that Democrats abandon their "stay the course" policy in Iraq and denounce the war, just as his generation of Democrats had opposed the Vietnam War. Hart condemned Democrats for remaining "tongue-tied or trying to trump a war president by calling for deployment of more troops." The antiwar protests during the summer of 2005 were undermined by the involvement of fringe groups, however, and the prominence of 1960s sentiments. After covering an antiwar march in Washington during the fall of 2005, Lawrence Kaplan criticized the "hollowness at the core of the antiwar movement," which was driven by veteran Vietnam War protesters (Joan Baez led the crowd's rendition of "Where Have All the Flowers Gone?"), and concluded that the marchers were too concerned with condemning Israel, the military, capitalism, colonialism, and Wal-Mart. Others criticized the protesters for promoting "the resistance" in Iraq, for using war-weariness as a means to advance their own particular causes, and for trying to transform Iraq "into another incarnation of Vietnam."[24]

Some intellectuals voiced open frustration with the inability to distinguish between a Vietnam-era contempt for the exercise of U.S. military power and noble foreign policy goals. Human rights advocate Larry Diamond defended his work for the United States in Iraq and skewered his critics, who attacked his "pact with the devil": "Let them see some of the roughly 300 mass graves of opponents of the regime who were brutally slaughtered in the hundreds of thousands. Then they will find out who the devil really is." Liberal columnist Richard Cohen feared that the left had ceded foreign policy moralism to the GOP. In a widely discussed essay, the global affairs writer Ian Buruma criticized leftist intellectuals who were "much keener to denounce the U.S. than to find ways to liberate Iraqis and others from their murderous Fuehrers." Martin Peretz attacked the "unmistakable but macabre schadenfreude among many critics of the war, who want nothing of history except to be proved right." Some on the left could not overlook the Bush administration's means of overthrowing one of the world's most sadistic despots, regardless of the end achieved. British commentator Nick Cohen, when criticizing the leftist icon Noam Chomsky's latest book condemning U.S. foreign policy, lamented that leftists viewed Saddam's victims "with indifference or active hostility because they have committed the unforgivable sin of cooperating with the Americans. For the first time in its history the Left has nothing to say to the victims of fascism." The editors of the *Nation*, for example, ignored the victory over despotism in Iraq and called for a "revived antiwar movement, which not only calls for a withdrawal from Iraq but opposes and prevents new bloody adventures." During the 2004 GOP convention in New York City, the *Nation* published an article calling on protestors to "Bring Najaf to New York." A dejected Christopher Hitchens noted that the antiwar movement had adopted "symbols from Fallujah as the emblems of its resistance."[25]

Despite all the denunciations of the Bush administration for its radicalism, the left suffered more for its affiliations and irrationality. The criticism of the Democratic Party's antiwar sympathies advanced by Beinart and others highlighted the cost to the party of maintaining certain alliances. George Will compared liberalism's travails with the absurd elements of the left to "conservatism's 1960s embarrassment from the claimed kinship of the John Birch Society, whose leader called President Eisenhower a Kremlin agent." Birchers, however, had remained marginal, while Michael Moore and the Hollywood left had been openly embraced as mainstream by the Democrats. John Kerry's daughter revealed the Democrats' dependence on Hollywood when she turned to noted film director Steven Spielberg to improve her father's poor public performances. Howard Dean also trotted out Martin Sheen and Rob Reiner before the Iowa caucuses, apparently believing that small-town Iowans would be impressed with how "Meathead" thought they should vote. *Boston Globe* columnist Scot Lehigh said that for the Democrats to make a comeback they must "say goodbye to Hollywood."[26]

Overall, the politics of the antiwar left, Hollywood, and the Blue Coasts failed to impress many voters in the middle of the country. During the 2004 campaign, the managing editor of the South Dakota newspaper the *Huron Daily Plainsman* criticized the antiwar sentiments of Michael Moore and Whoopi Goldberg and concluded that "for some strange reason, I guess the left doesn't want to believe Saddam Hussein was an evil dictator who murdered thousands of people." The *New Republic* conceded after the election that "it is clear that many Americans feel the Democratic Party is governed by out-of-touch liberal elites who look down on red-state America as a backward fiefdom ruled by cultural reactionaries." Some liberals did little to change this perception. One New Yorker interviewed after the election about the regional divide dismissed midwestern voters as "very 1950s. When I go back there, I feel I'm in a time warp." In 2005, newly elected Democratic chairman Howard Dean pronounced that the "base" of the party was "merlot Democrats."[27]

Reliving the battles of Vietnam and the 1960s also meant con-
fronting the cultural divisions that deepened in late-twentieth-century
America. One Vietnam veteran said that the "very act of remembering
Vietnam places one in the midst of a culture war." Two historians of
the era noted the persistence of these battles, attributing the phenomenon to their belief that "the cultural civil war of the 1960s produced
no clear victor." But cultural conservatism did win battles on the
Great Plains, a fact that bedeviled the left. Thomas Frank's widely
discussed election-year book *What's the Matter with Kansas?* argued
that "deranged" Red State Americans on the plains had been misled
by the right's promotion of military strength and cultural conservatism,
to the detriment of their economic interests. Some out-of-staters who
helped the Daschle campaign in South Dakota agreed with Frank.
The senior political editor for *CBS News* reported that a "couple of
Washington Democrats who traveled to South Dakota to campaign
for Tom Daschle reported to me that they were stunned when they
went into very poor trailer parks to find voters cared more about
killing babies and gay people getting married than about jobs and
health care. 'Why can't they see that by voting for John Thune they
are voting against their economic self-interest?' they wondered." The
editor also noted that such "bewildered liberals pat their rich friends
on the back for voting against their self-interest when they vote
Democratic and have rarely complained about religious figures in
politics when their names were Martin Luther King, Robert Drinan,
Daniel Berrigan or William Sloan Coffin."[28]

Thomas Frank's broadside against the "deranged" souls of the Great
Plains echoed earlier dismissals of conservative politics as "a kind of
pathology," in the words of historian Alan Brinkley. Voters' identification with conservatism was explained by academic theories of "status
anxiety" or by the power of the "paranoid style" in politics. These
liberal critiques persisted long after their genesis in the 1950s; some
on the left continued to hope that more Americans would embrace
"cosmopolitanism" and transcend the "provincialism" of Red America's
"village mind." Some commentators viewed such liberal attitudes as
elitist and damaging to social traditions, however, and many voters
agreed. In the summer of 2005, the *Washington Post* reported that
Democratic pollsters concluded that voters "see the Democrats as weak

on national security, and on cultural and moral issues, they view Democrats as both inconsistent and hostile to traditional values."[29]

Frank and other critics argued that working-class Americans should pay less attention to social issues and that the left should advocate more social and economic programs. Frank's views reflected the long-range vision of leftist intellectuals such as Richard Rorty, who said that "in the final stages of democracy we won't need religion anymore." Similarly, Democratic operatives, according to Ed Kilgore of the Democratic Leadership Council (DLC), were "forever trying to change the subject" and "telling the American people, 'You stupid crackers, stop thinking about the moral order of the universe and chow down on this prescription drug benefit.'" But as Daschle discovered, a focus on federal entitlement programs and promises of federal largesse can be trumped by moral questions, many of which first emerged in the 1960s and continue to resonate in Red America. Despite the desires of coastal elites, South Dakota is not France. Newly elected Senator Barack Obama of Illinois, who criticized Democratic tolerance for the "licentiousness" of the 1960s, urged Democrats to stop attempting to avoid moral questions. Others on the left deemed their colleagues' dire predictions of a GOP-led religious tyranny absurd. Popular historian Michael Lind explained that "when an American president closes an address by saying 'God bless America,' this is not a signal that the US is about to become a theocracy. It is the equivalent of saying 'May the force be with you.'" To the ongoing frustration of activists on the left, some voters made economic class issues subordinate to moral concerns.[30]

Democrats also suffered from the broader unraveling of the dispositions and demographics of the New Deal order. Most fundamentally, the New Deal–era faith in government activism had faded. When Daschle went to Washington as a congressional staffer in 1973, only 32 percent of Americans agreed with the statement that "the best government is one which governs least." In 1981, 60 percent of Americans agreed with the statement, which explained why Daschle first ran as a conservative, derided the bloated federal government, and voted for the Reagan tax cuts. Many of the seniors who supported the New Deal's federal programs after living through the misery of the Great Depression (South Dakota was enveloped by drought-driven dust storms and had the highest percentage of people on relief in the entire country) are also passing. Since the year 2000, thirty thousand people have died in South Dakota, a state where close elections are decided by a few thousand votes or less—most of the deaths occurred among members of the New Deal generation. When Daschle first ran for the Senate in 1986, he skewered his opponent for allegedly endangering Social Security, perhaps the New Deal's most prominent institutional legacy. In 2004, Daschle again accused Thune of promoting the "elimination" of Social Security by supporting private investment accounts, but this was no longer a fatal charge. One study noted that the weakening of the Democratic Party could be traced to "fervent New Deal Democrats dying off while less Democratic-leaning cohorts enter the electorate."[31]

Other parts of the once-powerful New Deal coalition are also shrinking. The number of small farmers, for example—who formed the core of George McGovern's first successful campaign for Congress in 1956—continues to dwindle. Whereas there were 45,000 farms in South Dakota when Daschle first went to Washington as a congressional aide in the early 1970s, in 2004 there were only 30,000. The declining number of small farmers and union members, once-confirmed pillars of the New Deal order, also helped Bush to prevail in neighboring Iowa in 2004. Bush was also shockingly competitive in Minnesota, which had in earlier years voted for the Democratic presidential candidates Walter Mondale and Michael Dukakis (the only state that voted for both) and supported the pro-union, pro-farmer liberalism of Senators Hubert Humphrey, Eugene McCarthy, and Paul Wellstone. Between 1996 and 2004, American unions lost nearly one million members, and the percentage of unionized workers dropped by 2 percent. In 2005, some of the nation's largest unions voted to defect from the AFL-CIO federation, a decision that further alarmed Democratic strategists. The population of blue urban areas, another source of strength for the New Deal coalition, also failed to keep pace with red states, in which fertility rates are higher. Women are giving birth to twice as many children per capita in Utah, for example, as they are in Howard Dean's Vermont. In 1960, John Kennedy's Massachusetts had more electoral votes than Florida, and Illinois had more than Texas; Florida and Texas now have more. In 2005, for the second straight year, Massachusetts lost population. Blue cities such as Boston and San Francisco are considered the worst places in the country to do business, causing many businesses to relocate to red states.[32]

The collapsing credibility of major media outlets also poses a challenge to the revival of liberalism, which has tended to benefit from the solicitousness of the media. Near the end of the 2004 campaign, law professor and blogger Glenn Reynolds wrote that the "Fourth Estate" was "unraveling before our very eyes, which I think is the biggest story of this election so far." (In November, Reynolds said, "It still is.") Although the travails of the *New York Times* were much discussed among elites in 2003, the CBS "memogate" fiasco had made mass media bias into conventional wisdom by the end of the 2004 campaign. President Bush openly made sport of CBS, an unlikely prospect in earlier decades (when figures such as Walter Cronkite commanded widespread respect). At a press conference in September with the Iraqi prime minister, Bush mockingly asked, "Is anybody here from CBS?" During one of the presidential debates, while chiding Kerry, Bush said, "I'm not so sure it's credible to quote leading news organizations"—while looking at the moderator from *CBS News.* Daniel Henninger said after the election that "Big Media lost big. But it was more than a loss. It was an *abdication of authority.* . . . It did so by choosing to go into overt opposition to one party's candidate, a sitting president. It stooped to conquer. . . . Big Media chose precisely the wrong moment to give itself over to an apparent compulsion to overthrow the Bush presidency." In an editorial entitled "End of an Era," the editors of *USA Today* opined that Dan Rather's National Guard documents story criticizing President Bush "was a textbook example of how to undermine journalistic credibility." One columnist instructed his fellow liberals in the blogosphere to stop criticizing the mainstream media, which "played straight into conservative hands" by undermining the public's faith in major media outlets.[33]

The blogger scrutiny of the *Sioux Falls Argus Leader* also indicated that Internet criticism can be especially effective where local news-papers maintain information monopolies. One commentator explained that instead of a "priestly caste" of journalists deciding "what we should read or what are the current talking points, we'll do it for ourselves." Blogging became an act of subversion, an attempt to reorder politics by undermining the major-media mandarins who controlled the flow of information to voters. This was not, of course, Czeslaw Milosz defying Stalinism in postwar Poland. It happened in the nation with the greatest freedom-of-speech liberties in history, ubiquitous Internet access, and free blogging software. The subversion was directed not against an oppressive government, however, but against local pro-Democratic newspaper monopolies, which will never again have the same stranglehold on information that they once maintained. Recognizing the perils that blogging posed for future Democratic candidates, Harry Reid (the new Senate leader) forced his caucus to address their influence and their role in the Daschle-Thune race at a retreat as the 109th Congress convened. Thune's caucus also wanted to hear from him about blogs.[34]

The Internet and blogs broadened the democratic discourse as well. While conservatives naturally benefited from the rise of another medium through which to criticize the establishment media, groups and individuals on the left, which often felt suffocated by leaders of the Democratic Party, also made their voices heard through the Internet. The changes wrought by the Internet, in addition to enhancing the public's ability to sift through the memories of the past and to discern the weaknesses of certain parties and candidates, served as another reminder to skeptics about the capacity for renewal and deliberation in American democracy. Social critics who have taken a dim view of American democracy in recent times, although they have raised important questions, should reconsider the depth of their pessimism. Often their views are taken from a high altitude, which obscures the gory details of democratic elections. While certainly not attaining a standard of perfection, the Daschle-Thune race did draw in thousands of citizens, present a vigorous debate over policy differences, and foster the growth of new sources of political information. The defeat of Senator Daschle, the most powerful Democrat in the country, constituted evidence of what political scientists term "vertical accountability" in a political system. After the election, the editors of the *Grand Forks Herald* concluded that "Thune hammered away at Daschle's record" and that Thune's "claims and assertions held up." Democracy functioned. Although a theoretical ideal of democratic practice may always be elusive, a more realistic appraisal of elections could dilute the corrosive cynicism about American democracy. Displeasure with democratic outcomes, including the defeat of one's preferred candidates, must not be confused with a failure of the democratic process itself. In a world of failed states, Islamic terror, and democratic breakdowns, American democracy deserves more credit than it receives.[35]

EPILOGUE

Perhaps wars weren't won any more. Maybe they went on forever.
—Ernest Hemingway

As President Bush began his second term, commentators consistently compared him to Woodrow Wilson, some believing that he would meet a similar fate: Wilson's idealistic crusade to "make the world safe for democracy" ended in ruin after a domestic revolt against his policies. Bush called on the memory of Reagan, however, and invoked the democratization of Eastern Europe, hoping that 1989, not 1919, would be the controlling precedent. The Democrats who opposed Bush were haunted by the memories of the 1960s, hobbled by incoherent foreign policy views and weakened by divisions in the ranks between purists and pragmatists. Capping a string of electoral setbacks dating to 1980, the leader of the opposition to Bush's policies, Senator Tom Daschle, had been defeated by a child of the Reagan revolution, John Thune. Whether the Reagan tradition would persist and Bush's hopes for democratization would yield results or the Democrats would come roaring back in the wake of Bush's Wilsonian demise remained an open question. Whatever the future held, the elections of 2004 demonstrated the continuing strength of the post-1980 GOP revival, which had its roots in the tumult of the 1960s.

Despite the hoary legacies that burdened the Democrats, after the 2004 elections the Republicans suffered politically as the war in Iraq continued. Democrats increasingly lashed out at the Bush administration, which they claimed had misled the nation about the threat posed by Saddam Hussein in 2002 and had mismanaged the subsequent occupation. In the fall of 2005, Tom Daschle called for the withdrawal of U.S. troops from Iraq, and John Kerry, in contrast to his position during the 2004 campaign, renounced his 2002 vote in favor of the war. The Bush administration responded that Democrats had made similarly dire predictions about the Iraqi threat when voting for war in 2002; the U.S. goals remained establishing a stable government in Iraq, training Iraqi security forces, and squelching the insurgency. Despite the successful elections in Iraq, however, by the end of 2005 some Americans had lost faith in the Bush administration's foreign policy goals as U.S. casualties mounted.[1]

As the war ground on, the specter of Vietnam was ever present and persistently invoked by the media. *New York Times* reporter John Burns wrote that "thoughts of Vietnam were hard to avoid." A few days before the Iraqi elections in January 2005, Senator Edward Kennedy gave a major policy speech invoking the ghosts of Vietnam and calling for U.S. troops in Iraq to come home. The day before the Iraqi elections, the *New York Times* ran a long news analysis comparing Iraq to Vietnam. After the election, the *Times* ran an article about the flawed Vietnamese elections of 1967. A *Times* article describing the infiltration of foreign terrorists into Iraq during the spring of 2005 was entitled "Iraq's Ho Chi Minh Trail." When reviewing Bush's democratization efforts, Michael Ignatieff, writing in the *Times Magazine*, asserted, "If Iraq fails, it will be his Vietnam, and nothing else will matter much about his time in office." Throughout 2005, Iraq-as-debacle remained the media's master narrative.[2]

The Bush administration also faced mounting problems on the domestic front as 2005 came to a close. The GOP could boast of a growing economy, passing long-stalled bills through the Senate, and confirming a new chief justice of the Supreme Court. In August, however, the administration was denounced for what critics deemed a passive response to Hurricane Katrina's destruction of New Orleans, which caused the greatest dislocation of Americans since the Civil War. In October, Bush's second nominee to the Supreme Court, White House counsel Harriet Miers, withdrew her nomination after charges of cronyism and criticism of her competence—much of the flak stemming from conservatives. House Majority Leader Tom Delay was then indicted for campaign finance violations, and Vice President Dick Cheney's chief of staff was indicted for perjury in the Valerie Plame/CIA leak investigation. Historian Michael Beschloss began comparing Bush's standing to the second-term slumps of FDR, Eisenhower, Reagan, and Clinton.[3]

The GOP's troubles fired Democratic hopes of winning back Congress in 2006. In addition to criticizing the war in Iraq and what they called the "culture of corruption" in Washington, Democratic Party strategists planned to set forth a united agenda for the 2006 midterm elections. But while they made their plans, polls showed that the same number of voters (39 percent) viewed the Democrats favorably as viewed them unfavorably. And although Bush's approval rating dropped to 40 percent or below during the fall of 2005, 70 percent of Americans thought Democratic criticism hurt the war effort. Some moderate Democrats recoiled in early December when Democratic chairman Howard Dean compared the Iraq effort to Vietnam and said that the "idea that we are going to win is an idea that unfortunately is just plain wrong." *Time* magazine columnist Joe Klein said Dean "seemed downright gleeful about the bad news. He seemed to be rooting for defeat." A *New Republic* analysis noted the "deep fissures" between liberal and moderate Democrats over the war, and headlines such as "Democratic Lawmakers Splinter on Iraq" began to appear in the national press. The *Washington Post* reported that even Democrats who hoped to benefit from the unpopularity of the Iraq War thought the Democratic leadership would "'blow it' by playing to the liberal base of the party." In a reflection of red-state sentiment, North Dakota Democratic Congressman Earl Pomeroy said that Dean did not "make policy announcements on behalf of all the Democrats" and should "shut up."[4]

The political passions of the 2004 elections persisted and intensified in the run-up to the midterm elections of 2006. They also reinforced the contrasts between the major parties that defined post-1960s American politics. The year 2006 opened with a battle over another Bush nominee to the Supreme Court, which replayed many of the previous decades' skirmishes over the federal judiciary and what conservatives viewed as liberal judicial activism. Senate liberals such as John Kerry and Edward Kennedy called for a filibuster of Samuel Alito, which caused a rift with Senate moderates, who were already under tremendous pressure from liberal interest groups to filibuster the appointment. Activists in North Dakota, for example, said that Democratic senator Kent Conrad "voted with the side of fascism" when he favored Alito.

But New York senator Chuck Schumer conceded that a Democratic filibuster was "harder than it was last term" under Senator Daschle because of diminished Democratic power in the Senate. The *New York Times* called the successful confirmation of Alito a "watershed for the conservative movement," which had been working since the Reagan administration to roll back liberal influences on the federal courts. Senator John Thune cast the deciding vote that ensured Alito's confirmation.[5]

In addition to exposing the rift between liberals and moderate Democrats within the Senate, the Alito vote also symbolized the opening of the chronic divide in post-1960s American politics. *New York Times* columnist David Brooks argued that if Alito, a product of the Italian middle class in New Jersey, had been born a little earlier, he probably would have become a member of the New Deal political coalition, which included northern white ethnic voters. But Alito had viewed the liberal rebellion of the 1960s at close range when he attended Princeton University, and he recoiled. Instead of manning the barricades with the rebels, Alito saw them as "very privileged people behaving irresponsibly. And I couldn't help making a contrast between some of the worst of what I saw on the campus and the good sense and the decency of the people in my own community." Princeton also purged Alito's ROTC unit from campus. Alito deemed the expulsion "a very bad thing for Princeton to do," and he finished his ROTC classes at a state college. When Senate liberals berated Alito for his views relating to police authority (which Senator Kennedy deemed "Gestapo-like"), antiterrorism laws, military recruitment on campus, affirmative action, and abortion, they underscored the reasons that had led many voters to abandon the Democratic Party since the 1960s.[6]

In addition to the ongoing battles over social and cultural issues, national security remained a prominent and vexing problem for Democrats throughout 2006. At the beginning of the year, some Democrats vigorously protested the existence of a National Security Agency antiterrorist surveillance program after its existence was revealed by the *New York Times*. The Bush administration responded that only telephone calls between suspected terrorists overseas and callers in the United States were monitored, but many critics conflated the program with the Nixon era's binge of domestic wiretapping of political enemies. One senior editor at *Newsweek* compared the Bush administration's "spying" program to those operated by "South Africa's apartheid regime," and some Democrats considered the program grounds for impeaching President Bush—indeed, they called on John Dean, who had testified to Congress in 1973 during the Watergate hearings, to make the case for censure or impeachment. Despite the outrage on the left, when Democratic senator Russ Feingold sought to censure President Bush for allowing the program, his fellow senators quickly demurred. Feingold accused his Democratic colleagues of cowering, but one Democratic strategist doubted that censure would have popular appeal: "If someone proposed stringing up Bush like they did Mussolini, that would have a lot of support in the base of the party, too. But it's not smart." Joe Klein downplayed the liberals' "civil-liberties fetishism" as a "hangover from the Vietnam era" and Nixon's reign of misdeeds. One survey found that 60 percent of Americans favored the surveillance program, and many criticized the *New York Times* for disclosing the existence of a clandestine antiterrorist program. Later in the year, the *Times* revealed another program designed to track and eliminate terrorists' attempts to transfer money electronically, a disclosure that prompted another wave of criticism from those who thought the disclosure compromised national security and wondered why the media outlet had chosen to reveal the details of its operation to the terrorists. The *New York Times* ombudsman later concluded that the newspaper should not have published the money-transfers story, because of the "apparent legality of the program in the United States, and the absence of any evidence that anyone's private data had actually been misused."[7]

The war in Iraq remained the central point of friction in American foreign policy. In late 2005, some prominent Democrats such as House Minority Leader Nancy Pelosi called for the withdrawal of U.S. troops within six months, a move rejected by other Democrats. For much of 2006, Democrats debated the when, if, and how of withdrawing troops from Iraq. John Kerry and John Edwards, the Democratic standard-bearers in 2004, both renounced their votes to authorize the Iraq War. Kerry's advocacy of withdrawal, according to the *New York Times*, "left the Democrats divided, and open to renewed Republican accusations that they are indecisive and weak—the same ridicule that Republicans heaped on Mr. Kerry in 2004, when his 'I was for it before I was against it' statement about a vote on money for the war became a punchline." Throughout 2006, Tom Daschle also became more vocal in his opposition to the Iraq War.[8]

Some Democrats calling themselves members of the "Sept. 11 generation" sought to promote an aggressive foreign policy to challenge "the generation of Democrats who came of age during the 1960s and who were instrumental in finishing off 'Cold War liberalism' because of its failures in the jungles of Vietnam." Peter Beinart of the *New Republic* continued to spearhead the call for a bold Democratic foreign policy, and observers noted his break with the liberal past. Joe Klein said that Beinart was "not a member of the baby boom generation. His political sensibility was not molded by Vietnam, the civil rights movement or hallucinogens. He is not afflicted by the excesses, delusions, indulgences or grandiosity of the current leaders of the Democratic Party." Other observers, when criticizing the persistent shadow cast by Vietnam, noted that the left still featured "Seymour Hirsh chronicling the demonic breakdowns of command, and Neil Young releasing antiwar songs."[9]

When antiwar liberals promoted a primary challenge to moderate Democratic senator Joe Lieberman of Connecticut, they compared it to the 1968 antiwar candidacies of Eugene McCarthy and Robert Kennedy, both of whom had challenged cold warrior Hubert Humphrey for the Democratic nomination. When political newcomer Ned Lamont defeated Lieberman in the Connecticut Senate primary in August by focusing on Lieberman's support for the war in Iraq, pundits viewed it as a major victory for liberals, antiwar bloggers, and what political analyst Matt Bai termed "exasperated and ideologically disappointed baby boomers." *Slate* columnist Jacob Weisberg noted that the "Lamont-Lieberman battle was filled with echoes and parallels from the Vietnam era." Lamont declared victory while flanked by Jesse Jackson and Al Sharpton, and *Newsweek* warned that the "revival of the romance of the antiwar left is a potential disaster for the Democrats."[10]

Peter Beinart published his book *The Good Fight* in 2006 and clashed with the hardened antiwar faction within the Democratic Party. Beinart criticized liberals for antiwar-inspired "Lieberman-hatred" and for viewing the Iraq War "through the prism of Bush—which is why they can muster so little anger at America's jihadist enemies and so little enthusiasm when Iraqis risk their lives to vote." He called for more than "Bush-hatred" from liberals. Markos Moulitsas Zuniga, the "Kos" of the well-known liberal blog Daily Kos, responded by calling Beinart a "dumbass" who wrote for a "dying" magazine that sought "to destroy the new people-powered movement for the sake of its Lieberman-worshipping neocon owners." Kos said that if liberals still subscribed to the *New Republic,* once the forerunner of progressive reform in the country, "it really is time to call it quits. If you see it in a magazine rack, you might as well move it behind *National Review."* Jonathan Chait of the *New Republic* responded by criticizing the "paranoid mentality" of Kos and his supporters and their sectarian resistance to pro-war viewpoints that many viewed as lending legitimacy to the Bush administration. Other liberals, after witnessing such exchanges, feared that the "raw hatred" and "anger festering on the Democratic left" would undermine moderate Democrats. When historian Todd Gitlin advocated that liberals take patriotism more seriously, his message was not warmly received by some in his target audience. "The night of the long knives had begun," he lamented. He asked, "Why is the left so determined to eat its own?"[11]

Deep divisions over issues such as foreign policy complicated Democrats' efforts to formulate a coherent political message in 2006. Jacob Weisberg, echoing many critics, condemned the Democrats for failing to "articulate a positive agenda for reform and change." The promised unveiling of a Democratic program was delayed several times because of tactical and philosophical divisions magnified by leaders who sought to subordinate the release of a Democratic agenda to repetitive charges of Republican incompetence and corruption. When Democratic leaders finally held an event to unveil their national security ideas, the *Washington Post* reported that the "Democrats rehashed their usual litany of security cliches, declaring their opposition to terrorism, proclaiming their support for the troops." Others, by contrast—including congressional staffers, liberal writers, professors, and think tank researchers—were aggressively seeking to craft a new message that Democrats could embrace. The *New York Times* reported that the in-depth discussion of this new vision marked a "psychological shift for many in the party; a frequent theme is that Democrats must stop being afraid, stop worrying that their core beliefs are out of step with the times, stop ceding so much ground to the conservatives."[12]

While Democratic strategists debated deeper philosophical issues about the future direction of the party, Democratic tacticians exploited

Republican stumbles. Democrats began 2006 by focusing their message on GOP "ethics and corruption" in the wake of the Jack Abramoff scandal and the indictment of the vice president's chief of staff for perjury over "Plamegate." One Democratic Party strategist said of the Republicans: "They're on fire. Don't say anything. Let them destroy themselves." Leading Democrats sought to focus on Republican "competence" and avoid ideological debates. Liberal columnist Anna Quindlen complained about the Democrats' strategy of reacting and waiting: "The plan seems to be to wait until the Republicans falter, then to move in for the kill. It's not pretty, it's not inspiring and it's not working."[13]

Despite such complaints, Democrats racked up a number of political advantages in 2006. Wealthy liberals agreed to fund new think tanks and interest groups to influence federal policy, and new journals of liberal opinion came to life. In addition to large-scale fund-raising and organizational efforts, political passion favored the Democrats as the loathing of President Bush among them deepened. In addition to organizing a "religious left," Democrats also sought to appeal to religious conservatives. Howard Dean appeared on Pat Robertson's *700 Club* to argue that Democrats "have an enormous amount in common with the Christian community, and particularly with the evangelical Christian community." Democrats aggressively targeted vulnerable Republican senators such as Rick Santorum of Pennsylvania, who called his contest "the revenge of Tom Daschle race." Democrats also sought to squelch primary contests and arrange the most electable congressional candidates. New York senator Chuck Schumer, who led Democratic efforts to retake the Senate, promoted a pragmatic recognition of the difficult situation faced by Democrats in red states in commenting that "when I go into a drawing room in Manhattan and they say, 'You got to appeal to our base!' I say, 'There is no base in North Dakota!'"[14]

Senator Schumer's shrewd recognition of the segmentation of the electorate and the narrowness of the Democratic base reflected the difficulties faced by liberals who sought to win a convincing majoritarian mandate. Broad-based political appeal eluded liberals, whose shrill outbursts exposed the near-exhaustion of liberalism's capacity to inspire. During the summer of 2006, Howard Dean compared the GOP's Senate candidate in Florida to Joseph Stalin—which may have found favor in the drawing rooms described by Senator Schumer but otherwise sounded absurd. While the liberalism of the 1960s still resonates in parts of the country, many of the great causes of the 1960s have been eclipsed, either by being adequately addressed or by being discredited in the minds of many voters. The valiant struggle to liberate blacks from systemic Jim Crow segregation, for example, could once motivate the young to enlist in an honorable liberal cause, but embracing Chevy Chase's denunciation of the president as a "dumbf——" failed to inspire. "This politics," historian Garry Wills once said of the Nixon era, "will not summon us with trumpets." *New Yorker* columnist George Packer thought that "liberalism seemed to have achieved what it could and stopped being a vital force for reform." He lamented that liberalism "was becoming a set of fixed positions that went along with a certain way of life peculiar to a narrow social class."[15]

The limited scope and appeal of the politics of the drawing room did not prevent Democrats from profiting throughout 2006 from Republican woes. Controversies erupted over the administration's decision to allow a Dubai company to manage some U.S. ports, and Vice President Dick Cheney's accidental shooting of another hunter while pursuing quail. High fuel prices, the war in Iraq, and a legislative stalemate over immigration policy contributed to an ongoing erosion of the Bush administration's standing among both the electorate and his Republican base. The *Washington Post* also reported that insiders thought the Bush White House was "physically and emotionally exhausted, battered by scandal and drained by political setbacks," an image that contributed to a staff shake-up in the spring. Some neoconservatives abandoned the administration's Iraq policy, while other longtime conservative activists railed against the failure to slow federal spending. Despite his tumbling popularity, however, polls indicated that President Bush was still more popular than John Kerry and Al Gore and that nearly 60 percent of Americans did not "believe the Democrats offer a clear set of alternative policies."[16]

Republican stumbles did not eliminate the Democrats' long-term quandary. Winning on a platform of Republican incompetence and corruption would not legitimize a reinvigorated Democratic agenda. It risked wedding Democrats to a more efficient execution of GOP policies and set Democrats up for charges of flip-flopping if they pursued liberal policies after winning, a turn that had hobbled the effectiveness of the Clinton administration in its early years. Democrats and the American left in general needed to provide, as the philosopher Richard Rorty once counseled, the details of a reform agenda and then prevail in the voting booth. Continuing to operate within the political contours carved by Reaganism did not appeal to the Democratic base, which favored the symbols and icons of 1960s activism, or liberal intellectuals, who thought that Democratic moderates legitimized the narrow parameters of American politics set by Reagan. Democratic strategist Michael Tomasky demanded that Democrats "stop focusing on their grab bag of small-bore proposals that so often seek not to offend and that accept conservative terms of debate." Some liberals were less than thrilled when leading Democrats such as Senator Barack Obama of Illinois reached out to religious conservatives. The presumptive front-runner for the Democratic presidential nomination in 2008, Senator Hillary Clinton of New York, also took fire for embracing a ban on flag burning and for not renouncing her support for the war in Iraq. Pragmatists, however, endorsed the Democratic embrace of conservative causes. The chairwoman of the New Hampshire Democratic Party said, "We make a mistake if we think that just because people are fed up with George Bush they want George McGovern."[17]

By late summer of 2006, according to a *Washington Post*/ABC News poll, 81 percent of Democrats had come to believe that the war in Iraq was not worth fighting, and the approval ratings of congressional incumbents dropped to the lowest level since 1994. As the midterm elections of 2006 approached, commentators predicted large Democratic gains as the war in Iraq continued to grind on, President Bush's popularity hovered in the 30 percent range, and Republican woes persisted. In early October, Democrats fiercely criticized Republican House leaders for not disciplining Mark Foley, a Republican congressman from Florida who had sent racy messages to a young male intern. The violence in Iraq also intensified and increasingly undermined Republican candidates. In late October, *Newsweek* reported that the "Iraq war is all but overwhelming every other topic on the table now."[18]

On election day, the Democrats won back the House and the Senate. Many commentators attributed Republican losses to the sinking popularity of President Bush and frustration with the war in Iraq. In addition to the Mark Foley scandal, the conventional wisdom regarding Republican losses was succinctly captured by political analyst Chuck Todd: "Two words: Bush and Iraq." Congressman Rahm Emanuel of Illinois, who led Democratic efforts to retake the House, said that "Iraq was the driving factor behind everything." Republican pollster Bill McInturff said, "Iraq [was] front and center of this election, and people voted for change." Political analyst Stuart Rothenberg pointed to the Republican loss of independent voters and declared President Bush the "biggest loser" on election day, stating that "he is the reason Republicans took a bath." Exit polls showed that 37 percent of voters who voted against Republicans did so as a protest against Bush personally. Defeated Republican congressman Jim Leach of Iowa pointed to the "six-year itch," in addition to Bush and the war. In all the sixth-year elections since World War II, the party in power had lost an average of thirty-one House and six Senate seats. In keeping with political history, the Republicans lost twenty-nine House and six Senate seats in the fall of 2006. "In elections when the president's popularity was low because of war, scandal or recession," the editor of *Roll Call* noted, "the average is 47 House seats and eight Senate seats," making Republican losses less stinging than they could have been.[19]

Many of the Democrats who were victorious in fall 2006 did little to advance the cause of political liberalism. Incoming Democratic senators, according to Chuck Todd, were "socially moderate" and "all seem to evoke a hawkishness on defense even while criticizing Iraq." The Democratic victory, according to British reporter Tim Reid, was "built on the back of moderate, often conservative candidates" who were "well to the right of the party's current caucus on cultural issues." The victorious Senate candidate in Montana, Jon Tester, is an "anti-abortion, pro-gun, three-generation farmer with a buzz cut, three missing fingers on his left hand and no big fan of Hillary Clinton," and the victorious Virginia candidate, Jim Webb, "hates liberals and likes guns so much he gave one to his son at the age of 8" and championed "Southern redneck culture." Webb—a one-time Republican, a Vietnam veteran, and Ronald Reagan's secretary of the navy—once said, "Jane Fonda can kiss my a[—] . . . I wouldn't go across the street to watch her slit her wrist." The Democrat who defeated Republican senator Rick Santorum of Pennsylvania was described by the *New York Times* as an "ardent opponent of abortion."

The *Washington Post* reported, "What the election was not, in the view of strategists in both parties, was a powerful affirmation of the Democratic Party, despite its takeover of the House and Senate." In Connecticut, antiwar liberals hoped that a victory by their champion, Ned Lamont, would legitimize the movement against the war, but he was decisively defeated by hawkish Senator Lieberman, who reentered the race as an independent.[20]

The nature of the Democratic victory in fall 2006 sharply limited Democrats' ability to pursue an ideological agenda. Matt Bai reported that "even leading Democrats had to admit that the election had everything to do with Republican failures and almost nothing to do with them." Democrats "avoided new ideas," which Bai deemed a "smart electoral tactic," but it left Democrats with "only vague slogans ('a new direction') around which to build a governing agenda." The *Washington Post* described the Democrats' national security agenda as "more goals than details. Who could disagree with promises to 'eliminate Osama Bin Laden, destroy terrorist networks like al-Qaeda, finish the job in Afghanistan and end the threat posed by the Taliban' or 'redouble efforts to stop nuclear weapons development in Iran and North Korea?'" Peter Beinart of the *New Republic* called the Democratic agenda vague and unremarkable.[21] During the early months of 2007, some Democratic leaders sought to avoid advancing liberal causes on the domestic front and adhered to a plan to "keep the party's ideological faithful happy through a series of hearings during which they would excoriate the Bush administration." Despite the attempt to contain promotion of an unpopular liberal agenda, the new Democratic Congress still received lower approval ratings than President Bush. The relentless focus on Iraq, Democratic Congressman Rahm Emanuel conceded, made the new Congress appear to be a "one-trick pony."[22]

Despite the election of more moderate Democrats in the fall of 2006 and the party's effort to avoid ideological clashes, long-serving liberal Democrats who were poised to ascend to committee chairmanships vowed to take a hard line against the Bush administration. Representative John Murtha of Pennsylvania, who began supporting an immediate withdrawal from Iraq in 2005, also challenged the deal-making foreign-policy moderate Representative Steny Hoyer of Maryland to become majority leader of the Democratic House. The incoming Speaker of the House, Nancy Pelosi, a San Francisco liberal, made the unexpected decision to publicly support Murtha. Pelosi's support of Murtha "set off a furor" in Washington as moderates supporting Hoyer objected to her intervention and reformers who had criticized the GOP's "culture of corruption" began revealing Murtha's past ethical scrapes. Murtha was defeated, and the *New York Times* editorialized that Pelosi "managed to severely scar her leadership even before taking up the gavel as the new speaker of the House." Pelosi's gambit did appeal to the progressive "netroots" and liberal activists, however, who demanded attention to their agenda. Political analyst Thomas Edsall worried that such demands would "revive the internecine warfare that has plagued the party since 1968."[23]

The new Democratic Congress risked strengthening the party's antiwar image. Some Democrats called for Congress to cut off funds for the war in Iraq, some called for a withdrawal of U.S. troops to begin immediately, and others called for a troop withdrawal within months. What some Democrats called a "phased redeployment," the editors of the *New York Times* called "a euphemism for withdrawal." Immediately after the election, the sixty-two Democratic members of the Congressional Progressive Caucus invited an increasingly vocal George McGovern to speak to them about how to withdraw from Iraq. McGovern again compared Iraq to Vietnam and, according to the Associated Press, said that the "threat of terrorism developed because—not before—the United States went into Iraq." McGovern called on Democratic presidential front-runner Hillary Clinton to be "more gutsy" and to stop "running away from liberalism." The *New York Times* reported that other Democrats feared "getting caught up in the party's Vietnam history." Senator John Kerry sounded another Vietnam-era theme during the fall elections when he instructed students to "do your homework" and "be smart" so that they did not "get stuck in Iraq." Matt Bai, who deemed Kerry's remark "inexcusably smug," detected a frustration among voters with political leaders "who seem stuck in the same ideological debate they were having in 1975" and hoped for an end to the "era of baby-boomer politics—with its culture wars, its racial subtext, its archaic divisions between hawks and doves and between big government and no government at all." Odds favored the continuation of the long-running battle between Reaganism and the '60s generation and their younger disciples.[24]

In early 2007, liberals and antiwar activists pressured the new Democratic Congress to end the war in Iraq. Many Democrats criticized the Bush administration's planned "troop surge," designed to stabilize Baghdad and, according to the *New York Times*, generally sought "to map out a strategy that will appease the antiwar left." Representative John Murtha sought to cease funding of the war and others promoted nonbinding congressional resolutions condemning the surge. Divisions erupted over these strategies, however. Thomas Edsall criticized the "loophole-ridden resolution that showcases the party's generic antiwar stance" and Congressman David Obey (Dem.-Wis.) ridiculed the "idiot liberals" who sought to "defund the war." The *Los Angeles Times* reported that some Democrats feared "exposing the party to charges that it is undermining the military." The Democratic Congress finally passed a bill that required the withdrawal of American troops within several months, but it prompted a presidential veto. Throughout the legislative debate, however, the new Congress made clear it sought the withdrawal of American troops from Iraq. In April 2007, Senate Majority Leader Harry Reid simply pronounced, "This war is lost." Reid said he had compared Iraq to Vietnam in a discussion with President Bush and had told the president to avoid following the precedent of Lyndon Johnson.[25]

Although Democratic pragmatists tried to resist the gravitational pull of the 1960s, its power in Democratic circles continued to be felt. The icon of that earlier era, George McGovern, continued to speak out against the Iraq War throughout 2006, asserting that "you can just cross out Vietnam and write in Iraq. It's the same thing." McGovern also praised a convention of Americans who had fled to Canada in the 1960s to avoid the draft. The iconic folk group Peter, Paul, and Mary, who had played in 1972 in Sioux Falls (where George McGovern conceded after losing forty-nine states) played once again at the opening of the McGovern Library in Mitchell in October 2006. Liberal columnist David Corn said that the looming fight for the Democratic nomination in 2008 "could become something of a replay of 1968," when Eugene McCarthy led a rebellion that helped crack the post–World War II foreign policy consensus. In late 2005, McCarthy passed away at age eighty-nine, but his powerful memory lived on. David Broder noted that the "McCarthy volunteers remained in politics, fueling a generation of Democratic activism." Tom Daschle supported McCarthy's presidential bid in 1968 and worked for McGovern's presidential campaign in 1972. In 2006, Daschle gave speeches against the war in New Hampshire, where the antiwar McCarthy crusade had begun in 1968. Daschle also went to Iowa and declared his interest in running for president, four decades after McCarthy's historic campaign. Daschle's bid symbolized the frustration of American liberals. His political success first came when he abandoned the politics of Peter, Paul, and Mary; his defeat came when he embraced it again.[26] Daschle ultimately abandoned his presidential bid and endorsed Senator Barack Obama, who sought, according to the *New York Times*, to transcend the "tired ideological battles of the 1960s" and defeat "uberboomer Hillary Rodham Clinton" for the Democratic nomination. At times, however, Obama appeared more liberal than the woman from Wellseley's Class of '69.[27]

The world of Democratic politics dominated by Eugene McCarthy and George McGovern in the 1960s and 1970s, in which Tom Daschle first found his political footing, toppled in 1980 with the ascendancy of political conservatism and the election of Ronald Reagan. In a measure of the shift in American politics, McCarthy even endorsed Reagan for president. John Thune represented the ongoing resonance of Reaganism and embraced the Reagan tradition in his successful bid to defeat the Democrats' leader. The Reagan position still held in 2004 in South Dakota, but its strength remains to be determined in the varied fronts of American politics. Historians will wait to see whether the Democratic breakthrough in 2006 would mark the beginning of the end of the Reagan era or whether Republicans could stand their ground. Perhaps the rival political generations of the 1960s and 1980s and their descendants would remain locked in a perpetual generational showdown, the importance of which should cause the republic's historians to dwell on its historic origins.

NOTES

BOOK EPIGRAPH

Alexis de Tocqueville, "Some Characteristics of Historians in Modern Times," in *Democracy in America* (1835; New York: Barnes and Noble Books, 2003), 487, 490.

PREFACE

Epigraph source: Frederick Jackson Turner, "The Significance of History" (1891), in John Mack Faragher, ed., *Rereading Frederick Jackson Turner: "The Significance of History" and Other Essays* (New Haven, Conn.: Yale University Press, 1994), 21.

1. Henry Adams to Francis Parkman, 1884, quoted in Cushing Strout, *The Pragmatic Revolt in American History: Carl Becker and Charles Beard* (New Haven, Conn.: Yale University Press, 1958), 15. For a recent attempt to seriously analyze the necessary qualities of a workable democracy, see Larry Diamond and Leonardo Morlino, eds., *Assessing the Quality of Democracy* (Baltimore, Md.: Johns Hopkins University Press, 2005).

2. Mark T. Gilderhus, *History and Historians: A Historiographical Introduction*, 2nd ed. (Englewood Cliffs, N.J.: Prentice-Hall, 1992), 16 (Thucydides quote); John Lukacs, *Churchill: Visionary, Statesman, Historian* (New Haven, Conn.: Yale University Press, 2002), 105 (Churchill quote).

3. Richard Hofstadter, *The Progressive Historians: Turner, Beard, Parrington* (New York: Vintage Books, 1968), 30; Cushing Strout, *The Pragmatic Revolt in American History: Carl Becker and Charles Beard* (New Haven, Conn.: Yale University Press, 1958), 4 (Beard quote); Christopher Lasch, "Consensus: An Academic Question?" *Journal of American History* 76, no. 2 (September 1989): 458. Arthur Schlesinger, Jr.,

wrote that there were "compensating advantages in writing so soon [after historic events]—in particular, the opportunity to consult those who took part in great events and thus to rescue information which might otherwise elude the written record." Schlesinger, *The Age of Roosevelt: The Crisis of the Old Order* (Boston: Houghton Mifflin, 1957), ix.

4. Michael Kazin, "The Agony and Romance of the American Left," *American Historical Review* 100, no. 5 (December 1995): 1490; Jesse Lemisch, "2.5 Cheers for Bridging the Gap between Activism and the Academy," *Radical History Review* 85, no. 1 (Winter 2003): 241 ("tear gas" quote); Michael Walzer, *The Company of Critics: Social Criticism and Political Commitment in the Twentieth Century*, 2nd ed. (New York: Basic Books, 2002), xiii, 8, 16.

5. Robin W. Winks, ed., *The Historian as Detective: Essays on Evidence* (New York: Harper and Row, 1970), 523 ("outspoken liberal" quote); George Packer, "The Revolution Will Not Be Blogged," *Mother Jones*, May/June 2004; James Nuechterlein, "Liberalism and Theodore White," *Commentary*, September 1982 (White quote); Joyce Hoffmann, *Theodore White and Journalism as Illusion* (Columbia: University of Missouri Press, 1995). For more on Arthur Schlesinger, Jr., in the Kennedy White House, see Tevi Troy, *Intellectuals and the American Presidency: Philosophers, Jesters, or Technicians?* (Lanham, Md.: Rowman and Littlefield, 2002), 17–42.

6. Douglas Brinkley, *Tour of Duty: John Kerry and the Vietnam War* (New York: William Morrow, 2004); Alex Beam, "Historian's 'Duty': PR for Kerry?" *Boston Globe*, April 29, 2004; Paul Farhi, "Ad Says Kerry 'Secretly' Met with Enemy; But He Told Congress of It," *Washington Post*, September 22, 2004; Ann Gerhart, "The Political Guns of August Are Firing; Brinkley Wrote about John Kerry's Battles in Vietnam; Now He's Fighting His Own," *Washington Post*, August 28, 2004; Tom Infield and Ron Hutcheson, "Anti-Kerry Veterans: Biography Spurred TV Ads," *Kansas City Star*, August 26, 2004 (captain quote); Evan Thomas, "The Vets Attack," *Newsweek*, November 15, 2004.

7. Thomas Carlyle, "On History" (1830), reprinted in Fritz Stern, ed., *The Varieties of History: From Voltaire to the Present* (New York: Meridian Books, 1968), 93; Carl Becker, "Everyman His Own Historian," *American Historical Review* 37, no. 2 (January 1932): 236.

8. Alan Brinkley, *Liberalism and Its Discontents* (Cambridge, Mass.: Harvard University Press, 1998), 277; Neil Jumonville, *Henry Steele Commager, Midcentury Liberalism, and the History of the Present* (Chapel Hill: University of North Carolina Press, 1999), 244; Leo Ribuffo, *Right Center Left: Essays in American History* (New Brunswick, N.J.: Rutgers University Press, 1992), 13, 18 ("influence" and "perfidy" quotes); Leo Ribuffo, "Confessions of an Accidental (or Perhaps Overdetermined) Historian," in Elizabeth Fox-Genovese and Elisabeth Lasch-Quinn, eds., *Reconstructing History: The Emergence of a New Historical Society* (New York: Routledge, 1999), 162 ("moralizing" quote).

9. Todd Gitlin, *The Intellectuals and the Flag* (New York: Columbia University Press, 2006), 2; Richard Hofstadter, *The Age of Reform: From Bryan to FDR* (New York: Vintage Books, 1955), 13. On the decline of political history, see William Leuchtenburg, "The Pertinence of Political History: Reflections on the Significance of the State in America," *Journal of American History* 73, no. 3 (December 1986): 586–600. For a review of recent attempts to revive political history, see Meg Jacobs and Julian E. Zelizer, "The Democratic Experiment: New Directions in American Political History," in Meg Jacobs, William J. Novak, and Julian E. Zelizer, eds., *The Democratic Experiment: New Directions in American Political History* (Princeton, N.J.: Princeton University Press, 2003), 1–19; Robert B. Westbrook, *John Dewey and American Democracy* (Ithaca, N.Y.: Cornell University Press, 1991), 551 (Walzer quote); Richard White, "What Are We Afraid Of?" *OAH Newsletter* 34 (August 2006). The release of new books on the history of American conservatism is noted in Donald T. Critchlow, "What's Wrong with the New Conservative History?" *History News Network*, April 30, 2007. The 2007 Organization of American Historians annual conference in Minneapolis also featured several panels relating to the history of American conservatism.

10. Frederick Jackson Turner, "The Significance of History" (1891), in John Mack Faragher, ed., *Rereading Frederick Jackson Turner: "The Significance of History" and Other Essays* (New Haven, Conn.: Yale University Press, 1994), 23, 29; Elisabeth Lasch-Quinn, "Democracy in the Ivory Tower? Toward a Restoration of an Intellectual Community," in Elizabeth Fox-Genovese and Elisabeth Lasch-Quinn, eds., *Reconstructing History: The Emergence of a New Historical Society* (New York: Routledge, 1999), 24–25; Alan B. Spitzer, *Historical Truth and Lies about the Past: Reflections on Dewey, Dreyfus, de Man, and Reagan* (Chapel Hill: University of North Carolina Press, 1996), 4 (White quote).

11. Sean Wilentz, "Freedoms and Feelings: Taking Politics out of Political History," review of Andrew Burstein, *The Passions of Andrew Jackson* (New York: Alfred A. Knopf, 2003), in *New Republic*, April 7, 2003 ("denigration" and "sound" quotes); Sean Wilentz, "Roundtable on *The Rise of American Democracy: Jefferson to Lincoln*," Society for the Historians of the Early American Republic Annual Conference, July 2006 ("essential" quote).

INTRODUCTION: POLITICS AND MEMORY

Epigraph source: Benedetto Croce, quoted in Gerald N. Grob and George Athan Billias, *Interpretations of American History: Patterns and Perspectives*, 6th ed. (New York: Free Press, 1991), 1.

1. Sheryl Gay Stolberg, "Chasing a Coveted Democratic Prize across the Plains," *New York Times*, October 24, 2004 (italics added); "Tom and John Slug It

Out; The Second-Most Important Race in America," *Economist*, October 28, 2004; David Rogers, "The 'Keystone' State: South Dakota? As Democrat Sen. Daschle Fights for His Seat, Republicans Lustily Eye Control of Congress," *Wall Street Journal*, October 11, 2004; Chris Cillizza, "Roll Call's 10 Best Senate Races," *Roll Call*, May 9, 2005; Dean E. Murphy, "Can History Save the Democrats?" *New York Times*, November 7, 2004 (Wilentz quote); Todd S. Purdum, "The Year of Passion," *New York Times*, October 31, 2004.

2. Editorial, "Daschle's Dead Zone," *Wall Street Journal*, July 22, 2004.

3. For additional background on South Dakota, see Jon Lauck, John E. Miller, and Edward Hogan, "The Contours of South Dakota Political Culture," *South Dakota History* 34, no. 2 (Summer 2004): 157–78; Jon D. Schaff, Erin Hogan Fouberg, and Thomas D. Isern, "Comments on 'The Contours of South Dakota Political Culture,'" *South Dakota History* 36, no. 2 (Summer 2006): 208–23.

4. Jonah Goldberg, "Democrats' Long List of Flops Breeds Even Greater Failure," *Kansas City Star*, November 11, 2000 ("20 million" quote).

5. Todd S. Purdum and David D. Kirkpatrick, "Campaign Strategist Is in Position to Consolidate Republican Majority," *New York Times*, November 5, 2004; Jeffrey Goldberg, "Central Casting: The Democrats Think about Who Can Win in the Midterms—and in 2008," *New Yorker*, May 29, 2006 (Wilentz quote); Theodore J. Lowi, *The End of the Republican Era* (Norman: University of Oklahoma Press, 2006 [1995]), 267.

6. Francis Parkman, *Montcalm and Wolfe: The Decline and Fall of the French Empire in North America* (New York: Collier Books, 1962 [1884]). General Louis-Joseph de Montcalm-Grozon and General James Wolfe commanded the armies of France and England, respectively, during the French and Indian War, which was fought for control of North America. Francis Parkman told their story in his well-known book *Montcalm and Wolfe*, which stressed how each general represented and symbolized his respective nation.

7. C. Vann Woodward, "The Future of the Past," *American Historical Review* 85, no. 3 (February 1970): 714; David Farber, ed., *The Sixties: From Memory to History* (Chapel Hill: University of North Carolina Press, 1994), 1; Arnold R. Isaacs, *Vietnam Shadows: The War, Its Ghosts, and Its Legacy* (Baltimore, Md.: Johns Hopkins University Press, 1997), 44–45; Tom Brokaw, *The Greatest Generation* (New York: Random House, 1998).

8. John Kerry, with David Thorne, ed., *The New Soldier* (New York: Macmillan, 1971) (italics added); David M. Halbfinger, "Three Decades Later, Vietnam Remains a Hot Issue," *New York Times*, August 29, 2004; Todd S. Purdum, "What They're Really Fighting About; A Debate about Vietnam Revives an Old Cultural Battle and Points to Iraq," *New York Times*, August 29, 2004; Edward Epstein, "'Winter Soldier' Testimony Still Fuels Discontent; Bitterness Lingers over Young Kerry's Senate Appearance," *San Francisco Chronicle*, October 17, 2004; Mackubin Thomas

Owens, "Fahrenheit 1971," *Weekly Standard*, September 6, 2004 (Naval War College professor quote and quotes from *The New Soldier*; italics added); John Lukacs, *Historical Consciousness* (New York: Harper and Row, 1968), 33. On the battle over memories of Vietnam, see Christian Appy and Alexander Bloom, "Vietnam War Mythology and the Rise of Public Cynicism," in Alexander Bloom, ed., *Long Time Gone: Sixties America Then and Now* (New York: Oxford University Press, 2001), 62–71.

9. Evan Thomas, "How Bush Did It," *Newsweek*, November 15, 2004 ("symbol" quote); Martin Peretz, "Good Riddance," *Wall Street Journal*, November 10, 2004; Jodi Wilgoren, "Truth Be Told, the Vietnam Crossfire Hurts Kerry More," *New York Times*, September 24, 2004; Evan Thomas, "Fits and Starts," *Newsweek*, November 15, 2004 ("living proof" quote).

10. Matthew Dallek, *The Right Moment: Ronald Reagan's First Victory and the Decisive Turning Point in American Politics* (New York: Free Press, 2000), 241.

11. Richard Hofstadter, *The Progressive Historians: Turner, Beard, Parrington* (New York: Vintage Books, 1968), 5; Daniel Boorstin, *The Image: A Guide to Pseudo-Events in America* (New York: Harper Collins, 1961), 17 ("in the moment" quote); Arthur Schlesinger, Jr., "On the Inscrutability of History," *Encounter* 27 (November 1966): 14 (italics added).

12. Milan Kundera, *The Book of Laughter and Forgetting* (New York: Penguin Books, 1981), 3; Aldous Huxley, *Brave New World* (New York: Harper Collins, 1998 [1932]), 51; Anne Applebaum, *Gulag: A History* (New York: Anchor Books, 2003), 569, 571; Craig S. Smith, "Where 642 Died, a Wound Too Deep for Time to Heal," *New York Times*, June 11, 2004 (prime minister quote; italics added). See Sarah Farmer, *Martyred Village: Commemorating the 1944 Massacre at Oradour-sur-Glane* (Berkeley: University of California Press, 1999).

13. Paul Roberts, "2004: The Year of the Blog," *CIO Magazine*, February 15, 2005; "'Blog' Picked as Word of the Year," BBC News, December 1, 2004.

CHAPTER 1. THE CANDIDATES AND THEIR TIMES

Epigraph source: John B. Judis, *The Paradox of American Democracy: Elites, Special Interests, and the Betrayal of Public Trust* (New York: Pantheon Books, 2000), 81.

1. Thune's "holy grail" comment is from personal observation during the campaign. Joseph C. Anselmo, "Both Sides Say Energy Bill Outcome Too Close to Call," *Congressional Quarterly Daily Monitor*, November 20, 2003 ("reluctantly" comment); Joseph C. Anselmo and Martha Angle, "Senate Fails to End Filibuster against Energy Policy Bill," *Congressional Quarterly Daily Monitor*, November 21, 2003; Sheryl Gay Stolberg, "Daschle, Democrats' Leader, Faces Tough Race at Home," *New York Times*, January 11, 2004; John Stanton and April Fulton, "Daschle Unlikely to Work to Get Energy Bill Votes," *Congress Daily*, November 20, 2003.

2. Meg Kinnard, "Daschle Fills First Ad with Ethanol Pals," *National Journal*, July 9, 2003; Editorial, "Energy Bill Frustrating," *Argus Leader*, November 20, 2003; "Daschle Lends Clout to Energy Bill," *Argus Leader*, November 21, 2003 (spokesman quote).

3. Herbert Hoover, "Territorial Politics and Politicians," in Harry Thompson, ed., *A New History of South Dakota* (Sioux Falls: Center for Western Studies, 2005), 137 ("water that laughs" translation). Thune quotations are from personal observation during his campaign.

4. Monica Davey, "Fatal Crash Charges Threaten Political Career," *New York Times*, September 7, 2003.

5. Monica Davey, "One Top Political Figure Testifies for Another in South Dakota," *New York Times*, December 5, 2003; T. R. Reid, "Daschle Takes Witness Stand for Janklow," *Washington Post*, December 5, 2003; Peter Harriman, "Janklow Runs on Dynamic, Controversial Past," *Argus Leader*, September 29, 2002; Monica Davey, "In South Dakota, Janklow Era Starts to Fade as Parties Focus on Filling Seat," *New York Times*, December 10, 2003.

6. David Shribman, "Republican Feud for Senate Seat in South Dakota Pits Frontier Populist against Stoic Incumbent," *Wall Street Journal*, August 12, 1985; "Janklow, Daschle Discuss Their Friendship," Associated Press, February 18, 1999.

7. Jay Timmons interview, September 21, 2005; "South Dakota Senate: Play It Again, John," *Rothenberg Political Report*, July 18, 2003; Chris Cillizza, "Now Charged Janklow May Quit," *Roll Call*, September 2, 2003; David Kranz, "Janklow's Situation Will Have Effect on Senate Race," *Argus Leader*, August 31, 2003; David Kranz, "Janklow's Political Influence Outlives His Career," *Argus Leader*, August 15, 2004; Bob Mercer, "Long Rivalry between Janklow, Abdnor-Thune and Daschle Reaches Final Act," *Aberdeen American News*, October 29, 2004; Denise Ross, "Daschle, Thune's Prospects Not Dim in Event of a Loss," *Rapid City Journal*, August 21, 2004.

8. Jacob S. Hacker and Paul Pierson, "The Center No Longer Holds," *New York Times Magazine*, November 20, 2005; Thomas J. Whalen, *Kennedy v. Lodge: The 1952 Massachusetts Senate Race* (Boston: Northeastern University Press, 2000), 30 (Kennedy quote).

9. Stuart Rothenberg, "South Dakota: One Man Out," *Political Report*, March 12, 1982; William Pratt, "Socialism on the Northern Plains, 1900–1924," *South Dakota History* 18, nos. 1 and 2 (Spring/Summer 1988): 11–12; Howard Lamar, *Dakota Territory, 1861–1889: A Study in Frontier Politics* (New Haven, Conn.: Yale University Press, 1956), 260 (Lamar quote); Howard Lamar, "Public Values and Private Dreams: South Dakota's Search for Identity, 1850–1900," *South Dakota History* 8, no. 2 (Spring 1978): 139; Harry Thompson, ed., *A New History of South Dakota* (Sioux Falls: Center for Western Studies, 2004), 305; Edwin Torrey, *Early Days in Dakota* (Minneapolis: Farnham Printing and Stationery Company, 1925),

174–78; Daryl Webb, "'Just Principles Never Die': Brown County Populists, 1890–1900," *South Dakota History* 22, no. 4 (Winter 1992): 366–99.

10. Jon Walker, "'Regular Guy' to Outspoken Leader," *Argus Leader*, October 17, 2004 ("artist" quote); Anthony H. Richter, "A Heritage of Faith: Religion and the German Settlers of Dakota," *South Dakota History* 21, no. 2 (Summer 1991): 165–66; Bob Jones, "Mad Daschle," *World Magazine*, October 12, 2002; CNBC News Transcripts, *Tim Russert Show*, August 4, 2001 ("dream" quote).

11. Theresa House, "The Future of the Democratic Party," *Harvard Political Review*, January 25, 2003 (Burns quote); John Lukacs, *Democracy and Populism: Fear and Hatred* (New Haven, Conn.: Yale University Press, 2005), 28.

12. Fred Breukelman, "Convo Rescinds Inconsistent Platform," *South Dakota Collegian*, May 1, 1968 (Daschle quotes); Ron Kroese, "Trotskyists Bring Campaign to State," *South Dakota Collegian*, May 22, 1968.

13. Tom Daschle, with Michael D'Orso, *Like No Other Time: The 107th Congress and the Two Years That Changed America Forever* (New York: Crown Publishers, 2003), 117 ("riots" quote); Mark Kurlansky, *1968: The Year That Rocked the World* (New York: Ballantine Books, 2004), 278–86 ("flags," "hand-to-hand combat" and Ribicoff quotes); James Traub, "The Things They Carry," *New York Times Magazine*, January 4, 2004.

14. Sheryl Gay Stolberg and Carl Hulse, "Daschle Reflects on Past and Looks Ahead," *New York Times*, December 12, 2004 ("activism" quote); Rick Perlstein, "Who Owns the Sixties?" *Lingua Franca*, May/June 1996, 30–37; Elizabeth Becker, "A McGovern Liberal Who's Content to Stick to the Label," *New York Times*, July 23, 2001 (McGovern quote); Philip Brasher, "Daschle's Leadership Goals Linked to Childhood," Associated Press, May 3, 1994 ("liberal politics" quote); David Kranz and Chuck Raasch, "Few Thought Aberdeen Native Could Climb So Far," *Argus Leader*, April 8, 2001. Daschle credited McGovern with "inspiring him toward public life." Kevin Woster, "Dignitaries Start McGovern Library Drive," *Argus Leader*, April 20, 2002.

15. Julian Zelizer, *On Capitol Hill: The Struggle to Reform Congress and Its Consequences, 1948–2000* (Cambridge, England: Cambridge University Press, 2004), 156–76; "Abourezk Staff—Functional Outline—1975," Box 856, Abourezk Papers, Richardson Library, University of South Dakota ("primary responsibility" quote); "Dove on 1st Flight," *Washington Star*, January 17, 1973 (Abourezk quote); "Night of the Long Winds: A Chaotic Filibuster Characterizes Carter's Problems with Congress," *Time*, October 10, 1977; Richard L. Lyons, "Mondale Helps Break Gas Pricing Filibuster," *Washington Post*, October 4, 1977; Myra MacPherson, "Calling It Quits on the Hill: Why Abourezk Is Leaving the Club of 100," *Washington Post*, June 1, 1977; Dominic Sandbrook, *Eugene McCarthy: The Rise and Fall of Postwar American Liberalism* (New York: Alfred A. Knopf, 2004), 268–69; Weston Kosova, "Daschle's Dash," *New Republic*, May 23, 1994 ("schmoozing" quote); Sidney

Blumenthal, *The Permanent Campaign: Inside the World of Elite Political Operatives* (Boston: Beacon Press, 1980), 37.

16. Memo from Gail to Mike, August 12, 1976, Box 1041, Abourezk Papers, Richardson Library, University of South Dakota ("involved" quote); Bob Jones, "Mad Daschle," *World Magazine,* October 12, 2002 ("gatekeepers" quote).

17. Joe McGinniss, *The Selling of the President* (New York: Simon and Schuster, 1969); John Lukacs, *A New Republic: A History of the United States in the Twentieth Century* (New Haven, Conn.: Yale University Press, 2004), 281–82; William Leuchtenburg, *A Troubled Feast: American Society since 1945* (Boston: Little, Brown, 1983), 275 ("student-council" quote); Bruce Schulman, *The Seventies: The Great Shift in American Culture, Society and Politics* (Cambridge, Mass.: Da Capo Press, 2002), 122 (Doonesbury information); Leo Ribuffo, "'Malaise' Revisited: Jimmy Carter and the Crisis of Confidence," in John Patrick Diggins, ed., *The Liberal Persuasion: Arthur Schlesinger Jr. and the Challenge of the American Past* (Princeton, N.J.: Princeton University Press, 1997), 165.

18. Peter Carroll, *It Seemed Like Nothing Happened: America in the 1970s* (New Brunswick, N.J.: Rutgers University Press, 1982), 189–91 ("Kama Sutra" and Carter "thousand faces," "respect," and "errors" quotes); John Howard, "Old School: In Kerry's Corner, a Consultant with Populist Bent," *Wall Street Journal,* July 6, 2004 (Shrum quote); Steven M. Gillon, *The Democrats' Dilemma: Walter F. Mondale and the Liberal Legacy* (New York: Columbia University Press, 1992), 201 (Mondale quote); Thomas E. Patterson, *Out of Order* (New York: Vintage Books, 1994), 32; Michael Crowley, "Last, Best Hope," *New Republic,* March 26, 2001; David Kranz, "Janklow: Election Is a Referendum on His Record," *Argus Leader,* October 29, 1998 (Janklow quote).

19. Bruce Schulman, *The Seventies: The Great Shift in American Culture, Society and Politics* (Cambridge, Mass.: Da Capo Press, 2002), 121–22, 185; Steven Gillon, *The American Paradox: A History of the United States since 1960* (Boston: Houghton Mifflin, 2003), 218; David A. Horowitz, *Beyond Left and Right: Insurgency and the Establishment* (Urbana and Chicago: University of Illinois Press, 1997), 296–99. On Carter's religiosity, see Leo Ribuffo, *Right Center Left: Essays in American History* (New Brunswick, N.J.: Rutgers University Press, 1992), 214–48.

20. William Leuchtenburg, *A Troubled Feast: American Society since 1945* (Boston: Little, Brown, 1983), 232 ("Eisenhower" quote); Bruce Schulman, *The Seventies: The Great Shift in American Culture, Society and Politics* (Cambridge, Mass.: Da Capo Press, 2002), 177 ("Alda" and "New Age" quotes); John F. Harris, *The Survivor: Bill Clinton in the White House* (New York: Random House, 2005), 398; Christopher Lasch, *The Culture of Narcissism: American Life in an Age of Diminishing Expectations* (New York: W. W. Norton, 1979), 14 ("therapeutic sensibility" quote); Michael Barone, *Hard America, Soft America: Competition vs. Coddling and the Battle for the Nation's Future* (New York: Crown Forum, 2004), 14; George Lakoff, *Moral Politics:*

How Liberals and Conservatives Think (Chicago: University of Chicago Press, 1996), 13; Noam Scheiber, "Wooden Frame," *New Republic,* May 23, 2005.

21. "Memo to Senator McGovern," November 12, 1978, Box 855, McGovern Papers, Princeton University ("drift" quote); Memo, "Media Events Related to Issues," FF Udall, DB 664, Abourezk Papers, Richardson Library, University of South Dakota ("redneck" comment); Thomas Byrne Edsall and Mary D. Edsall, *Chain Reaction: The Impact of Race, Rights, and Taxes on American Politics* (New York: W. W. Norton, 1991), 129 ("brick wall" quote); Bruce Schulman, *The Seventies: The Great Shift in American Culture, Society and Politics* (Cambridge, Mass.: Da Capo Press, 2002), 124; Editorial, "Spending Views of Ins and Outs," *Argus Leader,* September 9, 1978 ("bloated" quote); Editorial, "Daschle, Abdnor Recommended," *Argus Leader,* November 1, 1978 ("conservative ideas" and "calls" quotes); Memo to the McGovern Campaign from Cambridge Survey Research, October 31, 1979, Box 428, no file number, McGovern papers, Princeton University (Caddell poll); Memo to the McGovern Campaign from Cambridge Survey Research, n.d., Box 428, no file number, McGovern papers, Princeton University; "Daschle Blames Oil, Gas Lobbies," *Argus Leader,* October 2, 1978; "House Candidates All Support 100% Parity," *Argus Leader,* October 18, 1978; Jon Lauck, "George S. McGovern and the Farmer: South Dakota Politics, 1953–1962," *South Dakota History* 32, no. 4 (Winter 2002): 331–53.

22. Memo to the McGovern Campaign from Cambridge Survey Research, October 31, 1979, Box 428, no file number, McGovern papers, Princeton University (source of Caddell poll and "potent" quote); Sister Maurice Crowley et al. to Tom Daschle, October 6, 1978, DB 7573, Abdnor Papers, South Dakota State Historical Society; David Kranz and Chuck Raasch, "Few Thought Aberdeen Native Could Climb So Far," *Argus Leader,* April 8, 2001 ("free fall" quote); Jeffrey Stinson, "Candidates Firming Up Campaign Strategies," *Argus Leader,* October 5, 1978 ("nice guy" quote); Tim Schreiner, "1st District Outcome 'Sealed,'" *Argus Leader,* November 8, 1978; Sheryl Gay Stolberg, "Daschle, Democrats' Leader, Faces Tough Race at Home," *New York Times,* January 11, 2004.

23. Jon Walker, "Barnes: Daschle Didn't Help Dems," *Argus Leader,* November 20, 1982; Stuart Rothenberg, "South Dakota: One Man Out," *Political Report,* March 12, 1982 ("gimmicks" and "perceptions" quotes); Helen Dewar, "On Capitol Hill, Symbols Triumph; Substance Suffers amid Frustrating Fiscal Pressures, Political Fears," *Washington Post,* November 26, 1991 (Daschle quote); Alan Ehrenhalt, *Congressional Quarterly,* December 1, 1985 (source of first Struble quote); Dean Rindy, "Zen and the Art of Campaign Media: Define Your Commercials—For They Will Define You," *Campaigns and Elections,* July 1992 (source of second Struble quote); *The Federalist,* no. 68, quoted in Thomas E. Patterson, *Out of Order* (New York: Vintage Books, 1994), 38 ("little arts" quote).

24. Bill Harlan and Ken Baka, "Democrats See Another Era of Golden Years on the Horizon," *Rapid City Journal,* July 13, 1986; Mellman memo to the Daschle Campaign, September 5, 1986, Box 7574, Abdnor Papers, South Dakota State Historical Society (source of Mellman poll and "farm issue" and "important" quotes). Agricultural historian William Pratt, in an indication of the prominence of the farm issue in 1986, believes that "the 1980s may have witnessed the last significant progressive rural insurgency in American history." Pratt, "Using History to Make History? Progressive Farm Organizing during the Farm Revolt of the 1980s," *Annals of Iowa* 55 (Winter 1996): nn. 56, 45. Chet Brokaw, "Daschle Outspends Abdnor, Janklow," Associated Press, April 17, 1986; Bob Imrie, "Campaigns: Spending Reports Detail Races," *Argus Leader,* July 19, 1986.

25. Reverend Terry Miller to Tom Daschle, October 23, 1986, DB 7573, Abdnor Papers, South Dakota State Historical Society.

26. Book and Thimble Club, *Proving Up: Jones County History* (Murdo, S.Dak.: Book and Thimble Club, 1969), 85; Paula Nelson, *After the West Was Won: Homesteaders and Town-Builders in Western South Dakota, 1900–1917* (Iowa City: University of Iowa Press, 1986), 15 (*Murdo Coyote* quote); Frederick C. Luebke, "Ethnic Group Settlement on the Great Plains," *Western Historical Quarterly* 8, no. 4 (October 1977): 417 (information on German and Norwegian immigration). See also Paula M. Nelson, "Traveling the Hope Highway: An Intellectual History of the West River Country of South Dakota," in William Lang, ed., *Centennial West: Essays on the Northern Tier States* (Seattle: University of Washington Press, 1991), 244–64. The family of noted Norwegian American novelist O. E. Rolvaag similarly took the name of "the little cove where they lived, Rolvaag." See "A Biographical Note," in O. E. Rolvaag, *Peder Victorious* (Lincoln: University of Nebraska Press, 1982 [1929]), 321.

27. Greg Latza, *Blue Stars: A Selection of Stories from South Dakota's World War II Veterans* (Sioux Falls: Peoplescapes Publishing, 2004), 24–25; Kevin Woster, "Vet Shys from 'Hero' Label," *Rapid City Journal,* May 29, 2006.

28. Robert Fogel, *The Fourth Great Awakening and the Future of Egalitarianism* (Chicago: University of Chicago Press, 2000), 25; Will Herberg, *Protestant Catholic Jew: An Essay in American Religious Sociology* (Chicago: University of Chicago Press, 1960), 46–71; Rich Thune to author, January 3, 2005; Dorothy Hubbard Schwieder, *Growing Up with the Town: Family and Community on the Great Plains* (Iowa City: University of Iowa Press, 2002), 2.

29. John E. Miller, *Laura Ingalls Wilder's Little Town: Where History and Literature Meet* (Lawrence: University Press of Kansas, 1994), 124, 128; Lisa McGirr, *Suburban Warriors: The Origins of the New American Right* (Princeton, N.J.: Princeton University Press, 2001), 13, 46; William F. Gayk, "The Taxpayers' Revolt," in Rob King, Spencer Olin, and Mark Poster, eds., *Postsuburban California: The Transformation of Orange County since World War II* (Berkeley: University of California Press, 1991), 286 ("hotbed" quote); Rich Thune to author, January 3, 2005; John Thune

interview, January 5, 2005; Gil Troy, *Morning in America: How Ronald Reagan Invented the 1980s* (Princeton, N.J.: Princeton University Press, 2005), 17 (Schneider quote).

30. Jonathan Rieder, "The Rise of the 'Silent Majority,'" in Steve Fraser and Gary Gerstle, eds., *The Rise and Fall of the New Deal Order, 1930–1980* (Princeton, N.J.: Princeton University Press, 1989), 244; David Kranz, "Newcomer Takes on 2-Term Congressman in House Contest," *Argus Leader,* October 20, 2000 (Harold Thune quote); Rich Thune to author, January 3, 2005.

31. John Thune interview, January 5, 2005. For Humphrey's upbringing in Doland, see Charles L. Garrettson III, "Home of the Politics of Joy: Hubert H. Humphrey in South Dakota," *South Dakota History* 20, no. 3 (Fall 1990): 165–84; Albert Eisele, *Almost to the Presidency: A Biography of Two American Politicians* (Blue Earth, Minn.: Piper, 1972), 11–26.

32. "SD—At Large: Two Polls—Two Big Leads for Hillard," *Hotline,* May 10, 1996; "South Dakota," *Roll Call,* May 2, 1996; Tom Daschle, with Michael D'Orso, *Like No Other Time: The 107th Congress and the Two Years That Changed America Forever* (New York: Crown Publishers, 2003), 65–72.

33. Michael Barone, *Almanac of American Politics, 2006* (Washington, D.C.: National Journal Group, 2006), 1527–28; John Fund, *Stealing Elections: How Voter Fraud Threatens Our Democracy* (San Francisco: Encounter Books, 2004), 77–94.

34. ABC News, *The Note,* January 6, 2003 ("chance" quote); Chuck Raasch and David Kranz, "Daschle Discusses His Possible Bid for President," *Argus Leader,* December 20, 2002; Chuck Raasch, Mike Madden, and David Kranz, "He's Running," *Argus Leader,* January 7, 2003.

35. Peter Baker, Juliet Eilperin, Guy Gugliotta, John F. Harris, Dan Morgan, Eric Pianin, and David Von Drehle, "The Train That Wouldn't Stop; Key Players Thwarted Attempts to Derail Process," *Washington Post,* February 14, 1999 (Podesta quote); Eric Pianin, "After an Often-Tumultuous Tenure, Daschle Exits Quietly; Defeated Democratic Leader Uncertain about Next Move," *Washington Post,* December 12, 2004 ("signal" quote); John F. Harris, *The Survivor: Bill Clinton in the White House* (New York: Random House, 2005), 347 (Conrad quote).

36. Michael Barone interview, January 11, 2005 ("all for one" and "hang" quotes); Michael Crowley, "Last, Best Hope: Tom Daschle's Struggle to Save the Dems," *New Republic,* March 26, 2001; Richard Leiby, "The Reliable Source," *Washington Post,* July 21, 2004 (Novak quote); Sheryl Gay Stolberg, "The 2004 Campaign: The Senate; Daschle, Democrats' Leader, Faces Tough Race at Home," *New York Times,* January 11, 2004 ("paranoid" quote); Exclusive Excerpt from David Frum, *The Right Man* (New York: Random House, 2003), "He felt not merely angry, but surprised—and betrayed," *The Hill,* January 8, 2003; Kirk Victor, "Deconstructing Daschle," *National Journal,* June 1, 2002 ("bleeding" quote); Alison Mitchell, "A Low-Key Leader with 'Steel in His Spine,'" *New York Times,* May 27, 2001 (Byrd quote).

37. Eric Pianin, "After an Often-Tumultuous Tenure, Daschle Exits Quietly; Defeated Democratic Leader Uncertain about Next Move," *Washington Post,*

December 12, 2004; Stuart Rothenberg, "Democratic Rhetoric Can't Hide Nation's Cultural Divide," *Roll Call*, August 2, 2004; Ryan Lizza, "Wisdom of the Losers," review of George McGovern, *The Essential America: Our Founders and the Liberal Tradition* (New York: Simon and Schuster, 2004), Mario M. Cuomo, *Why Lincoln Matters: Today More Than Ever* (New York: Harcourt, 2004), and Gary Hart, *The Fourth Power: A Grand Strategy for the United States in the Twenty-First Century* (New York: Oxford University Press, 2004), in *New York Times Book Review*, July 18, 2004.

38. *The 9/11 Commission Report* (New York: W. W. Norton, 2004), 47–70.

39. E. J. Dionne, Jr., "Another Set of Scare Tactics," *Washington Post*, November 15, 2005; Ronald Brownstein and Emma Vaughn, "Timing Entwined War Vote, Election," *Los Angeles Times*, November 28, 2005 (Kennedy quote).

40. Amy Keller, "Members Gave More Cash in '04," *Roll Call*, January 18, 2005; Paul Magnusson, "What Makes Jon Corzine Run; His Rise in the Senate Has Been Meteoric—So Why Is He Aiming to Be Governor of Jersey?" *BusinessWeek*, September 27, 2004.

41. Evan Thomas and Babak Dehghanpisheh, "Inside Red Dawn: Saddam Up Close," *Newsweek*, December 29, 2003 ("regards" quote); Joe Klein, "Saddam's Revenge," *Time*, September 26, 2005; Jill Lawrence, "Saddam's Capture Forces Dean to Reshape Message," *USA Today*, December 16, 2003 (Dean quotes); David Brooks, "The Great Surrender," *New York Times*, December 23, 2003; Dan Balz and Richard Morin, "Bush Gets Year-End Boost in Approval; Poll Shows Dean Surging among Democratic Rivals," *Washington Post*, December 23, 2003.

42. Tom Daschle, with Michael D'Orso, *Like No Other Time: The 107th Congress and the Two Years That Changed America Forever* (New York: Crown Publishers, 2003), 5, 219.

43. Editorial, "Spare the Rod?" *New Republic*, December 15, 2003.

44. Jon Lauck, "Daschled Hopes: The South Dakota Senator Looks Back on His Brief Stint as Majority Leader," review of Tom Daschle, with Michael D'Orso, *Like No Other Time: The 107th Congress and the Two Years That Changed America Forever* (New York: Crown Publishers, 2003), in *Weekly Standard*, December 29, 2003; Zell Miller, *A National Party No More: The Conscience of a Conservative Democrat* (Atlanta: Stroud and Hall, 2003), 10, 62; Michael Barone, "The Jacksonian Persuasion," *U.S. News and World Report*, September 2, 2004; "The 3rd Annual Year in Ideas," *New York Times Magazine*, December 14, 2003; Dick Polman, "Political Reality: Democrats May Look Away from Dixie in 2004 Election," *Chattanooga Times Free Press*, December 14, 2003.

45. Editorial, "Daschle's Campaign Manager Wants to Reassure You That Tom Supports Bush 75% of the Time!" Buzzflash.com, December 11, 2003. One analysis noted that Dailykos.com "frequently attacks Democrats such as Tom Daschle." Benjamin Wallace-Wells, "Kos Call: For America's Number One Liberal Blogger Politics Is Like Sports; It's All about Winning," *Washington Monthly*, January/

February 2006; Kirk Victor, "Second-Guessing Daschle," *National Journal*, December 13, 2003; Geoff Earle, "Reid Makes It Clear He's No Daschle," *The Hill*, December 1, 2004; Editorial, "Spare the Rod?" *New Republic*, December 15, 2003.

46. Matthew Rothschild, "Russ Feingold—The *Progressive* Interview," *Progressive*, May 2002 ("brutal" quote); Nat Hentoff, "Senator Tom Daschle, the Enforcer," *Jewish World Review*, June 17, 2002; Sheryl Gay Stolberg, "Daschle, Democrats' Leader, Faces Tough Race at Home," *New York Times*, January 11, 2004 ("winning" quote); Byron York, "'Buyer's Remorse' in South Dakota," *National Review*, December 10, 2002.

47. Mike Madden, "Republicans See Chance to Unseat Daschle," *Argus Leader*, December 17, 2003; Scott MacKay, "Daschle Gets Rhode Island Money for South Dakota Race," *Providence Journal*, December 18, 2003 (Daschle quote); Alexandra Starr, "Dick Wadhams," *Slate*, June 10, 2005 ("kamikaze" quote).

CHAPTER 2. THE LAUNCH

Epigraph source: Editorial, "The Challenge of a Lifetime," *Mitchell Daily Republic*, January 7, 2004.

1. William E. Gienapp, *Abraham Lincoln and Civil War America: A Biography* (Oxford: Oxford University Press, 2002), 63; Thomas E. Patterson, *Out of Order* (New York: Vintage Books, 1994), 9 ("ugliest" quote); Thune's Lincoln Day speech is quoted from personal observation; Sheryl Gay Stolberg, "Former Representative to Challenge Daschle," *New York Times*, January 6, 2004 ("difference" quote).

2. Terry Woster, "Thune: 'A Race That Needed to Be Run,'" *Argus Leader*, October 10, 2004 ("weary" and "compressed" quotes); David Kranz, "Thune Makes It Official: I Will Run," *Argus Leader*, January 6, 2004 ("cousin" quote); "Who's Afraid of Dick Wadhams," *Hotline*, December 12, 2003 ("attack dog" quote); Editorial, "Scale Tips in Daschle's Favor in Race for Senate," *Argus Leader*, November 2, 1986.

3. Byron York, *The Vast Left Wing Conspiracy* (New York: Crown Forum, 2005), 189–219.

4. Carson Walker, "Thune Urges Republicans to Unite behind House Candidate," Associated Press, January 24, 2004 (Whalen quote).

5. Jim VandeHei, "Slowed by 3rd Place Finish, Questions about Electability," *Washington Post*, January 20, 2004 ("pin cushion" quote). Large numbers of Iowa voters told reporters that "'electability' was their greatest concern." Peter Beinart, review of Jerome Armstrong and Markos Moulitsas Zuniga, *Crashing the Gate: Netroots, Grassroots, and the Rise of People-Powered Politics* (White River Junction, Vt.: Chelsea Green Publishing Company, 2006), in *New York Times Book Review*, March 26, 2006; Evan Thomas et al., *Election 2004* (New York: Public Affairs, 2004), 22 ("miracle" quote).

6. Robin Toner, "The 2004 Campaign: Political Memo; Whoever Is Chosen, Democrats Spoil for a Fight," *New York Times*, January 30, 2004 ("centrism" quote); Claude R. Marx, "The Rise and Fall of Howard Dean," in Larry J. Sabato, ed., *Divided States of America: The Slash and Burn Politics of the 2004 Presidential Election* (New York: Pearson-Longman, 2006), 45; James Traub, "The Things They Carry," *New York Times Magazine*, January 4, 2004 (O'Hanlon quote).

7. Jim Drinkard and William M. Welch, "AARP Accused of Conflict of Interest," *USA Today*, November 21, 2003.

8. Geoff Earle, "String of Losses Stir Dem Grumblings as Talk of Dorgan Challenge Subsides," *The Hill*, January 27, 2004.

9. James E. McMillan, ed., *The Ernest McFarland Papers: The United States Senate Years, 1940–1952* (Prescott, Ariz.: Sharlot Hall Museum Press, 1995), 410.

10. Chris Cillizza and Brody Mullins, "Thune Will Keep Lobbying; Criticism of Daschles May Wane," *Roll Call*, January 26, 2004; John Fund, "The Daschle Family Business," *Wall Street Journal* (OpinionJournal.com), January 27, 2004; David Kranz, "Linda Daschle Had Planned to Quit Lobbying Job," *Argus Leader*, January 12, 2003.

11. David Kranz, "Thune Spells Out Differences with Daschle in Talk Show," *Argus Leader*, February 8, 2004 ("attack" quote); Paul Kane and Damon Chappie, "Ban on Family Lobbying Eyed," *Roll Call*, January 28, 2004 ("looks like" quote).

12. Tom Daschle, with Michael D'Orso, *Like No Other Time: The 107th Congress and the Two Years That Changed America Forever* (New York: Crown Publishers, 2003), 206; *Catholic World News*, March 23, 2005; Evelyn Nieves, "S.D. Makes Abortion Rare through Laws and Stigma; Out-of-State Doctors Come Weekly to 1 Clinic," *Washington Post*, December 27, 2005.

13. Rick Lyman and Michael Janofsky, "The 2004 Campaign: Battlegrounds; Safest Prediction for the Outcome in North Dakota's Primary Is 'Cold,'" *New York Times*, January 29, 2004; Rick Lyman, "The 2004 Campaign: Campaign Trail; Democrats Finally Calling for North Dakota's Votes," *New York Times*, February 1, 2004.

14. Robert F. Worth, "Wealth of Others Helped Shape Kerry's Life," *New York Times*, October 10, 2004; Chuck Todd, "Campaign 2004: The Hidden Story," in Larry J. Sabato, ed., *Divided States of America: The Slash and Burn Politics of the 2004 Presidential Election* (New York: Pearson-Longman, 2006), 30–31; Samuel Z. Goldhaber, "John Kerry: A Navy Dove Runs for Congress," *Harvard Crimson*, February 18, 1970 ("United Nations" quote).

15. Evan Thomas et al., *Election 2004* (New York: Public Affairs, 2004), 22 (Trippi quote).

16. Bill Lofy, *Paul Wellstone: The Life of a Passionate Progressive* (Ann Arbor: University of Michigan Press, 2005), 107 (Wellstone quote); Jacob M. Schlesinger,

"Kerry Staggers His Foes in South, but Fight Goes On," *Wall Street Journal,* February 11, 2004; Howard Kurtz, "Divide and Bicker; The Dean Campaign's Hip, High-Tech Image Hid a Nasty Civil War," *Washington Post,* February 29, 2004 ("fraud" quote).

17. Late Edition, CNN, January 25, 2004 ("deserter" and "AWOL" accusations); "Kerry, Edwards Both Top Bush in Poll," CNN.com, February 18, 2004.

18. Mike Madden, "Bush Leads Democrats in S.D. Poll," *Argus Leader,* February 14, 2004; Dave Kranz, "Daschle Has Slight Lead, New Poll Finds," *Argus Leader,* February 13, 2004.

19. Amy Fagan, "Clinton Advises Senate Democrats; Focuses on Recapturing Power," *Washington Times,* January 30, 2004 (Daschle quote); "Clinton to Help Daschle Raise Campaign Money," Associated Press, February 9, 2004; Peter Baker, Juliet Eilperin, Guy Gugliotta, John F. Harris, Dan Morgan, Eric Pianin, and David Von Drehle, "The Train That Wouldn't Stop; Key Players Thwarted Attempts to Derail Process," *Washington Post,* February 14, 1999.

20. David Kranz, "Clinton to Help Daschle Raise Money at Dinner," *Argus Leader,* February 9, 2004 (Sabato quote).

21. Brody Mullins, "Chamber Targets Daschle; Business Group Takes More Aggressive Approach in Elections," *Roll Call,* February 2, 2004 (Thune endorsement and "special interests" quote); Brody Mullins, "PAC Dollars Favor Daschle," *Roll Call,* May 5, 2004. Lobbyist and PAC contributions to Daschle after 1998 totaled $1.7 million. Eric Pfeiffer, "Study: $103 Million Given to Congress," *Washington Times,* May 23, 2006; Denise Ross, "Daschle Satisfied with War Progress," *Rapid City Journal,* February 20, 2004 ("Iraq War" quote); Daschle's State of the Union response, January 21, 2004.

22. Politicalaims.com, February 22, 2004.

23. "Russell Means Says He Will Back Thune in Senate Race," Associated Press, February 5, 2004; Means's "plantation" quote is from personal observation; John Fund, "Daschle Faces Revolt on the Reservation," *Wall Street Journal* (OpinionJournal.com), January 19, 2004 (Giago quote).

24. Steve Young and Terry Woster, "Bill to Ban Abortions Reaches Last Hurdle," *Argus Leader,* March 15, 2004.

25. Stevenson Swanson, "Same-Sex Marriage Leaping into Election," *Chicago Tribune,* February 15, 2004.

26. Carson Walker, "South Dakota Political Leaders Split on Gay Marriage Ban," Associated Press, February 24, 2004 (Herseth quote); Denise Ross, "A Race against the Clock; Herseth, Diedrich Battle for Votes as Election Looms," *Rapid City Journal,* March 28, 2004.

27. Douglas Waller, "Ready to Mix It Up," *Time,* February 23, 2004 (Daschle quote); *Congressional Quarterly,* February 2, 2004 (Grassley quote).

CHAPTER 3. WHIPSAW

Epigraph source: Wayne LaPierre quoted in Sheryl Gay Stolberg, "Looking Back and Ahead after Senate's Votes on Guns," *New York Times,* March 4, 2004.

1. Exchange between Daschle and Thune communicated by Thune to author.

2. Sheryl Gay Stolberg, "A Swing to the Middle on Gun Control," *New York Times,* March 7, 2004; Jim VandeHei, "Democrats Will Try a Hybrid of Old, New Policies," *Washington Post,* February 15, 2004.

3. John R. Milton, *South Dakota: A History* (New York: W. W. Norton, 1977), 161 ("man" quote); James Marten, "'We Always Looked Forward to the Hunters Coming': The Culture of Pheasant Hunting in South Dakota," *South Dakota History* 29, no. 2 (Summer 1999): 89, 112 ("gift" and "greatest" quotes); Paul M. Barrett, "High Plains Drifter: In the Besieged World of Gun Manufacturers, Geography Is Destiny," *Wall Street Journal,* December 15, 1999; Dave Kranz, "NRA Asks Members to Thank Democrats," *Argus Leader,* February 20, 2004.

4. Sheryl Gay Stolberg, "Senate to Vote on Shielding Gun Makers," *New York Times,* February 24, 2004.

5. Klaus Marre, "Riders Sink the Gun Bill in 90–8 vote," *The Hill,* March 3, 2004 ("no" quote); Brian DeBose, "Senate Rejects Gun-Maker Legislation," *Washington Times,* March 3, 2004.

6. Sheryl Gay Stolberg, "Looking Back and Ahead after Senate's Votes on Guns," *New York Times,* March 4, 2004 (LaPierre quote; italics added); Eleanor Clift, "Capitol Letter: Shadow President," *Newsweek,* May 18, 2004.

7. Collin Levey, "Democrats Get in Touch with Their Inner Bubba," *Seattle Times,* November 6, 2003 ("NASCAR dads" information); Donald Lambro, "Democrats Urged to Move to Center," *Washington Times,* October 30, 2003; Dave Kranz, "Thune, Johnson Backers Dispute Records on Guns," *Argus Leader,* September 24, 2002; Jennifer Sanderson, Ad Watch, *Argus Leader,* September 23, 2004.

8. Randy Hascal, "Costs Stymie Growth, Business Owners Tell Daschle," *Argus Leader,* April 4, 2004 (Daschle quote); *Crain's Insider,* April 28, 2004 ("honored" quote).

9. Liz Sidoti, "Kerry Ads Explain His Priorities; Bush Ad Calls Kerry Liberal," Associated Press, April 21, 2004; Drudgereport.com, February 27, 2004; Richard E. Cohen, "Kerry Rated Most Liberal Member of Senate," *National Journal,* February 27, 2004; Scott Lehigh, "Taking the Campaign up a Notch," *Boston Globe,* April 7, 2004 (Kerry quote); Scott Shepard, "Flip-Flop Charge Hard to Shake," *Atlanta Journal-Constitution,* April 13, 2004 (Bush quote).

10. Jonathan Chait, "Make You Ralph," *New Republic,* March 8, 2004; James W. Ceaser and Andrew E. Busch, *Red over Blue: The 2004 Elections and American Politics* (Lanham, Md.: Rowman and Littlefield, 2005), 13 (study quote).

11. Chris Cillizza, "Cheney Helps Thune Raise $250k," *Roll Call,* March 10, 2004 (Cheney quote); "Daschle Has Big Lead in Campaign Cash," Associated Press, February 3, 2004.

12. Bob Mercer, "Herseth Sprints to Early Lead," *Aberdeen American News,* March 6, 2004; Theodore White, *The Making of the President 1968* (New York: Atheneum Publishers, 1969), 412.

13. Jon Walker, "Vice-President Stumps for Thune," *Argus Leader,* March 9, 2004 (Thune and Daschle campaign quotes); Brian DeBose, "Delay to Press Democrats on Energy; GOP Says Daschle Is Stalling Bill," *Washington Times,* March 26, 2004; "Daschle Claims Votes to Cut Off Debate on Energy Measure," *Congress Daily,* March 3, 2004.

14. Carson Walker, "GOP Eyes American Indian Vote in Traditional Democratic Stronghold," Associated Press, March 5, 2004 (Daschle and Means quotes).

15. Terry Woster, "One Vote Scuttles Ban on Abortions," *Argus Leader,* March 16, 2004; "South Dakota Poll Says Just over Half Support Abortion Restrictions," Associated Press, March 31, 2004.

16. Bob Mercer, "Daschle, Johnson Center of Attention," *Aberdeen American News,* March 27, 2004 (source of all quotes).

17. "Statement of Democratic Leader Daschle on the War on Terrorism," press release, March 24, 2004; Denise Ross, "Daschle Satisfied with War Progress," *Rapid City Journal,* February 19, 2004; Editorial Note, "Statement of Senator Tom Daschle on the Administration Attacking Good People for Telling the Truth," Buzzflash.com, March 23, 2004.

18. Editorial, "Back Off, Senator; Daschle's Anti-war Remarks Come Too Late, Serve No Constructive Purpose," *Argus Leader,* March 19, 2003 (Daschle quote); "South Dakota Senate," *Hotline,* March 27, 2003 (polling data); Chuck Baldwin, "Editor's Note," *Argus Leader,* April 6, 2003 (letter policy).

19. Walter Pincus and Dana Milbank, "Kay Cites Evidence Of Iraq Disarming; Action Taken in '90s, Ex-Inspector Says," *Washington Post,* January 28, 2004 ("testy" quote); Dailykos.com, April 1, 2004; Christopher Hitchens, "Fallujah," *Wall Street Journal,* April 2, 2004; John F. Burns, "The Long Shadow of a Mob," *New York Times,* April 4, 2004 (Kimmitt quote).

20. Roxanne Roberts, "Out and About," *Washington Post,* March 29, 2004 (Daschle quote); Evan Thomas, "The Vietnam Question," *Newsweek,* April 19, 2004 (Byrd quote); Editorial, "The Story Line in Iraq," *New York Times,* April 11, 2004 (Kennedy quote); John MacArthur, "The Decline and Fall of Liberal Courage," *Providence Journal-Bulletin,* April 12, 2003 ("gumption" and "courage" quotes).

21. Brenda Wade Schmidt, "Second S.D. Guardsman in One Week Dies in Iraq," *Argus Leader,* April 26, 2004.

22. Ann Scott Tyson, "Youths in Rural U.S. Are Drawn to Military," *Washington Post,* November 4, 2005; Ben Shouse, "War in Iraq Strikes Home in Winner

with Heavy Price," *Argus Leader*, April 21, 2004 ("amazing" and "escalating" quotes).

23. Sheryl Gay Stolberg, "Democrats Issue Threat to Block Court Nominees," *New York Times*, March 27, 2004 (Daschle quote); Helen Dewar, "Bush Warned on Appointments," *Washington Post*, March 27, 2004; *60 Minutes*, CBS News, March 28, 2004.

24. Tom Daschle, with Michael D'Orso, *Like No Other Time: The 107th Congress and the Two Years That Changed America Forever* (New York: Crown Publishers, 2003), 211; Editorial, "Daschle's Duplicity," *New York Post*, April 4, 2004; Ross Mackenzie, "The Democratic Filibuster Invites 'Systemic Collapse,'" *Richmond Times Dispatch*, June 12, 2003 ("baffling" quote).

25. Morton Kondracke, "Welfare Impasse Is a Tragic Case of Partisan Posing," *Roll Call*, April 5, 2004; Editorial, "Politics Halts CARE Act," *Rapid City Journal*, October 21, 2004; Thomas Ferraro, "Daschle to Block Nominees," *Reuters*, March 31, 2004.

26. Robert Novak, "Frist Pushed to Play Hardball," *Chicago Sun-Times*, April 25, 2004; Carl Hulse, "A Longtime Courtesy Loses in the Closely Split Senate," *New York Times*, April 24, 2004; Paul Kane, "Frist Going to Daschle's Turf," *Roll Call*, April 12, 2004 ("obstruction" and "thorn" quotes); Sheryl Gay Stolberg, "Daschle Has Race on His Hands and Interloper on His Turf," *New York Times*, May 23, 2004; "Daschle Takes Potshots at Pressler," *Hotline*, August 14, 1990 ("terrible" quote); Tim Curran, "A Battle Brewing on Great Plains: Pressler, Johnson Headed for '96 Senate Showdown," *Roll Call*, April 3, 1995.

27. Jill Lawrence, "Kerry Takes Cut at Republicans, then Buries Hatchet with Dean," *USA Today*, March 11, 2004 (Kerry quote); Jeff Jacoby, "Kerry's UN Fetish," *Boston Globe*, April 22, 2004; "Bush, Kerry in Dead Heat if Vote Held Now, Poll Says," *Orlando Sentinel*, March 21, 2004; David F. Halbfinger, "Kerry Role in Antiwar Veterans Is Delicate Issue in His Campaign," *New York Times*, April 24, 2004.

28. Jeff Jacoby, "The Kerry Medals Mystery," *Boston Globe*, April 29, 2004; Patrick Healy, "Kerry Rejects Medals Dispute," *Boston Globe*, April 27, 2004 (Kerry's *Good Morning America* quote); James Ridgeway, "John Kerry Must Go," *Village Voice*, May 4, 2004; Roland Watson, "Kerry Campaign Fails to Profit from Bush Woes," *Times* (London), April 29, 2004; Howard Kurtz, "A Kerry-Worrying Trend; Is It Too Soon to Panic? Evidently Not," *Washington Post*, May 10, 2004.

29. Brian Faler, "Daschle Gets His Own Nader," *Washington Post*, April 5, 2004; Chris Cillizza, "Independent Could Sway Dakota Senate Race," *Roll Call*, March 31, 2004 (spokesman quote); Talkingpointsmemo.com, March 30, 2004.

30. David Kranz, "Bush-Giuliani Could Be Stronger Ticket Than Bush-Cheney," *Argus Leader*, March 21, 2004; Denise Ross, "Poll: Daschle Getting Narrow Nod over Thune," *Rapid City Journal*, April 2, 2004.

31. Harold Campbell, "MTI Says Daschle Ad Not an Endorsement," *Mitchell Daily Republic*, April 27, 2004.

32. KELO-Land News, April 27, 2004. Quotes and information on Daschle campaign tactics come from personal experience.

33. Mike Glover, "Bush Is Drawing Distinctions—and Getting under Kerry's Skin," Associated Press, March 31, 2004 (Kerry quotes).

34. Evelyn Nieves, "Daschle Gains Support of Rival; Indian Activist Drops Senate Bid," *Washington Post*, April 20, 2004; John Fund, "Political Diary," *Wall Street Journal* (OpinionJournal.com), April 21, 2004; Chris Cillizza, "Independent Could Sway Dakota Senate Race," *Roll Call*, March 31, 2004.

35. Editorial, "Candidates Show Earnings," *Rapid City Journal*, May 9, 2004; Editorial, "Show Us Your Taxes," *Mitchell Daily Republic*, October 2, 1982.

CHAPTER 4. MAY DAYS: THE SENATE SHUTS DOWN

Epigraph source: Tom Daschle, quoted in Howard Fineman, "The Reasons Not to Run? Pizza, for One," *Newsweek*, January 20, 2003.

1. Robert May, "Young American Males and Filibustering in the Age of Manifest Destiny: The U.S. Army as a Cultural Mirror," *Journal of American History* (December 1991): 857; Catherine Fisk and Erwin Chemainsky, "The Filibuster," *Stanford Law Review* 49 (January 1997): 192; Jacqueline Calmes, "Dilatory Debate: A Tactic as Old as the Senate," *Congressional Quarterly*, September 5, 1987.

2. Barbara Sinclair, *Party Wars: Polarization and the Politics of National Policy Making* (Norman: University of Oklahoma Press, 2006), 215; Thomas E. Mann, "Estrada Caught in 'Poisonous' War Based on Ideology," *Roll Call*, March 5, 2003; Adam Nagourney, Richard W. Stevenson, and Neil A. Lewis, "Glum Democrats Can't See Halting Bush on Courts," *New York Times*, January 15, 2006 (nominees quote); Elsa Walsh, "Minority Retort; How a Pro-gun, Anti-abortion Nevadan Leads the Senate's Democrats," *New Yorker*, August 8, 15, 2005.

3. John Stanton and April Fulton, "Daschle Unlikely to Work to Get Energy Bill Votes," *Congress Daily*, November 20, 2003; Joseph C. Anselmo and Allison Stevens, "Regional Issues Leave Energy Bill a Hair Too Unwieldy for Senate," *Congressional Quarterly Daily Monitor*, November 21, 2003 (Daschle quote); Bob Cusack, "'I'm Going to Make This Place Work': Grassley," *The Hill*, January 27, 2004 (Grassley quotes).

4. John Stanton and April Fulton, "Daschle Unlikely to Work to Get Energy Bill Votes," *Congress Daily*, November 20, 2003; Joseph C. Anselmo, "Senate GOP Leaders May Delay Further Action on Energy Bill," *Congressional Quarterly Daily Monitor*, November 23, 2003; Morton M. Kondracke, "Welfare Impasse Is a Tragic

Case of Partisan Posing," *Roll Call*, April 5, 2004; Tom Daschle, letter to the editor, *Wall Street Journal*, October 1, 2003.

5. Joseph C. Anselmo, "Energy Filibuster Idea Gaining Steam in the Senate," *Congressional Quarterly Daily Monitor*, November 18, 2003; Joseph C. Anselmo, "Both Sides Say Energy Bill Outcome Too Close to Call," *Congressional Quarterly Daily Monitor*, November 20, 2003 ("happy" and "nutshell" quotes); Joseph C. Anselmo and Martha Angle, "Senate Fails to End Filibuster against Energy Policy Bill," *Congressional Quarterly Daily Monitor*, November 21, 2003 ("going to know" quote); "Daschle Lends Clout to Energy Bill," *Argus Leader*, November 21, 2003.

6. Helen Dewar, "Senate Partisanship Worst in Memory; Key Legislation Languishes as Democrats and Republicans Jockey for Power," *Washington Post*, May 2, 2004; Bob Cusack, "'I'm Going to Make This Place Work': Grassley," *The Hill*, January 27, 2004.

7. *Congressional Record*, April 29, 2004 (McCain quote; italics added); Chuck Grassley, "End the Block and Blame Game," *Congressional Record*, May 20, 2004; Editorial, "Energy Follies," *Washington Post*, April 29, 2004; Shailagh Murray, "Senate Votes to Restore Ban on Internet Tax," *Wall Street Journal*, April 30, 2004.

8. Brody Mullins, "Bush's Push for Energy; President Expected to Provide a Boost for Stalled Initiative," *Roll Call*, January 20, 2004; Helen Dewar, "Bid to Revive Energy Legislation via Unrelated Bills Fails in Senate," *Washington Post*, April 30, 2004; "Daschle Spins Ethanol Defeat into High-Octane Political Charge," *Congress Daily*, April 30, 2004; David Ivanovich, "Energy Bill Falls Short Again; MTBE Pulled Out, but Senate Balks," *Houston Chronicle*, April 30, 2004.

9. Mike Madden, "Ethanol Measure Discarded," *Argus Leader*, April 30, 2004.

10. Jim VandeHei, "Democrat in Bush Country; A GOP Target, Daschle Begins Race of His Life in S.D.," *Washington Post*, May 31, 2003 ("attack" quote); Joseph C. Anselmo and Allison Stevens, "Regional Issues Leave Energy Bill a Hair Too Unwieldy for Senate," *Congressional Quarterly Weekly*, November 23, 2003 (Richardson quote).

11. Terry O'Keefe, "Daschle Wants Ethanol Bill," *Watertown Public Opinion*, May 6, 2003 ("disposal" quote).

12. Chuck Grassley, "End the Block and Blame Game," *Congressional Record*, May 20, 2004 (source of quotes; italics added).

13. Helen Dewar, "Senate Partisanship Worst in Memory; Key Legislation Languishes as Democrats and Republicans Jockey for Power," *Washington Post*, May 2, 2004; Paul Barton, "Lawmakers Say Split in Senate Frustrating," *Arkansas Democrat-Gazette*, May 9, 2004 ("do-nothing" quote); Gebe Martinez, "Casualties of Capitol Hill War; Partisanship Stalls Bills, Dooms Opportunities to Get Things Done," *Houston Chronicle*, May 9, 2004; Carl Hulse and Robert Pear, "Feeling Left Out on Major Bills, Democrats Turn to Stalling Others," *New York Times*, May 3, 2004; Richard Rosenfeld, "What Democracy? The Case for Abolishing the United

States Senate," *Harper's Magazine*, May 2004; Chuck Grassley, "End the Block and Blame Game," *Congressional Record*, May 20, 2004.

14. John Fund, "Political Diary," *Wall Street Journal* (OpinionJournal.com), May 13, 2004 (Specter quote); Jesse J. Holland, "Judiciary Committee Memo Snooping, Investigation Stirs Uproar," Associated Press, February 13, 2004.

15. Alexander Bolton, "Frist Finger on 'Nuclear' Button," *The Hill*, May 13, 2004 (spokesman quote); Jesse Holland, "White House, Senate Democrats Reach Deal," Associated Press, May 18, 2004.

16. Terence Samuel, "A Dakota Shoot-'Em-Up," *U.S. News and World Report*, May 24, 2004; Terry Woster, "Tight for Sure," *Argus Leader*, May 20, 2004; Stephen Dinan, "South Dakota Becomes Turf War; Frist Stumps for Daschle Foe," *Washington Times*, May 23, 2004 (Frist quote); *Congressional Record*, April 28, 2004 (Byrd quote); Carl Hulse, "A Longtime Courtesy Loses in the Closely Split Senate," *New York Times*, April 24, 2004; Sheryl Gay Stolberg, "Daschle Has Race on His Hands and Interloper on His Turf," *New York Times*, May 23, 2004 ("strained" quote); Charles Babington and Jeffrey Birnbaum, "Battle on Daschle's Turf Underscores Partisanship; Senate Majority Leader Frist Ruffles Feathers by Campaigning in Home State of Democratic Counterpart," *Washington Post*, May 23, 2004 ("bruised" quote); *Hardball*, MSNBC, November 7, 2005 ("wrong" quote).

17. Denise Ross, "Senator Stumps for Thune," *Rapid City Journal*, May 23, 2004.

18. Chris Cillizza and John Bresnahan, "Lobbyists Warned on S.D. Race," *Roll Call*, December 17, 2001 (lobbyist quotes); "South Dakota; Daschle Proposes, Thune Rejects Third Party Ban," *Roll Call*, June 15, 2004; Brody Mullins, "Insurers' Dinner Backfires," *Roll Call*, June 17, 2004 ("terrorism insurance" quote); Editorial, "ISO Political Payback," *Washington Times*, June 21, 2004.

19. Stephen Kinzer, "Both Parties Seek National Momentum in South Dakota Race," *New York Times*, May 20, 2004; *Capitol Gang*, CNN, May 22, 2004 (Kranz quote); Terry Woster, "Tight for Sure," *Argus Leader*, May 20, 2004 (source of poll).

20. Pam Belluck, "Governor Moves on Non-Massachusetts Couples," *New York Times*, May 19, 2004 ("Las Vegas" quote); Matt Foreman [director of National Gay and Lesbian Task Force], Editorial, *Washington Blade*, May 7, 2004; Lou Chibbaro, "Democrats Disavow Claim They Might 'Cave' on FMA," *Washington Blade*, May 14, 2004; Patrick Healy, "Kerry Aims to Keep Peace with Gays," *Boston Globe*, May 15, 2004 ("tenuous peace" quote).

21. David Kranz, "Johnson, Thune Debate about Iraq," *Argus Leader*, October 8, 2002 ("over the top" and "despicable" quotes); *Evening News*, KDLT-TV, May 25, 2004 ("sorry" quote); David Kranz, "'Taliban' Remark Draws Apology from Johnson," *Argus Leader*, May 26, 2004; Editorial, "The Cost of Freedom," *Rapid City Journal*, May 31, 2004; Editorial, "Not Quite an Apology," *Mitchell Daily Republic*, May 27, 2004; Editorial, "Johnson's Apology Isn't Good Enough," *Argus Leader*, May 26, 2004.

22. Tom Daschle, "Can We Talk? Free Speech and Civil Discourse in Turbulent Times," May 10, 2004, Landon Lecture Series, Kansas State University ("demonizing" quote); "Daschle Decries 'Meanness' in Politics," Associated Press, May 24, 2004; "Politicos Turn Up Heat on Johnson," *Rapid City Journal*, May 26, 2004 ("all that needs to be said" quote); Editorial, "The Cost of Freedom," *Rapid City Journal*, May 31, 2004.

23. John Hanna, "Daschle: Abuse 'Bigger' Than Question of Rumsfeld Resignation," Associated Press, May 11, 2004; Jodi Wilgoren, "Kerry Ties Prisoner Abuse to Bush's Handling of War," *New York Times*, May 15, 2004 (Daschle quote); Joan Vennochi, "Kennedy's Two-Edged Mystique," *Boston Globe*, May 27, 2004 (Kennedy quote); "Kerry Pulls Ahead of Bush in New Poll," *Agence France Presse*, May 16, 2004; "Bush Leads Kerry in Public Ppinion Poll," Associated Press, May 20, 2004.

24. Denise Ross, "Poll Shows Big Daschle Lead," *Rapid City Journal*, May 25, 2004 (source of Zogby poll information); Sheryl Gay Stolberg, "Daschle Has Race on His Hands and Interloper on His Turf," *New York Times*, May 23, 2004; Chris Cillizza, "Latest Poll Has Daschle Leading by 13 Points," *Roll Call*, June 1, 2004; "Enter Bill Frist; The Senate Race in South Dakota," *Economist*, May 29, 2004; Geoff Earle, "Dems Look beyond Daschle," *The Hill*, June 2, 2004; *The Chris Matthews Show*, MSNBC, June 6, 2004.

CHAPTER 5. THE POLITICS OF ASSOCIATION AND MEMORY

Epigraph source: Herbert Baxter Adams, quoted in Steven Gillon, "The Future of Political History," *Journal of Policy History* 9, no. 2 (1997): 241.

1. David Kranz, "Independent Style: Stephanie Herseth Adds Her Own Distinctive Voice to a Family Legacy of Politics," *Argus Leader*, May 16, 2004 ("difference" quote); Editorial, "Herseth Is the Choice," *Argus Leader*, May 23, 2004; Editorial, "Herseth for Congress," *Aberdeen American News*, May 30, 2004; David Kranz, "Women, Sioux Falls Key to Victory for Herseth," *Argus Leader*, June 2, 2004 ("liberal label" and "avoidance" quotes); Stephen Kinzer, "Both Parties Seek National Momentum in South Dakota Race," *New York Times*, May 20, 2004 (Diedrich quote); David Kranz, "Herseth Hasn't Altered Support for Bush on Iraq," *Argus Leader*, July 3, 2004; Bob Mercer, "Turnout a GOP Key," *Watertown Public Opinion*, March 5, 2004 (Herseth quote).

2. Stuart Rothenberg, "South Dakota Special: Will Herseth Benefit from Buyer's Remorse?" *Roll Call*, May 10, 2004 ("popularity" quote); Steve Hemmingsen, "How Did It Get That Close?" Keloland.com, June 2, 2004; Stephen Kinzer, "Both Parties Seek National Momentum in South Dakota Race," *New York Times*, May 20, 2004 ("star quality" quote).

3. David Kranz, "'Nice' Image Appeals to Many S.D. Voters," *Argus Leader,* April 29, 2004 ("truthful" quote); Charlie Cook, "Off to the Races: South Dakota's Monumental Election," *National Journal,* May 4, 2004; Stuart Rothenberg, "South Dakota Special: Will Herseth Benefit from Buyer's Remorse?" *Roll Call,* May 10, 2004.

4. Joe Kafka, "Herseth Wins Close Contest for South Dakota's House Seat," Associated Press, June 2, 2004 (Herseth quote); Carson Walker, "Diedrich to Have Heart Surgery," Associated Press, June 15, 2004.

5. Patrick O'Connor, "Imported Volunteers Helped Dems in S.D.; Mobilization for Herseth Outdid National GOP," *The Hill,* June 16, 2004; Herseth's spokesman "confirmed that the netroots played a major part in her special election victory." Chris Cillizza, "Crying Foul, Netroots Note Some Big Wins," March 30, 2006, blog.washingtonpost.com/thefix/; Rob Morse, "Web Forum Shapes Political Thinking; Dean Consultant in Berkeley Builds 'Blog' into Influential Tool," *San Francisco Chronicle,* January 15, 2004; DailyKos.com, June 2, 2004.

6. DailyKos.com, May 26–June 2, 2006 (quotes from blog comments); DailyKos.com, May 24, 2004 (child abuse information).

7. KELO-Land.com, June 2, 2004 (Hemmingsen quote); John Fund, "Political Diary," *Wall Street Journal* (OpinionJournal.com), May 21, 2004 (source of polling information); Carl Hulse, "Could Herseth's Victory in South Dakota Hurt Daschle?" *New York Times,* June 2, 2004; Peter Savodnik, "Narrow Loss Will Do, Says Diedrich in S.D.," *The Hill,* June 1, 2004 (Stroschein quote).

8. Maria Newman, "'I Will Not Yield,' Bush Tells Troops; Broadcast Speech Offers Thanks and Warns of Violence to Come," *International Herald Tribune,* June 17, 2004.

9. "Ronald Reagan, 1911–2004: Excerpts from the Funeral Service," *Atlanta Journal-Constitution,* June 12, 2004. Thatcher quotation is from my notes on the ceremony.

10. Natan Sharansky, "The Prisoners' Conscience," *Jewish World Review,* June 8, 2004 (source of quote); Natan Sharansky, *The Case for Democracy: The Power of Freedom to Overcome Tyranny and Terror* (New York: Public Affairs, 2004).

11. David Sanger, "Bush Tells U.S. Troops 'Life Is Better' in Iraq," *New York Times,* June 17, 2004; "Public Support for War Resilient; Bush's Standing Improves," Pew Research Center for the People and the Press, June 17, 2004 (source of polling information); Elisabeth Bumiller, "Trying on Reagan's Mantle, But It Doesn't Exactly Fit," *New York Times,* June 14, 2004.

12. Anne E. Kornblut, "Campaigns Seize on Reagan's Legacy," *Boston Globe,* June 9, 2004 (Daschle quote); Anthony Lewis, "Abroad at Home: Onward, Christian Soldiers," *New York Times,* March 10, 1983; John Oakes, "The Reagan Hoax," *New York Times,* November 1, 1981; Steven Hayward, *The Age of Reagan: The Fall of the Old Liberal Order, 1964–1980* (New York: Random House, 2001), 697

(King and Reeves quotes); Daniel Henninger, "Ronald Reagan Started a War That Rages Today," *Wall Street Journal,* June 11, 2004 (Schlesinger quote).

13. Dave Boyer and Bill Sammon, "Bush Praises Reagan as He Turns 91; Daschle Criticizes Ex-president over Tax Cuts, Deficits," *Washington Times,* February 7, 2002 (birthday information); Michael S. Gerber, "State Legislatures Back Bush Initiatives for National Reforms at the State Level," *The Hill,* April 16, 2003; Charles Krauthammer, "Reagan Revisionism," *Washington Post,* June 11, 2004; Adam Nagourney, "Reagan Legacy Looming Large over Campaign," *New York Times,* June 7, 2004 (Jordan quote).

14. Sheryl Stolberg, "Pondering a Legacy Not (Yet) Carved in Stone," *New York Times,* June 8, 2004; Peter Kirsanow, "Shining Countenance on a Hill: Reagan Belongs on Mount Rushmore," *National Review Online,* June 10, 2004.

15. KELO-Land.com, June 15, 2004 (Hemmingsen quote).

16. Arthur Schlesinger, Jr., *The Disuniting of America: Reflections on a Multicultural Society* (New York: W. W. Norton, 1992), 45–72; Walter Isaacson, "I'm Okay, You're Okay," *Washington Post Book World,* July 4, 2004; Fred Barnes, "The Shrinking Clinton: Big Book, Small Legacy," *Weekly Standard,* June 28, 2004; Charles Krauthammer, "Clinton Writ Small," *Washington Post,* June 25, 2004; Michiko Kakutani, "A Pastiche of a Presidency, Imitating a Life, in 957 Pages," *New York Times,* June 20, 2004; *Newsweek,* July 5, 2004 (Lewinsky quote).

17. Robert Brent Toplin, *Michael Moore's* Fahrenheit 9/11: *How One Film Divided a Nation* (Lawrence: University Press of Kansas, 2006), 13 ("torches" quote); Jim Geraghty, *Voting to Kill: How 9/11 Launched the Era of Republican Leadership* (New York: Touchstone, 2006), 214–31; Philip Shenon, "Michael Moore Is Ready for His Close-Up," *New York Times,* June 20, 2004 ("libel" quote); Hanna Rosin and Mike Allen, "'Fahrenheit 9/11' Is a Red-Hot Ticket; At the Film's U.S. Premiere, the White House Takes the Heat," *Washington Post,* June 25, 2004 (italics added); Christopher Hitchens, "Unfairenheit 9/11: The Lies of Michael Moore," *Slate,* June 21, 2004 (italics added).

18. "Review and Outlook: McCain-Moore," *Wall Street Journal,* June 28, 2004; Frank Rich, "The Best Goebbels of All?" *New York Times,* June 27, 2004; Michael Isikoff and Mark Hosenball, "Terror Watch: More Distortions from Michael Moore," *Newsweek,* June 30, 2004.

19. David Brooks, "All Hail Moore," *New York Times,* June 26, 2004 (Moore quotes); Robert Brent Toplin, *Michael Moore's* Fahrenheit 9/11: *How One Film Divided a Nation* (Lawrence: University Press of Kansas, 2006), 127–28; Michael Barone, "The Company They Keep," *U.S. News and World Report,* July 12, 2004.

20. Jason Zengerle, "Crashing the Party," *New Republic,* June 24, 2004 ("standing ovation," Zengerle, and McAuliffe quotes); David Brooks, "All Hail Moore," *New York Times,* June 26, 2004; "Moore's Law," *Economist,* July 3, 2004; Michael Barone, "The Company They Keep," *U.S. News and World Report,* July 12, 2004.

21. Christopher Hitchens, "Unfairenheit 9/11: The Lies of Michael Moore," *Slate,* June 21, 2004; Andrew Sullivan, "William Raspberry and Michael Moore: Be Like Mike," *New Republic,* June 29, 2004.

22. Denise D. Tucker, "'Fahrenheit 9/11' a Hit with Critics of Iraq War," *Argus Leader,* June 26, 2004; Hanna Rosin and Mike Allen, "'Fahrenheit 9/11' Is a Red-Hot Ticket; At the Film's U.S. Premiere, the White House Takes the Heat," *Washington Post,* June 25, 2004; Eric Alterman, "The Hollywood Campaign: Want Big Money to Get Elected to Congress? If You're a Democrat, You Need to Head for the Hills—Beverly Hills," *Atlantic Monthly,* September 1, 2004 ("pillars" quote). In 1992, Bill Clinton denounced the black activist Sister Souljah for her statement calling for the killing of whites. In 1954, Joseph Welch denounced Senator Joe McCarthy for his outlandish charges of communist control of the U.S. Army.

23. "Powell Assails Barbarism of Johnson's Killers," Associated Press, June 18, 2004; Peter Harriman, "Daschle Praises New Iraqi Leaders," *Argus Leader,* June 20, 2004 (Daschle quotes).

24. Evan Osnos, "U.S. Transfers Power to Iraq," *Chicago Tribune,* June 29, 2004 (Bremer quote); Greg Sheridan, "Western Elections Hit by Iraq Ripple Effects—Saddam on Trial," *Western Australian,* July 3, 2004 ("death" quote); David Halbfinger, "After Iraq Transfer, Kerry Again Prods Bush to Win Help from Abroad," *New York Times,* June 29, 2004 (Kerry and Bush spokesman quotes); David E. Sanger, "Fresh Starts: One for Iraq, One for Bush," *New York Times,* June 29, 2004; Ryan Lizza, "WWJKD?" *New Republic,* May 24, 2004.

25. Senator Daschle, who had long advocated campaign finance reform, was criticized by the *Washington Post* for supporting the circumvention of the McCain-Feingold campaign-financing law by encouraging such organizations as 527 entities: "As the Senate prepared to vote on the campaign finance law last year, Mr. Daschle noted that 'there are those who are already looking for ways to work around this bill.' What he failed to say was that he and his colleagues would soon take their place among them." Editorial, "Once More into the Swamp," *Washington Post,* May 10, 2003; Adam Nagourney and Janet Elder, "Bush's Rating Falls to Its Lowest Point, New Survey Finds," *New York Times,* June 29, 2004.

CHAPTER 6. DISINTERMEDIATION: THE DAKOTA BLOG ALLIANCE AND THE *SIOUX FALLS ARGUS LEADER*

Epigraph source: "The Campaign Desk," cjr.org, *Columbia Journalism Review,* January 19, 2004. At a minimum, according to a recent study, a successful democracy requires "alternative sources of information." Larry Diamond and Leonardo Morlino, eds., *Assessing the Quality of Democracy* (Baltimore, Md.: Johns Hopkins University Press, 2005), xi.

1. Randell Beck, "Grumpy Season Is Here," *Argus Leader,* July 18, 2004. Wadhams told me the substance of the telephone calls.

2. Randell Beck, "Web Log Junkies Welcome Here," *Argus Leader,* July 25, 2004 (editor quote); George Packer, "The Revolution Won't Be Blogged," *Mother Jones,* May/June 2004 (Lessig quote).

3. Robert J. Samuelson, "Picking Sides for the News," *Newsweek,* June 28, 2004.

4. Jacques Steinberg, "Newspaper Editors Move to Tighten Safeguards," *New York Times,* March 22, 2004; Memo from Bill Hilliard, Bill Kovach, and John Seigenthaler to Craig Moon, "The Problems of Jack Kelley and *USA Today*" (independent review); James Bandler, "Report Cites 'Virus of Fear' at *USA Today,*" *Wall Street Journal,* April 23, 2004 ("coddling" and "Golden Boy" quotes); *Editor and Publisher,* April 22, 2004 (Sulzberger quote); Daniel Okrent, "It's Been 11 Weeks: Do You Know Where Your Ombudsman Is?" *New York Times,* February 15, 2004; James Bandler, "New York Times Finds Its Watchdog Has a Strong Bite," *Wall Street Journal,* July 12, 2004.

5. Edward Driscoll, "Welcome to the Post-Bias Media," *Tech Central Station,* May 5, 2004 ("predilections," Rooney, Zelnick, and Cronkite quotes); Daniel Okrent, "Is the *New York Times* a Liberal Newspaper?" *New York Times,* July 25, 2004. See also Tim Groseclose and Jeff Milo, "A Measure of Media Bias" (September 2003), 1–29, report from the Department of Political Science at the University of California–Los Angeles and Harris School of Public Policy at the University of Chicago. This report found a "strong liberal bias."

6. Jim Finkle, "Turner Compares Fox's Popularity to Hitler," *Broadcasting and Cable,* January 25, 2004; Howard Kurtz, "Liberal Radio Network Hits Air with Left Jab; Programming Debuts with Al Franken," *Washington Post,* April 1, 2004 ("apologists" quote); Eliza Newlin Carney, "Extreme Makeover," *National Journal,* February 26, 2005; Siobhan Gorman, "News You Can Choose," *National Journal,* October 9, 2004.

7. Al Neuharth, "Cowardly Senators Duck Iraq and Vote," *USA Today,* November 7, 2003; Al Neuharth, "If Kerry Loses, Who Leads Dems in '08?" *USA Today,* July 23, 2004 (source of first Neuharth quote); Ben H. Bagdikian, *The Media Monopoly* (Boston: Beacon Press, 1983), 67, 74 (source of second and third Neuharth quotes); *Nashville Scene,* no date, http://www.nashvillescene.com/Grading_the_Daily/ gannett1.html. For additional criticism of Gannett, see Doug Underwood, *When MBAs Rule the Newsroom* (New York: Columbia University Press, 1993), 95–105.

8. *Argus Leader* purchases include the *Baltic Beacon,* the *Brandon Valley Challenger,* the *Dell Rapids Tribune,* the *Garretson Weekly,* and the *Tea-Harrisburg Champion.* Randell Beck, "Growth of Web Logs Forces Public to Read Skeptically," *Argus Leader,* March 6, 2005 (source of first Beck quote); *Argus on Air,* KELO AM, June 18, 2003 (source of second Beck quote); Howell Raines, "My Times," *Atlantic Monthly,* May 2004.

9. Rebecca Blood, "Weblogs: A History and Perspective," September 2000; Esther Scott, "'Big Media' Meets the 'Bloggers': Coverage of Trent Lott's Remarks at Strom Thurmond's Birthday Party," Kennedy School of Government Case Program, C14-0401731.0 (2004); Edward Driscoll, "Welcome to the Post-Bias Media," *Tech Central Station*, May 5, 2004; Glenn Reynolds, "The Blogs of War," *National Interest*, March 30, 2004; Tim Worstal, "More Bias, Please," *Tech Central Station*, November 12, 2004 ("disintermediation" explanation).

10. Joe Trippi, *The Revolution Will Not Be Televised: Democracy, the Internet, and the Overthrow of Everything* (New York: Regan Books, 2004); Alan Wolfe, "The New Pamphleteers," *New York Times Book Review*, July 11, 2004. For more, see Daniel Drezner and Henry Farrell, "The Power and Politics of Blogs," paper presented to the 2004 American Political Science Association; Bruce Bimber, "The Internet and Political Transformation: Populism, Community, and Accelerated Pluralism," *Polity* 31, no. 1 (Fall 1998): 133–60; Chris Wright, "Parking Lott: The Role of Web Logs in the Fall of Sen. Trent Lott," Culture, Communication and Technology Program, Georgetown University vol. 3, Fall 2003, 1–30; Mark Glaser, "'Watchblogs' Put the Political Press under the Microscope," *Annenberg Online Journalism Review*, February 11, 2004; Barb Palser, "Journalism's Backseat Drivers," *American Journalism Review*, August/September 2005.

11. Joseph Epstein, "Are Newspapers Doomed?" *Commentary* 121, no. 1 (January 2006): 49; Dave Kranz, no headline, *Austin Daily Herald*, September 6, 1974 (Kranz quote); Michael Schudson, *Watergate in American Memory: How We Remember, Forget, and Reconstruct the Past* (New York: Basic Books, 1992), 103, 111 ("overwhelms" quote); Andreas Killen, *1973 Nervous Breakdown: Watergate, Warhol, and the Birth of Post-Sixties America* (New York: Bloomsbury, 2006), 66; Talkingpointsmemo.com, October 12, 2002. Jack Germond and Dan Balz are longtime political reporters; Germond, especially, was thought to be sympathetic to Democrats. Randell Beck, "Election Year's Daily Challenge," *Argus Leader*, June 27, 2004 (Beck quote); Randell Beck, "Curious E-mails Stir Lynch Mob," *Argus Leader*, October 17, 2004. David Kranz declined to be interviewed for this book.

12. Chris Bower and Matthew Stoller, "The Emergence of the Progressive Blogosphere: A New Force in Politics," New Politics Institute (August 10, 2005), 4.

13. Dave Kranz, untitled column, *Mitchell Daily Republic*, November 3, 1983 ("bias" quote; italics added); Dave Kranz, untitled column, *Mitchell Daily Republic*, September 4, 1976 ("speaker" quote).

14. "Delegation Chairmen Change Designation of Mock Convention," *South Dakota Collegian*, April 3, 1968 ("publicity chairman" quote); Dave Kranz, "Daschle Was Workhorse for Political Convention," *South Dakota Collegian*, May 1, 1968; William Powers, "The Massless Media," *Atlantic Monthly*, January/February 2005. Vandenberg was first elected to the Senate in 1928 and remained active in politics through the early 1950s.

15. David Kranz and Chuck Raasch, "Few Thought Aberdeen Native Could Climb So Far," *Argus Leader*, April 8, 2001; Dave Kranz, "Killing Brought Down Dream," *Argus Leader*, November 20, 1988; Dave Kranz untitled column, *Mitchell, Daily Republic*, January 18, 1978 ("eloquent" quote); David Kranz, "McCarthy Campaign Eye-Opener about Harsh Reality of Poverty," *Argus Leader*, December 13, 1987 ("politically active," "official language," "Neat," "cheered," and "forcing" quotes); Theodore H. White, *The Making of the President 1968* (New York: Atheneum Publishers, 1969), 140; Lewis Chesler, Godfrey Hodgson, and Bruce Page, *An American Melodrama: The Presidential Campaign of 1968* (New York: Viking Press, 1969), 8; Richard Corliss, "A Poet Who Took On the War," *Time*, December 19, 2005.

16. David Kranz, "Daschle Shows Courage in Voting for Pay Increase," *Argus Leader*, November 26, 1989; David Kranz, "Daschle's Friendship with Clinton Could Be Beneficial," *Argus Leader*, March 26, 1993 ("master politician" quote); David Kranz, "Potential Republican Opponent Assails Daschle's Ties to Clinton," *Argus Leader*, March 22, 1998 ("unbeatable" quote); David Kranz, "Convention Speech Helps Brighten Daschle's Star," *Argus Leader*, July 24, 1988 ("bleeds" quote).

17. David Kranz, "Voters May Be Growing Weary of Senate Campaign," *Argus Leader*, September 9, 1990 ("health records" quote); David Kranz, "Muenster Funds Running Low; Samuelson's Chances Rise," *Argus Leader*, September 30, 1990 ("memory" criticism); David Kranz, "Author Takes Heat for Jabs at Pressler," *Argus Leader*, September 20, 1996; Bob Mercer, "Abourezk Spread Rumor about Pressler; Book Alleges That Senator Is Gay," *Rapid City Journal*, September 21, 1996; David Tuller, "New Wave of Outings in Politics," *San Francisco Chronicle*, October 26, 1996; Karen Tumulty, "The Baiting Game; A New Twist on Sexual Politics: Some Democrats Are Hinting That Their GOP Opponents Are Gay," *Time*, October 14, 1996; "Former Senator Settles Libel Case over 1996 Book," *Chicago Tribune*, July 26, 1998; David Kranz, "S.D. Voters Losers When Pressler, Muenster Debate Campaign Purity," *Argus Leader*, April 18, 1990 (*Madison* bias quotes). After reporting the 1996 rumor about Pressler's sexual preference, the *Argus* editors wrote, "Even if true, it wouldn't have any bearing on [Pressler's] abilities as a senator." Editorial, "Evidence of Pressler's Side," *Argus Leader*, September 20, 1996.

18. *Argus on Air*, June 18, 2003, KELO AM.

19. Andrewsullivan.com, June 10, 2003; Instapundit.com, June 20, 2003; AndrewClem.com, June 21, 2003; Powerlineblog.com, June 21, 2003, and July 19, 2004; Noel Hamiel, "Disclosure Healthy, Even for Reporters, but College Activities Irrelevant," *Mitchell Daily Republic*, June 7, 2003.

20. "The 1990 Elections: State by State; Midwest," *New York Times*, November 7, 1990; Glenn R. Simpson and Craig Winneker, "Pressler Is Running for Re-election against Newspaper," *Roll Call*, July 30, 1990 (chief of staff and "hand in hand"

quotes); Lieutenant Governor Lowell Hanson, opinion-editorial, *Argus Leader,* January 15, 1986.

21. Karl Struble, "How to Beat an Incumbent: The Inside Story of the Hard-Fought Johnson vs. Pressler U.S. Senate Race in South Dakota," *Campaigns and Elections,* June 1997 (italics added).

22. David Kranz, "Politicos See No Danger of Daschle Losing Clout," *Argus Leader,* April 13, 2004; Stuart Rothenberg interview, *Washington Post,* March 3, 2004 (italics added); Geoff Earle, "String of Losses Stirs Dem Grumbling as Talk of Dorgan Challenge Subsides," *The Hill,* January 27, 2004 (Feinstein quote); Political Aims.com, February 15, 2004; SouthDakotaPolitics.blogs.com, January 26, 2004.

23. Denise Ross, "Major Political Players Descend on Pierre," *Rapid City Journal,* February 24, 2004; SouthDakotaPolitics.blogs.com, April 12, 2004; e-mail, Steve Hildebrand, "No Danger of Daschle Losing Clout," April 13, 2004 ("article" quote).

24. Dave Kranz, untitled column, *Mitchell Daily Republic,* September 4, 1976; SouthDakotaPolitics.blogs.com, April 14, 2004 (italics added).

25. SouthDakotaPolitics.blogs.com, April 19, 2004 ("hokey" and "friendly" quotes); SouthDakotaPolitics.blogs.com, August 10, 2004 ("priests" information).

26. Instapundit.com, April 19, 2004; Andrewsullivan.com, April 16, 2004; Powerlineblog.com, April 19, 2004; *American Spectator,* April 19, 2004; KELO Land.com, April 19, 2004 (Hemmingsen quote). David Broder is the longtime political reporter/analyst of the *Washington Post* and is considered to be the dean of American political commentators.

27. *Argus on Air,* April 21, 2004, KELO AM (Beck quotes); Andrew sullivan. com, April 22, 2004; *Editor and Publisher,* February 22, 2005 ("manipulate" quote).

28. Joseph Bottum, "Prairie Politics; Daschle, Thune, and the Race for South Dakota," *Weekly Standard,* September 27, 2004.

29. SouthDakotaPolitics.blogs.com, February 27, 2004; Chris Cillizza, "State Account Helped Thune," *Roll Call,* February 10, 2004; Mike Madden and David Kranz, "Thune Spending Questioned," *Argus Leader,* February 11, 2004; Chris Cillizza and Brody Mullins, "Thune Will Keep Lobbying; Criticism of Daschles May Wane," *Roll Call,* January 26, 2004; David Kranz and Peter Harriman, "Candidate Thune Plans to Continue Lobbyist Job," *Argus Leader,* January 27, 2004. Although the *Argus* ran the *Roll Call* stories about Thune the next day, the *Argus* ignored the *Roll Call* stories about Daschle. Chris Cillizza, "Daschle's Five-Year, $9.5M Spending Spree," *Roll Call,* February 26, 2004; Amy Keller, "Daschle Hit on Tax Break; Wife Claims 'Homestead' Exemption," *Roll Call,* August 18, 2003. See also Thomas E. Patterson, *Out of Order* (New York: Vintage Books, 1994), 53 (Lippmann quote).

30. Letter to Editor, Catherine Piersol, *Tempest,* June 10–23, 1992 (*"Village Voice"* quote); *Tempest,* September 1992 ("evil" quote); *Tempest,* October 28–November 10, 1992 ("wunderkind" and "demeanor" quotes); *Tempest,* October 1990 ("rhetoric"

and "ate" quotes); *Tempest*, July 3–16, 1991 ("powerful" quote). The *Tempest* columns cited here are by Lalley.

31. *Tempest*, July 31–August 13, 1991 ("sneer" quote); *Tempest*, March 18–31, 1992 ("fine city" quote); *Tempest*, January 26–February 8, 1994 ("mainstream" quote); Tempest, November 11–24, 1993 ("hatemongers" and "called" quotes); *Tempest*, October 28–November 10, 1992 ("commie" quote).

32. James Fallows, "The American Information Revolution," *New York Times Book Review*, May 30, 2004; Randell Beck, "Take Charge of Your Vote," *Argus Leader*, May 2, 2004 ("fanatic" quote); Randell Beck, "Election Year's Daily Challenge," *Argus Leader*, June 27, 2004 ("venomous" quote); Randell Beck, "New to the Area? This Will Help You Fit Right In," *Argus Leader*, January 4, 2004 ("bed" quote).

33. Randell Beck, "Web Log Junkies Welcome Here," *Argus Leader*, July 25, 2004 ("Hitler" and preceding quotes); AndrewSullivan.com, July 26, 2004; Instapundit .com, July 26, 2004; Powerlineblog.com, July 26, 2004; Oxblog.com, July 26, 2004; Peter Preston, "Media: Dawn of the Daily Blog?" *Observer*, January 9, 2005; John Fund, "Political Diary," *Wall Street Journal* (OpinionJournal.com), July 26, 2004; Randell Beck, "Editors Set Newspaper Compass," *Argus Leader*, June 8, 2003.

34. Editorial, "Steps Made to Open Government," *Argus Leader*, February 21, 2004; Editorial, "Openness Pays Off," *Argus Leader*, July 4, 2004.

35. Editorial, "Pardons Teach Lesson: Democracy Best Exercised in Light of Public Scrutiny," *Argus Leader*, May 30, 2004; Editorial, "S.D.'s Political Paradox," *Argus Leader*, August 24, 2004.

36. Randell Beck, "Leaders Must Be Accountable," *Argus Leader*, April 27, 2003 (source of all quotes).

37. Norm Brewer, "Pressler Goes His Own Way; Often Controversial Picture Painted of S.D. Senator," *Argus Leader*, June 24, 1990 (source of critics' quotes); Norm Brewer, "Early Pledges Fall by the Wayside," *Argus Leader*, June 24, 1990.

38. Editorial, "Blog Watch," *World Magazine*, May 8, 2004; Hugh Hewitt, "Trouble in South Dakota . . . for Tom Daschle. Local Bloggers Are Going to Make His Reelection Fight Tougher," *Weekly Standard*, July 8, 2004.

39. Lev Grossman and Anita Hamilton, "Meet Joe Blog," *Time*, June 21, 2004; Lalley, untitled column, *Tempest*, October 4–27, 1992; "Web Logs Discussed at Conference," Associated Press, August 15, 2004; John Fund, "A Prairie Revolt against the Lamestream Media," *Wall Street Journal*, August 17, 2004.

40. Michael Crowley, "Local Yokels," *New Republic*, March 14, 2005 ("shocked" quote); Instapundit.com, August 31, 2004; Jennifer Sanderson, "Blogging: A Venue to Rant and Rave," *Argus Leader*, August 9, 2004.

41. Daniel Okrent, "Weapons of Mass Destruction? Or Mass Distraction?" *New York Times*, May 30, 2004. Blogger's comment on *Argus* editor is from the author's notes.

42. Dick Wadhams interview, November 9, 2004; *Inside Washington,* July 10, 2004 (Thomas comment); Howard Fineman, "Living Politics: The 'Media Party' Is Over," *Newsweek,* January 11, 2005; Howard Kurtz, "Suddenly Everyone's a Critic," *Washington Post,* October 3, 2005.

43. "Gannett Honors *Argus Leader,*" *Argus Leader,* April 23, 2005. See also "The Collapse of Big Media," *Wilson Quarterly* 39, no. 2 (Spring 2005): 39–59; and Richard Posner, "Bad News," *New York Times Book Review,* July 31, 2005.

CHAPTER 7. THE END OF THE BEGINNING

Epigraph source: Bill Zehme, *The Way You Wear Your Hat: Frank Sinatra and the Lost Art of Livin'* (New York: HarperCollins, 1997), 30.

1. Kirk Victor, "Fighting for His Life," *National Journal,* October 15, 2004; Jennifer Sanderson, Ad Watch, *Argus Leader,* August 10, 2004; Denise Ross, "Daschle: Health Care a 'Quiet Crisis,'" *Rapid City Journal,* August 15, 2004; Kevin Dobbs, "Senators: Open VA to All Vets," *Argus Leader,* July 26, 2004.

2. Jennifer Sanderson, "GOP Criticizes Daschle TV Ad: Spot on Long-Distance Learning Should Be Pulled, Lawmakers Say," *Argus Leader,* August 6, 2004.

3. Ben Shouse, "Norton Praises on Partisan Lines," *Argus Leader,* August 13, 2004 (Norton quote); Chet Brokaw, "Conservation Groups Seek Court Order to Halt Prairie Dog Killing," Associated Press, September 22, 2004; Blaine Harden, "Prairie Dog Pops Up in S.D. Senate Race; Daschle, Foe Spar over Rodent's Future," *Washington Post,* October 10, 2004.

4. Sid Salter, "Daschle Luncheon Was Quiet Gathering," *Clarion-Ledger,* August 15, 2004.

5. Josh Benson, "The Democrats' A.T.M.," *New York Times,* August 8, 2004; Powerlineblog.com, September 3, 2004.

6. Terry Woster, "Debates May Not Change Election," *Argus Leader,* July 31, 2004; "Daschle Turns Down Thune Challenge," *Rapid City Journal,* August 3, 2004; Editorial, "Schedule Debates," *Rapid City Journal,* August 3, 2004; Editorial, "Time to Quit Debating Debates, Start Debating," *Argus Leader,* August 29, 1986 ("smoother" quote); David Kranz, "Thune, Daschle to Debate on 'Meet the Press,'" *Argus Leader,* August 4, 2004.

7. Richard Bale, "Senate Debates Debated," *Argus Leader,* August 15, 1986; *Daschle Digest,* July 21, 2004.

8. Terry Woster, "Thune: 'A Race That Needed to Be Run,'" *Argus Leader,* October 10, 2004 ("raucous" quote). Debate proceedings are from personal observation.

9. Denise Ross, "Chicken What? Daschle Seeks Apology from Thune on Statements to Staffer," *Rapid City Journal,* August 14, 2004; Editorial, "Still Time for More Debates," *Rapid City Journal,* August 29, 2004 ("manipulate" quote);

Editorial, "Debates Offer Opportunity to Listen," *Argus Leader,* August 25, 2004; *Mitchell Daily Republic,* September 3, 2004 ("security" quote); Editorial, "Our Challenge: Weekly Debates," *Rapid City Journal,* August 23, 2004.

10. David Kranz, "Thune Letter Marks First Shot in Fight about Clout," *Argus Leader,* January 30, 2004 ("clout" focus); David Kranz, "Best Bets: Janklow in Senate; Kneip for Governor," *Argus Leader,* January 5, 1986; "Where's the Aid?" *Argus Leader,* July 22, 2004; Peter Harriman, "S.D. Denied Drought Relief; 9 States Get Federal Help; Daschle Says Long-Term Assistance Needed," *Argus Leader,* July 17, 2004; "Bush Makes Parts of S.D. Disaster Area," *Argus Leader,* July 21, 2004.

11. Keloland.com, July 13, 2004 (Hemmingsen quote); Minnesota Public Radio, August 17, 2004; Jon Walker, "Daschle Seeks Small-Farms Agency; Thune: Idea Is Pure Politics," *Argus Leader,* August 17, 2004.

12. Stuart Rothenberg, "South Dakota: One Man Out," *Political Report,* March 12, 1982; Scott Waltman, "Senator Pushes for Dental Legislation," *Aberdeen American News,* July 16, 2004.

13. Lauren Shepherd, "No Gay-Union Outcry, Senators Say," *The Hill,* July 6, 2004 (spokesman quote); Jennifer Sanderson, "2 in 3 Back Marriage Amendment; War, Homeland Security Drives S.D. Voters' Concerns," *Argus Leader,* September 29, 2004; "Rounds Asks Daschle, Johnson to Support Federal Marriage Amendment," Associated Press, July 13, 2004.

14. 365gay.com, July 19, 2004; David Kranz, "New GOP Moderates Ready to Speak Up," *Argus Leader,* June 23, 2005; Hannah Seligson, "Task Force Honors Tom Daschle; Former South Dakota Senator Feted for Role in Killing Marriage Amendment," *Gay City News,* June 16–22, 2005; "Same-Sex Marriage Measure Fails," *World News Tonight with Peter Jennings,* ABC News Transcripts, July 14, 2004 ("sacred" quote).

15. Editorial, "Populism Redux," *Washington Post,* February 1, 2004 ("peddlers" quote).

16. Oliver Teves, "Philippines to Pull Peacekeepers from Iraq Next Month," Associated Press, July 10, 2004; "Review and Outlook: The Philippines Does a Spain," *Wall Street Journal,* July 15, 2004; Michael Isikoff, "Exclusive: Election Day Worries," *Newsweek,* July 19, 2004 (Daschle "sobering" statement); Editorial, "A Bad Idea, Rejected," *New York Times,* July 17, 2004 (Sandburg quote).

17. Charles Babington, "Senate Hopefuls Are Convention No-Shows; Some Fear Being Tied to Democratic Ticket," *Washington Post,* July 26, 2004; Will Lester, "Polls after Democratic Convention Showed Mixed Evidence on Whether Kerry Gained Ground," Associated Press, August 2, 2004; Jonathan Alter, "Hating Bush Is Not a Winning Ticket," *Newsweek,* August 2, 2004.

18. Jim VandeHei, "In Hindsight, Kerry Says He'd Still Vote for War; Challenged by President, Democrat Spells Out Stance," *Washington Post,* August 10, 2004; Mike Madden, "South Dakota Delegates Hit Boston," *Argus Leader,* July 27, 2004.

19. David S. Broder, "Punting on First Down," *Washington Post,* August 4, 2004; Evan Thomas, "Teaming Up," *Newsweek,* November 15, 2004 (Crowe quote); Ian Bishop and Vincent Morris, "Cambodia 'Mission' Never Happened: Shipmates," *New York Post,* August 10, 2004 ("seared" quote); Kerry lawyers to station managers, August 5, 2004 (available on the Internet).

20. Neil Sheehan, "A War without End," *New York Times,* August 27, 2004 (Bush and Sheehan quotes); Daniel Henninger, "Wounds of War Are Reopened by Kerry's Battle," *Wall Street Journal,* August 27, 2004; David S. Broder, "Swift Boats and Old Wounds," *Washington Post,* August 24, 2004; Deborah Orin, "Stop All Attack Ads: Bush—But Swift Vets Vow to Continue Anti-Kerry Campaign," *New York Post,* August 23, 2004 (Dole quote).

21. William F. Weld, "Kerry 'Will Have It Both Ways,'" *Newsweek,* August 2, 2004.

22. "Daschle Decides to Go It Alone against Formidable Challenger," *Congressional Quarterly,* May 15, 2004; Mary Ann Akers, "Heard on the Hill," *Roll Call,* March 3, 2005 (Kennedy quote).

23. Richard Corliss, "The World According to Michael," *Time,* July 5, 2004; Charles Hurt, "Daschle Cools on Plaudits for '9/11'; Says He Didn't Hug Filmmaker," *Washington Times,* July 10, 2004.

24. Mary Ann Akers, "Huggate Update," *Roll Call,* July 27, 2004.

25. Noelle Straub, "Gore Slams Bush 'Brown Shirts,'" *Boston Herald,* June 25, 2004; George Soros, commencement address, Columbia School of International and Public Affairs, May 17, 2004; Daniel Henninger, "Democrats Sell Apocalypse Now to Hollywood," *Wall Street Journal,* August 13, 2004; "High Stakes in November for Music Biz," Reuters, September 4, 2004.

26. Editorial, "Najaf and Falluja," *Wall Street Journal,* August 30, 2004; Editorial, "Kerry on Iraq," *Wall Street Journal,* August 13, 2004; Editorial, "Emergency Exit," *New Republic,* August 30, 2004; David E. Sanger, "For Now, Bush's Mocking Drowns Out Kerry's Nuanced Explanation of His War Vote," *New York Times,* August 12, 2004 (Bush quote); Editorial, "Unraveling Kerry's Iraq Plan," *New York Times,* September 9, 2004 ("tough" quote); Eric Lichtblau, "A Kerry Adviser Leaves the Race over Documents," *New York Times,* July 21, 2004; John F. Harris and Allan Lengel, "Berger Will Plead Guilty to Taking Classified Paper," *Washington Post,* April 1, 2005.

27. Peter Beinart, "Civil War," *New Republic,* November 8, 2002; Christian Walk, "Sen. Daschle Speaks in Elk Point," KTIV News, July 11, 2004; Daschle Statement, *Congressional Record,* October 10, 2002 ("threat" quote); Trent Lott, *Herding Cats: A Life in Politics* (New York: ReganBooks, 2005), 239; John MacArthur, "The Decline and Fall of Liberal Courage," *Providence Journal-Bulletin,* April 12, 2003.

28. Editorial, "Daschle's Dead Zone," *Wall Street Journal,* July 22, 2004; Mike Madden, "Bush-Hug Ad No Problem for Kerry Camp," *Argus Leader,* September 3, 2004 (campaign manager quote); Jon Walker, "Senator Defends Hug as 'Private

Moment,'" *Argus Leader,* September 2, 2004 (Daschle quote); Mike Madden, "Daschle Ad Showing Bush Hug Rankles GOP," *Argus Leader,* September 1, 2004 (Duffy quote).

29. Charles Babington, "Daschle's Senate Role Dominates S.D. Race; Rival Says Minority Leader Answers to Liberals," *Washington Post,* August 26, 2004.

CHAPTER 8. THE FALL OFFENSIVE

Epigraph source: character in William Faulkner, *Requiem for a Nun* (New York: Random House, 1951), 80.

1. Denise Ross, "Campaigns Ads Go on the Attack," *Rapid City Journal,* August 24, 2004.

2. *ATLA's List,* May 2004; Jennifer Sanderson, Ad Watch, *Argus Leader,* September 25, 2004 (analysis of trial-lawyer contributions).

3. Rasmussenreports.com; Adam Nagourney and David M. Halbfinger, "Kerry Enlisting Clinton Aides to Refocus Campaign," *New York Times,* September 6, 2004.

4. Dave Kranz, no headline, *Austin Daily Herald,* September 6, 1974; James W. Ceaser and Andrew E. Busch, *Red over Blue: The 2004 Elections and American Politics* (Lanham, Md.: Rowman and Littlefield, 2005), 126 (source of study results).

5. Editorial, "A Media Watershed," *Wall Street Journal,* September 16, 2004.

6. Serenity Banks, "Lakota Publisher Announces He Will Run for U.S. Senate Seat," *Lakota Journal,* January 16–23, 2004 ("guts" quote); Evelyn Nieves, "Daschle Gains Support of Rival; Indian Activist Drops Senate Bid," *Washington Post,* April 19, 2004; *Lakota Journal,* April 23–30, 2004.

7. Serenity Banks, "To Be or Not to Be?" *Lakota Journal,* August 20–27, 2004; "Wind Cave Used as Bargaining Chip?" KOTA-TV, September 24, 2004; Doris Haugen, "Giago Expects Good to Come from Tribal Summit Meeting," Associated Press, September 24, 2004; Denise Ross, "Summit Set between S.D., Tribal Leaders," *Rapid City Journal,* September 10, 2004 (Hildebrand and Daschle quotes).

8. Editorial, "Summit Should Have Been Open," *Aberdeen American News,* September 29, 2004; Editorial, "Delegation, Indians Wrong on Secrecy," *Mitchell Daily Republic,* September 29, 2004; Editorial, "Let Public Observe," *Rapid City Journal,* September 15, 2004; Editorial, "The 'Closed Door' Summit Leaves Much to Be Questioned," *Lakota Journal,* October 1–8, 2004; Editorial, "District's Business Must Be Done in Public," *Argus Leader,* October 5, 2004.

9. *Crossfire,* CNN, September 20, 2004 (Rubin quote); "Sen. Daschle's Advice for Short People: Use Pillow, Appear Taller," *The Hill,* September 29, 2004.

10. *Morning Edition,* National Public Radio, December 22, 2003 ("vindicated" quote); Sheryl Gay Stolberg, "Daschle, Democrats' Leader, Faces Tough Race at Home," *New York Times,* January 11, 2004.

11. "Woodshed" quote is from the debate. Cara Hetland, "Close Senate Race in National Spotlight," *Minnesota Public Radio*, September 20, 2004; *Mitchell Daily Republic*, October 28, 2004 (source of Zogby poll); Jon Walker, "Daschle, Thune in virtual tie," *Argus Leader*, October 27, 2004 (source of Mason-Dixon poll).

12. Kirk Victor, "Fighting for His Life," *National Journal*, October 15, 2004; Mike Madden, "Lines Drawn in Gun-Ban Battle," *Argus Leader*, September 13, 2004; Jodi Wilgoren, "Kerry Faults Bush for Failing to Press Weapons Ban," *New York Times*, September 14, 2004; Denise Ross, "Senate OKs Drought Package," *Rapid City Journal*, September 15, 2004; William Welch, "Senate's No. 1 Dem Also Its Most Threatened," *USA Today*, October 25, 2004 ("conversion" quote); Mike Madden, "Campaigns Focus on 9-11 Vote," *Argus Leader*, October 11, 2004 ("cooperative" quote); David Rogers, "The 'Keystone' State: South Dakota? As Democrat Sen. Daschle Fights for His Seat, Republicans Lustily Eye Control of Congress," *Wall Street Journal*, October 11, 2004 ("wince" quote).

13. Howard Fineman, "To the Bitter End," *Newsweek*, October 25, 2004 ("Scarface" quote); David Kranz, "Presidential Coattails Debated in Daschle-Thune Race," *Argus Leader*, October 6, 2004 (Sabato quote).

14. Chet Brokaw, "Thune, Daschle Clash on Social Security Remedy," Associated Press, October 12, 2004.

15. Bob Mercer, "Long Rivalry between Janklow, Abdnor-Thune and Daschle Reaches Final Act," *Aberdeen American News*, October 29, 2004.

16. Eleanor Clift, "Capitol Letter: Don't Betray the Family," *Newsweek*, March 21, 2003.

17. "General Wants Daschle to Promote Vote on Flag-Burning Amendment," Associated Press, October 6, 2004; Denise Ross and Kevin Woster, "Brady Pushes for Vote on Flag Amendment," *Rapid City Journal*, October 6, 2004.

18. Richard Wolffe and Susannah Meadows, "Kerry's New Call to Arms," *Newsweek*, September 27, 2004 ("mess" and "betting" quotes); Jacob M. Schlesinger, "In a Risky Move, Kerry Shifts Focus to Iraq from the Economy," *Wall Street Journal*, September 23, 2004; Andrewsullivan.com, September 18, 2004; Victor Davis Hanson, "See Ya, Iraq?" *National Review*, September 16, 2004; Scott Johnson and Babak Dehghanpisheh, "It's Worse Than You Think," *Newsweek*, September 12, 2004 ("crazy" quote).

19. Jonathan Finer, "Bush: 'Mixed Signals Are Wrong Signals'; Kerry Attacked on Iraq, Terror, Education," *Washington Post*, September 23, 2004 (Allawi and Bush quotes).

20. Gwen Glazer, "Partisan Rhetoric Ramps Up in South Dakota Senate Race," *National Journal*, September 30, 2004.

21. Donald Lambro, "GOP Vows Same Democrats Won't 'Stand in the Way the Next Time,'" *Washington Times*, March 3, 1995; Adam Clymer, "Battle over the Budget: The Negotiator; Senate's Chief Undertaker of Republican Initiatives,"

New York Times, January 10, 1996; Editorial, "Daschle's Dead Zone," *Wall Street Journal,* July 22, 2004. "Accurate" quote is from campaign debate, heard by author.

22. Mike Robinson, "Senators Searching for Crime Bill Compromise," Associated Press, June 8, 1990 ("crazy" quote); Jennifer Sanderson, Ad Watch, *Argus Leader,* September 24, 2004.

23. *Argus Leader,* October 31, 2004 (source of poll information); David Kranz, "Thune Effectively Played on Perception of Detached Daschle," *Argus Leader,* November 7, 2004.

24. William M. Welch, "Senate's No. 1 Dem Also Its Most Threatened," *USA Today,* October 25, 2004.

25. J. Bottum, "Tom Daschle's Duty to Be Morally Coherent," *Weekly Standard,* April 17, 2003 ("smokescreen" and "cover" quotes); Politicalaims.com, August 22, 2003 (Sullivan quotes); Donald Lambro, "Democrats Urged to Move to Center," *Washington Times,* October 30, 2003 ("move on" quote); Bishop Robert Carlson, "The Responsibility to Have a Well-Informed Faith Life," *Bishop's Bulletin,* August 2004 ("standing" quote); Bishop Robert Carlson, opinion-editorial, "Abortion Is Injustice of Modern Era," *Argus Leader,* November 3, 2004.

26. Kevin Woster, "Abortion Letter Still an Issue," *Rapid City Journal,* October 6, 2004; Kevin Woster to author, March 28, 2005; Scott Waltman to author, November 30, 2004; "Will Daschle Survive Tough Senate Race? Seeking Fourth Term, He Touts Tax Cuts, Ethanol, Abortion Opposition," MSNBC.com, October 13, 2004.

27. Emily Arthur, "Group Criticizes Daschle's Position on Abortion Issue," *Aberdeen American News,* October 20, 2004; Denise Ross, "Group Says Daschle Not Anti-abortion," *Rapid City Journal,* October 20, 2004. Quote from Gray's press conference is from my notes.

28. Jon Walker, "Abortion at Core of Debate; Hopefuls Disagree on Whether They Agree," *Argus Leader,* October 19, 2004 (Thune quote).

29. Jon Walker, "Abortion at Core of Debate; Hopefuls Disagree on Whether They Agree," *Argus Leader,* October 19, 2004 (Thune quote); Chet Brokaw, "Senate Candidates Clash on Clout, Religion in Schools," Associated Press, October 18, 2004.

30. Helen Dewar, "On Capitol Hill, Symbols Triumph; Substance Suffers amid Frustrating Fiscal Pressures, Political Fears," *Washington Post,* November 26, 1991; Julian Borger, "US Elections 2004: A Senate Race the Democrat Must Win; Tom Daschle, Kerry's Most Important Ally in Washington, Must Defend South Dakota to Give His Party a Chance of Recapturing Upper House," *Guardian,* October 18, 2004.

31. *Forbes,* April 18, 2003; *New York Times,* October 25, 2004; Amy Keller, "Daschle Hit on Tax Break; Wife Claims 'Homestead' Deduction," *Roll Call,* August 18, 2003; Robert Novak, "Bush Honing His Smart Weapons," *Chicago Sun-Times,* August 17, 2004; Brian Faler, "D.C. House Is a Topic on Daschle's Home Turf," *Washington Post,* August 8, 2003. Jeff Gannon was the reporter who sought

and published information about the FOIA documents. After the election, he was severely criticized by Democrats for asking "softball" questions at White House press conferences, for not using his real name (James Guckert), for his lack of journalistic training, and for his personal life, but the facts in his stories about South Dakota were not challenged.

32. Bob Mercer, "Daschle Took Tax Breaks on Both Houses," *Mitchell Daily Republic*, October 28, 2004; KDLT Television, October 21, 2004 ("retire" quote); Lori Montgomery, "Rove Not Entitled to D.C. Homestead Deduction; Bush Adviser to Reimburse City for Back Taxes," *Washington Post*, September 3, 2005.

33. Jon Walker, "As Lobbyist, Linda Daschle Navigates Ethical Minefield," *Argus Leader*, October 3, 2004; Stephanie Mencimer, "Tom Daschle's Hillary Problem: If the Senator Majority Leader Runs for President What Will Voters Think of His Lobbyist Wife?" *Washington Monthly*, January/February 2002; Timothy Noah, "Why Dems Should Be Glad Daschle Won't Run," *Slate*, January 7, 2003; Doug Ireland, "I'm Linda, Fly Me: The Real Reason Tom Daschle Didn't Run for President," *LA Weekly*, January 17–23, 2003.

34. Jon Walker, "Group: Wife of Candidate Not Fair Game," *Argus Leader*, October 26, 2004 ("conflicts" quote); Denise Ross, "Who's Paying for Campaign? Out-of-State Funds Fueling Senate Race," *Rapid City Journal*, October 26, 2004.

35. Editorial, "Gingrich's Wife's Job Raises Ethical Issue," *Argus Leader*, February 7, 1995.

36. Robert Penn Warren, *The Legacy of the Civil War* (New York: Random House, 1961), 3.

37. Jennifer Sanderson, "TV Ads Spur Battle about Control over Third-Party Campaign Tactics," *Argus Leader*, September 14, 2004 ("behalf" quote); *Meet the Press*, NBC News, September 19, 2004; Jennifer Sanderson, Ad Watch, *Argus Leader*, September 9, 2004 (DSCC quote); Scott Waltman, "Daschle Reneges on Outside Help Pledge," *Aberdeen American News*, October 28, 2004; Chris Cillizza, "DSCC Joins Fray in S.D.; Ad Violates Promise to Shun Third-Party Help," *Roll Call*, October 28, 2004; Sheryl Gay Stolberg, "Promises, Promises," *New York Times*, October 27, 2004.

38. Bill Harlan, "Poll: Republicans Inch Ahead," *Rapid City Journal*, October 27, 2004 (source of Zogby poll); Jon Walker, "Daschle, Thune in Virtual Tie," *Argus Leader*, October 27, 2004.

39. Jerry Seper, "Democrats File 9 Suits in Florida," *Washington Times*, October 27, 2004 ("scare" quote); Carson Walker, "Observer Alleges Vote Buying; Worker Says He Never Went to Pine Ridge," Associated Press, October 30, 2004 (U.S. attorney quote); Denise Ross, "Send in the Lawyers: Tuesday Might Not Bring Election Relief," *Rapid City Journal*, October 31, 2004; Peggy Lowe, "Democrat Playbook Opened to Criticism; Leaked Page Reveals Push to Use Tactic of 'Pre-Emptive Strike,'" *Rocky Mountain News*, October 15, 2004 (handbook quotes).

40. Lawsuit responses and protests communicated to author by observers. *Thomas A. Daschle v. John Thune et al.*, Civ. 04-4177, November 1, 2004, U.S. District Court, District of South Dakota, Southern Division; Carson Walker, "Judges Hold Out for a Democratic President," Associated Press, March 29, 2007.

41. Carson Walker, "Daschle Takes Thune to Court on Night before Election," Associated Press, November 2, 2004 ("intimidating" quote); hearing transcript, *Thomas A. Daschle v. John Thune*, November 1, 2004, 18; Kevin Woster, "Rumors of Vote Buying Continue," *Rapid City Journal*, November 1, 2004.

42. Vodkapundit.com, November 2, 2004.

43. Jody Bottum, "Suing Your Way to Defeat," *Weekly Standard*, November 2, 2004.

44. Jody Bottum, "Suing Your Way to Defeat," *Weekly Standard*, November 2, 2004; RapidCityJournal.com/politicalblog, November 2, 2004.

45. Charles Babington and Brian Faler, "In Response to Poll, Daschle Backers Amass," *Washington Post*, October 30, 2004; Christopher Jones, "Sabato's Crystal Ball Predicts Tight Race," *Cavalier Daily*, October 28, 2004 (Sabato quote); KSFY Television debate, October 18, 2004 ("troubled" quote); Jennifer Sanderson, "TV Ads Spur Battle about Control over Third-Party Campaign Tactics," *Argus Leader*, September 14, 2004.

46. Powerlineblog.com, November 1, 2004.

47. Bob Mercer, "Searching for Support, Daschle Turns to Indians," *Mitchell Daily Republic*, November 3, 2004.

48. "Daschle Interview," MSNBC.com, December 16, 2004 ("happen" quote).

CHAPTER 9. RECKONING

Epigraph source: George McGovern, quoted in Sheryl Gay Stolberg, "Gracious but Defeated, Daschle Makes History," *New York Times*, November 4, 2004.

1. Randell Beck, "Of Lutefisk, Ads and Long Nights," *Argus Leader*, November 7, 2004.

2. Sheryl Gay Stolberg, "Gracious but Defeated, Daschle Makes History," *New York Times*, November 3, 2004; William M. Welch, "Reid Eyes Top Senate Post after Daschle's Loss," *USA Today*, November 4, 2004; Christine Gorman, Jeffrey Kluger, Michael D. Lemonick, and Josh Tyrangiel, "New Faces: John Thune; The Giant Killer," *Time*, November 15, 2004; Chris Cillizza, "John Thune: A Star Is Born," *Roll Call*, November 17, 2004; Debra Rosenberg, David Noonan, and Sam Seibert, "Firmly in Control," *Newsweek*, November 15, 2004; Geoff Earle, "Frist Gains New Powers: Majority Leader Will Control Half of 'A' Panel Seats," *The Hill*, November 18, 2004.

3. Matthew Daly, "Former Speaker Foley Sees Parallels between His Defeat and Daschle's," Associated Press, November 19, 2004; Adam Nagourney and

Carl Hulse, "For Democrats, New Leader in Senate Is Not Typical," *New York Times*, November 14, 2004 ("glum" quote); Sheryl Gay Stolberg, "Chasing a Coveted Democratic Prize across the Plains," *New York Times*, October 24, 2004 ("psychological" quote); Revitalizesddems.blogspot.com, November 17–18, 2004 (source of Hauffe and first Epp quotes); Todd Epp, "What Happened? One Dem's View," *The Bird*, November 8, 2004 (source of second Epp quote); Ruth Conniff, "Reasons for Hope," *Progressive*, December 2004; "The Great Democratic Crack-Up," *Economist*, November 6, 2004.

4. Kimberley A. Strassel, "Life after Daschle," *Wall Street Journal*, November 5, 2004; Michael Tomasky, "What Now? A Discussion on the Way Forward for the Democrats," panel discussion, *Washington Monthly*, December 2004.

5. David Lightman, "Senate Voice of Outrage Silenced by Defeat; Tom Daschle Knew How to 'Stick It to Republicans,'" *Hartford Courant*, November 18, 2004 (Allen quotes); *Capital Gang*, CNN, November 6, 2004 (Hunt quote); Charlie Cook, "D.C.'s Own Reality Show," *National Journal*, November 16, 2004; Robin Toner, "Southern Democrats' Decline Is Eroding the Political Center," *New York Times*, November 15, 2004. Senator Mike Mansfield was Democratic majority leader in the Senate from 1961 to 1977.

6. Editorial, "Recircling the Democrats' Wagons," *New York Times*, November 9, 2004 ("redoubt" quote); Adam Nagourney and Anne E. Kornblut, "Dean Emerging as Likely Chief for Democrats," *New York Times*, February 2, 2005 ("wake" quote).

7. Albert Eisele and Jeff Dufour, "Under the Dome," *The Hill*, November 16, 2004 ("loosely" quote); Sheryl Gay Stolberg, "On Capitol Hill, the Majority Doesn't Always Rule," *New York Times*, November 7, 2004 ("Daschled" quote); Albert Eisele and Jeff Dufour, "Can the Verb 'to Specter' Be Far Behind?" *The Hill*, November 16, 2004; Richard Simon, "GOP Senate Improves Odds for Bush's Energy Plan," *Los Angeles Times*, November 5, 2004; Sheryl Gay Stolberg, "Congress Back to Face Unfinished Business," *New York Times*, November 21, 2004; Geoff Earle, "Kerry Returns to Hill, Dems Ponder Strategy," *The Hill*, November 10, 2004 (Durbin quote); Editorial, "Amid Unknowns, Federal Energy Bill a Certainty," *Great Falls Tribune*, November 10, 2004.

8. Gary J. Andres, "Capitol Hill Leadership Democrats Realigning," *Washington Times*, November 24, 2004 (lobbyist quote); Geoff Earle, "Reid Makes It Clear He's No Daschle," *The Hill*, December 1, 2004 (aide quote); Washingtonmonthly.com, November 3, 2004 (Sullivan quotes).

9. Stuart Taylor, Jr., "Who Might Get the Nod?" *National Journal*, December 11, 2004; Lyn Nofziger, "Bush's Trouble Ahead," *New York Times*, November 7, 2004; George Will, "Shock and Awe in the Senate," *Newsweek*, December 6, 2004; Adam Nagourney and Richard W. Stevenson, "Democrats See Wide Bush Stamp on Court System," *New York Times*, January 15, 2006.

10. Mark Leibovich, "Land of Hard Knocks; Long after It Gave Him Something to Escape, the Busted Boom Town of Searchlight Still Speaks to Harry Reid's Heart," *Washington Post*, July 17, 2005 ("laugh" quote); Matthew Continetti, "Permanent Minority Leader? Harry Reid Takes Over from Tom Daschle," *Weekly Standard*, November 29, 2004; David Espo, "Conservatives Celebrate Election Triumphs with Bold Congressional Moves," Associated Press, November 23, 2004 ("dance" quote); Sheryl Gay Stolberg, "Incoming Democratic Leader Eases into Higher Profile," *New York Times*, December 5, 2004 ("appropriate" comment); *Meet the Press*, NBC News, December 5, 2004 ("embarrassment" quote); Dan Balz, "Senate Democratic Leader Blasts Greenspan," *Washington Post*, March 4, 2005 ("hacks" quote); Geoff Earle, "Reid Makes It Clear He's No Daschle," *The Hill*, December 1, 2004; Rick Klein, "Senate Democrats Coordinate Message, Attack on Bush," *Boston Globe*, January 25, 2005; Elizabeth Drew, "He's Back," *New York Review*, February 24, 2005 ("radical" quote).

11. Editorial, "Recircling the Democrats' Wagons," *New York Times*, November 9, 2004 ("compromise" and "drubbing" quotes); Sheryl Gay Stolberg, "Incoming Democratic Leader Eases into Higher Profile," *New York Times*, December 5, 2004 ("complain" quote); News Summary, *New York Times*, August 9, 2005; Charles Babington and Justin Blum, "On Capitol Hill, a Flurry of GOP Victories; Key Measures Advance after Long Delays," *Washington Post*, July 30, 2005; David Rogers, "Congress Clears Long-Stalled Gun-Liability Bill," *Wall Street Journal*, October 21, 2005; Robert Novak, "For Politicians, Frist's Sin Is Not So Much What He Did, but When He Did It," *Chicago Sun-Times*, August 15, 2005; Adam Nagourney and Richard W. Stevenson, "Democrats See Wide Bush Stamp on Court System," *New York Times*, January 15, 2006.

12. Editorial, "John Thune for Senate," *Rapid City Journal*, October 28, 2004.

13. Leo Thorsness to author, November 12, 2004; Christine Gorman, Jeffrey Kluger, Michael D. Lemonick, and Josh Tyrangiel, "New Faces," *Time*, November 15, 2004; Eric Pianin, "After an Often-Tumultuous Tenure, Daschle Exits Quietly; Defeated Democratic Leader Uncertain about Next Move," *Washington Post*, December 12, 2004 ("irreconcilable" quote); Charles Babington, "Daschle's Senate Role Dominates S.D. Race; Rival Says Minority Leader Answers to Liberals," *Washington Post*, August 25, 2004 (source of voter quote); *Morning Edition*, National Public Radio, December 22, 2003; Tom Daschle, with Michael D'Orso, *Like No Other Time: The 107th Congress and the Two Years That Changed America Forever* (New York: Crown Publishers, 2003), 24; CNN.com, November 4, 2004 (source of exit poll); Sabato interview with author, January 11, 2005.

14. "Will Daschle Survive Tough Senate Race? Seeking Fourth Term, He Touts Tax Cuts, Ethanol, Abortion Opposition," MSNBC.com, October 13, 2004 ("allowed" quote); Jeremy Berg to author, November 1, 2004 ("egos" quote); Paul Pederson

to author, November 2, 2004 ("deck" quote); Jon Klemme to author, November 1, 2004 ("stupid" quote); Scott Waltman to author, November 30, 2004; Michael Freeman to author, November 1, 2004 (communications director quotes).

15. Bill Richardson to author, November 19, 2004; Chris Maynard to author, November 29, 2004; Sam Hurst, "Will Thune Change for the Better?" *Rapid City Journal,* November 17, 2004; Kevin Woster to author, November 19, 2004; Steven Hemmingsen, "The Opera Ain't Over . . . ," KELO-Land.com, November 30, 2004.

16. Editorial, "51–48," *New Republic,* November 15, 2004; Timothy Noah, "Whither Liberalism? Again?" *Slate,* November 3, 2004; Evan Thomas, "The Vets Attack," *Newsweek,* November 15, 2004 ("laughed" quote); Jeffrey Goldberg, "Central Casting: The Democrats Think about Who Can Win the Midterms—and in 2008," *New Yorker,* May 29, 2006 ("hog farmer" quote).

17. Robin Toner, "Swift Boats and the Lessons of Dukakis," *New York Times,* August 29, 2004 ("honest liberal" quote); Todd Epp, "What Happened? One Dem's View," *The Bird,* November 8, 2004.

18. David Newquist, *Northern Valley Beacon,* November 13, 2004 (staffers quotes); David Kranz, "'Blue Dog' Image Could Offer Blueprint for S.D. Democrats," *Argus Leader,* December 26, 2004.

19. Rob Regier to author, November 17, 2004; Joe Cella to author, November 17, 2004; CNN.com, November 4, 2004 (source of exit poll).

20. David Kranz, "Thune Effectively Played on Perception of Detached Daschle," *Argus Leader,* November 7, 2007; Patrick Lalley to author, November 18, 2004. The *Argus* (in contrast to the *Rapid City Journal,* which had called for weekly debates) had editorialized in early fall that enough debates had already occurred. The *Argus* also reported that debates would not be important to the race. Terry Woster, "Debates May Not Change Election," *Argus Leader,* July 31, 2004; Editorial, "The Daschle Two-Step," *Wall Street Journal,* September 21, 2004.

21. Jerome Bentz, letter to the editor, *Argus Leader,* November 23, 2004; Sam Hurst, "Will Thune Change for the Better?" *Rapid City Journal,* November 17, 2004; George Cunningham interview, December 22, 2004.

22. Denise Ross, "Campaign's Responses Fell Short," *Rapid City Journal,* November 9, 2004. Duffy made her comments in a letter to the *Rapid City Journal,* and they were reported on the *Journal* blog on November 12, 2004. She subsequently rescinded her letter.

23. Denise Ross, "Campaign's Responses Fell Short," *Rapid City Journal,* November 9, 2004; John Stanton, "Bloggers Targeted Daschle and the Press," *National Journal,* November 20, 2004.

24. Sam Hurst, "Will Thune Change for the Better?" *Rapid City Journal,* November 17, 2004; Randell Beck, "Of Lutefisk, Ads and Long Nights," *Argus Leader,* November 7, 2004; Chuck Raasch, "Stay in Touch with Roots," *Argus Leader,*

November 14, 2007; David Kranz, "Thune Effectively Played on Perception of Detached Daschle," *Argus Leader,* November 7, 2004; Doug Grow, "South Dakota Gives Sharp-Dressed Liberal the Boot," *Minneapolis Star Tribune,* November 7, 2004.

25. George Cunningham interview, December 22, 2004 ("populism" quote); Michael Kazin, *The Populist Persuasion: An American History* (New York: Basic Books, 1995), 245–66; Lynn Vincent, "Sweeps Week," *World Magazine,* November 13, 2004 ("roots" quote).

26. Richardson to author, November 19, 2004; *Reuters,* September 27, 2004 ("hell" quote); CNN.com, November 4, 2004 (source of polling information).

27. Andrew Ferguson, "Hate's Labour's Lost; How Michael Moore Led the Democrats Astray," *Weekly Standard,* November 15, 2004; John Files, "The Like-Minded Line Up for a 9/11 Film," *New York Times,* June 24, 2004 (Graham quote); Scot Lehigh, "Dems to Hollywood: The End," *Boston Globe,* December 15, 2004 (Mellencamp and Kerry quotes); Mark Steyn, "We Weren't Dumb Enough to Vote for Kerry," *Telegraph* (London), November 9, 2004; Richard Leiby, "The Reliable Source," *Washingon Post,* December 16, 2004 (Chase quote).

28. CNN.com, November 3, 2004 (source of polling information); Regier to author, November 17, 2004; Craig Okken to author, November 1, 2004 ("flood gates" quote); Melissa Evans, "Daschle Addresses Sympathetic Ears; Ex-Senate Leader Is Keynote Speaker at Fundraiser," *Santa Barbara News-Press,* October 3, 2005.

29. Doug Grow, "South Dakota Boots Sharp-Dressed Liberal," *Minneapolis Star Tribune,* November 7, 2004 ("faith" quotes); Thorsness to author, November 25, 2004; Roberts to author, November 25, 2004; E. J. Dionne, "The Religious Right and the New Republican Party," in William Chafe, Harvard Sitkoff, and Beth Bailey, eds., *A History of Our Time: Readings on Postwar America,* 6th ed. (New York: Oxford University Press, 2003), 367; Thomas Byrne Edsall and Mary D. Edsall, *Chain Reaction: The Impact of Race, Rights, and Taxes on American Politics* (New York: W. W. Norton, 1991), 133.

30. Brad Carson, "Vote Righteously!" *New Republic,* November 22, 2004; McGovern interview with author, November 25, 2003.

31. Memo from George Cunningham to George McGovern, November 12, 1978, Box 855, File Staff Memos, McGovern papers ("fences" quote); Democracy Corps memo, March 29, 2005 (source of polling information); William McGurn, "Bob Casey's Revenge," *First Things,* January 2005; Joseph Bottum, "The Myth of the Catholic Voter," *Weekly Standard,* November 1, 2004 (Kucinich antiabortion stance); Joseph Bottum, "Tom Daschle's Duty to Be Morally Coherent," *Weekly Standard,* April 17, 2003; David D. Kirkpatrick and Laurie Goodstein, "Groups of Bishops Using Influence to Oppose Kerry," *New York Times,* October 12, 2004; Christopher Dickey and Melinda Henneberger, "The Vision of Benedict XVI," *Newsweek,* May 2, 2005.

32. Ramesh Ponnuru, "Catholics Are Swingers: The Catholic Vote Revisited," *National Review Online,* December 1, 2004 ("bishops" information); Jodi Schwan, "Daschle Campaign Manager Discusses Election," KELO-Land Television, December 6, 2004 (campaign manager quote); Chuck Raasch, "Aide Says Daschle Didn't Fight Back," *Argus Leader,* February 11, 2006; David Kranz, "Carlson Moves to Center on Abortion," *Argus Leader,* March 8, 2005; Joseph Bottum, "The Myth of the Catholic Voter," *Weekly Standard,* November 1, 2004. See Mark Noll and Carolyn Nystrom, *Is the Reformation Over? An Evangelical Assessment of Contemporary Roman Catholicism* (Grand Rapids, Mich.: Baker Academic, 2005); Amy Sullivan, "Not God's Party: A New Poll Shows Democrats Are Losing (More) Religious Voters," *Slate,* August 29, 2006.

33. E. J. Dionne, Jr., "The Democrats' Rove Envy," *Washington Post,* December 15, 2004 (Dean quote). See also Matt Bai, "Who Lost Ohio?" *New York Times Magazine,* November 21, 2004.

34. Bob Mercer, "South Dakota Blues," *Weekly Standard,* November 22, 2004.

35. Steven Hemmingsen, "The Opera Ain't Over . . . ," KELOLand.com, November 30, 2004; Glenn Reynolds, "Politics and the Web," *Tech Central Station,* November 8, 2004; John Stanton, "Bloggers Targeted Daschle and the Press," *National Journal,* November 20, 2004 ("siege" and "truth" quotes).

36. Kimberley A. Strassel, "All about Tom," *Wall Street Journal,* October 15, 2004; Michael Barone interview, January 11, 2005; "Dropping the Anchorman," *Economist,* November 25, 2004. After the election, the Daschle v. Thune blog was nominated for "Best Election Coverage" for the 2004 Weblog Awards. Daschle v. Thune placed ninth out of fifteen nominees.

37. Editorial, "On Daschle and Dorgan," *Grand Forks Herald,* November 4, 2004. Ingraham quotes are from personal observation.

38. Richardson to author, November 19, 2004; Dan Pfeiffer, Daschle communications director, e-mail to campaign staff, September 13, 2004; Gene Edward Veith and Lynn Vincent, "Year of the Blog," *World Magazine,* December 4, 2004; Kevin Woster, "Blogs Change Campaigns," *Rapid City Journal,* March 7, 2005.

39. Michael Barone, "The 51 Percent Nation," *U.S. News and World Report,* November 15, 2004; Randell Beck, "Blogger Campaign," *Argus Leader,* March 6, 2005; David Kranz, "McCarthy Campaign Eye-Opener about Harsh Reality of Poverty," *Argus Leader,* December 13, 1987; Randell Beck to author, March 22, 2005.

40. Albert Eisele and Jeff Dufour, "Under the Dome," *The Hill,* November 16, 2004 ("$20 million" quote); Alan B. Spitzer, *Historical Truth and Lies about the Past: Reflections on Dewey, Dreyfus, de Man, and Reagan* (Chapel Hill: University of North Carolina Press, 1996), 8; Grant, *Personal Memoirs of U.S. Grant* (Old Saybrook, Conn.: Konecky and Konecky, 1885), 629. Authors Steve Jarding and Dave "Mudcat" Saunders also blame "lies and distortions" for Daschle's defeat; Jarding

and Saunders, *Foxes in the Henhouse: How the Republicans Stole the South and the Heartland* (New York: Touchstone, 2006), 122.

41. Jodi Schwan, "Daschle: One on One," KELO-Land News, December 14, 2004 ("merit" quote); Jennifer Sanderson, "A Talk with Tom Daschle; 'It Was All Worth Doing'; Senator Says He Won't Lobby or Seek Office," *Argus Leader,* December 12, 2004 ("judge" quote); William M. Welch, "S.D. Senator Packs Up after 26 Years on Hill," *USA Today,* December 13, 2004 ("lineman" and "quarterback" quotes).

42. KELO-Land Television, December 12, 2004; Editorial, "John Thune for Senate," *Rapid City Journal,* October 28, 2004.

43. Jon Walker, "Out but Not Finished," *Argus Leader,* November 4, 2004 ("respect" quote); Bob von Sternberg, "In Light of Day, Thune Shakes Up Capitol Hill," *Minneapolis Star Tribune,* November 4, 2004 ("choking" and "sad" quotes); "Daschle: 'I Feel Good Walking Out of These Doors,'" *Today Show* interview, MSNBC.com, December 16, 2004 ("melts" quote); Editorial, "Senator Frist Tightens the Screws," *New York Times,* November 27, 2004.

44. Robert Penn Warren, *The Legacy of the Civil War* (New York: Random House, 1961), 43; Peter Harriman, "6 Months Later, Campaign-like Mud Still Flying," *Argus Leader,* May 28, 2005; Kevin Woster, "Long after Vote, Thune-Daschle Campaign Continues," *Rapid City Journal,* July 9, 2005; "Daschle: A Campaign So Indelible You'd Have to Sand Blast It Away," *Hotline,* July 19, 2005; Editorial, "Now, Let's Stand United," *Argus Leader,* November 4, 2004; Daily caucus.com, November 23, 2004 (source of cartoon); Dakotatoday.typepad .com, January 31, 2005 ("fascism" quote); Browncountydemocrats.blogspot.com, February 12, 2005 ("fuehrer" quote); Mary Ann Akers, "Heard on the Hill," *Roll Call,* December 6, 2004; Dontworryaboutthegovernment.blogspot.com, April 5 and 7, 2005 (T-shirts information); Hanna Rosin, "Right with God," *Washington Post,* March 6, 2005 ("beast" quote); Chris Cillizza, "Coalition to Battle Social Security Plan," *Roll Call,* February 17, 2005.

45. Nicole Duran, "Daschle Loyalists Keep Heat on Thune," *Roll Call,* May 25, 2005 ("wait" quote); Chris Cillizza, "527 Aims for Six-Year Drumbeat on Senate GOP," *Roll Call,* June 23, 2005; Paul Kane, "527 Eyes Senate GOPers," *Roll Call,* March 16, 2006; Paul Weyrich, "History Does Repeat Itself," *National Ledger,* June 20, 2005; Mike Allen, "Thune Delivers on Campaign Vow; Senator's Future Brightens as S.D. Base Survives the Cut," *Washington Post,* August 27, 2005 (Hildebrand quote).

46. Editorial, "Rise and Fall," *Richmond Times-Dispatch,* November 10, 2004 ("epitomize" quote); Lionel Trilling, *The Liberal Imagination: Essays on Literature and Society* (New York: Charles Scribner's Sons, 1950), 242 (Milton quote).

47. Memo from George Cunningham to George McGovern, May 3, 1980, Box 855, Staff Memos, McGovern papers ("undiluted" quote).

48. Louis Menand, *American Studies* (New York: Farrar, Straus, and Giroux, 2002), 247.

49. David Kranz, "Did Daschle Give a Campaign Speech?" *Argus Leader,* April 7, 2005; David Kranz, "Departing Augustana President Tagged for Political Future," *Argus Leader,* May 15, 2005 ("doors" quote); "Daschle to Join Dole at Law Firm," *Argus Leader,* March 14, 2005; Morton M. Kondracke, "Democratic Think Tank Mixes Ideas with Bush-Bashing," *Roll Call,* October 17, 2005; Paul Kane, "Daschle to Keep Hand in Politics," *Roll Call,* February 7, 2005 ("force" quote); Paul Kane, "Daschle Seeks to Get Back in Game," *Roll Call,* September 19, 2005; Mary Clare Jalonick, "Daschle Donates to Dems," Associated Press, January 6, 2006; Dianna Marrero, "Daschle Keeps Option Open for Run for President," *Argus Leader,* December 14, 2005; Nestor Ramos, "Daschle Considers 2008 Run," *Argus Leader,* January 18, 2006; "Daschle Still Eyes '08," *National Journal,* January 14, 2006; Susan Kuczka, "Daschle Calls for Iraq Troop Withdrawal," *Chicago Tribune,* November 3, 2005; Mike Glover, "Daschle Argues Bush Presidency 'Is Essentially Over,'" Associated Press, November 5, 2005. After the election, Daschle had said he would not run for any office in the future and would not work as a lobbyist. Jennifer Sanderson, "It Was All Worth Doing; Senator Says He Won't Lobby or Seek Office," *Argus Leader,* December 12, 2004.

50. "Thune Defends Tone of Campaign," Associated Press, November 6, 2004 ("resources" quote); Steve Hemmingsen, "My Name Is Steve and I'm a Politico-Holic," Keloland.com, December 9, 2004 (source of staff information); "Tom and John Slug It Out," *Economist,* October 28, 2004 ("profiles" information); C. Wright Mills, *The Sociological Imagination* (New York: Oxford University Press, 1959), 181.

51. Thune quotation is from personal observation.

CHAPTER 10. DASCHLE VERSUS THUNE AS SYNECDOCHE

Epigraph source: Editorial, "51–48," *New Republic,* November 15, 2004.

1. Gail Russell Chaddock, "Money Lessons from a Year on the Campaign," *Christian Science Monitor,* November 9, 2004. See also Byron York, *The Vast Left Wing Conspiracy* (New York: Crown Forum, 2005), 49–104; Evan Thomas, "Down to the Wire," *Newsweek,* November 15, 2004; John Harwood, "Hopeful Liberals See Signs of a Political Comeback," *Wall Street Journal,* June 3, 2004.

2. Arianna Huffington, "The Architects of Defeat," *Los Angeles Times,* November 11, 2004 (Carville quote); E. J. Dionne, Jr., "The Democrats' Rove Envy," *Washington Post,* December 14, 2004; Scot Lehigh, "Seeing Red and Wondering Why," *Boston Globe,* November 10, 2004 (Gergen quote).

3. Richard W. Stevenson, "For the President, Power Is There for the Taking," *New York Times,* May 15, 2005; Dan Balz and Mike Allen, "Four More Years

Attributed to Rove's Strategy; Despite Moments of Doubt, Adviser's Planning Paid Off," *Washington Post*, November 7, 2004 ("lonely victory" quote); "How to Pick a President," *Economist*, October 7, 2004; Tom Mertes, "A Republican Proletariat," *New Left Review*, 30 (November–December 2004): 46 ("blue plutocracy" phrase); Jon Wiener, "Working-Class Republicans and 'False Consciousness,'" *Dissent* 52, no. 2 (Spring 2005): 55–58.

    4. "Poll Shows GOP on the Move: More Ink to Follow?" *Editor and Publisher*, December 14, 2004 (6% advantage information); William A. Galston and Elaine C. Kamarck, *The Politics of Polarization: A Third Way Report* (Washington, D.C.: Third Way, 2005), 50 (Democratic party identification advantage); Richard Lowry, "Bush's Well-Mapped Road to Victory," *National Review*, November 29, 2004 ("legacy" quote); Adam Nagourney, "What If They Lose?" *New York Times*, October 24, 2004 (Rosenberg quote).

    5. Dan Balz, "Partisan Polarization Intensified in 2004 Election; Only 59 of the Nation's 435 Congressional Districts Split Their Vote for President and House," *Washington Post*, March 29, 2005; David S. Broder, "The Cost of Being Blue," *Washington Post*, November 29, 2004; John F. Harris, "Was Nov. 2 a Realignment—Or a Tilt?" *Washington Post*, November 28, 2004 ("gasp" quote); E. J. Dionne, Jr., "Moderates, Not Moralists," *Washington Post*, November 9, 2004; Peter Dreier, "Why Bush Won and What to Do Next," *Dissent* 51, no. 4 (Fall 2004): 15–21; Rick Perlstein, *Before the Storm: Barry Goldwater and the Unmaking of the American Consensus* (New York: Hill and Wang, 2001); Todd Gitlin, "A Gathering Swarm," *Mother Jones*, January/February 2005.

    6. Todd D. Purdum, "A Steamroller That May Lose Its Steam," *New York Times*, November 28, 2004 ("Athens" quote); David Brooks, "How to Reinvent the GOP," *New York Times Magazine*, August 29, 2004 ("unstable" quote); Franklin Foer, "The Grumblers," *New Republic*, September 13 and 20, 2004; Thomas B. Edsall, "Now in Power, Conservatives Free to Differ," *Washington Post*, February 20, 2005; John Micklethwait and Adrian Wooldridge, *The Right Nation: Conservative Power in America* (New York: Penguin Press, 2004), 264 ("stockbrokers" quote); Chuck Todd, "Are Democrats Creeping into Contention?" *National Journal*, June 22, 2005 ("devour" quote).

    7. Editorial, "51–48," *New Republic*, November 15, 2004; Peter Beinart, "What Went Wrong?" *New Republic*, November 15, 2004.

    8. Bernard Moon, "A Lesson for the Liberal Elite," *Boston Globe*, November 30, 2004 (Rooney quote); Jane Smiley, "Why Americans Hate Democrats—A Dialogue," *Slate*, November 4, 2004.

    9. Garry Wills, "The Day the Enlightenment Went Out," *New York Times*, November 4, 2004; Bill Moyers, "There Is No Tomorrow," *Minneapolis Star Tribune*, January 30, 2005; Sean Salai, "Florida Kerry Supporters Meet for Group Therapy," *Boca Raton News*, December 2, 2004 ("fascists" quote); Jeffrey Goldberg, "Central Casting: The Democrats Think about Who Can Win in the Midterms—and in 2008,"

New Yorker, May 29, 2006 ("Brown Shirts" quote); The Week, *National Review,* November 29, 2004; Brandon Bosworth, "News Scraps," *American Enterprise Online,* January/February 2005 (source of DU poll). Todd Gitlin also commented, "For many in the cosmopolitan class, middle to upper middle in income, college educated and beyond, university and culture-industry based, patriotism lost its allure decades ago." Todd Gitlin, *The Intellectuals and the Flag* (New York: Columbia University Press, 2006), 129; Michelle Cottle, "The Battle Is Over, but the War Goes On," *Time,* November 29, 2004 ("theocracy" quote); David Brooks, "The Values-Vote Myth," *New York Times,* November 6, 2004.

10. Editorial, "Stand and Fight," *Nation,* November 22, 2004. See also Joshua Frank, *Left Out! How Liberals Helped Re-elect George W. Bush* (Monroe, Me.: Common Courage Press, 2005); Mark Hertsgaard, "Left in the Wings: The Looming Fight for the Heart and Soul of the Democratic Party," *San Francisco Chronicle,* October 10, 2004 ("left wing" quote); "The Great-Democratic Crack-Up," *Economist,* November 6, 2004 ("harbingers" quote); Denise Ross, "McGovern: Democrats Should Stay the Course," *Rapid City Journal,* November 11, 2004 ("convictions" quote); Sidney Blumenthal, *Our Long National Daydream: A Political Pageant in the Reagan Era* (New York: Harper-Collins, 1988), 25; DailyKos.com, December 9, 2004 ("idiots" and "Flat Earth" quotes); Noam Schieber, "&c.," *New Republic,* September 5, 2005 ("radioactive" quote); Amy Sullivan, "Fire the Consultants," *Washington Monthly,* January/February 2005. See also Noam Scheiber, "Exit Poll: The People Who Really Run the Democratic Party," *New Republic,* February 24, 2003.

11. Katha Pollitt, "Mourn," *Nation,* November 22, 2004 ("Debs" quote); Dan Gerstein, "More Muscle, More God, Less Shrum," *Wall Street Journal,* November 11, 2004; Howard Fineman, "Now Playing: 'Anybody But Dean,' Part 2," *Newsweek,* January 31, 2005; Editorial, "Scream 2," *New Republic,* December 13, 2004; Jonathan Chait, "A Suicidal Selection; With Dean as Party Chairman, the Democrats Wouldn't Need Enemies," *Los Angeles Times,* February 4, 2005; Maggie Haberman, "Dean's Howling for Shot to Lead DNC into Future Battle to Head Democrats," *Daily News,* January 30, 2005 ("hate" quote).

12. Adam Nagourney and Anne E. Kornblut, "Dean Emerging as Likely Chief for Democrats," *New York Times,* February 2, 2005 ("scream" quote); Ryan Lizza, "The Outsiders," *New Republic,* February 14, 2005; Dan Balz, "Democrats' Grass Roots Shift the Power; Activists Energized Fundraising, but Some Worry They Could Push the Party to Left," *Washington Post,* February 20, 2005 ("activists" and "triangulation" quotes); Ronald Brownstein, "The Internet and Democrats," *National Journal,* July 1, 2005; Rick Perlstein, "Party Cannibals," *Nation,* February 7, 2005 (Truman quote); Will Marshall, "Valuing Patriotism," *Blueprint Magazine,* July 23, 2005 ("choosier" and "fringe" quotes).

13. Brian Faler, "A Scathing Chairman Dean Finds Republicans 'Evil,' 'Corrupt' and 'Brain-Dead,'" *Washington Post,* April 25, 2005; Howard Fineman and Tamara Lipper, "Scream 2: The Sequel," *Newsweek,* June 20, 2005; Jim Abrams, "Rhetoric

Takes Nasty Turn in Congress," Associated Press, June 21, 2005; "Salazar Says He Misspoke Calling Focus 'Anti-Christ,'" *Denver Post,* April 28, 2005; Jeff Jacoby, "A New Low in Bush-Hatred," *Boston Globe,* September 10, 2006; David D. Kirkpatrick and Carl Hulse, "At Center of Senate Showdown, a Boxer Takes on a Surgeon," *New York Times,* May 15, 2005; Tony Batt, "Reid Doesn't Back Down from Friday Remark about Bush," *Las Vegas Review-Journal,* May 11, 2005; Charles Babington, "Battle of the Judicial Nominee Resumes; GOP Leaders Eye Action on Filibuster," *Washington Post,* March 2, 2005 (Byrd quote); Geoff Earle, "Durbin Says He's Sorry; McCain: Apology Should Be Enough to End Controversy," *The Hill,* June 22, 2005; Marc Cooper, "Thinking of Jackasses: The Grand Delusions of the Democratic Party," *Atlantic Monthly,* April 2005; Washingtonmonthly.com, June 13, 2005 (Drum quote); "Beyond Red and Blue," Pew Research Center, May 10, 2005.

14. John F. Harris, "New Group to Tout Democrats' Centrist Values; Third Way Plans to Focus on 'Moderate Majority,'" *Washington Post,* November 11, 2004; Jules Witcover, *Party of the People: A History of the Democrats* (New York: Random House, 2003), 632–33, 641–44 (Jackson quote); Steve Gillon, *The Democrats' Dilemma: Walter F. Mondale and the Liberal Legacy* (New York: Columbia University Press, 1992), 189 (O'Neill quote); Dan Balz, "Sen. Clinton Calls for Party Truce, United Front; Prospective '08 Candidates Say Democrats Must Do More Than Oppose Bush Policies," *Washington Post,* July 26, 2005.

15. Harold Meyerson, "What Are Democrats About?" *Washington Post,* November 17, 2004 (Begala quote); Ryan Lizza, "Bad Message," *New Republic,* November 22, 2004 ("rewrite" and strategist quotes); Evan Thomas, "Trench Warfare," *Newsweek,* November 15, 2004 ("What is our message?" quote).

16. E. J. Dionne, Jr., "Lessons for Democrats," *Washington Post,* December 31, 2004; Democracy Corps memo, February 1, 2005 (source of poll information and "McDonald's" quote); Marc Humbert, "Clinton Advisor: Kerry Ran Inconsistent Campaign," Associated Press, March 17, 2005 (Lewis quote); "Democrats' Own Mood Poll Scares Them," United Press International, June 29, 2005 (Greenberg quote); Michael Barone, "The Hardest Numbers," *U.S. News and World Report,* April 11, 2005; Martin Peretz, "Not Much Left," *New Republic,* February 28, 2005 ("bookless" quote); Robert Reich, "Story Time," *New Republic,* March 28, 2005 ("narrative" comment); William Voegli, "The Endless Party," *Claremont Review of Books,* Winter 2004; Marc Cooper, "Code Blue," *LA Weekly,* February 18–24, 2005; John Powers, "A Vision of Our Own," *LA Weekly,* January 21–27, 2005 ("reactionary" quote).

17. Sandra Mathers, "Obama Lends Star Power to Nelson," *Orlando Sentinel,* July 10, 2005 (Obama quote); Christopher Graff, "Dean Says Democrats Must Take Offensive," Associated Press, August 8, 2005; Jeffrey Goldberg, "The Unbranding; Can the Democrats Make Themselves Look Tough?" *New Yorker,* March 21, 2005

("marketing" quote); Matt Bai, "The Framing Wars," *New York Times Magazine,* July 17, 2005; Joshua Green, "It Isn't the Message, Stupid," *Atlantic Monthly,* May 2005 ("denial" quote).

18. Martin Peretz, "Not Much Left," *New Republic,* February 28, 2005; Chris Cillizza, "Republicans Page Dr. Cheney," *Washington Post,* October 4, 2005 (Rangel quote); Deepti Hajela, "Clinton Says House Run Like 'Plantation,'" Associated Press, January 17, 2006.

19. Bill Bradley, "A Party Inverted," *New York Times,* March 30, 2005; Rick Perlstein, "How Can the Democrats Win?" *Boston Review,* Summer 2004; Nicholas Confessore, "King of the Hill? The Unlikely Ascendancy of Thomas Daschle," *American Prospect,* January 29, 2001 (Daschle quote); E. J. Dionne, *They Only Look Dead: Why Progressives Will Dominate the Next Political Era* (New York: Simon and Schuster, 1997), 9.

20. Peter Beinart, "A Fighting Faith," *New Republic,* December 13, 2004.

21. David Frum's Diary, *National Review Online,* November 22, 2004; Tom Daschle, with Michael D'Orso, *Like No Other Time: The 107th Congress and the Two Years That Changed America Forever* (New York: Crown Publishers, 2003), 126–27.

22. Mackubin Thomas Owens, "Fahrenheit 1971," *Weekly Standard,* September 6, 2004 ("mystical" quote); William Voegeli, Claremont Institute, December 8, 2004; Peter Beinart, "Left Behind," *New York Times Book Review,* March 6, 2005 ("estranged" quote); Mark Danner, "How Bush Really Won," *New York Review,* January 13, 2005. See also Kevin Mattson, "Revisiting the Vital Center," *Dissent* 52, no. 1 (Winter 2005): 105–9.

23. Paul Glastris, "What Now? A Discussion on the Way Forward for Democrats," *Washington Monthly,* December 2004 ("comfortable" quote); Washington monthly.com, December 2, 2004 (Drum quote); Scott Hananel, "MoveOn to Democratic Party: 'We Bought It, We Own It,'" Associated Press, December 9, 2004; Peter Baker and Shailagh Murray, "Democrats Split over Position on War; Activists More Vocal as Leaders Decline to Challenge Bush," *Washington Post,* August 22, 2005; Peter Beinart, *The Good Fight: Why Liberals—and Only Liberals— Can Win the War on Terror and Make America Great Again* (New York: Harper-Collins, 2006), 187 (source of polling data); Martin Peretz, "Not Much Left," *New Republic,* February 28, 2005.

24. Gary Hart, "Who Will Say 'No More'?" *Washington Post,* August 24, 2005; Lawrence F. Kaplan, "Mall Rats," *New Republic,* October 10, 2005; Tim Dickinson, "Give Peace a Chance; Is the Anti-war Movement Too Fractured to Be Effective?" *Rolling Stone,* October 6, 2005 ("incarnation" quote).

25. Fareed Zakaria, "Who the Devil Really Is," *Newsweek,* December 20, 2004 (Diamond quotes); Richard Cohen, "Ceding Idealism to the GOP," *Washington Post,* October 25, 2005; Christopher Hitchens, "Bush's Secularist Triumph: The Left Apologizes for Religious Fanatics; The President Fights Them," *Slate,* November 9,

2004; Ian Buruma, "Wielding the Moral Club; The Left Is Miring Itself in Anti-Americanism," *Financial Times Weekly Magazine*, September 13, 2003; Martin Peretz, "The Politics of Churlishness," *New Republic*, April 11, 2005; Nick Cohen, "By the Left . . . About Turn: The Reality of Iraq Shatters Chomsky's Looking Glass World," review of Noam Chomsky, *Hegemony or Survival: America's Quest for Global Dominance* (New York: Owl Books, 2004), in *Guardian*, December 14, 2003; Editorial, "Stand and Fight," *Nation*, November 22, 2004 ("adventures" quote); Jeff Jacoby, "Iraq through Iraqis' Eyes," *Boston Globe*, December 16, 2004; Naomi Klein, "Bring Najaf to New York," *Nation*, November 22, 2004; Christopher Hitchens, "Where Aquarius Went," review of Barry Miles, *Hippie* (New York: Sterling Publishing, 2004), Marcia A. Eymann and Charles Wollenberg, eds., *What's Going On? California and the Vietnam Era* (Oakland: Oakland Museum of California and University of California Press, 2004), and Eleanor Agnew, *Back from the Land: How Young Americans Went to Nature in the 1970s, and Why They Came Back* (New York: Ivan R. Dee, 2004), in *New York Times Book Review*, December 19, 2004.

26. George F. Will, "Redefining Liberalism; Democrats Must Revert to Resisting Oppression," *Washington Post*, December 12, 2004; Evan Thomas, "Teaming Up," *Newsweek*, November 15, 2004; Scot Lehigh, "Dems to Hollywood: The End," *Boston Globe*, December 15, 2004. Sheen and Reiner were well-known actors during the McGovern era; Reiner's character in the television series *All in the Family* was nicknamed "Meathead."

27. Darian Dudrick, "The Disgusting Influence of America," *Huron Daily Plainsman*, September 5, 2004; Notebook, *New Republic*, December 13, 2004; Joseph Berger, "A Blue City (Disconsolate, Even) Bewildered by a Red America," *New York Times*, November 4, 2004 ("1950s" quote); Michael Powell and Sonya Geis, "Democrats Sample the Merlot, but Find It's Not for Everyone," *Washington Post*, October 16, 2005.

28. Mackubin Thomas Owens, "Fahrenheit 1971," *Weekly Standard*, September 6, 2004 ("culture war" quote); Maurice Isserman and Michael Kazin, *America Divided: The Civil War of the 1960s*, 2nd ed. (New York: Oxford University Press, 2004), 301; Thomas Frank, *What's the Matter with Kansas? How Conservatives Won the Heart of America* (New York: Metropolitan Books, 2004); Dotty Lynch, "Postmortems 'R' Us," CBS News, December 8, 2004.

29. Alan Brinkley, *Liberalism and Its Discontents* (Cambridge, Mass.: Harvard University Press, 1998), 279, 295 ("cosmopolitanism" and "provincialism" quotes); Dan Balz, "For Democrats, a Troubling Culture Gap," *Washington Post*, August 10, 2005.

30. Peter Steinfels, "Beliefs: A Leading Gadfly of Contemporary Philosophy Calls for a Renewal of the Left in America That Has No Room for God or Religion," *New York Times*, July 11, 1998 (Rorty quote); Ed Kilgore, "What Now? A Discussion on the Way Forward for Democrats," *Washington Monthly*, December 2004; Jonathan Alter, "Barack Obama: The Dems' Freshest Face Has a New

Challenge: To Help His Party Relocate Its Moral Core," *Newsweek*, December 27–January 3, 2004; Michael Lind, "Red-State Sneer," *Prospect*, January 2005; William A. Galston and Elaine C. Kamarck, *The Politics of Polarization: A Third Way Report* (Washington, D.C.: Third Way, 2005), 43; Ross Douthat, "Theocracy, Theocracy, Theocracy," *First Things*, August/September 2006.

31. Benjamin Wallace-Wells, "Party Down," *Washington Monthly*, October 2004; Samuel P. Huntington, "The Democratic Distemper," in Nathan Glazer and Irving Kristol, eds., *The American Commonwealth: 1976* (New York: Basic Books, 1976), 17; Chet Brokaw, "Daschle, Thune Face Off," Associated Press, October 13, 2004 ("elimination" statement); William A. Galston and Elaine C. Kamarck, *The Politics of Polarization: A Third Way Report* (Washington, D.C.: Third Way, 2005), 4 ("cohorts" quote).

32. Jon Lauck, "George Stanley McGovern and the Farmer: South Dakota Politics, 1953–1962," *South Dakota History* 32, no. 4 (Winter 2002), 331–53; John B. Judis, "Labored Steps," *New Republic*, March 21, 2005; Steven Greenhouse, "Democrats Concerned by Prospects of a Labor Schism," *New York Times*, July 24, 2005; Jeff Jacoby, "Mass. Exodus," *Boston Globe*, January 15, 2006; M. D. Harmon, "Birth Rates Have a Political Implication, and It's Not Good for Leftists," *Portland Press Herald* (Maine), March 24, 2006; Michael Lind, "Red-State Sneer," *Prospect*, January 2005.

33. Glenn Reynolds, "The Revolution Will Be Posted," *New York Times*, November 2, 2004; Evan Thomas, "The Vets Attack," *Newsweek*, November 15, 2004 ("anybody here" quote); James Poniewozik, "Bush v. Kerry v. the Media," *Time*, November 15, 2004 ("credible" quote); Daniel Henninger, "2004's Biggest Losers: How Dan Rather and Media's Kings Lost Their Crowns," *Wall Street Journal*, November 12, 2004 (italics added); Editorial, "End of an Era," *USA Today*, November 23, 2004; Franklin Foer, "Bad News," *New Republic*, December 26, 2005–January 9, 2006 ("hands" quote); Lakshmi Chaudhry, "Rage against the MSMachine," *Nation*, July 31, 2006.

34. Tim Worstall, "More Bias, Please," *Tech Central Station*, November 12, 2004 ("caste" and "talking" quotes); "Senate Dems Talk Religion and Bloggers at Retreat," *Congress Daily*, January 6, 2005; Michael Crowley, "Local Yokels," *New Republic*, March 14, 2005.

35. Larry Diamond and Leonardo Morlino, *Assessing the Quality of Democracy* (Baltimore, Md.: Johns Hopkins University Press, 2005), xix; Editorial, "On Daschle and Dorgan," *Grand Forks Herald*, November 4, 2004.

EPILOGUE

Epigraph source: Ernest Hemingway, *A Farewell to Arms* (New York: Scribner, 2003 [1929]), 118.

1. George F. Will, "The Politics of Trash Talk," *Newsweek,* May 24, 2004; Dana Milbank, "An Iraq Policy, Better Late Than Never," *Washington Post,* October 27, 2005.

2. John F. Burns, "Shadow of Vietnam Falls over Iraq River Raids," *New York Times,* November 29, 2004 ("thoughts" quote); Lolita C. Baldor, "Kennedy Calls for Troop Withdrawal in Iraq," Associated Press, January 28, 2005; Todd S. Purdum, "Flashback to the 60s: A Sinking Sensation of Parallels between Iraq and Vietnam," *New York Times,* January 29, 2005; Michael Wines, "Democracy Has to Start Somewhere," February 6, 2005 (Vietnamese elections); John F. Burns, "Iraq's Ho Chi Minh Trail," *New York Times,* June 5, 2005; Michael Ignatieff, "Who Are Americans to Think That Freedom Is Theirs to Spread?" *New York Times Magazine,* June 26, 2005; Christopher Hitchens, "Beating a Dead Parrot; Why Iraq and Vietnam Have Nothing Whatsoever in Common," *Slate,* January 31, 2005.

3. David Von Drehle and Jacqueline Salmon, "Displacement of Historic Proportions," *Washington Post,* September 2, 2005. In the summer of 2003, the press reported that Valerie Plame, the wife of war critic Joe Wilson, worked for the CIA. Commentators speculated that the "Plame leak" was orchestrated by the Bush White House to discredit and silence Wilson. A special prosecutor was appointed to investigate whether "outing" a CIA employee violated federal espionage laws. Vice President Cheney's chief of staff, "Scooter" Libby, was indicted for and convicted of perjury as a result of the investigation, but no espionage laws were found to have been violated. During the week in October 2005 when Libby was indicted, the story received more airtime than any other story on the network news. The Libby indictment fueled intense Democratic criticism and press speculation about the involvement of other high-ranking White House officials, especially Karl Rove. The source of the leak was determined to have been Deputy Secretary of State Richard Armitage, who was skeptical of the war. David Broder of the *Washington Post* deemed the affair overblown and called on reporters to apologize to Karl Rove. See Rem Rieder, "Whatever," *American Journalism Review,* August/September 2006 (network news information); David Broder, "One Leak and a Flood of Silliness," *Washington Post,* September 7, 2006; Editorial, "End of an Affair: It Turns Out That the Person Who Exposed CIA Agent Valerie Plame Was Not Out to Punish Her Husband," *Washington Post,* September 1, 2006. For the second-term slump of presidencies, see Michael Beschloss, "The Five-Year Itch," *Newsweek,* November 7, 2005.

4. Morton Kondracke, "Despite Woes, GOP Hopes to Make 2006 a 'Status Quo' Election," *Roll Call,* November 28, 2005 (source of favorable/unfavorable poll); "Dean: U.S. Can't Win Iraq War," CNN.com, December 6, 2005; Jonathan Weisman, "Democratic Lawmkers Splinter on Iraq," *Washington Post,* December 2, 2005; Joe Klein, "Why Washington Is Playing with Fire," *Time,* December 19, 2005; Jim VandeHei and Shalaigh Murray, "Democrats Fear Backlash at Polls for

Antiwar Remarks," *Washington Post,* December 7, 2005; Michael Crowley, "Tug of War," *New Republic,* December 26, 2005; Erin P. Billings, "Iraq Tests Party Unity," *Roll Call,* December 8, 2005; John Stanton, "Reid Seeks to Keep Caucus on Same Page," *Roll Call,* December 8, 2005; Dan Balz, "Pelosi Hails Democrats' Diverse War Stances," *Washington Post,* December 16, 2005; Peter Savodnik, "Dean Still Gives Dems Heartburn," *The Hill,* December 15, 2005.

5. Adam Nagourney and Richard W. Stevenson, "Democrats See Wide Bush Stamp on Court System," *New York Times,* January 15, 2006; Charles Babington, "Democrats Split over Filibuster on Alito," *Washington Post,* January 27, 2006; John Mercurio, "The Left Left, So What's Left?" *National Journal,* February 2, 2006 ("fascism" quote); Michael Crowley, "Swiss Miss," *New Republic,* February 13, 2006; David D. Kirkpatrick, "In Alito, G.O.P. Reaps Harvest Planted in '82," *New York Times,* January 30, 2006 ("watershed" quote); David Kranz, "Supporters in Shriver Square Praise, Energize Munson," *Argus Leader,* February 2, 2006.

6. David Brooks, "Losing the Alitos," *New York Times,* January 12, 2006 ("privileged" and "Gestapo-like" quotes); Terry Eastland, "Inside 'Concerned Alumni of Princeton,'" *Weekly Standard,* January 23, 2006 ("bad thing" quote).

7. Michael Powell, "Dems Split as Impeachment Whispers Get Louder," *Newsweek,* March 25, 2006; William Kristol, "The Paranoid Style in American Liberalism," *Weekly Standard,* January 2, 2006 ("apartheid" quote); Joe Klein, "How to Stay Out of Power," *Time,* January 8, 2006. The drama surrounding the eavesdropping program also lessened when the fact that congressional leaders knew of its existence was revealed. Douglas Jehl, "Among Those Told of Program, Few Objected," *New York Times,* December 23, 2005; Paul Kane, "Boxer Raises Impeachment," *Roll Call,* December 20, 2005; Charles Babington, "Senators Debate Move to Censure Bush," *Washington Post,* April 1, 2006; Dana Milbank, "The Feingold Resolution and the Sound of Silence," *Washington Post,* March 15, 2006; Carl Hulse, "Democrats Beat Quick Retreat on Call to Censure President," *New York Times,* March 14, 2006; Laurie Kellman, "Feingold Accuses Democrats of 'Cowering,'" *Associated Press,* March 15, 2006; Eleanor Clift, "Democrats' Dilemma," *Newsweek,* March 17, 2006 ("Mussolini" quote); Fox News/Opinion Dynamics poll of 900 registered voters, January 12, 2006; Carl Hulse, "House Assails Media Report on Tracking of Finances," *New York Times,* June 30, 2006; Howard Kurtz, "Piling On the *New York Times* with a Scoop," *Washington Post,* June 28, 2006; Jacob Weisberg, "Not So SWIFT," *Slate,* July 12, 2006; Byron Calame, "Can 'Magazines' or the *Times* Subsidize News Coverage?" *New York Times,* October 22, 2006 (ombudsman quote).

8. Gloria Borger, "A Confederacy of Dunces," *U.S. News and World Report,* December 19, 2005; Rick Klein, "Democrats May Unite on Plan to Pull Troops," *Boston Globe,* February 20, 2006; Adam Nagourney and Robin Toner, "Clinton and Kerry Show Democratic Divide on Iraq," *New York Times,* June 14, 2006; Kate

Zernike, "Senate Rejects Calls to Begin Iraq Pullback," *New York Times*, June 23, 2006; Adam Nagourney, "War Handicaps Senators in '08 White House Race," *New York Times*, June 2, 2006; John Edwards, "The Right Way in Iraq," *Washington Post*, November 13, 2005; Kate Zernike, "On Iraq, Kerry Again Leaves Democrats Fuming," *New York Times*, June 21, 2006 ("divided" quote).

9. Jacob Heilbrun, "Neocons in the Democratic Party," *Los Angeles Times*, May 28, 2006 ("generation" quotes); Norman Geras, "Why the Left Needs to Get It Right," *Times* (London), May 18, 2006; Joe Klein, "The Truman Show," review of Peter Beinart, *The Good Fight: Why Liberals, and Only Liberals, Can Win the War on Terror and Make America Great Again* (New York: HarperCollins, 2006), in *New York Times Book Review*, June 11, 2006; Kurt Anderson, "The Vietnam Obsession," *New York Magazine*, June 19, 2006 ("Hirsh" quote).

10. Harold Meyerson, "Lieberman v. the Democrats," *Washington Post*, June 21, 2006; Shailagh Murray, "Lamont Relied on Net Roots—And Grass Roots," *Washington Post*, August 9, 2006; Matt Bai, "What Are the Lieberman Foes For?" *New York Times Magazine*, August 11, 2006 ("baby boomers" quote); Jacob Weisberg, "Dead with Ned: Why Lamont's Victory Spells Democratic Disaster," *Slate*, August 9, 2006; Jonathan Alter, "The Putting of First Things First," *Newsweek*, August 7, 2006.

11. Peter Beinart, "Both Sides," *New Republic*, January 16, 2006; DailyKos.com, January 5, 2006; Jonathan Chait, "Excommunicated: Daily Kos Strikes Again," *New Republic*, June 22, 2006; David Brooks, "Respect Must Be Paid," *New York Times*, June 25, 2006 (Kos quotes); Richard Cohen, "Digital Lynch Mob," *Washington Post*, May 9, 2006 ("raw hatred" quote); Todd Gitlin, "The Urge to Purge," *Los Angeles Times*, April 9, 2006.

12. Chuck Todd, "What the Heck Do Democrats Run On?" *National Journal*, January 18, 2006; Sheryl Gay Stolberg, "Democrats Outline Agenda, Mostly Sparing the Specifics," *New York Times*, January 27, 2006; Jacob Weisberg, "The Three Stooges: Nancy Pelosi, Harry Reid, and Howard Dean," *Slate*, March 8, 2006; Erin P. Billings, "Democrats Stalled on Message Rollout," *Roll Call*, February 6, 2006; Michael Grunwald, "Who Needs New Ideas, Anyway," *Washington Post*, April 2, 2006 ("rehashed" quote); Shailagh Murray and Charles Babington, "Democrats Struggle to Seize Opportunity," *Washington Post*, March 7, 2006; Ronald Brownstein, "Democratic Plan to Beef Up U.S. Security Lacks Specifics," *Los Angeles Times*, March 30, 2006; John Stanton, "Topic A Shifts from Ports to 'Incompetence,' Policy," *Roll Call*, March 7, 2006; Robin Toner, "Optimistic, Democrats Debate the Party's Vision," *New York Times*, May 9, 2006 ("shift" quote).

13. Michael Crowley, "Swiss Miss," *New Republic*, February 13, 2006; Erin P. Billings, "Democrats Prepare to Launch 'Honesty' Message," *Roll Call*, January 9, 2006; David Ignatius, "A Party Waiting to Pounce," *Washington Post*, March 29,

2006 ("fire" quote); Ronald Brownstein, "Debating Bush Censure Serves Dueling Purposes," *Los Angeles Times*, March 26, 2006; Susan Schmidt and James V. Grimaldi, "The Fast Rise and Steep Fall of Jack Abramoff," *Washington Post*, December 29, 2005. Jack Abramoff was a lobbyist accused of arranging campaign donations to Republicans in exchange for legislative favors. Several Democrats were also implicated by Abramoff. At the time of this book's preparation for publication, the full extent and political implications of the Abramoff affair were not clear. Brian Ross and Rhonda Schwartz, "Abramoff Reports to Prison; Officials Focus on Reid, Others," ABC News, November 15, 2006. On the Democrats' strategy, see Anna Quindlen, "Enough of the Waiting Game," *Newsweek*, December 12, 2005.

14. Ruth Marcus, "The New Temptation of Democrats," *Washington Post*, May 23, 2006; Caryle Murphy and Alan Cooperman, "Religious Liberals Gain New Visibility," *Washington Post*, May 20, 2006 (Dean quote); Thomas B. Edsall, "Rich Liberals Vow to Fund Think Tanks; Aim Is to Compete with Conservatives," *Washington Post*, August 7, 2005; Dan Balz, "The Democrats Reassess; Effort to Win Battle of Ideas Includes New Web Site and Journal," *Washington Post*, June 21, 2006; David Goodman, "Economic Sabotage, Whisper Campaigns, and Threats: How the Democrats Took Paul Hackett Out," *Mother Jones*, February 16, 2006; Robin Toner, "To Democrats Hungry for Senate, a Pennsylvania Seat Looks Ripe," *New York Times*, March 5, 2006 (Santorum quote); Ryan Lizza, "The Bush-Cheney Era Ends Here," *New York Magazine*, April 10, 2006 (Schumer quote); Janet Hook, "Meet the Powers behind the Democrats' Strategy," *Los Angeles Times*, July 5, 2006.

15. Tim Grieve, "Hitler, Stalin and . . . Joe Lieberman," *Salon*, July 28, 2006; Richard Leiby, "The Reliable Source," *Washington Post*, December 16, 2004 (Chase quote); Garry Wills, *Nixon Agonistes: The Crisis of the Self-Made Man* (New York: New American Library, 1969), 535; George Packer, *Blood of the Liberals* (New York: Farrar, Straus and Giroux, 2000), 298.

16. Adam Nagourney and Megan Thee, "Poll Gives Bush His Worst Marks Yet," *New York Times*, May 10, 2006; Karen Tumulty and Mike Allen, "Republicans on the Run," *Time*, March 26, 2006 (source of poll and "alternative" quote); James Traub, "The Submerging Republican Majority," *New York Times Magazine*, June 18, 2006; Peter Baker, "Senior White House Staff May Be Wearing Down," *Washington Post*, March 13, 2006; Francis Fukuyama, "After Neoconservatism," *New York Times Magazine*, February 19, 2006; Richard Viguerie, "Bush's Base Betrayal," *Washington Post*, May 21, 2006; Bruce Bartlet, *Imposter: How George W. Bush Bankrupted America and Betrayed the Reagan Legacy* (New York: Doubleday, 2006). For a more positive interpretation of Bush's conservatism, see Fred Barnes, "Strong-Government Conservatism: How George W. Bush Has Redefined the American Right," *Weekly Standard*, January 23, 2006.

17. Richard Rorty, *Achieving Our Country: Leftist Thought in Twentieth-Century America* (Cambridge, Mass.: Harvard University Press, 1998), 104. Russell Jacoby complains that with the "demise of a radical opposition, passion and idealism also depart; only commercial regulations and tariffs remain contentious." Jacoby, *The End of Utopia: Politics and Culture in an Age of Apathy* (New York: Basic Books, 1999), 9. Eric Lott also criticizes the "disappearance of a liberal alternative to hawkish conservatism." Lott, *The Disappearing Liberal Intellectual* (New York: Basic Books, 2006), 26. See Michael Tomasky, "Party in Search of a Notion," *American Prospect*, May 2006; Howard Kurtz, "Senator Steps in It," *Washington Post*, June 30, 2006; Richard Cohen, "Star-Spangled Pandering," *Washington Post*, December 15, 2005; Anne E. Kornblut, "Senator Clinton and Liberals Split over Flag Desecration," *New York Times*, June 28, 2006; Arianna Huffington, "Don't Be a Hack, Hillary," *Los Angeles Times*, June 29, 2006; Jeffrey Goldberg, "Central Casting: The Democrats Think about Who Can Win the Midterms—and in 2008," *New Yorker*, May 29, 2006 (chairwoman quote).

18. Peter Baker and Claudia Deane, "House Incumbents at Risk, Poll Finds; Percentage of Americans Who Approve of Their Representative Has Fallen Sharply," *Washington Post*, August 8, 2006 (polling information); Stuart Rothenberg, "Democrats Poised to Take Control of the House," *Roll Call*, September 5, 2006; Stuart Rothenberg, "A True Blowout Is Now Possible," *Roll Call*, October 6, 2006; David Broder and Dan Balz, "Poll Shows Strong Shift of Support to Democrats," *Washington Post*, October 10, 2006; Charlie Cook, "Reaping the Whirlwind?" *National Journal*, October 28, 2006; Evan Thomas, "A Secret Life: Mark Foley's Explicit E-mails Could Bring Down the GOP," *Newsweek*, October 16, 2006; Christina Bellatoni, "Democrats Shopped Foley Story to Papers," *Washington Times*, December 12, 2006; Peter Slevin and Michael Powell, "War Now Works against GOP; Iraq Often Seen as Hindrance in Campaigns," *Washington Post*, October 26, 2006; Kate Zernike and Carl Hulse, "Security and War Center Stage as Campaign Break Nears," *New York Times*, September 26, 2006; Howard Fineman, "Benchmark Strategy," *Newsweek*, October 25, 2006 ("overwhelming" quote).

19. Chuck Todd, "Congress Gets a Case of the Blues," *National Journal*, November 8, 2006; Adam Nagourney, "Democrats Turned War into an Ally," *New York Times*, November 9, 2006 (Emanuel quote); Ronald Brownstein, "GOP Ceded the Center and Paid the Price," *Los Angeles Times*, November 8, 2006 (McInturff quote); Stuart Rothenberg, "As Predicted, a Wave Washes Republicans Out to Sea," *Roll Call*, November 9, 2006; Matt Bai, "The Last 20th-Century Election?" *New York Times Magazine*, November 19, 2006 (37% figure); Adam Nagourney, "Democrats Turned War into an Ally," *New York Times*, November 9, 2006 (Leach quote); Mike Allen, "The Architect Speaks," Time-blog.com, November 10, 2006 (source of information on post–WW II congressional losses); Mort Kondracke,

"Moderates Fed Up with Polarization," *Roll Call*, November 9, 2006 ("war, scandal, or recession" quote).

20. Chuck Todd, "Congress Gets a Case of the Blues," *National Journal*, November 8, 2006; Tim Reid, "Meet the Blue Dogs: Pro-gun, Anti-abortion—and Democrat," *Times* (London), November 9, 2006 ("moderate candidates" and "caucus" quotes and quotes about Montana and Virginia candidates); Timothy Egan, "A Redder Kind of Democrat in a Close Montana Contest," *New York Times*, November 4, 2006; Timothy Egan, "Fresh Off the Farm in Montana, a Senator-to-Be," *New York Times*, November 13, 2006; David Brooks, "The Fighting Democrat," *New York Times*, November 5, 2006 ("Fonda" quote); Carl Hulse, "New Democrats Pose Challenge," *New York Times*, November 9, 2006 ("ardent" quote); Dan Balz, "Midterm Election Leaves Political Landscape Blurry," *Washington Post*, November 13, 2006 ("affirmation" quote); Shaila Dewan and Anne E. Kornblut, "In Key Races, Democrats Run to the Right," *New York Times*, October 30, 2006; Janet Hook, "A Right Kind of Democrat," *Los Angeles Times*, October 26, 2006; Kate Zernike, "Seats in Danger, Democrats Proclaim Their Conservatism," *New York Times*, October 24, 2006; David Broder, "Connecticut Crucible for a War Debate," *Washington Post*, October 26, 2006.

21. Matt Bai, "The Last 20th-Century Election?" *New York Times Magazine*, November 19, 2006; Michael Kinsley, "Pelosi's Platform," *Washington Post*, November 7, 2006; Editorial, "What Democrats Would Do," *Washington Post*, October 29, 2006; John M. Broder, "Democrats Are Divided on a Solution for Iraq," *New York Times*, October 27, 2006; Peter Beinart, "Speak Not," *New Republic*, September 4, 2006; Morton Kondracke, "Democrats Decide They Don't Need 'Contract' to Win," *Roll Call*, September 28, 2006; Sebastion Mallaby, "A Party without Principles," *Washington Post*, October 2, 2006.

22. Stuart Rothenberg, "The Sounds of Silence from Democrats on the Hot-Button Issues," *Roll Call*, April 28, 2007 ("faithful" quote); Edmund L. Andrews, "The Democrats' Cautious Tiptoe around the President's Tax Cuts," *New York Times*, January 4, 2007; Carl Hulse, "New Majority's Choice: Should GOP Policies Be Reversed?" *New York Times*, January 5, 2007; Juliet Eilperin and Michael Grunwald, "Democrats' Cause Is Tempered by Political Realities," *Washington Post*, April 9, 2007; John Harwood, "Shift in Congress Brings Little Change, Most Americans Say," *Wall Street Journal*, April 27, 2007 (Emanuel quote).

23. Dick Morris, "Ultra-liberals Rise on Moderate Wings," *The Hill*, November 15, 2006; Charles Babington, "Hawkish Democrat Joins Call for Pullout," *Washington Post*, November 18, 2005; Janet Hook and Richard Simon, "Power Struggles Unravel Democrats' Unity," *Los Angeles Times*, November 14, 2006; Jonathan Weisman, "In Backing Murtha, Pelosi Draws Fire; Her Ethics Vow Is Questioned," *Washington Post*, November 14, 2006 ("furor" quote); Ruth Marcus,

"Unfit for Majority Leader," *Washington Post,* November 15, 2006; Carl Hulse, "Backing This Hopeful for No. 2 Job Is Risky for Pelosi," *New York Times,* November 14, 2006; Josephine Hearn, "Pelosi Pulls Out the Stops for Murtha," *The Hill,* November 15, 2006; Massimo Calabresi and Perry Bacon, Jr., "Inside Pelosi's Power Play," *Time,* November 14, 2006; Editorial, "Speaker Pelosi Tempts Disaster," *New York Times,* November 17, 2006 ("scar" quote); Howard Fineman, "Pelosi Loses Big on Hoyer-Murtha Race," *Newsweek,* November 16, 2006; Jonathan Weisman and Lois Romano, "Pelosi Splits Democrats with Push for Murtha; Speaker-to-Be Accused of Strong-Arm Tactics," *Washington Post,* November 16, 2006; Thomas Edsall, "West Wing," *New Republic,* November 20, 2006 ("internecine" quote).

24. Ann Scott Tyson, "U.S. Commander in Iraq to Face Democrats Eager for Troop Cuts," *Washington Post,* November 15, 2006; John M. Broder, "Democrats Are Divided on a Solution for Iraq," *New York Times,* October 27, 2006 ("cut off funds" threat); Sheryl Gay Stolberg and Mark Mazzetti, "Democrats Push for Troop Cuts within Months," *New York Times,* November 13, 2006; Greg Miller, "Democratic Lawmakers Will Seek a Phased Withdrawal from Iraq," *Los Angeles Times,* November 13, 2006; Editorial, "Democrats and Iraq," *New York Times,* November 12, 2006 ("euphemism" quote); Oskar Garcia, "McGovern to Meet with Congress on War," Associated Press, November 10, 2006; David Kranz, "McGovern Book Outlines Exit Strategy from Iraq," *Argus Leader,* August 24, 2006; Faith Bremer, "McGovern Tells House Liberals His Plan to Bring Troops Home," *Argus Leader,* November 17, 2006; Eleanor Clift, "'Ready for Change': George McGovern Shares His Views on the Anti-war Movement, the Lieberman Defeat and Why Hillary Clinton Needs to Be Gutsier," *Newsweek,* August 11, 2006 ("gutsy" and "running away" quotes); David D. Kirkpatrick, "'Antiwar' and Other Fighting Words," *New York Times,* October 29, 2006 ("Vietnam history" quote); Karen Tumulty, "John Kerry, Still One Step Behind," *Time,* October 31, 2006; Matt Bai, "The Last 20th-Century Election?" *New York Times Magazine,* November 19, 2006 ("smug," "ideological debate," and "baby-boomer politics" quotes).

25. Jonathan Weisman, "Activists on the Left Applying Pressure to Democratic Leaders," *Washington Post,* January 3, 2007; Janet Hook, "Democrats Feel Liberals' Antiwar Heat," *Los Angeles Times,* January 10, 2007; Michael Luo, "Antiwar Caucus Wants to Be Heard Now," *New York Times,* March 4, 2007; Jeff Zeleny and Carl Hulse, "Democrats Plan Symbolic Votes against Iraq Plan," *New York Times,* January 10, 2007; Dan Balz, "Democrats Split on How to End the War," *Washington Post,* February 4, 2007; Sheryl Gay Stolberg and John M. Broder, "Congressional Democrats Wrestle over How to Force Bush to Alter Iraq Policy," *New York Times,* February 24, 2007 ("appease" quote); Janet Hook, "Democrats Face a Struggle over War Strategy," *Los Angeles Times,* February 16, 2007 ("exposing" quote); Thomas Edsall, "A Smoke-Filled War Room," *Washington*

Post, March 22, 2007; Robin Toner, "Democrats Steer the War in Fits and Starts," *New York Times*, March 10, 2007 ("idiot" quote); Editorial, "Not the 'Real Vote,'" *Washington Post*, February 17, 2007; Jonathon Weisman and Lyndsey Layton, "Murtha Stumbles on Iraq Funding Curbs," *Washington Post*, February 25, 2007; Carl Hulse, "Democrats Back Date for Start of Iraq Pullout," *New York Times*, April 24, 2007; Jeff Zeleny, "Leading Democrat in Senate Tells Reporters, 'This War Is Lost,'" *New York Times*, April 20, 2007.

26. David Kranz, "McGovern Says Iraq, Vietnam Same War," *Argus Leader*, March 26, 2006 (McGovern quote); Con Marshall, "McGovern Blasts Bush, War in Iraq and S.D. Abortion Law," *Rapid City Journal*, April 3, 2006; "McGovern Praises Canada on Vietnam Draft Dodgers," Reuters, July 8, 2006; Dave Kranz, "College Heads Lose Elections, but Their Wives Don't," *Argus Leader*, May 30, 2006; David Corn, "2008 Looking Like 1968," TomPaine.com, April 12, 2006; David S. Broder, "A Reticent Senator Who Inspired," *Washington Post*, December 12, 2005; Francis X. Clines, "Eugene J. McCarthy, Senate Dove Who Jolted '68, Dies at 89," *New York Times*, December 11, 2005; Kevin Woster, "Daschle Sets Timeline on Bid for President," *Rapid City Journal*, March 14, 2006; Diana Marrero and Jon Walker, "Daschle Weighing Run for President," *Argus Leader*, May 18, 2006; Kevin Landigan, "Dems' Defeated Leader Eyeing Wins," *Nashua Telegraph*, June 9, 2006; Ed Henry, "Daschle Still Has Eye on '08," CNN.com, September 25, 2006.

27. "Daschle Endorses Sen. Barack Obama," *Argus Leader*, February 22, 2007; John M. Broder, "Shushing the Baby Boomers," *New York Times*, January 21, 2007 ("uberboomer" quote); Tamar Lewin, "Wellesley Class Sees 'One of Us' Bearing Standard," *New York Times*, April 14, 2007; Jeff Zeleny, "As Candidate, Obama Carves Antiwar Stance," *New York Times*, February 26, 2007; Steven Thomma, "Obama More Liberal Than Kucinich, Analysis Reveals," McClatchy Newspapers, March 19, 2007; Anne E. Kornblut, "Obama, Clinton Sparring Early; Candidates' Scrutiny Unusually Intense," *Washington Post*, March 12, 2007.

INDEX

60 Minutes: Bill Clinton on, 101; forged documents scandal, 163; forged documents used by, 111; on Janklow-Daschle relationship, 15; Judge Pickering story, 68–69

527 organizations: critical of Tom Daschle, 145; Daschle investigates use of, 277n25; development of, 41; Focus South Dakota, 205; for Kerry campaign, 108, 213; Soros finances, 156; spending levels for, 217

Abdnor, James: attends Thune's swearing in, 216; vs. Bill Janklow, 15; early influence on Thune, 28–29; joins Thune on election night, 188; loses to Janklow, 25; receives honorary doctorate, 77; Daschle demands debates, 146; on voting lawsuit, 183

Aberdeen, S.Dak., 17, 176, 178

Aberdeen American News: on Black Hills settlement promise, 165; on Daschle's use of third-party help, 181–82; endorses Herseth, 93; press conference coverage of AML, 176

Abortion: bishop of Sioux Falls and, 33, 46, 173–74, 205–206; Daschle on, 24, 25–26, 33, 46, 56, 171, 204; National Abortions Rights Action League (NARAL), 173–74; partial birth, 33, 173; polling on, 24; S.Dak. legislation, 46, 52, 63

Abourezk, James, 117; early career of, 20; foreign policy views of, 227–28

Abramoff, Jack, and scandal, 244, 306–307n13

Absentee ballot requests, 168

Abu Ghraib prisoner abuse scandal, 90–91, 98

Advertisement fatigue, 72

Agenda journalism, 127

Air America Radio, 111

Alaska National Wildlife Refuge (ANWR), 79–80

Alito, Samuel, 239–40

Allard, Wayne, 40

Allawi, Ayad, 170–71

Allen, George, 13, 190

Al-Qaeda, 33, 106, 152, 228

Al-Sadr, Moqtada, 157

Alston and Bird (D.C. lobbying firm), 215

Alter, Jonathan, 153

Al-Zarkawi, Abu Musab, 107

Ambrose, Stephen, 97

American Association of Retired Persons (AARP), 43

American Federation of State, County, and Municipal Employees (AFSCME), 47, 65

American Indian Movement, 15, 52

American Indian voters: for Herseth, 95; Russell Means endorses John Thune, 52; Native American voting drive, 186; outreach to, 42; poll watcher lawsuits, 182–85; *Rapid City Journal* proposes reservation debate, 148; Thune meets Indians at Pine Ridge Reservation, 62; Thune visits various reservations to encourage, 42, 55, 62–63, 80, 225; turnout by, 95; turnout in Thune-Johnson race, 31. *See also* Giago, Tom

American Prospect, The, 45

Americans for Democratic Action (ADA), 227

American Spectator, 122

Antiterrorist surveillance program, 240–41

Antiwar liberals, 242

Antiwar sentiment, 225, 227; protests, 228–30

Argus blog: creation of, 109–10; end of, 129, 146; formation of, 126

Argus Leader. See Sioux Falls Argus Leader

Argus Leader/KELO-Land poll, 91

Argus Leader/KELO poll, 89

Argus on Air, 117, 123

Arkansas Democrat-Gazette, 84

Arlington, S.Dak., 72

313